THE BOSTON CONSULTING GROUP ON STRATEGY

THE BOSTON CONSULTING GROUP ON STRATEGY

EDITED BY
CARL W. STERN AND
MICHAEL S. DEIMLER

WILEY

John Wiley & Sons, Inc.

Bruce Doolin Henderson

1915-1992

Contents

PART THREE The Practice of Business Strategy

The Customer: Segmentation and Value Creation   137

Innovation and Growth   173

Foreword

Looking back, it's hard to imagine that a few short essays could have had so much impact on business thinking. Addressed to the chief executives of large enterprises, *Perspectives* developed a devoted following, even circulating in bootleg copies in some companies. *Perspectives* challenged executives to think about their businesses strategically rather than simply operationally. They combined economic insight with an understanding of how management decisions can be distorted by organizational compromise. Their radically simple logic was unsettling.

Perspectives helped many people understand for the first time that:

- Being number one or number two in a business is a *necessity*.

- The prevailing management practices in diversified companies had to be scrapped and replaced with real *portfolio* management.

- Japan's competitive strength came from *strategic intent* as much as from macroeconomics or culture.

- Beating the *competition* is more important than beating the last quarter.

- *Cash flow* is pivotal in determining a business's real rate of return.

- Regulation can have a *devastating* effect on market mechanisms.

Few if any of these insights were wholly original. They owed much to a wide assortment of executives, economists, thinkers, and academics in many fields, as well as BCG's learning from work on real problems for farsighted corporations. But these notions had seldom been crafted into such coherent prescriptions, or argued as provocatively.

And they were prescient. Most of the forces driving the evolution of business strategy in the last several decades can be found in these essays: technology's declining costs and increasing power, the rise of Japan and then Asia in manufacturing, the restructuring of American industry to enhance shareholder value, and organizational learning and knowledge management, to name only a few.

In creating these *Perspectives,* Bruce Henderson, BCG's founder, invented a demanding form. He said each took six to ten drafts, with relentless self-editing. The results forced the reader to think and rewarded repeated reading.

Although most *Perspectives* credited one or two authors, these writers were in fact the tip of a much larger iceberg: unconstrained give and take among members of the firm and its clients. In the early 1960s, when BCG was small, the entire firm gathered every Monday morning in the library (with its still empty shelves) to debate a current issue. Even the newest associate might be called on to defend a point of view. The goal was clear: to penetrate beneath the surface to the real determinants of competitive success. This drive to transcend the conventional carried over to our work for clients. Best practice is fine, but there is always something better.

The best ideas have many parents, and are but the forerunners of what's to come. In this spirit, we publish this selection of *Perspectives* as both a memorial to Bruce Henderson and a tribute to the clients, employees, and friends, past and present, of The Boston Consulting Group.

JOHN S. CLARKESON
President and Chief Executive Officer, 1985–1997
Chairman of the Board, 1998–2003
Co-Chairman of the Board, 2004–Present

Preface

Bruce Henderson and Perspectives

"Few people have had as much impact on international business in the second half of the twentieth century as the founder of The Boston Consulting Group" is how the *Financial Times* characterized the legacy of Bruce Henderson just after his death on July 20, 1992. Bruce would have been pleased with the epitaph: Impact was what Bruce's life was all about.

From his earliest days, Bruce was obsessed with making a difference, with leaving something behind. An engineer by training, he never tired of quoting Archimedes to aspiring staff: "Give me a lever and a place to stand, and I'll move the world."

Bruce was at once a relentless contrarian and a passionate proselytizer, a combination that can only be explained by his unique background. Born on a Tennessee farm on April 30, 1915, he began his business life early and auspiciously, as a Bible salesman for his father's publishing company. He earned his undergraduate engineering degree from Vanderbilt University. He attended Harvard Business School, but opted to leave in 1941—ninety days before graduation—to join Westinghouse Corporation, where he became one of the youngest vice presidents in the company's history. In 1953, President Eisenhower chose him to serve on a five-member team charged with evaluating the foreign aid program to Germany under the Marshall Plan. In 1959, Bruce left Westinghouse to head Arthur D. Little's management services unit, and in 1963 he accepted the improbable challenge from the CEO of the Boston Safe Deposit and Trust Company to start a consulting arm of the bank. This was to become The Boston Consulting Group.

Bruce—and The Boston Consulting Group under his leadership— aspired to nothing less than changing the way the business world thought about competition. The vehicle was strategy. Although some of the fundamental precepts had been well developed and well accepted in the military sphere, they were surprisingly absent from business thinking when Bruce founded BCG in 1963. Developing the discipline of business strategy secured a place of honor for Bruce in the business pantheon and propelled BCG from a one-man operation to the 5,000-professional, worldwide organization it is today.

Bruce was an intense, curious, argumentative man with a voracious appetite for experience and ideas. He had an astonishing ability to borrow from a wide range of disciplines, synthesize and integrate disparate concepts, and then explore their implications for business. He drew enormous energy and excitement from pushing ideas to their logical limits. He was fond of quoting Jay Forrester: "While most people understand first-order effects, few deal well with second- and third-order effects. Unfortunately, virtually everything interesting in business lies in fourth-order effects and beyond."

His medium of choice was *Perspectives:* concise pieces designed to stimulate senior management thinking on a range of business issues. Bruce liked to refer to them as "a punch between the eyes." In *Henderson on Corporate Strategy* (HarperBusiness, 1984), he described their stylistic intent as follows:

> Statements that senior business managers would find believable are not supported. Only provocative material is argued. The subject matter is chosen to be deliberately provocative, significant in implication, and relevant to the policy decisions of corporate competition.

To date, over 400 *Perspectives* have been published. They have been translated into at least six languages and circulated to senior executives around the globe.

This book comprises 82 *Perspectives,* 4 *Harvard Business Review* articles, and 8 other pieces written by various members of The Boston Consulting Group between 1968 and 2005. It traces the evolution of BCG's thinking on strategy and documents the many significant contributions BCG has made to the field. But more than just a historical record, this collection represents a reference for business concepts that stand on their own. It demonstrates how timeless truly insightful ideas are. A fitting tribute, we hope, to the memory of Bruce Henderson—a great thinker and an inspirational leader.

CARL W. STERN
MICHAEL S. DEIMLER

Acknowledgments

Our deepest debt is to the many clients of The Boston Consulting Group. Virtually every idea expressed in these pages had its genesis in client work. All of us at BCG are gratified that so many outstanding executives have found it fruitful to work through some of their toughest management issues with us, and we are honored by the abiding trust that these enduring relationships represent.

This book is a tribute to Bruce D. Henderson, founder of The Boston Consulting Group, and to all BCG authors, past and present. BCG has a highly self-critical culture. The healthy debate that greets and hones new ideas can occur only if a few intrepid individuals are willing to hang themselves out a bit, to hold their ideas—and inevitably themselves—up for scrutiny. We salute their intellectual curiosity and their courage.

It is also a tribute to the many generations of BCG staff and alumni. Behind every author is an engaged group of professionals who helped develop and burnish the ideas-in-process in the best Hendersonian tradition.

A few of our colleagues deserve specific acknowledgment. Bolko von Oetinger and George Stalk played central roles in motivating and initiating this project. Mark Voorhees, Ted Buswick, and Bill Matassoni provided invaluable writing, editorial guidance, and support. Hans-Paul Bürkner and John Clarkeson offered unstinting encouragement and backing. We also thank Richard Narramore for superbly guiding us through the editorial process.

Finally, we thank our families—for their love and for their forbearance.

C. W. S.

M. S. D.

PART ONE

The Nature of Business Strategy

WHAT IS STRATEGY? For one thing, it is probably the business world's most used and abused word. We have strategies for everything: from advertising to logistics to human resources to custodian engineering. This is a shame, for the concept of strategy is both profound and useful.

Bruce Henderson captured it classically: "All competitors who persist over time must maintain a unique advantage by differentiation over all others. Managing that differentiation is the essence of long-term business strategy."

Bruce never stopped searching for a grand, unified theory of strategy. His quest took him far afield—ultimately into the realm of modern biology and evolution. *Strategic and Natural Competition*, one of Bruce's last *Perspectives*, represents the culmination of his thinking on the nature of strategy. His reasoning from emerging empirical findings on evolution anticipated the interdisciplinary approaches so prevalent today. Note also Bruce's concluding challenge on the task that lay ahead "to both control and expand the potential of our own future?" And thereby to better society and our lives.

STRATEGIC AND NATURAL COMPETITION

BRUCE D. HENDERSON, 1980

Strategic competition leads to time compression. Competitive shifts as a result of strategy can take place in a few short years. The same evolution by natural competition might require generations.

Strategic competition is a relatively new phenomenon in business. It may well have the same impact upon business productivity that the industrial revolution had upon individual productivity.

The basic elements of strategic competition are:

- The ability to understand competitive interaction as a complete dynamic system that includes the interaction of competitors, customers, money, people, and resources.

- The ability to use this understanding to predict the consequences of a given intervention in that system and how that intervention will result in new patterns of stable dynamic equilibrium.

- The availability of uncommitted resources that can be dedicated to different uses and purposes in the present even though the dedication is permanent and the benefits will be deferred.

- The ability to predict the risk and return with sufficient accuracy and confidence to justify the commitment of such resources.

- The willingness to deliberately act to make the commitment.

This description of strategy sounds like the basic requirements for making any ordinary investment. It is that. But it is far more. Strategy is all-encompassing in its commitment. Strategy by definition involves the commitment and dedication of the whole firm. Failure of any competitor to react and then deploy and commit his own resources against the strategic competition of another competitor can result in a complete inversion of the competitive relationships and a major shift in the equilibrium between them. That is why strategic competition leads to time compression. Natural competition has none of these characteristics.

Natural competition is wildly expedient in its moment-to-moment interaction. However, it is inherently extremely conservative in its change in characteristic behavior. By contrast, strategic competition is deliberate, carefully considered, and tightly reasoned in its commitments, but the consequences may well be radical change in a relatively short time.

Natural competition is evolutionary.

Strategic competition is revolutionary.

Natural competition is really low-risk incremental trial and error. Small changes that seem to be beneficial are gradually adopted and maintained. Other small changes are tried and added. It is learning by trial and error without the need for either commitment or foresight. It is the adaptation now to the way that things are now. It is the basic pattern of evolution. It is Darwinian natural selection. It functions even if controlled by pure chance or pure expediency. For these very reasons it is inevitably very conservative, gradual, and produces nearly imperceptible change near term regardless of the ultimate consequences long term.

Strategic competition by its very commitments seeks to make a very large change in competitive relationships. Its revolutionary character is moderated only by two fundamental inhibitions. Strategic failure can be as sweeping in its consequences as strategic success. And characteristically an alert defense has a major competitive advantage over the attacker. Strategic success usually depends upon the culture, perceptions, attitudes, and characteristic behavior of competitors and their mutual awareness of each other.

This is why in geopolitics and in military strategy as well as in business strategy the pattern of competition contains long periods of natural competition punctuated by relatively sudden and major shifts in relationships as a result of strategy. It is the age-old pattern of war and peace even though competition continues during peace.

Currently, normal modern business behavior seems to fall between the extremes of these two modes. However, a shift toward strategic competition seems to be the secular trend. The successful use of strategic competition by the most aggressive direct competitor can make the same foresight and dedication of resources the prerequisite for survival of others. Eventually, the mastery of strategic competition will be a requirement for adapting to that kind of environment in which most of the change is the result of strategic commitments.

Natural competition should be respected. It is the process that produced the infinite and exquisite complexity, variety, and interaction of all the forms of life on planet Earth. This was accomplished by pure chance, with no plan, foresight, or objectives. The starting point was the equivalent of sterile chemical soup. However, it took millions of years of nearly infinitesimal changes and adaptations.

Natural competition must be completely understood. It is the foundation. It is the system and pattern of interaction upon which any form of strategic competition must build and modify. Understanding of natural competition is required in order to predict the effect on those relationships as the result of intervention in the feedback loops of that system.

Differences between competitors is the prerequisite for survival in natural competition. Those differences may not be obvious. But competitors who make their living in exactly the same way in the same place at the same time are highly unlikely to remain in a stable equilibrium. However, any differences may give one competitor or the other an advantage over all others in some part of the common competitive environment. The value of that difference becomes a measure of the survival prospects as well as the future prosperity of that competitor.

There is nearly an infinite number of combinations of competitive factors in an environment that has a large number of variables. It should not be surprising that the world is filled with a vast variety of competitors, all different, which seem to exist in a moving but stable equilibrium. The range of size, behavior, and characteristics is not accidental; it is inevitable. It is also stable even though ever changing in detail. Those differences are the a priori requirement for the survival of each and every one of them in their particular subsection of the environment. That is natural competition as it always has been.

Strategic competition is not new. The elements of it have been recognized and used in warfare since the human race became able to combine intelligence, imagination, accumulated resources, and deliberately coordinated behavior. The distilled wisdom of many centuries has been expressed in many maxims such as "concentrate strength against weakness."

But most military strategy has been focused on the battle itself or the war rather than on the equilibrium of the relationship that continued through both peace and war. Geopolitics is this larger perspective of the continued competition of this dynamic equilibrium over time. Yet there is still a very limited general theory about geopolitical dynamic equilibrium.

The general theory of business competition is almost certainly in its infancy. But the elements of a general theory that integrates all of the elements seem to be developing. The integration itself is the critical development.

The classic economic theories of business competition seem to be so simplistic and sterile that they are obstacles to progress and understanding rather than contributions. They seem to be based on views of competition as a static equilibrium in a static economy rather than a dynamic equilibrium. They are based on theoretical concepts of cost behavior that have never been observed in reality and that directly contradict observable and quantifiable evidence. They make assumptions about competitive behavior that are neither observable nor useful in predicting competitive behavior. The frame of reference of "perfect competition" is a theoretical concept that has never existed and probably could not exist. Unfortunately, these classical theories have been used to develop public policy that is equally unrealistic.

Development of a general theory of business competition will permit the prediction of the consequences of any kind of business competition. It can be the base of both strategic competition and constructive public policy. The general public would benefit on both counts. The development of a general theory of business competition will require the testing and revision of many interlocking hypotheses.

We would now hypothesize that:

- Effective competition will result in a range of sizes of competitors from very large to very small. This spectrum of sizes will be stable over time.

- Competitors who survive and prosper will have unique advantages over any and all other competitors in specific combinations of time, place, products, and customers.

- For any given competitor, there will be different competitors who will provide the constraints for almost every combination of relevant factors. Therefore the frontiers or boundaries of competitive parity will be constantly changing as any one of the competitors changes, adapts, grows, or redeploys.

- Perpetual conflict will exist along those frontiers where competitive ability is at parity.

- Very little conflict will exist where clear superiority is visible. The military analogy of the battlefront is useful in visualizing this.

- Business competition inherently has multiple fronts with a different competitor on each front.

- Any redeployment of resources will change the balance of competitive parity on at least two fronts. If one is strengthened, others will be weakened.

- Whenever a front or zone of competitive parity becomes stable or static, then "bourgeois" competition will develop. Such bourgeois competition exists when the defense always acts as a hawk and the offense always acts as a dove. This is a mutual recognition of mutually predictable behavior.

- The fewer the number of competitive variables that are critical, the fewer will be the number of competitors. If only one factor is critical, then no more than two or three competitors are likely to co-exist. Only one will survive if the available market shrinks. This is the "Rule of Three and Four."

- The greater the number of potentially important variables, the larger will be the number of coexisting competitors but the smaller will be their absolute size.

- The more variable the environment, the fewer the number of surviving competitors. In this case, the ability to cope with the greater change in environment becomes the overriding and controlling factor.

- The entry of a new competitor depends on the ability of that competitor to develop and identify a clear superiority compared to all existing competitors in some subsection of the total market. Sequence of entry is important.

These and other hypotheses are direct derivatives from the observable facts and generally accepted theories of evolution in the biological and ecological sense. They are the pattern of natural competition.

The earlier work of The Boston Consulting Group attempted to develop a general theory of competition based on the following:

- Observable patterns of cost behavior

- Considerations of the dynamics of sustainable growth and capital use

- The role of the capital markets in permitting these effects to be leveraged or discounted

- The relationship between these in a system of competition

We recognized early the inappropriateness of accounting theories developed for other purposes as a model of economic behavior. We then developed the concepts that can be summarized as "cash in and out is all that counts."

From this start, the concepts of the experience curve, the growth share tradeoff, and the product portfolio were developed. This was further extended by analysis of shared experience, business risk versus financial risk tradeoffs, the cost of proliferation, and cultural and behavioral extrapolation for competitors.

Many of these ideas are now commonly accepted assumptions and part of the business language.

This conceptual framework of business competition is far from complete. The knowledge and insight into competitive systems is expanding at an exponential rate. It is parallel to the expansion of our knowledge and insight into the physical sciences in the last century.

We believe that insight into strategic competition has the promise of a quantum increase in our productivity and our ability to both control and expand the potential of our own future.

PART TWO

The Development of Business Strategy

Foundations

IN THE MID-1960s, Bruce Henderson and a team from his fledgling firm were retained by a leading semiconductor fabricator. Their brief: Find out what was driving the industry's chaotic pricing behavior. The team discovered that prices were not in fact behaving chaotically at all—they were paralleling costs in a systematic decline of 25 percent each time accumulated volume doubled. The experience curve was born, and the development of business strategy began.

It was not the experience curve itself that was noteworthy—an analogous phenomenon, learning curve reductions in direct labor costs, had been documented during World War II. It was the implications that were truly revolutionary. If total value-added costs fell predictably with accumulated experience—and relative accumulated experience was in most circumstances very close to relative market share—it meant that systematic cost differences, proportional to relative market share, should arise between competitors. At the time, neither business doctrine nor economic theory recognized such a possibility.

The ramifications were far-reaching. Competitive advantage mattered, and it could be gained and managed in a deliberate way. Market share was an extraordinarily valuable asset that should not be liquidated casually.

This notion put pricing and capacity decisions in a new light. Pricing to recover product development costs and optimizing capacity utilization in a growing business, both well-established business practices, amounted to selling off the future for a transitory gain. On the other hand, preemptive pricing and capacity addition could be used to buy market share, lowering relative costs while making a business seem less attractive to competitors.

The same was true of financial policies. Most thought of debt as a way to lever a given ROA up into a higher ROE—with attendant financial risk. Experience curve thinking turned that around, pointing out that, at a given ROE, debt would permit a lower ROA. Employed aggressively, debt could fund preemptive pricing and capacity additions, and thereby buy market share and ultimately lower business risk. Similarly, dividends were exposed as potentially costly in competitive terms, as they lower the sustainable growth rate and hence market-share gains.

But perhaps the most powerful implication of the value of market share was for resource allocation. Most large companies, then as now, comprised a portfolio of businesses that varied in competitive position and growth potential. Experience curve logic suggested that the common practice—for each business to fund its own growth—was suicidal. High-growth businesses were unable to generate enough cash to keep pace with the market and were forced to liquidate share, while mature businesses generated more than they could invest productively. Better to use the excess cash flow of these mature cash cows to fund a play for dominance by the "stars" and "question marks" while growth in their markets remained high. If these businesses could establish and hold leadership positions, they would become cash cows themselves when growth in their markets slowed. The growth-share matrix provided a framework for implementing such a virtuous cash-flow cycle.

Bruce Henderson wrote prolifically on the experience curve and its implications in the 1960s and 1970s. A selection of the best of these *Perspectives* follows. In assessing them, a question we must ask is: Their historical value aside, how do they hold up in today's more complex competitive world?

Clearly, accumulated experience is not the only route to cost advantage. Indeed, it seems irrelevant to the economics of many industries today (although, in its purest form, it has enjoyed something of a renaissance in recent years as a basis for advantage under time- and capability-based strategies). Further, cost differentials and relative market shares cannot be viewed as the sole source and measure of competitive advantage—innovation, customer franchises, and brand value are equally important.

But if "competitive advantage, whatever its source" is substituted for "accumulated experience" and "relative market share," then most of the concepts introduced in these classic *Perspectives* remain sound. The portfolio, in particular, although admittedly widely misperceived and misused as a generic business-categorization tool, remains sound as a framework for resource allocation.

The fundamental insight—that competitive advantage can be gained and must, therefore, be managed, both in fact and in the minds of competitors—remains fresh and valid. Just how much so was brought home forcefully in the recent Internet boom and bust. Pundits declared that the acceleration of everything rendered the notion of competitive advantage obsolete (along with traditional methods of equity valuation!). While there is no denying that today's fluid markets make competitive advantage ever harder to gain and sustain, the record confirms that a business without competitive advantage is essentially worthless. Competitive advantage remains an asset of enormous value, to be sought assiduously and defended ferociously.

THE EXPERIENCE CURVE REVIEWED: HISTORY

BRUCE D. HENDERSON, 1973

Experience curve is the name applied in 1966 to overall cost behavior by The Boston Consulting Group. The name was selected to distinguish this phenomenon from the well-known and well-documented learning curve effect. The two are related, but quite different.

It has been known for many years that labor hours per unit decline on repetitive tasks. This effect was particularly easy to observe in such things as aircraft production in wartime. The rate of labor decrease was characteristically approximately 10 to 15 percent per doubling of experience. This expectation has long been a part of military contracting.

The so-called learning curve effect apparently had somewhat limited application, however. It applied only to direct labor. Unless the job changed, this meant *the time required* to obtain a given cost decline tended to double each cycle of experience. This masked the far-reaching implication of the possibilities of job element management with volume changes.

The Boston Consulting Group's first effort to formulate the experience curve concept was an attempt to explain cost behavior over time in a process industry. Long-continued, successful cost reduction by the client had resulted only in the company's survival as a marginal competitor. The correlation between competitive profitability and market share was strikingly apparent. The pattern of the learning curve was an attractive initial hypothesis to explain this. The company was chasing its larger competitors down the cost curve.

Later, a study of the cost of television components showed striking differences in the rate of cost improvement between monochrome parts and color parts. This was difficult to explain, since the same factory, the same labor, and the same processes were involved at the same time. Again, the idea of progress down a cost curve provided a plausible hypothesis.

Semiconductors provided the evidence on which to build the experience curve concept itself. The wide variety of semiconductors offered a chance to compare differing growth rates and price decline rates in a similar environment. Price data supplied by the Electronic Industries Association was compared with accumulated industry volume. Two distinct patterns emerged.

In one pattern, prices in current dollars remained constant for long periods and then began a relatively steep and long-continued decline in constant dollars. In the other pattern, prices in constant dollars declined steadily at a constant rate of about 25 percent each time accumulated experience doubled. That was the experience curve in 1966.

Work with clients since 1966 has proven the universality of the experience curve relationships. A real understanding, however, required many, many client assignments.

Application of the experience curve to problem solving and policy determination discloses many technical questions:

- What is an appropriate unit of experience where the product itself changes, too? The transport airplane is an example.

- What is the relationship between experience effects on similar but different products such as semiconductors?

- How are technological changes integrated into experience effects?

- What effect does capital investment intensity have?

- Does the same effect appear in overhead and marketing functions?

Accounting data is frequently misleading for cost analysis. The choice of treatment as expense versus capital can distort apparent cost change.

Over time, the experience curve has become recognized as essentially a pattern of cash flow. The average cost is by definition the total expenditure divided by the total output. The unit cost is the rate of change in that ratio. Projection of this relationship is frequently both simpler and more accurate for cost forecasting than even the most elaborate conventional accounting analysis.

Understanding of the underlying causes of the experience curve is still imperfect. The effect itself is beyond question. It is so universal that its absence is almost a warning of mismanagement or misunderstanding. Yet the basic mechanism that produces the experience curve effect is still to be adequately explained. (The same thing is true of gravitation.)

It can be observed that if high return on investment thresholds are used to limit capital investment, then costs do not decline as expected.

It can also be observed that extensive substitution of cost elements and exchange of labor for capital is characteristic of progress down a cost experience curve.

Direct costs per megawatt, steam turbine generators, 1946–1963. Each dot corresponds to a year. The horizontal scale Is the total cumulative output of the specific firm involved to that year.

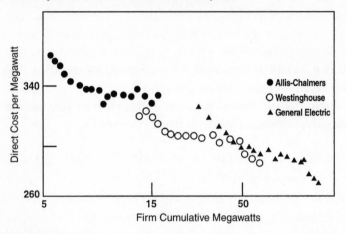

SOURCE: Confidential information from General Electric, Westinghouse, and Allis-Chalmers was made available in public records as the result of antitrust litigation.

The experience curve is a contradiction of some of the most basic assumptions of classic economic theory. All economics assumes that there is a finite minimum cost that is a function of scale. This is usually stated in terms of all cost/volume curves being either L-shaped or U-shaped. It is not true except for a moment in time.

The whole concept of a free enterprise competitive equilibrium assumes that all competitors can achieve comparable costs at volumes much less than pro rata shares of market. That is not true either.

Our entire concept of competition, antitrust, and nonmonopolistic free enterprise is based on a fallacy if the experience curve effect is true.

The experience curve effect can be observed and measured in any business, in any industry, for any cost element, anywhere.

Most of the history of insight into the experience curve effect and its significance is still to be written.

THE EXPERIENCE CURVE REVIEWED: WHY DOES IT WORK?

BRUCE D. HENDERSON, 1974

"Cost of value added declines approximately 20 to 30 percent each time accumulated experience is doubled."

This is an observable phenomenon. Whatever the reason, it happens. Explanations are rationalizations.

The whole history of increased productivity and industrialization is based on specialization of effort and investment in tools. So is the experience curve. It is a measure of the potential effect of specialization and investment.

Learning

Workers learn. If they learn to do a task better, they can do it in less time. This is equivalent to producing more in the same time. Characteristically, output can increase 10 to 15 percent each time total output is doubled. This is the well-known learning curve measure of man-hour productivity increase.

Based on the learning curve, labor costs should decline only 10 to 15 percent each time accumulated experience doubles.

Specialization

When scale of activity increases so that numbers of people are involved, then it becomes possible to specialize.

If two people are doing the same thing, it becomes possible to break the task into two parts. One person does all of one half. The other person does all of the other half. Each will therefore do his respective task twice as often for a given total output.

The learning curve just described predicts that with twice the experience the labor time should be reduced 10 to 15 percent.

Increase in scale permits such specialization. Consequently, each worker will approach a total experience at any point in time that would be twice as much as the worker could have achieved without specialization. Doing half as much but twice as often equals the same amount of effort but twice the experience with the task. Consequently, specialization permits 10 to 15 percent less time per unit or 10 to 15 percent more output in a given time.

If the scale doubles simultaneously with total experience, then these two effects should occur simultaneously. Costs decline 10 to 15 percent because of learning plus 10 to 15 percent because of specialization. The sum of 20 to 30 percent cost decline is alone an approximation of the total experience curve effect.

Where growth in output increases at any constant rate, then change in scale and change in total experience can and often do occur in parallel.

Investment

By definition, a profitable investment is one where money spent now results in a future payout that is larger than the original investment. All the return on investment comes in more output for the same total cost, but deferred.

If the cost of money is extremely high, then virtually no investment can be justified. If the cost of money were zero, then any investment that would recover the investment and something more by eternity could be justified.

The cost decline in experience curves is a partial function of rate of investment. The control on this element is the cutoff rate on added investment. If the cutoff rate is high, costs decline slowly. If the cutoff rate is low, costs decline rapidly.

Return on investment does result in cost reduction. Without investment, capacity increase cannot occur and neither can cost reduction at constant capacity.

A significant part of the experience curve cost reduction is the result of return on investment.

Scale

The experience curve effect is the result in part of increased scale. Yet there is no justification for increased scale unless there is growth. There is no need to add capacity at all.

With growth there is constant addition of capacity. Each added increment of unit capacity becomes a smaller percent of the total capacity unless size of the increment is increased also. Both capacity utilization and scale effect are affected by growth.

The effect of scale is well known, though very difficult to measure precisely. There is, however, a formula that is known to approximate scale effect in the process industries:

"Capital cost increases by the six-tenths power of the increase in capacity."

This exponential change is equivalent to an increase of 52 percent in capital cost to provide a 100 percent increase in capacity. The total capital cost became 152 percent instead of 100. The total output became 200 instead of 100. The average became $^{152}\!/_{200}$ = 76 percent of 100 percent. That is a very common and typical experience curve cost decline rate.

Average production unit size normally increases in proportion to rate of total output or even faster. If it does, then capital cost should go down as fast or even faster than in proportion to a 76 percent experience curve.

Since capital tends to displace labor over time, this scale effect becomes increasingly important with growth in volume and experience.

There are limits on scale due to load factors and logistics provided there is a finite total market. But if the total market grows, then scale can be expected to grow too.

Scale effect applies to all operations, not just to process plants. Marketing, accounting, and all the overhead functions have scale effects also.

Scale effect alone is sufficient to approximate the experience curve effect where growth is constant and scale grows with volume.

For most products, a 70 to 80 percent slope is normal, with the steeper slope for those where the maximum value is added and where shared experience with slower growth areas is least. However, it is probable that few products decline in cost as fast as they could if optimized.

It is known that costs are more likely to decline if it is generally expected that they should and will.

It must be remembered that experience curve costs are not accounting conventions. They are cash-flow rates divided by output rates. Accounting data is an approximation of this but generally tends to show lower average costs since assets are deferred recognition of cash expenditures.

This means that cost of capital and return on capital from value added are both included in experience curve costs. Trading profits or losses from price levels are excluded from this cost calculation.

Experience curve costs on the foregoing basis are probably more accurate representations of cost than any accounting convention, since they are based on cash flow only, not projections, and because such costs include the cost of capital.

The reasons for the experience curve effect are not particularly important. The important fact is that the experience curve is a universally observable phenomenon. If costs do not go down in a predictable fashion, then and only then do the underlying reasons become important. Analysis will usually show the reasons to be inadequate investment, improper value-added definitions, or occasionally just mismanagement.

Summary

The experience curve is the result of the combined effect of learning, specialization, investment, and scale. The effect of each of these is an approximation, and so the experience curve effect itself is also an approximation.

The combination of these factors should permit a considerably steeper experience cost curve than is actually observed. However, some additional overhead cost is introduced by the need to coordinate and plan these changes.

All elements of cost do not have the same experience base. Also, some cost elements share experience with other products.

Consequently, only new and unique products with completely new cost elements can be expected to go down the cost experience curve with the maximum slope.

THE EXPERIENCE CURVE REVIEWED: PRICE STABILITY

BRUCE D. HENDERSON, 1974

Whenever real (deflated) prices fail to parallel real (deflated) cost trends, then market shares will shift. When market share shifts, then relative costs of competitors will shift also. The market leader with the largest share will lose share eventually if prices do not go down as fast as costs.

When prices decline faster than the leader's costs on trend, then there is always some competitor who is growing faster than the industry average. That competitor's margin will usually stay constant while all other competitors' margins shrink.

Price and market share are stable only when prices are declining in parallel to costs and prices are low enough to prevent gain in share by high-cost competitors.

Crushed and broken limestone.

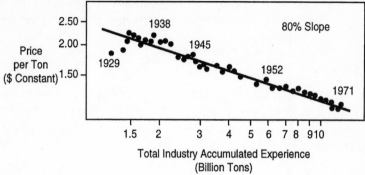

SOURCE: U.S. Bureau of Mines.

Costs characteristically decline 20 to 30 percent in real terms each time accumulated experience doubles. This means that when inflation is factored out, costs should always decline. The decline is fast if growth is fast and slow if growth is slow.

It is obvious that prices must approximately parallel costs over time. Otherwise, margins would constantly widen on trend, or conversely, they would continually narrow and then become negative. But costs net of inflation do continually decline as a function of experience. This experience curve effect can be observed in all manner of products and services.

Two characteristic patterns can be observed in almost all kinds of prices. In one, the prices parallel costs after removing inflation. Examples are crushed rock and integrated circuits.

Integrated circuits.

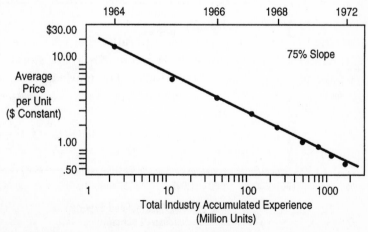

SOURCE: Published Data of Electronics Industry Association.

Freestanding gas ranges.

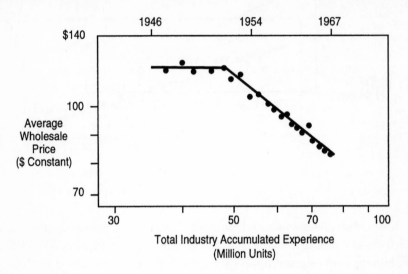

In the other pattern, prices remain nearly constant, declining very slowly. Then at some point in time, prices begin to decline much more sharply than in the previous pattern. Examples are gas ranges and polyvinylchloride.

Characteristically, the price during the initial flat portion of the curve is a constant price in the "then current" value. But if inflation is removed, the real price declines slowly in "constant" money value.

Polyvinylchloride.

Total Industry Accumulated Experience

B₁: Loses share
B : Holds share

A constant price is a strategic target. The increasing margin of the leader is an attractive inducement to enter and to grow even faster. Yet any reduction in share of the leader also reduces his rate of accumulation of experience and slows his rate of cost reduction. The new entry starts at high costs but reduces those costs rapidly because of the faster rate of growth.

Competitors are racing each other down the cost curve by accumulating experience. If X grows enough faster than Y, the relative costs can be reversed. The interaction between the competitors produces a continuing shift in their relative margins.

Differences in growth rate determine the potential rate of shift in margin between two competitors. For practical purposes there can be only one price or "price equivalent" at equilibrium between vendors of equivalent products. If any competitor is willing to sell at a lower price, he will tend to gain share and grow faster and thereafter improve his relative margin unless all others match the price change.

Prices are stable only when three conditions are met:

- The growth rate for all competitors is approximately the same.

- Prices are paralleling costs.

- Prices of all competitors are roughly equal for equal value.

A change in price will not change price stability, except temporarily, unless it changes relative growth rate of competitors. Temporary price changes matched by competitors have essentially no effect on relative cost or on stability.

However, a price change that affects competitors' relative growth rates will affect price stability eventually. Paradoxically, long-term effects tend to be the reverse of short-term effects. An increase in price tends to encourage growth in capacity as well as to affect financial

Total Experience for Each Competitor

resources. Rarely will all competitors be affected equally by any price change. If any competitor changes growth rate, prices will be destabilized if any competitor tries to maintain previous profit margins. The competitor who loses share will eventually have to charge relatively more and vice versa.

Characteristically in the United States, a majority of new or fast-growing products go through a two-phase cycle. The first phase has steady prices or very slowly declining prices in constant dollars. This phase is followed by another phase of a long period of steeply declining prices. Usually, only one competitor will be able to preserve profit margins. It is always the fastest-growing competitor.

The break in price is characteristically triggered by some combination of the following:

- A very successful and aggressive new entry willing and able to maintain a modest profit margin
- Growth of new entries at a rate that eventually preempts all growth from the original leader
- An economic recession that produces temporary significant over-capacity

Two-phase pattern.

Total Accumulated Industry Experience

Characteristic pattern if B is allowed an initial price advantage and if B gains market share rapidly while holding constant margin.

The fastest-growing competitor has the fastest decrease in costs. As soon as costs are below the current price he has an option. He can maintain constant margins and convert decreasing costs into lower prices. The alternative is to hold prices and let the margin widen. The first option tends to perpetuate the cost decline in addition to perpetuating the high growth rate. The other alternative stabilizes prices but stops shifts in cost and market share.

If the fastest-growing competitor maintains a constant margin, he can then lower prices faster than anyone else's costs can decline. The strong probability is created that competition with shrinking margins will not invest to maintain margin. Small competitors are often conceded a price differential until they become large and low-cost competitors.

By contrast almost all prices in Japan follow a pattern in which prices steadily decline in parallel to costs. Market share tends to be more stable in Japan than in the United States. In Japan the efficient producer tends to grow faster than the higher-cost competitor. In the United States the reverse is often true.

Price stability is determined by the willingness of the leader and low-cost competitor to set prices low enough to keep any competitor from growing faster than the market. Price stability is maintained by the low-cost competitor maintaining prices parallel to his costs. Any other policies will destabilize prices and shift market share.

THE PRICING PARADOX

BRUCE D. HENDERSON, 1970

The profit equation has three variables—price, volume, and cost. Of these, price is the most common candidate for manipulation since nothing else need change to produce profits for everyone, provided everyone changes prices together. That togetherness is what gives birth to dreams of "industry statesmanship," as a way to better profits through higher prices.

In fact, both volume and cost are easier to change than industry price levels. Efforts to change industry prices can cause them to ebb and flow like the tide, with equal net effect on mean sea level. Above-normal prices inevitably attract additional capacity until prices become depressed. Depressed prices inhibit capacity replacement or additions until prices rise. This is a corollary of the economic truism that competition will force prices down to approach costs or it will cause costs to rise to approach prices.

The consequences of a price advance are predictable. At best, other producers will follow the leader and there will be a substantial price rise. But this in turn sets up a ready-made umbrella for the new capacity of these other competitors who must force their way into the market to fill their added capacity.

The usual result is an artificial list price that hides real price cuts at the expense of the market leader. Because of the price leader's price rise, his profit erosion is obscured temporarily until he decides at some later date that he must retain his share of market. In the meantime, he has subsidized the invasion of his market share by competitors and justified their investment in more capacity.

Short term, the others may not follow his price leadership. Consequently, he must not only retract the price increase, but suffer some market-volume loss also.

Over the longer term, the consequences are quite different. Long term, share of the market is determined by who has the capacity and who can use it fully. Long term, the maintenance or addition of capacity is nearly always a function of profits in the past and their effect on profit expectations in the future.

Over the long term, profit and profit expectations are based upon anticipated relative costs and operating rates. As a consequence, short-term higher prices for the industry tend to encourage capacity additions and to provide the cash flow to justify that expansion.

All of this is simple classic economics, but the strategic implications are not immediately obvious:

- If you have the lowest cost at nominal capacity, then it is to your advantage to keep prices down at all times sufficiently to dissuade competition from making additional-capacity investments, unless, of course, you can raise them and still stay at nominal capacity.

- Also, it is to your advantage to invest in added capacity yourself as long as you can do so and maintain your cost advantage. This requires that the added capacity be operated at a load factor high enough to provide cost levels no higher than competitors' average costs. In fact, in an active technology you must make capacity additions to maintain a cost advantage.

- If your fixed costs are higher but your operating costs are lower than competitors', then you are more sensitive to changes in operating rate. It is to your advantage to accept any kind of price depression short term that provides a high operating rate. Only under these conditions can you maintain a relative cost advantage. For the same reason, you can accept a lower price level than can your competitors without out-of-pocket loss. This situation is usually true of the new facility.

If you are the low-cost producer with the newest facilities, then any price that is required to operate your facility at nominal capacity is not only justified but a prerequisite for maintaining your relative cost advantage. Any higher price is relatively disadvantageous. Conversely, the interests of high-cost producers must be to keep prices high or to obtain a higher operating rate.

Competitive strategy comes into play in the efforts to induce competitors to accept practices that shift *relative* costs.

The producer with the new low-cost facility must induce competitors to believe that he can and will depress prices indefinitely—until prices are below their cost, if need be—to the point that his new facilities are operating at average industry capacity. In fact, he has the power to do this. He benefits most, however, if he does not need to depress prices to fill his new capacity.

The producer with the higher-cost facilities but in possession of the market must attempt to convince competitors that high prices for the industry are to everyone's advantage. In this way, he can offset his relative cost disadvantage. He may also find it necessary to convince competitors that it will be too costly to wrest away his existing market share by price action. If he can induce competitors to use nonprice means of competing, then their added costs may defer for a long time their realization of the inherent advantage of newer and more efficient capacity.

Short term, the really critical elements of strategy are those that induce a competitor, for whatever reason, to accept a lower operating rate. This imposes a relative cost handicap that has no offsetting virtues.

Long term, the critical elements are those that determine the willingness of competitors to make further capital investment in capacity. Any uncertainty, risk, or competitive policy that can delay this kind of decision produces a higher profit level on average for those who are already in production.

Viewed in this light, the following conclusions can be drawn:

- Short-term price increases tend to depress industry profits long term by accelerating the introduction of new capacity and depressing market demand.

- Short-term price increases favor the high-cost producer relatively more than the low-cost producer.

- The lower-cost producer has everything to gain and little to lose by depressing prices until he is operating at nominal capacity.

- The perfect strategy for the lowest-cost producer is one that persuades others to permit him to obtain maximum capacity use with minimum price depression—at the others' expense in terms of operating rate and profit.

- The perfect strategy for the high-cost producer is one that persuades others that market shares cannot be shifted except over long periods of time and, therefore, that the highest practical industry prices are to everyone's advantage.

Paradoxically, it is often the strongest and lowest-cost producer who leads the way in establishing higher prices, even though he himself may be operating below his optimum capacity. When this happens, it must be considered a strategic victory for the higher-cost producer in the market.

If all of this seems obvious, it is difficult to explain the concern of businessmen, security analysts, and others regarding industry price levels. It would appear that the factor of vital concern should be relative costs—or rather, relative profit margins. The concentration of attention on short-term profits, which are often transient profits, frequently produces the very opposite long-term effect on performance from that desired.

THE MARKET-SHARE PARADOX

BRUCE D. HENDERSON, 1970

Market share is very valuable. It leads to lower relative cost and therefore higher profits. Unfortunately, most efforts to improve market share depress profits, at least short term.

There are two principal reasons for a shift in market share between competitors. The most common is lack of capacity. The other reason is a willingness to lose share to maintain price.

Lack of capacity is a common occurrence. It must be. It is expensive to maintain unused capacity for very long. Even in the face of projected *industry* growth, it is not surprising that not all *individual* producers feel they can justify the incremental investment in added capacity. On the other hand, nothing is more obvious than the fact that your capacity limits your market share. If the market grows and your capacity does not, then whoever has the capacity takes the growth and increases their share of the market—at your expense.

The decision to add capacity is a fateful one. Add too soon, and extra costs are incurred with no benefits. Add too late, and market share is lost. Added capacity means more than bricks and machines. It also means capable personnel in the proper proportions in the proper place. The lead time required is long. The decision must anticipate the need.

The competitive implications of all this are made more complex by the cost differentials among competitors. Simple arithmetic shows that the high-cost producer must add capacity in direct proportion to the low-cost firm if relative market shares are to remain constant. But the high-cost producer's return on the capacity investment is lower than that of the more efficient firm because of the differential in profit margins.

The market-share paradox is that, if the low-cost firm would accept the high-cost producer's return on assets, the low-cost firm would preempt all market growth. And the resulting increase in his accumulated experience would further improve his costs and steadily increase the cost differential between the competitors thereafter. In short, *if the same investment criteria were used by all firms, then the low-cost firm would always expand capacity first and other firms never would.*

All firms do not use the same investment criteria. The fact that market share is stable proves this. However, this also means that shares are unstable if there is vigorous competition.

The low-cost producer can take market share, but only if he is willing to sacrifice near-term profit. The high-cost producer can obtain a significant return only because he is allowed to do so in order to maintain current prices.

The tradeoff is inviting. Since the low-cost firm typically has the largest market share, his higher-return expectations often lead him to sacrifice share to maintain near-term margins. The loss of a modest amount of the market may seem far less costly short term than meeting a price concession of a minor competitor or spreading the price reduction necessary to fill proposed new capacity over his entire sales volume.

Unfortunately, the tradeoff is cumulative. More and more share must be given up over time to maintain price. Costs are a function of market share because of the experience effect. Lost market share leads to loss of cost advantage. Eventually, there is no way to maintain profitability.

The rate of growth is the critical variable in resolving the market-share paradox and the tradeoff between share and near-term profits:

- Without growth, it is virtually impossible to shift market share. No one can justify adding capacity. Neither can anyone afford to lose share at the price of idle capacity. Under such constraints, since prices will tend to be very stable, the appropriate strategy is to maximize profits within existing market shares.

- With only very little growth, a higher near-term profit now may be worth considerably more than continued modest profit. Those who should hold share into the no-growth period are only those with enough share—and the resulting cost position—to anticipate satisfactory profits.

- With rapid growth, market share is both very valuable and very easy to lose. On the one hand, any improvement in share will be compounded by growth of the market itself and then again by improved margins as cost improvement accrues from increased volume, and hence experience. On the other hand, growth means that capacity must be added rapidly, in advance of the growth, or share will be lost automatically; to gain share, capacity addition must be based on preempting the growth component.

Any shift in market share should be regarded as either investment or disinvestment. The rate of return can and should be evaluated just as it would be in any other business situation. *Change in market share should be an investment decision.*

MORE DEBT OR NONE?

Bruce D. Henderson, 1972

Use more debt than your competition or get out of the business. Any other policy is either self-limiting, no-win, or a bet that the competition will go bankrupt before they displace you.

If you are the low-cost competitor, you can carry more debt with less risk than your competition. That debt could be converted into more profit by leverage. But it can also be converted into lower prices at the same profit, while both decreasing the risk from competitors and maintaining a lower overall risk level than the competition.

Failure of the low-cost competitor to use more debt than the competition is self-limiting. It is failure to compete. It is also a failure to maximize shareholder profits at risk levels below competition's risk.

A high-cost competitor must use more debt to survive and grow, unless his more efficient or fortunate competitors unwittingly hold a price umbrella. A higher permanent debt level is the only way for the high-cost competitor to compensate for higher costs while still maintaining competitive prices and growth rates.

Without higher debt, the high-cost competitor is in a no-win position. *The higher-cost competitor must lose market share if he maintains the same debt/equity ratio and uses the same dividend payout ratio as his lower-cost competition. It is inevitable.* Relative growth must inevitably be in proportion to return on equity under these conditions.

The varying product margins of multiproduct companies often obscure these basic relationships. Failure to focus on the specific financial policies of specific lead competitors and react accordingly compounds the lost opportunity.

Properly used, debt can increase debt capacity faster than it increases the assets in which the debt is invested. Properly used, debt can decrease risk, decrease price, and increase shareholder profit simultaneously.

Proper use of debt will usually require that each product support more debt than any competitor chooses to use. Failure to do so on average is either self-defeating restraint on competition or a no-win position justifying no further investment.

Proper use of debt will inevitably mean that the low-cost competitor drives out all competition, unless antitrust laws force prices to be held up to protect higher-cost competition.

Few companies minimize their risk by using debt properly.

THE RULE OF THREE AND FOUR

Bruce D. Henderson, 1976

A stable competitive market never has more than three significant competitors, the largest of which has no more than four times the market share of the smallest.

The following conditions create this rule:

- A ratio of 2 to 1 in market share between any two competitors seems to be the equilibrium point at which it is neither practical nor advantageous for either competitor to increase or decrease share. This is an empirical observation.

- Any competitor with less than one-quarter the share of the largest competitor cannot be an effective competitor. This, too, is empirical but is predictable from experience curve relationships.

Characteristically, this should eventually lead to a market-share ranking of each competitor one-half that of the next larger competitor, with the smallest no less than one-quarter the largest. Mathematically, it is impossible to meet both conditions with more than three competitors.

The Rule of Three and Four is a hypothesis. It is not subject to rigorous proof. It does seem to match well observable facts in fields as diverse as steam turbines, automobiles, baby food, soft drinks, and airplanes. If even approximately true, the implications are important.

The underlying logic is straightforward. Cost is a function of market share as a result of the experience curve effect.

If two competitors have nearly equal shares, the one who increases relative share gains both volume and cost differential. The potential gain is high compared to the cost. For the leader, the opportunity diminishes as the share difference widens. A price reduction costs more and the potential gain is less. The 2 to 1 limit is approximate, but it seems to fit.

Yet when any two competitors actively compete, the most probable casualty is likely to be the weakest competitor in the arena. That, logically and typically, is the low-share competitor.

The limiting share ratio of 4 to 1 is also approximate but seems to fit. If it is exceeded, then the probable cost differential produces very large profits for the leader at break-even prices for the low-share competitor. That differential, predicted by the experience curve, is enough to discourage further reinvestment and efforts to compete by the low-share competitor unless the leader is willing to lose share by holding a price umbrella.

There are two exceptions to this result:

- A low-share competitor can achieve a leadership position in a given market sector and dominate it costwise if there is enough shared experience between that sector and the rest of the market and he is a leader in the rest of the market.

- An otherwise prosperous company is willing for some reason to continually add more investment to a marginal minor product. This can be caused by accounting averaging, full-line policy, or mismanagement.

Whatever the reason, it appears that the Rule of Three and Four is a good prediction of the results of effective competition.

There are strategy implications:

- If there are large numbers of competitors, a shakeout is nearly inevitable in the absence of some external constraint or control on competition.

- All competitors who are to survive will have to grow faster than the market in order to even maintain their relative market shares with fewer competitors.

- The eventual losers will have increasingly large negative cash flows if they try to grow at all.

- All except the two largest-share competitors will either be losers and eventually eliminated or be marginal cash traps reporting profits periodically and reinvesting forever.

- Anything less than 30 percent of the relevant market or at least half the share of the leader is a high-risk position if maintained.

- The quicker any investment is cashed out or a market position second only to the leader gained, then the lower the risk and the higher the probable return on investment.

- Definition of the relevant market and its boundary barriers becomes a major strategy evaluation.

- Knowledge and familiarity with the investment policies and market-share attitudes of the market leader are very important since his policies control the rate of the inevitable shakeout.

- Shifts in market share at equivalent prices for equivalent products depend upon the relative willingness of each competitor to invest at rates higher than the sum of both physical market growth and the inflation rate. Anyone who is not willing to do so loses share. If everyone is willing to do so, then prices and margins will be forced down by overcapacity until someone begins to stop investing.

There are tactical implications that are equally important:

- If the low-cost leader holds the price too high, the shakeout will be postponed, but he will lose market share until he is no longer the leader.

- The faster the industry growth, the faster the shakeout occurs.

- Near equality in share of the two market leaders tends to produce a shakeout of everyone else unless they jointly try to maintain the price level and lose share together.

- The price/experience curve is an excellent indicator of whether the shakeout has started. If the price curve slope is 90 percent or flatter, the leader is probably losing share and still holding up the price. If the curve has a sharp break from 90 percent or above to 80 percent or less, then the shakeout will continue until the Rule of Three and Four is satisfied.

The market leader controls the initiative. If he prices to hold share, there is no way to displace him unless he runs out of the money required to maintain his capacity share. However, many market leaders unwittingly sell off market share to maintain short-term operating profit.

A challenger who expects to displace an entrenched leader must do it indirectly by capturing independent sectors or by investing far more than the leader will need to invest to defend himself.

There are public policy implications:

- The lowest possible price will occur if there is only one competitor, provided that monopoly achieves full cost potential even without competition and passes it on to the customer.

- The next-lowest potential price to the customer is with two competitors, one of which has one-third and the other two-thirds of the market. Then cost and price would probably be about 5 percent higher than the monopoly would require.

- The most probable, and perhaps the optimal, relationship would exist when there are three competitors and the largest has no more than 60 percent of the market and the smallest no less than 15 percent.

A rigorous application of the Rule of Three and Four would require identification of discrete homogeneous market sectors in which all competitors are congruent in their competition. More typically, competitors' areas of competition overlap but are not identical. The barriers between sectors are sometimes surmountable, particularly if there are joint cost elements with scale effects. Yet it is a commonly observable fact that most companies have only two or three significant competitors on any product that is producing a net positive cash flow. Other competitors are unimportant factors.

The Rule of Three and Four is not easy to apply. It depends on an accurate definition of relevant market. It requires many years to reach equilibrium unless the leader chooses to hold his share during the high-growth phase of product life. However, the rule appears to be inexorable.

If the Rule of Three and Four is inexorable, then common sense says: If you cannot be a leader in a product market sector, cash out as soon as practical. Take your writeoff. Take your tax loss. Take your cash value. Reinvest in products and markets where you can be a successful leader. Concentrate.

THE PRODUCT PORTFOLIO

BRUCE D. HENDERSON, 1970

To be successful, a company should have a portfolio of products with different growth rates and different market shares. The portfolio composition is a function of the balance between cash flows. High-growth products require cash inputs to grow. Low-growth products should generate excess cash. Both kinds are needed simultaneously.

Four rules determine the cash flow of a product:

- Margins and cash generated are a function of market share. High margins and high market share go together. This is a matter of common observation, explained by the experience curve effect.

- Growth requires cash input to finance added assets. The added cash required to hold share is a function of growth rates.

- High market share must be earned or bought. Buying market share requires an additional increment of investment.

- No product market can grow indefinitely. The payoff from growth must come when the growth slows, or it never will. The payoff is cash that cannot be reinvested in that product.

Products with high market share and slow growth are *cash cows*. Characteristically, they generate large amounts of cash, in excess of the reinvestment required to maintain share. This excess need not, and should not, be reinvested in those products. In fact, if the rate of return exceeds the growth rate, the cash *cannot* be reinvested indefinitely, except by depressing returns.

Products with low market share and slow growth are *pets*. They may show an accounting profit, but the profit must be reinvested to maintain share, leaving no cash throw-off. The product is essentially worthless, except in liquidation.

All products eventually become either cash cows or pets. The value of a product is completely dependent upon obtaining a leading share of its market before the growth slows.

Low-market-share, high-growth products are the *question marks*. They almost always require far more cash than they can generate. If cash is not supplied, they fall behind and die. Even when the cash is supplied,

The matrix.

Market Share

	High	Low
High (Growth)	★ Star	? Question Mark
Low (Growth)	$ Cash Flow	X Pet

if they only hold their share, they are still pets when the growth stops. The question marks require large added cash investment for market share to be purchased. The low-market-share, high-growth product is a liability unless it becomes a leader. It requires very large cash inputs that it cannot generate itself.

The high-share, high-growth product is the *star*. It nearly always shows reported profits, but it may or may not generate all of its own cash. If it stays a leader, however, it will become a large cash generator when growth slows and its reinvestment requirements diminish. The star eventually becomes the cash cow, providing high volume, high margin, high stability, security, and cash throw-off for reinvestment elsewhere.

The payoff for leadership is very high indeed if it is achieved early and maintained until growth slows. Investment in market share during the growth phase can be very attractive if you have the cash. Growth in market is compounded by growth in share. Increases in share increase the margin. High margin permits higher leverage with equal safety.

Optimum cash flow.

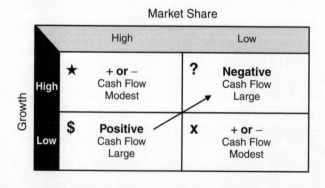

Market Share

	High	Low
★ **High** (Growth)	+ or – Cash Flow Modest	? **Negative** Cash Flow Large
$ **Low** (Growth)	**Positive** Cash Flow Large	X + or – Cash Flow Modest

Success sequence.

The resulting profitability permits higher payment of earnings after financing normal growth. The return on investment is enormous.

The need for a portfolio of businesses becomes obvious. Every company needs products in which to invest cash. Every company needs products that generate cash. And every product should eventually be a cash generator; otherwise it is worthless.

Only a diversified company with a balanced portfolio can use its strengths to truly capitalize on its growth opportunities. The balanced portfolio has:

- Stars whose high share and high growth assure the future

- Cash cows that supply funds for that future growth

- Question marks to be converted into stars with the added funds

Pets are not necessary. They are evidence of failure either to obtain a leadership position during the growth phase or to get out and cut the losses.

Disaster sequence.

THE REAL OBJECTIVES

Bruce D. Henderson, 1976

Investors want their money compounded with safety. Managers want opportunity and defendable security. Business growth seeks to provide both. It may not be so. Business growth has some characteristics that may defeat both investors and management expectations and hopes.

Growth requires added cash in proportion. Growth is an investment opportunity. But the opportunity from growth is real only if it provides a means of returning the invested cash after it has been compounded. This can begin to happen only when the growth has stopped, or substantially so. Growth can indeed lead to business security and stability. But this will be true only if the competitive advantage can be achieved and maintained before maturity and competitive equilibrium have set in.

Business success cannot be measured until the direct investor's cash input has been returned with his profit. Until then, all profit and all apparent success is merely a promise. Reported profit is only a signal. It is a misleading signal unless it represents the probable ultimate competitive position. Cash is all that counts. But cash really counts only when it is no longer needed to defend the competitive position. Competitors are the control on the ability to convert paper profits into real profit for investors.

The nature of competition changes drastically with continued growth. Cost elements shift dramatically in relative weight even though all may decline in real terms. Production costs shift from labor to raw materials and capital costs. Marketing costs shift from selling, education, and service to logistics. Distribution costs begin to overshadow production costs in some kinds of businesses, and the opposite happens in other kinds.

Competitive economics do shift with change in scale, growth rate, and product maturity. Early leaders may have quite different characteristics from those who are merely able to grow with the market until it matures. They in turn may be quite different from the ultimate real winners.

The ultimate success depends upon the ability to achieve and maintain superiority in the most heavily weighted cost components before product maturity and competitive equilibrium have been reached.

While this is the end objective, the means of reaching it may require several quite different kinds of competitive capabilities in the interim periods:

- Early success is no forecast of eventual superiority.

- Current reported profitability is no proof of success. It is only a forecast.

- Growth is evidence only of a compounding investment level in the hope of achieving eventual superiority.

In the final analysis, all true profit payable to the original investor must be represented by the cost superiority differential over the higher-cost marginal competitor who must reinvest his net cash generation just to hold his position.

Effective strategy analysis requires that you find a way to proceed and progress from wherever you start to a dependable competitive advantage at maturity and equilibrium. This in turn requires that you foresee both the shifting economics and the changing behavior of your competitors. If you succeed, then you must translate that insight into the action required now and at each stage as the market matures. Strategy success is action now consistent with a required sequence of actions until a defensible competitive superiority is achieved.

That is what competitive strategy is all about.

Milestones

"TO ADVANCE THE state of thinking about business strategy"—this aspiration, inspired by Bruce Henderson, became the soul of The Boston Consulting Group. In the 25 years since Bruce's breakthrough work on competitive advantage, BCG has continued to innovate. This section highlights *Perspectives* and other publications that represent milestone contributions to the field.

As BCG and its clients began to apply principles of competitive advantage, they learned that the world was not as monolithic as the experience curve implied. In particular, market leaders were not always able to achieve and maintain the kind of success their positions appeared to warrant. Indeed, we frequently saw smaller, more focused players outcompete the leader for the most attractive pieces of business, first becoming more profitable, then growing faster, and ultimately threatening the leader's position.

We observed that industry leaders tend to suffer a life cycle as pronounced as the industries they lead. As markets mature, they fragment into segments with distinct product and service needs, and price elasticities to match. For the producer, these needs translate into different costs to serve each segment. It seems particularly difficult for industry leaders, with their time-honed excellence across their markets as a whole, to spot the segments as they emerge, and to "deaverage" their costs, their product/service offering, and their prices accordingly. This opens an opportunity for competitors to establish a position, generally in the low-cost-to-serve segments.

BCG's focus on market segments and their unique economics led to an exploration of the fundamental trade-off between scale and complexity. Beyond the risks of average costing and average pricing, broad-line producers often find it difficult to achieve the economies of scale implied by their overall size. Lot sizes shrink, and the costs of managing variety mount. Competitors need to be alert to the relative advantages of broad market coverage and focus.

By the late 1970s, businesses clearly varied in inherent reward potential. Where slowing demand and increasingly global competition came together with limits to scale, competitive advantage became an elusive goal for many companies. In particular, mature industrial sectors in which products were largely undifferentiated and technology was no longer proprietary appeared to have reached stalemate. Their flat supply curves demonstrated the difficulty of any competitor achieving a sustainable competitive cost advantage. The only way to escape from stalemate was to transform the business—either by finding a way to reintroduce scale or, more commonly, by injecting a note of innovation and differentiation—to create a more promising competitive environment.

By the early 1980s, a solution to the scale/complexity dilemma began to emerge. Toyota innovated a production process that reduced setup times, work-in-process inventories, and indirect labor by a factor to 5 to 10. Flexible manufacturing allowed broad-line competitors to reduce dramatically the costs associated with handling product proliferation, breaking the compromise between scale and complexity.

But flexible manufacturing was about more than lower manufacturing costs and higher asset turns. The real payoff was in marketing. Producers could offer unprecedented variety in increasingly short cycle times. As a result, distributors could carry broad lines with lower inventories. And customers could get precisely what they wanted, precisely when they wanted it. Time-based competition, as we called it, was a marketer's dream come true.

Flexible manufacturing and time-based competition inspired a general concern with process excellence in all aspects of business operations in the late 1980s and early 1990s. One outgrowth was the recognition that transformational strategies could be built around horizontal capabilities, as Wal-Mart and others had done. Another was reengineering for cost reduction alone, which became the reigning management fad of the early 1990s, but without changes in marketing led to only short-lived gains in competitive advantage.

Reengineering lowered general cost levels and, in the best companies, rationalized core processes and increased organizational nimbleness. But its very ubiquity underlined its limits: A tool that every player uses may become essential for staying in the game, but it is unlikely to confer competitive advantage. Some industries even suffered a sort of reengineering stalemate, as general cost reductions were bid away in the form of lower prices. It was inevitable that attention would turn to how to *use* reengineered capability. The mid-1990s have seen a reinvigorated search for growth and, accordingly, a renewed focus on strategy.

It couldn't have come at a more opportune time. Artificial barriers, trade and regulatory, had been falling steadily for some time, and global markets were becoming the rule. But it was the emergence of the Internet that transformed the economics of information and accelerated the pace of change. Philip Evans and Tom Wurster prophesied in *Blown to Bits* (Harvard Business School Press, 2000) that relaxing the information-based ties that bind functions, departments, suppliers, and customers in companies' value chains would lead industries to deconstruct into value-added layers. Each layer would embody its unique economics and scope for competitive action. New competitors would emerge; existing competitors would have to transform themselves or wither away.

They were dead right. Globalization and deconstruction have altered traditional value chains beyond recognition. And the process is far from played out—the next decade seems a sure bet to see as much change as the last. It is an exciting era for the strategist. Deconstruction has added a new dimension to the concept of strategy, and the resulting instability of industry boundaries will lend the search for sustainable competitive advantage new urgency.

What's next? It may well be that the next breakthrough in strategy will be in the domain of organization design. Deconstruction has made all boundaries more porous, including those of the corporation itself. Competition today is among networks of geographically dispersed companies. How to make these networks work really well represents the next frontier. The final piece represents some early thinking on this emerging area.

LIFE CYCLE OF THE INDUSTRY LEADER

BRUCE D. HENDERSON, 1972

Companies who are pioneers develop great technical expertise. This is very valuable to their customers, particularly in the early stages of the development of the customer's own expertise. This is a source of great pride. It is considered to be proof of leadership. This reinforces emphasis on technical development. Technical pride leads to tailoring each order to the optimum specification.

This in turn leads to the evolution of a manufacturing organization that is geared to produce a very wide variety. Likewise, the marketing organization seeks out the unusual and the technically difficult orders where this kind of flexibility and excellence offers the greatest competitive advantage. This is where the wide profit margins are.

These things reinforce each other. The company's leadership and success reinforce the corporate culture. They preserve and strengthen this pattern of competition.

Almost all original leaders developed this way. They became leaders and prospered because they did. It is necessary. In the early stages of every product and every industry, customers must have this kind of service and resource. The leader is rewarded handsomely because his greater experience and scale result in proportionately lower costs (i.e., the experience curve effect).

However, as the market becomes very large, the leader comes under price pressure from much smaller and less well equipped competitors. The problem usually appears first with the largest and most knowledgeable customers. They have become expert themselves. They buy product, not service. Such sophisticated customers do not need the full range of technical services and manufacturing variety that are available. They begin to find smaller, less competent suppliers who can give them an acceptable product at a lower price. At this stage, such competitors are rarely profitable. However, since they are able to concentrate their experience in a particular sector, their costs come down rapidly in that sector and their competence in that sector increases rapidly.

This competition poses a serious problem for the original leader. Large markets always have a number of sectors that differ materially in their needs and characteristics. The costs of serving these sectors differ widely. It is often very difficult to set prices in a fashion that reflects the differences in services actually rendered or available.

If prices are high enough to cover the cost of the most expensive services available, then large portions of the total market will be lost to the specialized competitors who provide limited services and price accordingly. These prices are too low to cover costs for those customers who need and use the specialized service. A price midway between the two is worse than either, since it has the handicaps of both.

Under these conditions, market leaders usually try to price to preserve their average margin. This accelerates their margin shrinkage, because they tend to lose their volume base on price while increasing their proportion of high service, high cost, technical output.

This trend, if continued, changes the whole character of the leader with respect to costs, product characteristics, price policy, growth rates, and kinds of market sectors served. He becomes a high-price, high-cost, low-volume specialist. If the problem is not recognized and dealt with explicitly, it leads first to unprofitable business and then to inability to compete except in low-volume, high-margin specialties. By then, survival requires specialization in certain sectors and abandonment of the balance.

If the problem and its roots are recognized early enough, however, the leadership, the volume, and the profitability can be protected and preserved. But for this to happen, major changes in policy are required. These changes are to policies that are fundamentally different from those that brought early success. This is where most pioneers lose their leadership.

Price policy, product scope, marketing focus, manufacturing method, and production system must be fundamentally altered. This is a complex problem:

- Identifying market segment costs is very difficult. Many of these costs are joint costs. If one segment is served, the cost is often incurred in all segments. There is an infinite number of possible combinations of services and customer characteristics.

- Prices cannot always reflect different costs for those who do and those who do not need a service. If prices are not parallel to costs in all sectors, then a competitor can concentrate on a sector in which he has either a price advantage or a cost advantage.

- Competitors' costs in different sectors are never equivalent, even if average costs are the same. Since expected profit margins control investment, these differences will tend to produce differential growth rates. But cost differences are increased by shift in market share caused by differing growth rates.

- Changing marketing focus is of little help unless manufacturing facilities and production methods are modified to take advantage of the change. Yet optimization of one is often incompatible with optimization of the other.

- Modification of manufacturing to obtain the optimum cost in any segment may curtail or restrict the product line or the service capability and therefore shrink the volume and experience base overall.

- Marketing advantage, manufacturing costs, and volume potential are mutually dependent variables.

Overall optimization depends on competitors' characteristics, sector by sector.

It is a rare pioneer or industry leader that successfully makes the transition from generalized excellence across the board to focused competition segment by segment against specific competitors. There are too many forces that work against this adjustment:

- Marketing, engineering, and manufacturing all tend to take the policies and current character of the other two as a given and permanent constraint.

- The competitive success in concentration on certain sectors tends to continually concentrate the remaining business in those sectors that are the most complex, the most specialized, the least repetitive and, therefore, the least likely to permit future cost reduction based on experience. The more successful the company has been in the past, the more the entire structure and company tradition will tend to inhibit a change in style or concept of competition.

- In cyclical business, a few good years make everything seem all right. In the down cycle, the problems are blamed on business conditions.

- The management of such businesses, particularly publicly owned businesses, tends to be measured on near-term results. Major change in policy takes time, costs money, and does not demonstrate its value until long after the cost and effort are incurred. Management has a disincentive to change.

It is easy to understand why many pioneers and early leaders are displaced by lesser competitors.

The health and life cycle of the pioneer are determined by two factors. The first is his ability to recognize significant differences in customer segments and optimize his cost of serving each segment separately. The second is his appreciation of the cost value of experience that is common to more than one segment.

THE EVILS OF AVERAGE COSTING

RICHARD K. LOCHRIDGE, 1975

Average costing leads to the loss of market share. Given the normal accounting procedures of any business, some costs are assigned directly to particular products sold to specific customers. All others are averaged, that is, divided among all products and customers. This leads to a misstatement of real costs and a potential competitive threat.

Costs are a function of market share. The leading competitor in any business should have the lowest costs. This low-cost position allows the leader to make the most profit, charge the lowest prices, or add the most value to his product. He may do all three. In any case, there seems little reason to expect a low-share competitor to be able to compete effectively, let alone to gain share on the market leader.

In business after business, however, new entrants gain share on the leader and displace him. In some cases, this is because the return expectations of the leader are so high that a price umbrella is held over the competition. A competitor with a lower return expectation can enter the business and grow to a leadership position. In other cases, the new entrant practices an aggressive financial policy relative to the leader. With greater use of debt and higher retention, the new entrant, despite lower initial returns, can add capacity at a greater rate than the leader.

In many cases, however, the displacement of the leader is the result of average costing. Although costs are averaged across the entire business, overhead and other costs often differ greatly from one product to another. A focused factory can produce high-volume products much more cheaply than a plant designed for flexibility. As a result, broad product lines tend to raise the manufacturing cost of all products. Cost averaging ignores this and therefore overstates the real and potential cost of the high-volume products to a much greater extent than the cost of the low-volume products.

The broader the product line and the larger the number and variety of the customers, the greater the use of overhead cost averaging. Since the leader typically has the largest product line and the biggest customer base, he tends to do the most cost averaging.

The costs to serve different sets of customers are also averaged. Usually, all sales and marketing expenses are averaged across products in such a way that they are averaged across sets of customers as well. Yet different groups of customers have different needs. Large buyers tend to be sophisticated users of the products. They therefore place greater emphasis on price and delivery than on education, service, and support. The result is that it costs less to serve the larger customers than the smaller. This is intuitively obvious. However, costs are rarely classified by customer group; the real differences in cost of service are hidden by cost averaging.

Average costing leads to average pricing. Average pricing means that some customers are being overcharged while others are being subsidized. This is particularly true if the overcharged customers concentrate their purchases on higher-volume products. The problem is compounded when the leader institutes across-the-board price increases in times of inflation. Across-the-board increases, by their very nature, ignore the changes in product and customer mix that occur as markets mature.

The new entrant in the business is forced to focus because of his basic cost disadvantage. If he hopes to be successful, he focuses on those sectors of the market that are being overcharged. He will probably charge less than the leader to penetrate the market. It is only in these sectors that he can deliver product profitably because of the average pricing umbrella. It may be a strategy born of necessity rather than insight, but it still works.

The overcharged customers tend to be the largest and most price-sensitive sector of the market. The leader abandons them to the new entrant because his average costing reports them as less profitable accounts at the lower price levels. These customers also tend to be the fastest-growing sector of the business. The new entrant not only establishes a base-load business upon which to improve his relative cost position, he also grows faster than the leader.

Continued averaging by the leader produces a new set of customers who are being overcharged. The new entrant grows rapidly, improves his costs, and expands into these sectors as well. Eventually, the original leader is displaced. Despite a basic cost advantage to start with, average costing and average pricing lead to a loss in share. The strategic implications for the new entrant are clear:

- Focus on sectors in which the leader is negating his underlying cost advantage through averaging.

- Tailor your offering specifically to that sector's needs. Price to penetrate.

- Broaden the offering only as you improve your relative cost position and as the leader's continued averaging opens other sectors to attack.

The strategic implications for the market leader are also clear:

- Analyze your costs by groups of customers as well as by products.

- When you do have to allocate costs, intentionally bias the assignment of costs away from the rapidly growing, vulnerable segments.

- Differentiate your service to each sector of the market as required, and price accordingly.

- Avoid the evils of average costing.

SPECIALIZATION OR THE FULL PRODUCT LINE

MICHAEL C. GOOLD, 1979

Larger scale lowers costs. Product proliferation raises them. Proliferation can offset scale and more. Yet product families can have lower costs because of their scale than any individual product standing alone. This is true both in the factory and in the marketplace. Every company must choose between the benefits of breadth and those of focus.

In production, two factors are critical in this tradeoff. Every common component provides scale and cost improvement potential. Every deviation from identical cost elements adds overhead cost for coordination.

This proliferation of cost elements adds to both the cost of the variation and to the cost of the elements that are not varied.

If two products are completely unrelated, then they share no scale effect advantage. But neither do they create an overhead cost for coordination. This results in a tradeoff. A focused factory for each of two independent products can be very cost-effective. Combined production offers some increase in scale and shared experience but has inherently higher costs otherwise.

The same cost tradeoff exists in the marketing function. Each customer would prefer a product exactly tailored for him in its characteristics and service support. Every salesman would like to be able to offer this at no added cost. But there is an added cost for every variation both in the factory and in the marketplace. Only certain customers will find that the added value exceeds the added cost and be prepared to pay the higher price needed to maintain profit margins. This means that either demand will be low or profits will be reduced.

The infinite richness of possible tradeoffs and combinations of both product characteristics and customer preferences produces an apparently insuperable degree of complexity. The possibility of analysis and solution would indeed be remote if it were not for the characteristic Pareto (lognormal) distribution of the principal elements.

A limited number of customers usually provide the vast majority of the volume. A limited number of products usually provide the vast majority of the revenue. These combinations of products and customers are the core of the business. This is where analysis should start. This is the frame of reference that can be used to determine the added value and the added cost of extensions to either product line or customer base.

Other varieties of product and other customer classifications are characteristically marginal in their contribution to the firm. Far worse than this, they may create added cost that will be hidden by an average allocation to all products and customers. As a consequence, the essential core business may be deemphasized or overpriced, while the marginal extensions of the product line and customers served may be underpriced or overemphasized in their importance. This may be true even though a real competitive advantage exists in the core business while there is no comparable advantage in the extension coverage.

All the logic of cost effectiveness and competitive advantage favors the focused competitor who avoids product and customer proliferation of this type. That is why it so often seems to happen that a relatively modest sized competitor who is focused can sell at a lower price and still make better profits than his larger and seemingly more formidable competitor.

There is both a paradox and an opportunity here. Focus can result in superior costs. But if this superior cost position can be used as a basis for low costs in extensions to the product/customer range, profitable new opportunities may exist. Focus comes first on the core business areas, but it can still be the basis for a broad product line by building on shared experience and scale.

The basic rule is that you should never expand a product line or a customer base into a segment in which you do not expect to be able to obtain a competitive advantage over any other competitor in that segment. The practical definition of a segment is that combination of customers and products for which a given competitor does have such an advantage.

It is not enough to be able to sell into someone else's segment temporarily because your marginal revenue exceeds your out-of-pocket costs. Such raids and skirmishes are inevitable and endemic on the boundaries of nearly all segments of the market. For continued success, the fundamentals must be observed.

The fundamental rule has two parts. The first is that you should never attempt to serve a market segment (except on an opportunistic basis), unless you can reasonably expect to establish a true competitive advantage in the segment, as you define it, when compared to any other competitor. The other part of the fundamental rule says that when your competitive ability is based upon a relationship to an existing segment that you already dominate, then all marginal costs created by the added segment must be fully (or more than) compensated for by the marginal increase in revenue for the added products or services that represent the added segment.

These determinations cannot be made with reference to products and customers alone. The critical differences are between you and your competitor, and these differences affect your comparative ability to serve any given classification of product/customer pairing. Competitors define the market segments by their differences.

As competitors adjust to the facts of the marketplace and the behavior of each other, the definitions of the relevant segments change, too. Product lines, services, features, and customer characteristics and preferences, as well as the adaptations of competitors, all change. With all this change there must be a continuing reference point. That reference is the existing core of your business in which you have a clear competitive advantage over any competitor. If you cannot preserve that, you cannot protect and extend any of your business with advantage.

Focus of both production and marketing for the core business is essential. No costs are relevant to the core business except those that are in fact unavoidable for its own health. From that point, extension of the product line depends upon the ability to establish a true competitive advantage in new products or customer groups, without at the same time damaging the core business.

STALEMATE: THE PROBLEM

JOHN S. CLARKESON, 1984

Business competition does not always produce a winner. If the differences between competitors are minimal, their struggle may produce only losers. And conventional strategies may only make things worse.

The basis for profitability in a competitive system is competitive advantage. If no competitor can gain a significant and sustainable advantage over the rest, the result may be stalemate.

Under condition of stalemate, the profits of the participants are cyclical but low on average and few participants do much better or worse than the rest. And yet most competitors caught in a stalemate are slow to recognize the fact and reluctant to rethink their strategies. Many prefer to wait for demand to catch up with supply, for prices to return to "realistic levels," or for excess capacity to be shut. Others try to rationalize the industry by gaining a dominant share. In stalemate, both patience and determination usually go unrewarded.

Recognizing stalemate for what it is, however, can open up whole new avenues leading to superior returns.

Stalemate can occur wherever two or more enterprises compete on equal terms across the board and no one achieves that upper hand. This most often occurs where technology is not proprietary and the product is relatively undifferentiated. Further, if the capacity of a low-cost facility represents a small portion of the total needed to satisfy demand, then there are likely to be numerous competitors, each with a low-cost facility, and stalemate may be inevitable.

The industry conditions that result from stalemate are usually beyond the control of any of the participants. Prices are truly determined by the laws of supply and demand. They will tend to settle at or near the marginal cash costs of the highest-cost facility needed to supply demand. Unless you can offer an economically differentiated product that commands a higher price, you can be profitable only by achieving lower costs than the marginal producer.

The way to visualize this phenomenon is to develop an industry supply curve by arraying all the producing units in order of increasing cost (see figure). The difference between the costs of the highest- and lowest-cost producers is an indicator of the overall return potential of the industry. All other things being equal, a large difference, if it is stable, will be more profitable than a smaller difference. Careful data gathering and analysis of cost determinants can create remarkably accurate pictures of competitors' cost positions.

In stalemate, the difference between the highest- and the lowest-cost facility is too small; as a result, the profitability of the lowest-cost facility—and everyone else—is mediocre.

Large sectors of American industry have experienced sustained periods of stalemate over the past ten years, including segments of steel, basic chemicals, forest products, tires, electrical equipment, construction materials, and synthetic fibers and textiles. These industries have all earned less than the average of U.S. industry over the business cycle.

Increasingly, each of these industries has also faced significant international competition. The same characteristics that permit ease of entry for domestic competitors—available technology and know-how,

An industry supply curve. Each bar represents a producing facility. Its vertical dimension is the facility's cash cost per unit; its width is the plant's capacity.

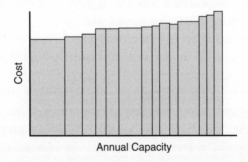

minimal marketing barriers—have attracted investment by offshore competitors with access to low-cost resources, including energy, labor, capital, or all three. Other industries are vulnerable to similar competition if the forces leading to stalemate are not avoided.

Stalemate is not confined to manufacturing. Any service where the customers' cost to switch is low can stalemate, as has happened in bank lending to large corporate accounts, in high-traffic transportation routes, and in nonspecialty retailing.

What is responsible for the shallow supply curves that characterize stalemate? One factor is the rate of technological progress and experience. As a technology matures, the difference in cost between successive generations of facilities or delivery systems will become smaller, especially when capital costs are included.

The other factor is the rate of investment. As an industry adds capacity—almost always at a rate faster than demand is growing—the oldest facilities are displaced.

Such investment behavior produces a steady decline in real costs and real prices. This is the practical basis of the experience effect: real costs are reduced by the substitution of more productive for less productive capacity. But in a stalemate situation, the improvements produced by experience do not result in significant differences among competitors.

This misunderstanding of the experience effect has led some competitors to pursue costly strategies to gain market share. In stalemate, market share is of little value. A new entrant with a new facility or delivery system will often have lower costs than a higher-share older competitor with a collection of production units of various ages.

Yet investment continues at a rapid rate. This testifies to weaknesses in the resource-allocation systems of many companies. These errors are due in part to inadequacies in the capital budgeting process, especially in long-term price forecasting.

Corporate management should identify where stalemate is present or likely to evolve in its current business portfolio. Strategies that exacerbate the competitive conditions should be avoided. The rules and procedures for allocating resources to stalemate businesses are different from the rules for other businesses; the nature of a winning strategy is different. Breaking stalemate requires a new approach to the business and a sharp departure from conventional patterns of competition.

What is the appropriate response to stalemate in your industry?

Acknowledging stalemate can be difficult. It requires confronting some deeply rooted patterns in the organization's behavior. Despite low historical returns, stalemated businesses are used to receiving significant investment, in part to try to improve returns.

It is necessary, therefore, to identify how these projects clear the hurdles intended to discourage low-return investments. The answer may lie in future price forecasts, which are often decisive in the calculated return. Prices do rise periodically to the level required to justify new investment, but seldom remain there long enough to produce the expected return. Forecasts can be made significantly more realistic by using analysis based on supply curves.

There are other pressures as well. One is the natural desire of operating management to close the book on marginal operations, including difficult labor relations, operating headaches, and other legacies. A greenfield investment often promises a fresh start. Yet some of the best investments during a period of rising real capital costs are available to those willing to rebuild and refocus older facilities.

One way not to break a stalemate is by a strategy of preemptive capacity addition, unless it alters the basic nature of the business. Other low-cost preemptive capacity moves are unlikely to change the slope of the supply curve. If you later try to harvest your investment with higher prices, no barrier exists to prevent competitors from entering and lowering prices again.

Finally, it is necessary to overcome the inertia that dictates reinvestment in a business simply because you can't think of an attractive alternative. Recognizing a stalemate for what it is often becomes the first step in committing to explore new avenues for corporate direction.

A stalemated business can be made more profitable once it is agreed that heavy future investment is neither necessary nor appropriate. Overheads maintained in anticipation of future growth can be pared back. Similarly, make-or-buy decisions can be reviewed. This is true especially of process engineering and systems development, where licensing and joint venture may appear more attractive when the business is viewed from a new perspective.

The second response to stalemate is to use supply-curve analysis to identify higher-return alternatives. A production system that is a middling performer in a large segment may be reconfigured into a low-cost producer when retargeted on a smaller segment. By examining competitors' options in supply-curve terms, you may be better able to anticipate competitive reactions.

The third response should be to reexamine a stalemated business for opportunities to restore competitive advantage. It usually requires a willingness to innovate. The starting point is to challenge each of the conditions that produced stalemate:

- *Restore competitive advantage.* While you may compete on equal terms in most of the activities that constitute your value added, there may be specific steps in which you have or can develop a significant edge over your competition. Developing a strategy around that activity—manufacture of a component, a distribution system, or a service—may create a new business opportunity. Union Carbide recently broke with tradition to promote the licensing of its new Unipol process for polyolefins rather than restrict its availability. Banc One sells its processing capabilities.

- *Differentiate.* Although many commodity products are not stalemated, the hallmark of most stalemates is the inability of any competitor to command a price premium. The requirement to load fully a world-scale facility at minimum cost naturally focuses many competitors on the large-volume, standard-product segments. Yet a few companies consistently find ways to uncover special needs of their customers, tailor the product or its delivery, and improve price realization. International Paper has upgraded a classic commodity, linerboard, by giving it barrier properties.

- *Develop proprietary technology.* While every competitor in a stalemate has learned a few tricks to produce his product more cheaply, the differences are marginal. An alternative open to some companies may be to attempt a breakthrough development, alone or in a venture with the leading third-party process equipment supplier, especially in the early stages of a next-generation technology. Michelin and Pilkington, in tires and flat glass, upset stalemates this way. The worst course is a halfway one—to spend enough to keep up with what outside suppliers will do anyway buy not enough to create a breakthrough.

When you do achieve a breakthrough, your decision on whether to license should be influenced by how long you believe it will be before a new stalemate results.

The best time to escape stalemate is before it happens. Early in the life cycle of any industry, the absence of industry standards, the high rate of growth, and the early profits available from developing new applications all obscure the fact that at maturity there may be no sustainable advantage. Seeing a stalemate coming can tell you when to take your profits and withdraw and when to show determination to win in the end. In stalemate, a shakeout will result only in survivors, not winners.

Stalemate is an ever more common fact of life. Finding new ways to create competitive advantage will be the measure of success for much of American business.

BUSINESS ENVIRONMENTS

RICHARD K. LOCHRIDGE, 1981

The economic environment and competitive dynamics of each era produce dramatic change in the requirements for strategic success. This is true despite the presence of fundamental strategy principles and laws of economics.

In the 1950s, dramatic growth and the postwar requirements for reindustrialization made a company's success depend on its ability to meet demand and to respond to changing market requirements. In the 1960s, increased competition and the internationalization of many industries made cost efficiency and market share critical determinants of success. The 1970s brought high inflation coupled with low growth, increased competition in traditional fields, added regulation, and dramatic growth in international trade, which again changed the rules of the game. Strategies in pursuit of market share and low-cost position alone met unexpected difficulty as segment specialists arose and multiple competitors reached economies of scale. The most successful companies achieved success by anticipating market evolution and creating unique and defensible advantage over their competitors in the new environment.

These external changes have led to a complex and sometimes confusing variety of competitive environments. In some cases, only the largest competitor makes adequate returns. In others, all competitors make low returns and there is little variance from best to worst. In still others, some of the most profitable are the smallest, focused competitors. No simple, monolithic set of rules or strategy imperatives will point automatically to the right course. No planning system guarantees the development of successful strategies. Nor does any technique. The business portfolio (the growth/share matrix) made a major contribution to strategic thought. Today it is misused and overexposed. It can be a helpful tool, but it can also be misleading, or worse, a straitjacket.

The strategy requirements of any business are ruled by the competitive environment and the potential for change in that environment. Two factors in particular give one a sense of the nature of that environment. The first is the size of the advantage that can be created over other competitors. The second is the number of unique ways in which that advantage can be created. The combination of these two factors gives a sense of the long-term value of a business and dictates the strategy requirements.

There is a fundamental difference between businesses in which the size of the potential advantage that can be created by a competitor over all other competitors is large and those in which it is small. The reward potential for a successful strategy is only large where the size of the advantage that can be created is also large. The long-term value of any business is determined by the size of its advantage over the marginal, but viable, competitor. When all or most competitors can achieve equal costs without price differentiation, then returns of the whole industry will be depressed to a level sufficient only to fund capacity additions to meet market growth requirements. Regardless of the reported returns, cash available to shareholders will be small or negative for all competitors in such industries. Only when real advantage exists can real returns accrue.

There is also a fundamental difference between businesses that offer only one or a few ways to achieve advantage and those that present several ways. When differentiation is costly and not valued by customers, low price and relative cost position determine success. This sort of environment has relatively straightforward strategy requirements. When a variety of approaches is possible, however, then so is a variety of strategies. Competitors can succeed by tuning their offering and costs exactly to meet a specific segment's demand. If advantage can be created by doing this, a small competitor can thrive as an industry specialist. When advantage cannot be created, or is dissipated with increased size, then the industry remains fragmented.

These two factors—the size of the advantage and the number of ways it can be achieved—can be combined into a simple matrix to help guide more creative strategy development. The specific requirements for success are different in each quadrant.

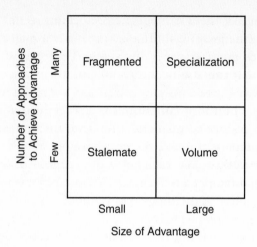

Corporate success requires that most of a company's businesses retain advantaged positions in volume and specialization businesses. Even high market share or relatively low cost position in stalemate and fragmented industries may not be exceptionally valuable. In fact, the value of success in businesses that best fit on the right side of this matrix is always higher than in those that fit best on the left. The market performance of stocks also reflects this reality.

Too many companies pursued strategies during the 1970s that were inappropriate to their specific competitive environments. Market share, for example, often lacks value in stalemated and fragmented businesses. In specialization businesses, focus and superior brand image may be more rewarding than mere size. This matrix is not a solution to all strategy. Most businesses, of course, present elements of each type of competitive environment. In any case, simple rules and models cannot substitute for creative, well-thought-through strategies.

Over time, the nature of the competitive environment can change. Businesses that start out as fragmented industries can evolve toward specialization and even on to the volume category. McDonald's did this in away-from-home eating. Businesses that start out as volume businesses can migrate toward stalemate. This has happened to much of the world's paper industry. Others that were clearly volume have moved toward specialization, as both the Japanese auto producers and a few European companies have proved to the large U.S. auto companies. Some have remained volume businesses by going toward world-scale economics, as Caterpillar has shown in construction equipment.

The challenge of the 1980s will be for companies to anticipate, or even cause, these major evolutions toward a new basis of competition. Those who are slow to react or fail to see the potential will be bypassed. New leaders will emerge. Returns for those who fail to adapt quickly will erode. The extraordinary performers of the coming decade will be those companies that can develop strategies to transform the basis of competition, to create advantaged positions in the new environment, and to preserve those positions from attack.

In a diversified company, the challenge is immense. A portfolio that is disadvantaged in specialized and volume businesses and has assets tied up in stalemate and fragmented industries will result in failure. The successful companies will be those with advantaged positions in volume and specialized businesses. Extraordinary success will accrue to those few strategists willing and able to create sustainable advantage, especially to those able to change the basis of competition.

REVOLUTION ON THE FACTORY FLOOR *

THOMAS M. HOUT AND GEORGE STALK JR., 1982

A revolution in manufacturing is completely transforming the economics of production. It is doing so by reducing the cost penalty of product diversity. The change is shaking up the rules of competition in industries ranging from automobiles to earthmoving equipment to housewares. Within companies, the traditional conflict between marketing, which wants to offer customers more models, and the factory, which has wanted to limit product line variety for the sake of production efficiency, is becoming a thing of the past.

A broad product line services a wider range of customers, but it inherently costs more than a narrow, high-volume-per-model line. More models mean more machine setups, hence more downtime. Work-in-process (WIP) inventories have to increase to keep assembly areas supplied to produce a changing mix of final products and to avoid even more costly setups from low-volume lots. Also, the more

* This article originally appeared in the *Wall Street Journal*, July 12, 1982.

diverse the product mix, the longer any given volume takes to get through a plant and the more scheduling and handling overhead it requires.

Today, however, the cost penalty for diversity is being sharply cut, thanks to a dramatic shortening of setup times in the factory. All plant operations—machining, welding, assembling, and so forth—require equipment setups. Setups that used to take hours can now take minutes as a result of new, sophisticated machine tools and microprocessor control and sensory technologies. With the aid of computer controls, machines can now switch rapidly from one preset tool-and-die configuration to another, without the need for trips to the toolroom or the trial runs and adjustments usually necessary after manual handling. The faster setups are the key to collapsing the structure of downtime, inventory and overhead cost that plagues the conventional factory.

Toyota pioneered these developments in the 1970s, largely to avoid the cost penalties it began to see as it doubled its model range. But there is nothing uniquely Japanese about radically cutting setup time. Global competitors on both sides of the Pacific—such as Komatsu and Caterpillar in construction equipment and Matsushita and General Electric in home appliances—are adopting essentially the same practices.

One large engine manufacturer, over a five-year period, roughly tripled its number of models while reducing WIP inventory by half, doubled the output per factory worker and cut material waste and rework by 40 percent. Across a broad range of products, reducing factory cost added after purchased materials by 15 percent to 35 percent from earlier levels is well within reach.

The marketing and competitive implications of these new plant economics are powerful. Because product variety costs less now, there will be more of it. Truck builders, for example, will pay less for the unusual engine their customers often want. Before, more product variety tended to increase finished goods inventories, causing carrying costs to rise. Now, however, shorter setups increase effective plant capacity and reduce the cycle time it takes for the complete model mix to move through the factory. This allows the manufacturers to increase their model range in finished goods stock and keep their delivery lead time constant without raising their inventory costs. Black-and-white television sets are a case in point. The model variety has risen, while prices have continued to fall.

A manufacturer may find other uses for his WIP inventory savings. He could, for instance, use them by placing more finished goods inventories at more field stocking points to widen his market presence. This is exactly how Toyota gained U.S. market share in forklift trucks in the 1970s. Toyota was the last to run out of stock in cyclical expansions.

The economies of scale which larger competitors in broad-line businesses have enjoyed are changing. The new setup economics will tend to reduce the cost benefits of size between two competitors with similar product mix. Traditionally, plant scale economies have been of two kinds—plantwide savings from greater automation and fixed overheads spread over more volume, and the benefits of more dedicated machines and assembly lines that never need setups. Shorter setups will have little effect on the first advantage but will significantly dilute the second. Full-line producers with smaller market shares may suffer less manufacturing disadvantage than before.

As with any change in the rules, the competitor who exploits more swiftly and completely will gain the advantage. Industry leaders typically have greater engineering resources and more opportunities for high-markup, low-volume specialty products which shorter setups would favor. (General Motors over Ford in cars and DuPont over Monsanto in synthetic fibers are examples.) But industry leaders may resist change. Engineering and production managers, for instance, may be heavily committed to their current systems. But the new setup economics is a powerful lever, and it's unlikely that a leader will be able to hold its lead without making these new investments.

This set of economic relationships is fairly straightforward, but making it work for you is not. It requires both capital and imagination—typically a doubling or tripling of equipment investment and a thorough rethinking of plant flows, layout, and line-balancing logic. The role of workers is also important. Greater flexibility and intelligence are demanded of both people and machines. Machine tools and material-handling devices must be redesigned. Experimentation is necessary: radical systems that work take time to develop.

Developing the actual working system will most likely demand some proprietary engineering advances. Off-the-shelf technology will go only so far. Unusual savings will often come only from an original, unique machine-tool configuration or a component redesigned to accommodate automatic handling. Companies whose cultures have devalued manufacturing will have trouble.

In addition, component suppliers have to make comparable changes in production operations if their deliveries are to match the manufacturer's shorter runs, lower inventories, and greater variety.

More frequent and rigorously scheduled deliveries are critical. Usually the manufacturer must educate the supplier, specify a tighter set of dimensional tolerances, and may even help underwrite his investment. In general, more supplier coordination and discipline are needed.

The payoffs from these investments, however, can be enormous. First, shorter setup time increases the use of machines and direct labor. It also reduces foreman and indirect labor time spent during setup. Second, shorter setups lower work-in-process inventory. They cut down on stock orders and the buffer inventory one needs ahead of and behind any operation. Third, simplifying traditionally long and complex setups reduces maintenance costs, raises production yields, and cuts down time spent solving problems. It's usually the difficulty, not the frequency, of setups that causes broken tools, high machine wear, and work rejected for being out-of-tolerance.

Reducing setup times by a factor of 5 or 10—quite common now for able manufacturers—dramatically increases the effective capacity of machines and plants. Each unit of output spends less time in the factory, reducing normal burden rates. Lower inventories eliminate not only their carrying costs but also the number of material handlers and schedulers who manage them.

Inventory turns go up by multiples, not mere percentages. Higher yields and lower maintenance reduce the cost per usable unit of output. The higher effective capacity allows slower machine running speeds with no loss of output, thus improving product quality by reducing machine wear.

Changing Will Be Better

Once the heavy investment is made by one competitor, the high interest rates associated with inventory carrying costs and uncertain, shifting demand patterns will differentiate him from the competitor who did not invest. Both will want to reduce inventories and change product mix quickly. The producer with a short setup time can achieve these without cost penalty; the other cannot. The latter can increase inventory turns via more setups only at the expense of more machine downtime and considerably more indirect labor time spent in setup.

The strategic payoff from the investment lies in marketing, and in better control of competitors. Shorter setup times enable a company to serve distribution channels better and to capture, at acceptable cost, higher-price, low-volume products. Broad-line producers everywhere will have to reckon with these new economics of diversity.

TIME—THE NEXT SOURCE OF COMPETITIVE ADVANTAGE *

GEORGE STALK JR., 1988

Like competition itself, competitive advantage is a constantly moving target. For any company in any industry, the key is not to get stuck with a single simple notion of its source of advantage. The best competitors, the most successful ones, know how to keep moving and always stay on the cutting edge.

Today, time is on the cutting edge. The ways leading companies manage time—in production, in new product development and introduction, in sales and distribution—represent the most powerful new sources of competitive advantage. Though certain Western companies are pursuing these advantages, Japanese experience and practice provide the most instructive examples—not because they are necessarily unique but because they best illustrate the evolutionary stages through which leading companies have advanced.

In the period immediately following World War II, Japanese companies used their low labor costs to gain entry to various industries. As wage rates rose and technology became more significant, the Japanese shifted first to scale-based strategies and then to focused factories to achieve advantage. The advent of just-in-time production brought with it a move to flexible factories, as leading Japanese companies sought both low cost and great variety in the market. Cutting-edge Japanese companies today are capitalizing on time as a critical source of competitive advantage: shortening the planning loop in the product development cycle and trimming process time in the factory—managing time the way most companies manage costs, quality, or inventory.

In fact, as a strategic weapon, time is the equivalent of money, productivity, quality, even innovation. Managing time has enabled top Japanese companies not only to reduce their costs but also to offer broad product lines, cover more market segments, and upgrade the technological sophistication of their products. These companies are time-based competitors.

From Low Wages to Variety Wars

Since 1945, Japanese competitors have shifted their strategic focus at least four times. These early adaptations were straightforward; the shift to time-based competitive advantage is not nearly so obvious. It does, however, represent a logical evolution from the earlier stages.

In the immediate aftermath of World War II, with their economy devastated and the world around them in a shambles, the Japanese concentrated on achieving competitive advantage through low labor costs. Since Japan's workers were still productive and the yen was devalued by 98.8 percent against the dollar, its labor costs were extraordinarily competitive with those of the West's developed economies.

Hungry for foreign exchange, the Japanese government encouraged companies to make the most of their one edge by targeting industries with high labor content: textiles, shipbuilding, and steel—businesses where the low labor rates more than offset low productivity rates. As a result, Japanese companies took market share from their Western competition.

But this situation did not last long. Rising wages, caused by high inflation, combined with fixed exchange rates to erode the advantage. In many industries, manufacturers could not improve their productivity fast enough to offset escalating labor costs. By the early 1960s, for instance, the textile companies—comprising Japan's largest industry—were hard-pressed. Having lost their competitive edge in world markets, they spiraled downward, first losing share, then volume, then profits, and finally position and prestige. While the problem was most severe for the textile business, the rest of Japanese industry suffered as well.

The only course was adaptation: in the early 1960s, the Japanese shifted their strategy, using capital investment to boost workforce productivity. They inaugurated the era of scale-based strategies, achieving high productivity and low costs by building the largest and most capital-intensive facilities that were technologically feasible. Japanese shipbuilders, for example, revolutionized the industry in their effort to raise labor productivity. Adapting fabrication techniques from mass production processes and using automatic and semiautomatic equipment, they constructed vessels in modules. The approach produced two advantages for the Japanese. It drove up their own productivity and simultaneously erected a high capital-investment barrier to others looking to compete in the business.

The search for ways to achieve even higher productivity and lower costs continued, however. And in the mid-1960s, it led top Japanese companies to a new source of competitive advantage—the focused factory. Focused competitors manufactured products either made nowhere else in the world or located in the high-volume segment of a market, often in the heart of their Western competitors' product lines. Focusing of production allowed the Japanese to remain smaller than established broad-line producers, while still achieving higher productivity and lower costs—giving them great competitive power.

Factory costs are very sensitive to the variety of goods a plant produces. Reduction of the product-line variety by half, for example, raises productivity by 30 percent, cuts costs 17 percent, and substantially lowers the break-even point. Cutting the product line in half again boosts productivity by 75 percent, slashes costs 30 percent, and diminishes the break-even point to below 50percent. (See "The Benefits of Focus.")

In industries like bearings, where competition was fierce in the late 1960s, the Japanese fielded product lines with one-half to one-quarter the variety of their Western competitors. Targeting the high-volume segments of the bearing business—bearings for automobile applications was one—the Japanese used the low costs of their highly productive focused factories to undercut the prices of Western competitors.

SKF was one victim. With factories scattered throughout Europe, each geared to a broad product line for the local market, the Swedish company was a big target for the Japanese. SKF reacted by trying to avoid direct competition with the Japanese: it added higher margin products to serve specialized applications. But SKF did not simultaneously drop any low-margin products, thereby complicating its plant operations and adding to production costs. In effect, SKF provided a cost umbrella for the Japanese. As long as they operated beneath it, the Japanese could expand their product line and move into more varied applications.

Avoiding price competition by moving into higher-margin products is called *margin retreat*—a common response to stepped-up competition that eventually leads to corporate suicide. As a company retreats, its costs rise as do its prices, thus "subsidizing" an aggressive competitor's expansion into the vacated position. The retreating company's revenue base stops growing and may eventually shrink to the point where it can no longer support the fixed cost of the operation. Retrenchment, restructuring, and further shrinkage follow in a cycle that leads to inevitable extinction.

Cutting variety yields higher productivity, lower costs, and reduced break-even points.

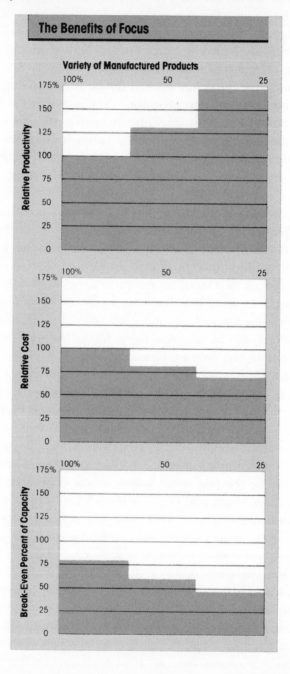

SKF avoided this fate by adopting the Japanese strategy. After a review of its factories, the company focused each on those products it was best suited to manufacture. If a product did not fit a particular factory, it was either placed in another, more suitable plant or dropped altogether. This strategy not only halted SKF's retreat but also beat back the Japanese advance.

At the same time, however, leading Japanese manufacturers began to move toward a new source of competitive advantage—the flexible factory. Two developments drove this move. First, as they expanded and penetrated more markets, their narrow product lines began to pinch, limiting their ability to grow. Second, with growth limited, the economics of the focus strategy presented them with an unattractive choice: either reduce variety further or accept the higher costs of broader product lines.

In manufacturing, costs fall into two categories: those that respond to volume or scale and those that are driven by variety. Scale-related costs decline as volume increases, usually falling 15 percent to 25 percent per unit each time volume doubles. Variety-related costs, on the other hand, reflect the costs of complexity in manufacturing: setup, materials handling, inventory, and many of the overhead costs of a factory. In most cases, as variety increases, costs increase, usually at a rate of 20 percent to 35 percent per unit each time variety doubles.

The sum of the scale- and variety-related costs represents the total cost of manufacturing. With effort, managers can determine the optimum cost point for their factories—the point where the combination of volume and variety yields the lowest total manufacturing cost for a particular plant. When markets are good, companies tend to edge toward increased variety in search of higher volumes, even though this will mean increased costs. When times are tough, companies pare their product lines, cutting variety to reduce costs.

In a flexible factory system, variety-driven costs start lower and increase more slowly as variety grows. Scale costs remain unchanged. Thus the optimum cost point for a flexible factory occurs at a higher volume and with greater variety than for a traditional factory. A gap emerges between the costs of the flexible and the traditional factory—a cost/variety gap that represents the competitive advantage of flexible production. Very simply, a flexible factory enjoys more variety with lower total costs than traditional factories, which are still forced to make the trade-off between scale and variety. (See "The Advantage of Flexible Manufacturing.")

For flexible factories, the optimum cost points occur at a higher volume
and with higher variety than for traditional factories.

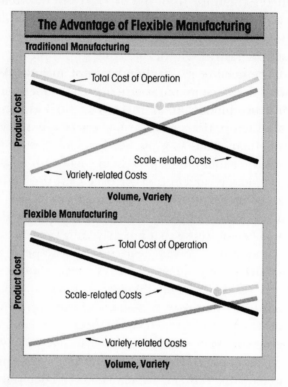

Yanmar Diesel illustrates how this process works. In 1973, with the
Japanese economy in recession, Yanmar Diesel was mired in red ink.
Worse, there was no promise that once the recession had passed, the
existing strategy and program would guarantee real improvement in
the company's condition.

As a Toyota supplier, Yanmar was familiar with the automaker's
flexible manufacturing system. Moreover, Yanmar was impressed
with the automaker's ability to weather the recession without losing
money. Yanmar decided to install the Toyota procedure in its own
two factories. The changeover took less than five years and produced
dramatic results: manufacturing costs declined 40 percent to 60 percent, depending on the product; factory break-even points dropped
80 percent to 50 percent; total manufacturing labor productivity
improved by more than 100 percent.

But it was Yanmar's newfound capability in product variety that sig-
naled the arrival of a unique strategic edge: During the restructuring

Yanmar more than quadrupled its product line. With focused factories, Yanmar could have doubled productivity in such a short time only by reducing the breadth of the product line by 75 percent. The Toyota system made Yanmar's factories more flexible, reducing costs and producing a greater variety of products.

As its inventor, Taiichi Ohno, said, the Toyota production system was "born of the need to make many types of automobiles, in small quantities with the same manufacturing process." With its emphasis on just-in-time production, total quality control, employee decision making on the factory floor, and close supplier relations, the Toyota system gave the many Japanese manufacturers who adopted it in the mid-1970s a distinct competitive advantage.

A comparison of a U.S. company with a Japanese competitor in the manufacture of a particular automotive suspension component illustrates the nature and extent of the Japanese advantage. The U.S. company bases its strategy on scale and focus: it produces 10 million units per year—making it the world's largest producer—and offers only 11 types of finished parts. The Japanese company's strategy, on the other hand, is to exploit flexibility. It is both smaller and less focused: it manufactures only 3.5 million units per year but has 38 types of finished parts.

With one-third the scale and more than three times the product variety, the Japanese company also boasts total labor productivity that is half again that of its American competitor. Moreover, the unit cost of the Japanese manufacturer is less than half that of the U.S. company. But interestingly, the productivity of the Japanese direct laborers is not as high as that of the U.S. workers, a reflection of the difference in scale. The Japanese advantage comes from the productivity of the overhead employees: with one-third the volume and three times the variety, the Japanese company has only one-eighteenth the overhead employees.

In the late 1970s, Japanese companies exploited flexible manufacturing to the point that a new competitive thrust emerged—the variety war. A classic example of a variety war was the battle that erupted between Honda and Yamaha for supremacy in the motorcycle market, a struggle popularly known in Japanese business circles as the H-Y War. Yamaha ignited the H-Y War in 1981 when it announced the opening of a new factory which would make it the world's largest motorcycle manufacturer, a prestigious position held by Honda. But Honda had been concentrating its corporate resources on the automobile business and away from its motorcycle operation. Now, faced with Yamaha's overt and public challenge, Honda chose to counterattack.

Honda launched its response with the war cry, "*Yamaha wo tsubusu!*" ("We will crush, squash, slaughter Yamaha!") In the no-holds-barred battle that ensued, Honda cut prices, flooded distribution channels, and boosted advertising expenditures. Most important—and most impressive to consumers—Honda also rapidly increased the rate of change in its product line, using variety to bury Yamaha. At the start of the war, Honda had 60 models of motorcycles. Over the next 18 months, Honda introduced or replaced 113 models, effectively turning over its entire product line twice. Yamaha also began the war with 60 models; it was able to manage only 37 changes in its product line during those 18 months.

Honda's new product introductions devastated Yamaha. First, Honda succeeded in making motorcycle design a matter of fashion, where newness and freshness were important attributes for consumers. Second, Honda raised the technological sophistication of its products, introducing four-valve engines, composites, direct drive, and other new features. Next to a Honda, Yamaha products looked old, unattractive, and out of date. Demand for Yamaha products dried up; in a desperate effort to move them, dealers were forced to price them below cost. But even that didn't work. At the most intense point in the H-Y War, Yamaha had more than 12 months of inventory in its dealers' showrooms. Finally Yamaha surrendered. In a public statement, Yamaha President Eguchi announced, "We want to end the H-Y War. It is our fault. Of course there will be competition in the future but it will be based on a mutual recognition of our respective positions."

Honda didn't go unscathed either. The company's sales and service network was severely disrupted, requiring additional investment before it returned to a stable footing. However, so decisive was its victory that Honda effectively had as much time as it wanted to recover. It had emphatically defended its title as the world's largest motorcycle producer and done so in a way that warned Suzuki and Kawasaki not to challenge that leadership. Variety had won the war.

Time-Based Competitive Advantage

The strength of variety as a competitive weapon raises an interesting question. How could Japanese companies accommodate such rapid rates of change? In Honda's case, there could be only three possible answers. The company did one of the following:

1. Began the development of more than 100 new models 10 to 15 years before the attack.

2. Authorized a sudden, massive spending surge to develop and manufacture products on a crash basis.

3. Used structurally different methods to develop, manufacture, and introduce new products.

In fact, what Honda and other variety-driven competitors pioneered was time-based competitiveness. They managed structural changes that enabled their operations to execute their processes much faster. As a consequence, time became their new source of competitive advantage.

While time is a basic business performance variable, management seldom monitors its consumption explicitly—almost never with the same precision accorded sales and costs. Yet time is a more critical competitive yardstick than traditional financial measurements.

Today's new-generation companies compete with flexible manufacturing and rapid-response systems, expanding variety and increasing innovation. A company that builds its strategy on this cycle is a more powerful competitor than one with a traditional strategy based on low wages, scale, or focus. These older, cost-based strategies require managers to do whatever is necessary to drive down costs: move production to or source from a low-wage country; build new facilities or consolidate old plants to gain economies of scale; or focus operations down to the most economic subset of activities. These tactics reduce costs but at the expense of responsiveness.

In contrast, strategies based on the cycle of flexible manufacturing, rapid response, expanding variety, and increasing innovation are time based. Factories are close to the customers they serve. Organization structures enable fast responses rather than low costs and control. Companies concentrate on reducing if not eliminating delays and using their response advantages to attract the most profitable customers.

Many—but certainly not all—of today's time-based competitors are Japanese. Some of them are Sony, Matsushita, Sharp, Toyota, Hitachi, NEC, Toshiba, Honda, and Hino; time-based Western companies include Benetton, The Limited, Federal Express, Domino's Pizza, Wilson Art, and McDonald's. For these leading competitors, time has become the overarching measurement of performance. By reducing the consumption of time in every aspect of the business, these companies also reduce costs, improve quality, and stay close to their customers.

Breaking the Planning Loop

Companies are systems; time connects all the parts. The most power-ful competitors understand this axiom and are breaking the debilitat-ing loop that strangles much of traditional manufacturing planning.

Traditional manufacturing requires long lead times to resolve con-flicts between various jobs or activities that require the same resources. The long lead times, in turn, require sales forecasts to guide planning. But sales forecasts are inevitably wrong; by definition they are guesses, however informed. Naturally, as lead times lengthen, the accuracy of sales forecasts declines. With more forecasting errors, inventories bal-loon and the need for safety stocks at all levels increases. Errors in fore-casting also mean more unscheduled jobs that have to be expedited, thereby crowding out scheduled jobs. The need for longer lead times grows even greater and the planning loop expands even more, driving up costs, increasing delays, and creating system inefficiencies.

Managers who find themselves trapped in the planning loop often respond by asking for better forecasts and longer lead times. In other words, they treat the symptoms and worsen the problem. The only way to break the planning loop is to reduce the consumption of time throughout the system; that will, in turn, cut the need for lead time, for estimates, for safety stocks, and all the rest. After all, if a company could ever drive its lead time all the way to zero, it would have to fore-cast only the next day's sales. While that idea of course is unrealistic, successful time-based competitors in Japan and in the West have kept their lead times from growing and some have even reduced them, thereby diminishing the planning loop's damaging effects.

Thirty years ago, Jay W. Forrester of MIT published a pioneering article in *HBR*, "Industrial Dynamics: A Major Breakthrough for Deci-sion Makers" (July–August 1958), which established a model of time's impact on an organization's performance. Using "industrial dynam-ics"—a concept originally developed for shipboard fire control sys-tems—Forrester tracked the effects of time delays and decision rates within a simple business system consisting of a factory, a factory ware-house, a distributors' inventory, and retailers' inventories. The num-bers in the illustration "Time in the planning loop" are the delays in the flow of information or product, measured in weeks. In this exam-ple, the orders accumulate at the retailer for three weeks, are in the mail for half a week, are delayed at the distributor for two weeks, go back into the mail for another half a week, and need eight weeks for

Time in the Planning Loop

Factory

Factory Warehouse

Retailers' Inventories

Distributors' Warehouse

Orders from Customers

Deliveries to Customers

processing at the factory and its warehouse. Then the finished product begins its journey back to the retailer. The cycle takes 19 weeks.

The system in this example is very stable—as long as retail demand is stable or as long as forecasts are accurate 19 weeks into the future. But if unexpected changes occur, the system must respond. The following chart, also taken from the Forrester article, shows what happens to this system when a simple change takes place: Demand goes up 10 percent, then flattens. Acting on new forecasts and seeking to cut delivery delays, the factory first responds by ramping up production 40 percent. When management realizes—too late—that it has overshot the mark, it cuts production 30 percent. Too late again it learns that it has overcorrected. This ramping up and cutting back continue until finally the system stabilizes, more than a year after the initial 10 percent increase.

What distorts the system so badly is time: the lengthy delay between the event that creates the new demand and the time when the factory finally receives the information. The longer that delay, the more distorted is the view of the market. Those distortions reverberate throughout the system, producing disruption, waste, and inefficiency.

These distortions plague business today. To escape them, companies have a choice: They can produce to forecast or they can reduce the time delays in the flow of information and product through the system. The traditional solution is to produce to forecast. The new approach is to reduce time consumption. Because time flows throughout the system, focusing on time-based competitive performance results in improvements across the board. Companies generally become time-based competitors by first correcting their manufacturing techniques, then fixing sales and distribution, and finally adjusting their approach to innovation. Ultimately, it becomes the basis for a company's overall strategy.

Time-Based Manufacturing

In general, time-based manufacturing policies and practices differ from those of traditional manufacturers along three key dimensions: length of production runs, organization of process components, and complexity of scheduling procedures.

When it comes to lot size, for instance, traditional factories attempt to maximize production runs while time-based manufacturers try to shorten their production runs as much as possible. In fact, many Japanese companies aim for run lengths of a single unit. The thinking behind this is as simple as it is fundamental to competitive success: Reduced run lengths mean more frequent production of the complete mix of products and faster response to customers' demands.

Factory layout also contributes to time-based competitive advantage. Traditional factories are usually organized by process technology centers. For example, metal goods manufacturers organize their factories into shearing, punching, and braking departments; electronic assemblers have stuffing, wave soldering, assembly, testing, and packing departments. Parts move from one process technology center to the next. Each step consumes valuable time: parts sit, waiting to move; then move; then wait to be used in the next step. In a traditional manufacturing system, products usually receive value for only .05 percent to 2.5 percent of the time that they are in the factory. The rest of the time products sit waiting for something to happen.

Time-based factories, however, are organized by product. To minimize handling and moving of parts, the manufacturing functions for a component or a product are as close together as possible. Parts move from one activity to the next with little or no delay. Because the production process eliminates the need to pile and repile parts, they flow quickly and efficiently through the factory.

In traditional factories, scheduling is also a source of delay and waste. Most traditional factories use central scheduling that requires sophisticated materials resource planning and shop-floor control systems. Even though these systems are advanced, they still waste time: Work orders usually flow to the factory floor on a monthly or weekly basis. In the meantime, parts can sit idle.

In time-based factories, local scheduling enables employees to make more production control decisions on the factory floor, without the time-consuming loop back to management for approval. Moreover, the combination of the product-oriented layout of the factory and local scheduling makes the total production process run more smoothly. Once a part starts through the production run, many of the requirements between manufacturing steps are purely automatic and require no intermediate scheduling.

These differences between traditional and time-based factories add up. Flexible factories enjoy big advantages in both productivity and time: Labor productivity in time-based factories can be as much as 200 percent higher than in conventional plants; time-based factories can respond eight to ten times faster than traditional factories. Flexible production means significant improvements in labor and net-asset productivity. These, in turn, yield reductions of up to 20 percent in overall costs and increases in growth for much less investment.

Toyota offers a dramatic example of the kinds of improvements that leading time-based competitors are making. Dissatisfied with the response time of a supplier, Toyota went to work. It took the supplier 15 days to turn out a component after arrival of the raw materials at its factory. The first step was to cut lot sizes, reducing response time to six days. Next Toyota streamlined the factory layout, reducing the number of inventory holding points. The response time fell to three days. Finally Toyota eliminated all work-in-progress inventories at the supplier's plant. New response time: one day. Toyota, of course, is not alone in improving manufacturing response times. Matsushita cut the time needed to make washing machines from 360 hours to just 2; Honda slashed its motorcycle fabricating time by 80 percent; in North America, companies making motor controllers and electrical components for unit air conditioners have improved their manufacturing response times by 90 percent.

Time-Based Sales and Distribution

A manufacturer's next challenge is to avoid dissipation of factory performance improvements in other parts of the organization. In Jay Forrester's example of the planning loop, the factory and its warehouse accounted for roughly one-half of the system's time. In actuality today, the factory accounts for one-third to one-half of the total time—often the most "visible" portion of time. But other parts of the system are just as important, if less apparent. For example, in the Forrester system, sales and distribution consume as much or more time than manufacturing.

What Forrester modeled, the Japanese experienced. By the late 1970s, leading Japanese companies were finding that inefficient sales and distribution operations undercut the benefits of their flexible manufacturing systems. Toyota, which at that time was divided into two separate companies, Toyota Motor Manufacturing and Toyota Motor Sales, again makes this point.

Toyota Motor Manufacturing could manufacture a car in less than two days. But Toyota Motor Sales needed from 15 to 26 days to close the sale, transmit the order to the factory, get the order scheduled, and deliver the car to the customer. By the late 1970s, the cost-conscious, competition-minded engineers at Toyota Manufacturing were angry at their counterparts at Toyota Motor Sales, who were frittering away the advantage gained in the production process. The sales and distribution function was generating 20 percent to 30 percent of a car's cost to the customer—more than it cost Toyota to manufacture the car!

Finally, in 1982 Toyota moved decisively to remedy the problem. The company merged Toyota Motor Manufacturing and Toyota Motor Sales. The company announced that it wanted to become "more marketing driven." While Toyota assured the public that the reorganization only returned it to its configuration in the 1950s, within 18 months all the Toyota Motor Sales directors retired. Their jobs were left vacant or filled by executives from Toyota Motor Manufacturing.

The company wasted no time in implementing a plan to cut delays in sales and distribution, reduce costs, and improve customer service. The old system, Toyota found, had handled customer orders in batches. Orders and other crucial information would accumulate at one step of the sales and distribution process before dispatch to the next level, which wasted time and generated extra costs.

To speed the flow of information, Toyota had to reduce the size of the information batches. The solution came from a company-developed computer system that tied its salespeople directly to the factory scheduling operation. This link bypassed several levels of the sales and distribution function and enabled the modified system to operate with very small batches of orders.

Toyota expected this new approach to cut the sales and distribution cycle time in half—from four to six weeks to just two to three weeks across Japan. (For the Tokyo and Osaka regions, which account for roughly two-thirds of Japan's population, the goal was to reduce cycle time to just two days.) But by 1987 Toyota had reduced system responsiveness to eight days, including the time required to make the car. In the Forrester example, this achievement is equivalent to cutting the 19-week cycle to six weeks. The results were predictable: shorter sales forecasts, lower costs, happier customers.

Time-Based Innovation

A company that can bring out new products three times faster than its competitors enjoys a huge advantage. Today, in one industry after another, Japanese manufacturers are doing just that to their Western competition:

- In projection television, Japanese producers can develop a new television in one-third the time required by U.S. manufacturers.

- In custom plastic injection molds, Japanese companies can develop the molds in one-third the time of U.S. competitors and at one-third the cost.

- In autos, Japanese companies can develop new products in half the time—and with half as many people—as the U.S. and German competition.

To accomplish their fast-paced innovations, leading Japanese manufacturers have introduced a series of organizational techniques that precisely parallel their approach to flexible manufacturing:

- In manufacturing, the Japanese stress short production runs and small lot sizes. In innovation, they favor smaller increments of improvement in new products, but introduce them more often— versus the Western approach of more significant improvements made less often.

- In the organization of product development work, the Japanese use factory cells that are cross-functional teams. Most Western new product development activity is carried out by functional centers.

- In the scheduling of work, Japanese factories stress local responsibility, just as product development scheduling is decentralized. The Western approach to both requires plodding centralized scheduling, plotting, and tracking.

The effects of this time-based advantage are devastating; quite simply, American companies are losing leadership of technology and innovation—supposedly this country's source of long-term advantage. Unless U.S. companies reduce their new product development and introduction cycles from 36 to 48 months to 12 to 18 months, Japanese manufacturers will easily out-innovate and outperform them. Taking the initiative in innovation will require even faster cycle times.

Residential air conditioners illustrate the Japanese ability to introduce more technological innovation in smaller increments—and how in just a few years these improvements add up to remarkably superior products. The Japanese introduce innovations in air conditioners four times faster than their American competitors; in technological sophistication the Japanese products are seven to ten years ahead of U.S. products.

Look at the changes in Mitsubishi Electric's three-horsepower heat pump between 1975 and 1985. From 1975 to 1979, the company did nothing to the product except change the sheet metal work, partly to improve efficiency but mostly to reduce materials costs. In 1979, the technological sophistication of the product was roughly equal to that of the U.S. competition. From this point on, the Japanese first established, and then widened, the lead.

In 1980, Mitsubishi introduced its first major improvement: a new product that used integrated circuits to control the air-conditioning cycle. One year later, the company replaced the integrated circuits with microprocessors and added two important innovations to increase consumer demand. The first was quick-connect Freon lines. On the old product (and on the U.S. product), Freon lines were made from copper tubing and cut to length, bent, soldered together, purged, and filled with Freon—an operation requiring great skill to produce a reliable air conditioner. The Japanese substituted quick-connect Freon lines—precharged hoses that simply clicked together. The second innovation was simplified wiring. On the old product (and still today on the U.S. product) the unit had six color-coded wires to connect. The advent of microprocessors made possible a two-wire connection with neutral polarity.

These two changes did not improve the energy-efficiency ratio of the product; nor were they intended to. Rather, the point was to fabricate a unit that would be simpler to install and more reliable, thereby broadening distribution and increasing demand. Because of these innovations, white-goods outlets could sell the new product, and local contractors could easily install it.

In 1982, Mitsubishi introduced a new version of the air conditioner featuring technological advances related to performance. A high-efficiency rotary compressor replaced the outdated reciprocating compressor. The condensing unit had louvered fins and inner fin tubes for better heat transfer. Because the balance of the system changed, all the electronics had to change. As a result, the energy-efficiency ratio improved markedly.

In 1983, Mitsubishi added sensors to the unit and more computing power, expanding the electronic control of the cycle and again improving the energy-efficiency ratio.

In 1984, Mitsubishi came out with another version of the product, this time with an inverter that made possible an even higher energy-efficiency ratio. The inverter, which requires additional electronics for the unit, allows unparalleled control over the speed of the electric motor, dramatically boosting the appliance's efficiency.

Using time-based innovation, Mitsubishi transformed its air conditioner. The changes came incrementally and steadily. Overall they gave Mitsubishi—and other Japanese companies on the same track—the position of technological leadership in the global residential air-conditioning industry.

In 1985, a U.S. air conditioner manufacturer was just debating whether to use integrated circuits in its residential heat pump. In view of its four- to five-year product development cycle, it could not have introduced the innovation until 1989 or 1990—putting the American company 10 years behind the Japanese. Faced with this situation, the U.S. air conditioner company followed the example of many U.S. manufacturers that have lost the lead in technology and innovation: It decided to source its air conditioners and components from its Japanese competition.

Time-Based Strategy

The possibility of establishing a response-time advantage opens new avenues for constructing winning competitive strategies. At most companies, strategic choices are limited to three options:

1. *Seeking coexistence with competitors.* This choice is seldom stable, since competitors refuse to cooperate and stay put.

2. *Retreating in the face of competitors.* Many companies choose this course; the business press fills its pages with accounts of companies retreating by consolidating plants, focusing their operations, outsourcing, divesting businesses, pulling out of markets, or moving upscale.

3. *Attacking, either directly or indirectly.* The direct attack involves the classic confrontation—cut price and add capacity, creating head-on competition. Indirect attack requires surprise. Competitors either do not understand the strategies being used against them or they do understand but cannot respond—sometimes because of the speed of the attack, sometimes because of their inability to mount a response.

Of the three options, only an attack creates the opportunity for real growth. Direct attack demands superior resources; it is always expensive and potentially disastrous. Indirect attack promises the most gain for the least cost. Time-based strategy offers a powerful new approach for successful indirect attacks against larger, established competitors.

Consider the remarkable example of Atlas Door, a 10-year-old U.S. company. It has grown at an average annual rate of 15 percent in an industry with an overall annual growth rate of less than 5 percent. In recent years, its pretax earnings were 20 percent of sales, about five times the industry average. Atlas is debt free. In its tenth year the company achieved the number one competitive position in its industry.

The company's product: industrial doors. It is a product with almost infinite variety, involving limitless choices of width and height and material. Because of the importance of variety, inventory is almost useless in meeting customer orders; most doors can be manufactured only after the order has been placed.

Historically, the industry had needed almost four months to respond to an order for a door that was out of stock or customized. Atlas's strategic advantage was time: It could respond in weeks to any order. It had structured its order-entry, engineering, manufacturing, and logistics systems to move information and products quickly and reliably.

First, Atlas built just-in-time factories. These are fairly simple in concept. They require extra tooling and machinery to reduce changeover times and a fabrication process organized by product and scheduled to start and complete all of the parts at the same time. But even the performance of the factory—critical to the company's overall responsiveness—still only accounted for 2½ weeks of the completed product delivery cycle.

Second, Atlas compressed time at the front end of the system, where the order first entered and was processed. Traditionally, when customers, distributors, or salespeople called a door manufacturer with a request for price and delivery, they would have to wait more than one week for a response. If the desired door was not in stock, not in the schedule, or not engineered, the supplier's organization would waste even more time, pushing the search for an answer around the system.

Recognizing the opportunity to cut deeply into the time expenditure in this part of the system, Atlas first streamlined, then automated its entire order-entry, engineering, pricing, and scheduling processes. Today Atlas can price and schedule 95 percent of its incoming orders while the callers are still on the telephone. It can quickly engineer new special orders because it has preserved on computer the design and production data of all previous special orders—which drastically reduces the amount of reengineering necessary.

Third, Atlas tightly controlled logistics so that it always shipped only fully complete orders to construction sites. Orders require many components. Gathering all of them at the factory and making sure that they are with the correct order can be a time-consuming task. It is even more time-consuming, however, to get the correct parts to the job site after they have missed the initial shipment. Atlas developed a system to track the parts in production and then purchased parts for each order, ensuring arrival of all necessary parts at the shipping dock in time—a just-in-time logistics operation.

When Atlas started operations, distributors were uninterested in its product. The established distributors already carried the door line of a larger competitor; they saw no reason to switch suppliers except, perhaps, for a major price concession. But as a start-up, Atlas was too small to compete on price alone. Instead, it positioned itself as the door supplier of last resort, the company people came to if the established supplier could not deliver or missed a key date.

Of course, with industry lead times of almost four months, some calls inevitably came to Atlas. And when it did get a call, Atlas commanded a higher price because of its faster delivery. Atlas not only got a higher price but its time-based processes also yielded lower costs: It thus enjoyed the best of both worlds.

In 10 short years, the company replaced the leading door suppliers in 80 percent of the distributors in the country. With its strategic advantage the company could be selective, becoming the house supplier for only the strongest distributors.

In the wake of this indirect attack, the established competitors have not responded effectively. The conventional view is that Atlas is a "garage shop operator" that cannot sustain its growth: Competitors expect the company's performance to degrade to the industry average as it grows larger. But this response—or nonresponse—only reflects a fundamental lack of understanding of time as the source of competitive advantage. The extra delay in responding only adds to the insurmountable lead the indirect time-based attack has created. While the traditional companies track costs and size, the new competitor derives advantage from time, staying on the cutting edge, leaving its rivals behind.

COMPETING ON CAPABILITIES: THE NEW RULES OF CORPORATE STRATEGY*

GEORGE STALK JR., PHILIP B. EVANS, AND LAWRENCE E. SHULMAN, 1992

In the 1980s, companies discovered time as a new source of competitive advantage. In the 1990s, they will learn that time is just one piece of a more far-reaching transformation in the logic of competition.

* Reprinted by permission of *Harvard Business Review.* "Competing on Capabilities: The New Rules of Corporate Strategy" by George Stalk, Philip Evans, and Lawrence E. Shulman (March–April 1992). Copyright 1992 by the Harvard Business School Publishing Corporation. All rights reserved.

Companies that compete effectively on time—speeding new products to market, manufacturing just-in-time, or responding promptly to customer complaints—tend to be good at other things as well: for instance, the consistency of their product quality, the acuity of their insight into evolving customer needs, the ability to exploit emerging markets, enter new businesses, or generate new ideas and incorporate them in innovations. But all these qualities are mere reflections of a more fundamental characteristic: a new conception of corporate strategy that we call *capabilities-based competition.*

For a glimpse of the new world of capabilities-based competition, consider the astonishing reversal of fortunes represented by Kmart and Wal-Mart: In 1979, Kmart was king of the discount retailing industry, an industry it had virtually created. With 1,891 stores and average revenues per store of $7.25 million, Kmart enjoyed enormous size advantages. This allowed economies of scale in purchasing, distribution, and marketing that, according to just about any management textbook, are crucial to competitive success in a mature and low-growth industry. By contrast, Wal-Mart was a small niche retailer in the South with only 229 stores and average revenues about half of those of Kmart stores—hardly a serious competitor.

And yet, only ten years later, Wal-Mart had transformed itself and the discount retailing industry. Growing nearly 25 percent a year, the company achieved the highest sales per square foot, inventory turns, and operating profit of any discount retailer. Its 1989 pretax return on sales was 8 percent, nearly double that of Kmart.

Today Wal-Mart is the largest and highest-profit retailer in the world—a performance that has translated into a 32 percent return on equity and a market valuation more than ten times book value. What's more, Wal-Mart's growth has been concentrated in half the United States, leaving ample room for further expansion. If Wal-Mart continues to gain market share at just one-half its historical rate, by 1995 the company will have eliminated all competitors from discount retailing with the exception of Kmart and Target.

The Secret of Wal-Mart's Success

What accounts for Wal-Mart's remarkable success? Most explanations focus on a few familiar and highly visible factors: the genius of founder Sam Walton, who inspires his employees and has molded a culture of service excellence; the greeters who welcome customers at the door; the motivational power of allowing employees to own part of the business; the strategy of "everyday low prices" that offers the customer a better deal and saves on merchandising and advertising costs. Economists also point to Wal-Mart's big stores, which offer economies of scale and a wider choice of merchandise.

But such explanations only redefine the question. Why is Wal-Mart able to justify building bigger stores? Why does Wal-Mart alone have a cost structure low enough to accommodate everyday low prices and greeters? And what has enabled the company to continue to grow far beyond the direct reach of Sam Walton's magnetic personality? The real secret of Wal-Mart's success lies deeper, in a set of strategic business decisions that transformed the company into a capabilities-based competitor.

The starting point was a relentless focus on satisfying customer needs. Wal-Mart's goals were simple to define but hard to execute: to provide customers access to quality goods, to make these goods available when and where customers want them, to develop a cost structure that enables competitive pricing, and to build and maintain a reputation for absolute trustworthiness. The key to achieving these goals was to make the way the company replenished inventory the centerpiece of its competitive strategy.

This strategic vision reached its fullest expression in a largely invisible logistics technique known as *cross-docking*. In this system, goods are continuously delivered to Wal-Mart's warehouses, where they are selected, repacked, and then dispatched to stores, often without ever sitting in inventory. Instead of spending valuable time in the warehouse, goods just cross from one loading dock to another in 48 hours or less.

Cross-docking enables Wal-Mart to achieve the economies that come with purchasing full truckloads of goods while avoiding the usual inventory and handling costs. Wal-Mart runs a full 85 percent of its goods through its warehouse system—as opposed to only 50 percent for Kmart. This reduces Wal-Mart's costs of sales by 2 percent to 3 percent compared with the industry average. That cost difference makes possible the everyday low prices.

But that's not all. Low prices in turn mean that Wal-Mart can save even more by eliminating the expense of frequent promotions. Stable prices also make sales more predictable, thus reducing stockouts and excess inventory. Finally, everyday low prices bring in the customers, which translates into higher sales per retail square foot. These advantages in basic economics make the greeters and the profit sharing easy to afford.

With such obvious benefits, why don't all retailers use cross-docking? The reason: It is extremely difficult to manage. To make cross-docking work, Wal-Mart has had to make strategic investments in a variety of interlocking support systems far beyond what could be justified by conventional ROI criteria.

For example, cross-docking requires continuous contact among Wal-Mart's distribution centers, suppliers, and every point of sale in every store to ensure that orders can flow in and be consolidated and executed within a matter of hours. So Wal-Mart operates a private satellite-communication system that daily sends point-of-sale data directly to Wal-Mart's 4,000 vendors.

Another key component of Wal-Mart's logistics infrastructure is the company's fast and responsive transportation system. The company's 19 distribution centers are serviced by nearly 2,000 company-owned trucks. This dedicated truck fleet permits Wal-Mart to ship goods from warehouse to store in less than 48 hours and to replenish its store shelves twice a week on average. By contrast, the industry norm is once every two weeks.

To gain the full benefits of cross-docking, Wal-Mart has also had to make fundamental changes in its approach to managerial control. Traditionally in the retail industry, decisions about merchandising, pricing, and promotions have been highly centralized and made at the corporate level. Cross-docking, however, turns this command-and-control logic on its head. Instead of the retailer pushing products into the system, customers "pull" products when and where they need them. This approach places a premium on frequent, informal cooperation among stores, distribution centers, and suppliers—with far less centralized control.

The job of senior management at Wal-Mart, then, is not to tell individual store managers what to do but to create an environment where they can learn from the market—and from each other. The company's information systems, for example, provide store managers with detailed information about customer behavior, while a fleet of airplanes regularly ferries store managers to Bentonville, Arkansas, headquarters for meetings on market trends and merchandising.

As the company has grown and its stores have multiplied, even Wal-Mart's own private air force hasn't been enough to maintain the necessary contacts among store managers. So Wal-Mart has installed a video link connecting all its stores to corporate headquarters and to each other. Store managers frequently hold videoconferences to exchange information on what's happening in the field, like which products are selling and which ones aren't, which promotions work and which don't.

The final piece of this capabilities mosaic is Wal-Mart's human resources system. The company realizes that its frontline employees play a significant role in satisfying customer needs. So it set out to enhance its organizational capability with programs like stock ownership and profit sharing geared toward making its personnel more responsive to customers. Even the way Wal-Mart stores are organized contributes to this goal. Where Kmart has 5 separate merchandise departments in each store, Wal-Mart has 36. This means that training can be more focused and more effective, and employees can be more attuned to customers.

Kmart did not see its business this way. While Wal-Mart was fine-tuning its business processes and organizational practices, Kmart was following the classic textbook approach that had accounted for its original success. Kmart managed its business by focusing on a few product-centered strategic business units, each a profit center under strong centralized line management. Each SBU made strategy—selecting merchandise, setting prices, and deciding which products to promote. Senior management spent most of its time and resources making line decisions rather than investing in a support infrastructure.

Similarly, Kmart evaluated its competitive advantage at each stage along a value chain and subcontracted activities that managers concluded others could do better. While Wal-Mart was building its ground transportation fleet, Kmart was moving out of trucking because a subcontracted fleet was cheaper. While Wal-Mart was building close relationships with its suppliers, Kmart was constantly switching suppliers in search of price improvements. While Wal-Mart was controlling all the departments in its stores, Kmart was leasing out many of its departments to other companies on the theory that it could make more per square foot in rent than through its own efforts.

This is not to say that Kmart managers do not care about their business processes. After all, they have quality programs too. Nor is it that Wal-Mart managers ignore the structural dimension of strategy: They focus on the same consumer segments as Kmart and still have to make traditional strategic decisions like where to open new stores. The difference is that Wal-Mart emphasizes behavior—the organizational practices and business processes in which capabilities are rooted—as the primary object of strategy and therefore focuses its managerial attention on the infrastructure that supports capabilities. This subtle distinction has made all the difference between exceptional and average performance.

Four Principles of Capabilities-Based Competition

The story of Kmart and Wal-Mart illustrates the new paradigm of competition in the 1990s. In industry after industry, established competitors are being outmaneuvered and overtaken by more dynamic rivals.

In the years after World War II, Honda was a modest manufacturer of a 50-cc engine designed to be attached to a bicycle. Today it is challenging General Motors and Ford for dominance of the global automobile industry.

Xerox invented xerography and the office copier market. But between 1976 and 1982, Canon introduced more than 90 new models, cutting Xerox's share of the midrange copier market in half. Today Canon is a key competitor not only in midrange copiers but also in high-end color copiers.

The greatest challenge to department store giants like Macy's comes neither from other large department stores nor from small boutiques but from The Limited, a $5.25 billion design, procurement, delivery, and retailing machine that exploits dozens of consumer segments with the agility of many small boutiques.

Citicorp may still be the largest U.S. bank in terms of assets, but Banc One has consistently enjoyed the highest return on assets in the U.S. banking industry and now enjoys a market capitalization greater than Citicorp's.

These examples represent more than just the triumph of individual companies. They signal a fundamental shift in the logic of competition, a shift that is revolutionizing corporate strategy.

When the economy was relatively static, strategy could afford to be static. In a world characterized by durable products, stable customer needs, well-defined national and regional markets, and clearly identified competitors, competition was a "war of position" in which companies occupied competitive space like squares on a chessboard, building and defending market share in clearly defined product or market segments. The key to competitive advantage was where a company chose to compete. How it chose to compete was also important but secondary, a matter of execution.

Few managers need reminding of the changes that have made this traditional approach obsolete. As markets fragment and proliferate, owning any particular market segment becomes simultaneously more difficult and less valuable. As product life cycles accelerate, dominating existing product segments becomes less important than being able to create new products and exploit them quickly. Meanwhile, as globalization breaks down barriers between national and regional markets, competitors are multiplying and reducing the value of national market share.

In this more dynamic business environment, strategy has to become correspondingly more dynamic. Competition is now a "war of movement" in which success depends on anticipation of market trends and quick response to changing customer needs. Successful competitors move quickly in and out of products, markets, and sometimes even entire businesses—a process more akin to an interactive video game than to chess. In such an environment, the essence of strategy is not the structure of a company's products and markets but the dynamics of its behavior. And the goal is to identify and develop the hard-to-imitate organizational capabilities that distinguish a company from its competitors in the eyes of customers.

Companies like Wal-Mart, Honda, Canon, The Limited, or Banc One have learned this lesson. Their experience and that of other successful companies suggests four basic principles of capabilities-based competition:

1. The building blocks of corporate strategy are not products and markets but business processes.

2. Competitive success depends on transforming a company's key processes into strategic capabilities that consistently provide superior value to the customer.

3. Companies create these capabilities by making strategic investments in a support infrastructure that links together and transcends traditional SBUs and functions.

4. Because capabilities necessarily cross functions, the champion of a capabilities-based strategy is the CEO.

A capability is a set of business processes strategically understood. Every company has business processes that deliver value to the customer. But few think of them as the primary object of strategy. Capabilities-based competitors identify their key business processes, manage them centrally, and invest in them heavily, looking for a long-term payback.

Take the example of cross-docking at Wal-Mart. Cross-docking is not the cheapest or the easiest way to run a warehouse. But seen in the broader context of Wal-Mart's inventory-replenishment capability, it is an essential part of the overall process of keeping retail shelves filled while also minimizing inventory and purchasing in truckload quantities.

What transforms a set of indvidual business processes like cross-docking into a strategic capability? The key is to connect them to real customer needs. A capability is strategic only when it begins and ends with the customer.

Of course, just about every company these days claims to be "close to the customer." But there is a qualitative difference in the customer focus of capabilities-driven competitors. These companies conceive of the organization as a giant feedback loop that begins with identifying the needs of the customer and ends with satisfying them.

As managers have grasped the importance of time-based competition, for example, they have increasingly focused on the speed of new product development. But as a unit of analysis, new product development is too narrow. It is only part of what is necessary to satisfy a customer and, therefore, to build an organizational capability. Better to think in terms of new product realization, a capability that includes the way a product is not only developed but also marketed and serviced. The longer and more complex the string of business processes, the harder it is to transform them into a capability—but the greater the value of that capability once built because competitors have more difficulty imitating it.

Weaving business processes together into organizational capabilities in this way also mandates a new logic of vertical integration. At a time when cost pressures are pushing many companies to outsource more and more activities, capabilities-based competitors are integrating vertically to ensure that they, not a supplier or distributor, control the performance of key business processes. Remember Wal-Mart's decision to own its transportation fleet in contrast to Kmart's decision to subcontract.

Even when a company doesn't actually own every link of the capability chain, the capabilities-based competitor works to tie these parts into its own business systems. Consider Wal-Mart's relationships with its suppliers. In order for Wal-Mart's inventory-replenishment capability to work, vendors have to change their own business processes to be more responsive to the Wal-Mart system. In exchange, they get far better payment terms from Wal-Mart than they do from other discount retailers. At Wal-Mart, the average "days payable," the time between the receipt of an invoice from a supplier and its payment, is 29 days. At Kmart, it is 45.

Another attribute of capabilities is that they are collective and cross-functional—a small part of many people's jobs, not a large part of a few. This helps explain why most companies underexploit capabilities-based competition. Because a capability is "everywhere and nowhere," no one executive controls it entirely. Moreover, leveraging capabilities requires a panoply of strategic investments across SBUs and functions far beyond what traditional cost-benefit metrics can justify. Traditional internal accounting and control systems often miss the strategic nature of such investments. For these reasons, building strategic capabilities cannot be treated as an operating matter and left to operating managers, to corporate staff, or still less to SBU heads. It is the primary agenda of the CEO.

Only the CEO can focus the entire company's attention on creating capabilities that serve customers. Only the CEO can identify and authorize the infrastructure investments on which strategic capabilities depend. Only the CEO can insulate individual managers from any short-term penalties to the P&Ls of their operating units that such investments might bring about.

Indeed, a CEO's success in building and managing capabilities will be the chief test of management skill in the 1990s. The prize will be companies that combine scale and flexibility to outperform the competition along five dimensions:

Speed. The ability to respond quickly to customer or market demands and to incorporate new ideas and technologies quickly into products.

Consistency. The ability to produce a product that unfailingly satisfies customers' expectations.

Acuity. The ability to see the competitive environment clearly and thus to anticipate and respond to customers' evolving needs and wants.

Agility. The ability to adapt simultaneously to many different business environments.

Innovativeness. The ability to generate new ideas and to combine existing elements to create new sources of value.

Becoming a Capabilities-Based Competitor

Few companies are fortunate enough to begin as capabilities-based competitors. For most, the challenge is to become one.

The starting point is for senior managers to undergo the fundamental shift in perception that allows them to see their business in terms of strategic capabilities. Then they can begin to identify and link together essential business processes to serve customer needs. Finally, they can reshape the organization—including managerial roles and responsibilities—to encourage the new kind of behavior necessary to make capabilities-based competition work.

The experience of a medical-equipment company we'll call Medequip illustrates this change process. An established competitor, Medequip recently found itself struggling to regain market share it had lost to a new competitor. The rival had introduced a lower-priced, lower-performance version of the company's most popular product. Medequip had developed a similar product in response, but senior managers were hesitant to launch it.

Their reasoning made perfect sense according to the traditional competitive logic. As managers saw it, the company faced a classic no-win situation. The new product was lower priced but also lower profit. If the company promoted it aggressively to regain market share, overall profitability would suffer.

But when Medequip managers began to investigate their competitive situation more carefully, they stopped defining the problem in terms of static products and markets. Increasingly, they saw it in terms of the organization's business processes.

Traditionally, the company's functions had operated autonomously. Manufacturing was separate from sales, which was separate from field service. What's more, the company managed field service the way most companies do—as a classic profit center whose resources were deployed to reduce costs and maximize profitability. For instance, Medequip assigned full-time service personnel only to those customers who bought enough equipment to justify the additional cost.

However, a closer look at the company's experience with these steady customers led to a fresh insight: At accounts where Medequip had placed one or more full-time service representatives on-site, the company renewed its highly profitable service contracts at three times the rate of its other accounts. When these accounts needed new equipment, they chose Medequip twice as often as other accounts did and tended to buy the broadest mix of Medequip products as well.

The reason was simple. Medequip's on-site service representatives had become expert in the operations of their customers. They knew what equipment mix best suited the customer and what additional equipment the customer needed. So they had teamed up informally with Medequip's salespeople to become part of the selling process.

Because the service reps were on-site full-time, they were also able to respond quickly to equipment problems. And of course, whenever a competitor's equipment broke down, the Medequip reps were on hand to point out the product's shortcomings.

This new knowledge about the dynamics of service delivery inspired top managers to rethink how their company should compete. Specifically, they redefined field service from a stand-alone function to one part of an integrated sales and service capability. They crystallized this new approach in three key business decisions.

First, Medequip decided to use its service personnel not to keep costs low but to maximize the life-cycle profitability of a set of targeted accounts. This decision took the form of a dramatic commitment to place at least one service rep on-site with selected customers—no matter how little business each account currently represented.

The decision to guarantee on-site service was expensive, so choosing which customers to target was crucial; there had to be potential for considerable additional business. The company divided its accounts into three categories: those it dominated, those where a single competitor dominated, and those where several competitors were present. Medequip protected the accounts it dominated by maintaining the already high level of service and by offering attractive terms for renewing service contracts. The company ignored those customers dominated by a single competitor—unless the competitor was having serious problems. All the remaining resources were focused on those accounts where no single competitor had the upper hand.

Next Medequip combined its sales, service, and order-entry organizations into cross-functional teams that concentrated almost exclusively on the needs of the targeted accounts. The company trained service reps in sales techniques so they could take full responsibility for generating new sales leads. This freed up the sales staff to focus on the more strategic role of understanding the long-term needs of the customer's business. Finally, to emphasize Medequip's new commitment to total service, the company even taught its service reps how to fix competitors' equipment.

Once this new organizational structure was in place, Medequip finally introduced its new low-priced product. The result: The company has not only stopped its decline in market share but also increased share by almost 50 percent. The addition of the lower-priced product has reduced profit margins, but the overall mix still includes many higher-priced products. And absolute profits are much higher than before.

This story suggests four steps by which any company can transform itself into a capabilities-based competitor: Shift the strategic framework to achieve aggressive goals. At Medequip, managers transformed what looked like a no-win situation—either lose share or lose profits—into an opportunity for a major competitive victory. They did so by abandoning the company's traditional function, cost, and profit-center orientation and by identifying and managing the capabilities that link customer needs to customer satisfaction. The chief expression of this new capabilities-based strategy was the decision to provide on-site service reps to targeted accounts and to create cross-functional sales and service teams.

Organize around the chosen capability and make sure employees have the necessary skills and resources to achieve it. Having set this ambitious competitive goal, Medequip managers next set about reshaping the company in terms of it. Rather than retaining the existing functional structure and trying to encourage coordination through some kind of matrix, they created a brand-new organization—Customer Sales and Service—and divided it into cells with overall responsibility for specific customers. The company also provided the necessary training so that employees could understand how their new roles would help achieve new business goals. Finally, Medequip created systems to support employees in their new roles. For example, one information system uses CD-ROMs to give field-service personnel quick access to information about Medequip's product line as well as those of competitors.

Make progress visible and bring measurements and reward into alignment. Medequip also made sure that the company's measurement and reward systems reflected the new competitive strategy. Like most companies, the company had never known the profitability of individual customers. Traditionally, field-service employees were measured on overall service profitability. With the shift to the new approach, however, the company had to develop a whole new set of measures—for example, Medequip's "share-by-customer-by-product," the amount of money the company invested in servicing a particular customer, and the customer's current and estimated lifetime profitability. Team members' compensation was calculated according to these new measures.

Do not delegate the leadership of the transformation. Becoming a capabilities-based competitor requires an enormous amount of change. For that reason, it is a process extremely difficult to delegate. Because capabilities are cross-functional, the change process can't be left to middle managers. It requires the hands-on guidance of the CEO and the active involvement of top line managers. At Medequip, the heads of sales, service, and order entry led the subteams that made the actual recommendations, but it was the CEO who oversaw the change process, evaluated their proposals, and made the final decision. His leading role ensured senior management's commitment to the recommended changes.

This top-down change process has the paradoxical result of driving business decision making down to those directly participating in key processes—for example, Medequip's sales and service staff. This leads to a high measure of operational flexibility and an almost reflexlike responsiveness to external change.

A New Logic of Growth: The Capabilities Predator

Once managers reshape the company in terms of its underlying capabilities, they can use these capabilities to define a growth path for the corporation. At the center of capabilities-based competition is a new logic of growth.

In the 1960s, most managers assumed that when growth in a company's basic business slowed, the company should turn to diversification. This was the age of the multibusiness conglomerate. In the 1970s and 1980s, however, it became clear that growth through diversification was difficult. And so, the pendulum of management thinking swung once again. Companies were urged to "stick to their knitting"—that is, to focus on their core business, identify where the profit was, and get rid of everything else. The idea of the corporation became increasingly narrow.

Competing on capabilities provides a way for companies to gain the benefits of both focus and diversification. Put another way, a company that focuses on its strategic capabilities can compete in a remarkable diversity of regions, products, and businesses and do it far more coherently than the typical conglomerate can. Such a company is a "capabilities predator"—able to come out of nowhere and move rapidly from nonparticipant to major player and even to industry leader.

Capabilities-based companies grow by transferring their essential business processes—first to new geographic areas and then to new businesses. Wal-Mart CEO David Glass alludes to this method of growth when he characterizes Wal-Mart as "always pushing from the inside out; we never jump and backfill." Strategic advantages built on capabilities are easier to transfer geographically than more traditional competitive advantages. Honda, for example, has become a manufacturer in Europe and the United States with relatively few problems. The quality of its cars made in the United States is so good that the company is exporting some of them back to Japan.

In many respects, Wal-Mart's move from small towns in the South to large, urban, northern cities spans as great a cultural gap as Honda's move beyond Japan. And yet, Wal-Mart has done it with barely a hiccup. While the stores are much bigger and the product lines different, the capabilities are exactly the same. Wal-Mart simply replicates its system as soon as the required people are trained. The company estimates that it can train enough new employees to grow about 25 percent a year.

But the big payoff for capabilities-led growth comes not through geographical expansion but through rapid entry into whole new businesses. Capabilities-based companies do this in at least two ways. The first is by cloning their key business processes. Again, Honda is a typical example.

Most people attribute Honda's success to the innovative design of its products or the way the company manufactures them. These factors are certainly important. But the company's growth has been spearheaded by less visible capabilities.

For example, a big part of Honda's original success in motorcycles was due to the company's distinctive capability in dealer management, which departed from the traditional relationship between motorcycle manufacturers and dealers. Typically, local dealers were motorcycle enthusiasts who were more concerned with finding a way to support their hobby than with building a strong business. They were not particularly interested in marketing, parts-inventory management, or other business systems.

Honda, by contrast, managed its dealers to ensure that they would become successful businesspeople. The company provided operating procedures and policies for merchandising, selling, floor planning, and service management. It trained all its dealers and their entire staffs in these new management systems and supported them with a computerized dealer-management information system. The part-time dealers of competitors were no match for the better-prepared and better-financed Honda dealers.

Honda's move into new businesses, including lawn mowers, outboard motors, and automobiles, has depended on re-creating this same dealer-management capability in each new sector. Even in segments like luxury cars, where local dealers are generally more service-oriented than those in the motorcycle business, Honda's skill at managing its dealers is transforming service standards. Honda dealers consistently receive the highest ratings for customer satisfaction among auto companies selling in the United States. One reason is that Honda gives its dealers far more autonomy to decide on the spot whether a needed repair is covered by warranty.

But the ultimate form of growth in the capabilities-based company may not be cloning business processes so much as creating processes so flexible and robust that the same set can serve many different businesses. This is the case with Wal-Mart. The company uses the same inventory-replenishment system that makes its discount stores so successful to propel itself into new and traditionally distinct retail sectors.

Take the example of warehouse clubs, no-frills stores that sell products in bulk at a deep discount. In 1983, Wal-Mart created Sam's Club to compete with industry founder Price Club and Kmart's own PACE Membership Warehouse. Within four years, Sam's Club sales had passed those of both Price and PACE, making it the largest wholesale club in the country. Sam's 1990 sales were $5.3 billion, compared with $4.9 billion for Price and $1.6 billion for PACE. What's more, Wal-Mart has repeated this rapid penetration strategy in other retail sectors, including pharmacies, European-style hypermarkets, and large, no-frills grocery stores known as superstores.

While Wal-Mart has been growing by quickly entering these new businesses, Kmart has tried to grow by acquisition, with mixed success. In the past decade, Kmart has bought and sold a number of companies in unrelated businesses such as restaurants and insurance—an indication the company has had difficulty adding value.

This is not to suggest that growth by acquisition is necessarily doomed to failure. Indeed, the company that is focused on its capabilities is often better able to target sensible acquisitions and then integrate them successfully. For example, Wal-Mart has recently begun to supplement its growth "from the inside out" by acquiring companies—for example, other small warehouse clubs and a retail and grocery distributor—whose operations can be folded into the Wal-Mart system.

It is interesting to speculate where Wal-Mart will strike next. The company's inventory-replenishment capability could prove to be a strong competitive advantage in a wide variety of retail businesses. In the past decade, Wal-Mart came out of nowhere to challenge Kmart. In the next decade, companies such as Toys "R" Us (Wal-Mart already controls as much as 10 percent of the $13 billion toy market) and Circuit City (consumer electronics) may find themselves in the sights of this capabilities predator.

The Future of Capabilities-Based Competition

For the moment, capabilities-based companies have the advantage of competing against rivals still locked into the old way of seeing the competitive environment. But such a situation won't last forever. As more and more companies make the transition to capabilities-based competition, the simple fact of competing on capabilities will become less important than the specific capabilities a company has chosen to build. Given the necessary long-term investments, the strategic choices managers make will end up determining a company's fate.

If Wal-Mart and Kmart are good examples of the present state of capabilities-based competition, the story of two fast-growing regional banks suggests its future. Wachovia Corporation, with dual headquarters in Winston-Salem, North Carolina, and Atlanta, Georgia, has superior returns and growing market share throughout its core markets in both states. Banc One, based in Columbus, Ohio, has consistently enjoyed the highest return on assets in the U.S. banking industry. Both banks compete on capabilities, but they do it in very different ways.

Wachovia competes on its ability to understand and serve the needs of individual customers, a skill that manifests itself in probably the highest "cross-sell ratio"—the average number of products per customer—of any bank in the country. The linchpin of this capability is the company's roughly 600 "personal bankers," frontline employees who provide Wachovia's mass-market customers with a degree of personalized service approaching what has traditionally been available only to private banking clients. The company's specialized support systems allow each personal banker to serve about 1,200 customers. Among those systems: an integrated customer-information file, simplified work processes that allow the bank to respond to almost all customer requests by the end of business that day, and a five-year personal banker training program.

Where Wachovia focuses on meeting the needs of individual customers, Banc One's distinctive ability is to understand and respond to the needs of entire communities. To do community banking effectively, a bank has to have deep roots in the local community. But traditionally, local banks have not been able to muster the professional expertise, state-of-the-art products, and highly competitive cost structure of large national banks like Citicorp. Banc One competes by offering its customers the best of both these worlds. Or in the words of one company slogan, Banc One "out-locals the national banks and out-nationals the local banks."

Striking this balance depends on two factors. One is local autonomy. The central organizational role in the Banc One business system is played not by frontline employees but by the presidents of the 51 affiliate banks in the Banc One network. Affiliate presidents have exceptional power within their own region. They select products, establish prices and marketing strategy, make credit decisions, and set internal management policies. They can even overrule the activities of Banc One's centralized direct-marketing businesses. But while Banc One's affiliate system is highly decentralized, its success also depends on an elaborate, and highly centralized, process of continuous organizational learning. Affiliate presidents have the authority to mold bank products and services to local conditions, but they are also expected to learn from best practice throughout the Banc One system and to adapt it to their own operations.

Banc One collects an extraordinary amount of detailed and current information on each affiliate bank's internal and external performance. For example, the bank regularly publishes "league tables" on numerous measures of operating performance, with the worst performers listed first. This encourages collaboration to improve the weakest affiliates rather than competition to be the best. The bank also continuously engages in workflow reengineering and process simplification. The 100 most successful projects, known as the "Best of the Best," are documented and circulated among affiliates.

Wachovia and Banc One both compete on capabilities. Both banks focus on key business processes and place critical decision-making authority with the people directly responsible for them. Both manage these processes through a support system that spans the traditional functional structure, and senior managers concentrate on managing this system rather than controlling decisions. Both are decentralized but focused, single-minded but flexible.

But there the similarities end. Wachovia responds to individual customers en masse with personalization akin to that of a private banker. Banc One responds to local markets en masse with the flexibility and canniness of the traditional community bank. As a result, they focus on different business processes: Wachovia on the transfer of customer-specific information across numerous points of customer contact; Banc One on the transfer of best practices across affiliate banks. They also empower different levels in the organization: the personal banker at Wachovia, the affiliate president at Banc One.

Most important, they grow differently. Because so much of Wachovia's capability is embedded in the training of the personal bankers, the bank has made few acquisitions and can integrate them only very slowly. Banc One's capabilities, by contrast, are especially easy to transfer to new acquisitions. All the company needs to do is install its corporate MIS and intensively train the acquired bank's senior officers, a process that can be done in a few months, as opposed to the much longer period it takes Wachovia to train a new cadre of frontline bankers. Banc One has therefore made acquisitions almost a separate line of business.

If Banc One and Wachovia were to compete against each other, it is not clear who would win. Each would have strengths that the other could not match. Wachovia's capability to serve individual customers by cross-selling a wide range of banking products will in the long term probably allow the company to extract more profit per customer than Banc One. On the other hand, Wachovia cannot adapt its products, pricing, and promotion to local market conditions the way Banc One can. And Wachovia's growth rate is limited by the amount of time it takes to train new personal bankers.

Moreover, these differences are deep-seated. They define each of the two companies in ways that are not easy to change. Capabilities are often mutually exclusive. Choosing the right ones is the essence of strategy.

STRATEGY AND THE NEW ECONOMICS OF INFORMATION*

PHILIP B. EVANS AND THOMAS S. WURSTER, 1997

A fundamental shift in the economics of information is under way—a shift that is less about any specific new technology than about the fact that a new behavior is reaching critical mass. Millions of people at home and at work are communicating electronically using universal, open standards. This explosion in connectivity is the latest—and, for business strategists, the most important—wave in the information revolution.

Over the past decade, managers have focused on adapting their operating processes to new information technologies. Dramatic as those operating changes have been, a more profound transformation of the business landscape lies ahead. Executives—and not just those in high-tech or information companies—will be forced to rethink the strategic fundamentals of their business. Over the next decade, the new economics of information will precipitate changes in the structure of entire industries and in the ways companies compete.

Early signs of this change are not hard to find. Consider the recent near-demise of *Encyclopædia Britannica,* one of the strongest and best-known brand names in the world. Since 1990, sales of *Britannica*'s multivolume sets have plummeted by more than 50 percent. CD-ROMs came from nowhere and devastated the printed encyclopedia business as we traditionally understand it.

How was that possible? *Britannica* sells for somewhere in the region of $1,500 to $2,200. An encyclopedia on CD-ROM, such as Microsoft Encarta, sells for around $50. And many people get Encarta for free because it comes bundled with personal computers or CD-ROM drives. The cost of producing a set of encyclopedias—printing, binding, and physical distribution—is about $200 to $300. The cost of producing a CD-ROM is about $1.50. This is a spectacular, if small, example of the way information technologies and new competition can disrupt the conventional value proposition of an established business.

Imagine what the people at *Britannica* thought was happening. The editors probably viewed CD-ROMs as nothing more than electronic versions of inferior products. Encarta's content is licensed from the Funk & Wagnalls encyclopedia, which was historically sold in supermarkets. Microsoft merely spruced up that content with public-domain illustrations and movie clips. The way *Britannica*'s editors must have seen it, Encarta was not an encyclopedia at all. It was a toy.

Judging from their initial inaction, *Britannica*'s executives failed to understand what its customers were really buying. Parents had been buying *Britannica* less for its intellectual content than out of a desire to do the right thing for their children. Today, when parents want to do the right thing, they buy their kids a computer.

The computer, then, is *Britannica*'s real competitor. And along with the computer come a dozen CD-ROMs, one of which happens to be—as far as the customer is concerned—a more-or-less perfect substitute for the *Britannica*. When the threat became obvious, *Britannica* did create a CD-ROM version—but to avoid undercutting its sales force, the company bundled it with the printed version and charged $1,000 for the stand-alone disc. Revenues continued to decline. The best salespeople left. And *Britannica*'s owner, a trust controlled by the University of Chicago, finally sold out. Under new management, the company is now trying to rebuild the business around the Internet.

Britannica's downfall is more than a parable about the dangers of complacency. It demonstrates how quickly and drastically the new economics of information can change the rules of competition, allowing new players and substitute products to render obsolete such traditional sources of competitive advantage as a sales force, a supreme brand, and even the world's best content.

When managers hear this story, many respond, "Interesting, but it has nothing to do with my business. *Britannica* is in an information business. Thank goodness, I'm not." They feel less secure, however, when they learn that the largest chunk of *Britannica*'s cost structure was not the editorial content—which constituted only about 5 percent of costs—but the direct sales force. *Britannica*'s vulnerability was due largely to its dependence on the economics of a different kind of information: the economics of intensive personal selling. A whole host of businesses fit that description, among them automobiles, insurance, real estate, and travel.

Every Business Is an Information Business

In many industries not widely considered information businesses, information actually represents a large percentage of the cost structure. About one-third of the cost of health care in the United States—some $300 billion—is the cost of capturing, storing, and processing information relating to, for example, patient records, physicians' notes, test results, and insurance claims.

More fundamentally, information is the glue that holds together the structure of all businesses. A company's value chain consists of all the activities it performs to design, produce, market, deliver, and support its product. The value chains of companies that supply and buy from each other collectively make up an industry's value chain, its particular configuration of competitors, suppliers, distribution channels, and customers.*

---

* For a complete discussion of the value chain concept, see Michael Porter's *Competitive Advantage* (Free Press, 1985). Differences in value chains—that is, differences in how competitors perform strategic activities or in which activities they choose to perform—are the basis for competitive advantage.

When we think about a value chain, we tend to visualize a linear flow of physical activities. But the value chain also includes all the information that flows within a company and between a company and its suppliers, its distributors, and its existing or potential customers. Supplier relationships, brand identity, process coordination, customer loyalty, employee loyalty, and switching costs all depend on various kinds of information.

When managers talk about the value of customer relationships, for example, what they really mean is the proprietary information that they have about their customers and that their customers have about their company and its products. Brands, after all, are nothing but the information—real or imagined, intellectual or emotional—that consumers have in their heads about a product. And the tools used to build brands—advertising, promotion, and even shelf space—are themselves information or ways of delivering information.

Similarly, information defines supplier relationships. Having a relationship means that two corporations have established certain channels of communication built around personal acquaintance, mutual understanding, shared standards, electronic data interchange (EDI) systems, or the synchronization of production systems.

In any buyer-seller relationship, information can determine the relative bargaining power of the players. Auto dealers, for example, know the best local prices for a given model. Customers—unless they invest a lot of time shopping around—generally do not. Much of the dealer's margin depends on that asymmetry of information.

Not only does information define and constrain the relationship among the various players in a value chain, but in many businesses it forms the basis for competitive advantage—even when the cost of that information is trivial and the product or service is thoroughly physical. To cite some of the best-known examples, American Airlines for a long time used its control of the SABRE reservation system to achieve higher capacity utilization than its competitors. Wal-Mart Stores has exploited its EDI links with suppliers to increase its inventory turns dramatically. And Nike has masterfully employed advertising, endorsements, and the microsegmentation of its market to transform sneakers into high-priced fashion goods. All three companies compete as much on information as they do on their physical product.

In many ways, then, information and the mechanisms for delivering it stabilize corporate and industry structures and underlie competitive advantage. But the informational components of value are so deeply embedded in the physical value chain that, in some cases, we are just beginning to acknowledge their separate existence.

When information is carried by things—by a salesperson or by a piece of direct mail, for example—it goes where the things go, and no further. It is constrained to follow the linear flow of the physical value chain. But once everyone is connected electronically, information can travel by itself. The traditional link between the flow of product-related information and the flow of the product itself, between the economics of information and the economics of things, can be broken. What is truly revolutionary about the explosion in connectivity is the possibility it offers to unbundle information from its physical carrier.

The Tradeoff between Richness and Reach

Let's back up for a minute to consider why this is such a revolutionary proposition. To the extent that information is embedded in physical modes of delivery, its economics are governed by a basic law: the tradeoff between richness and reach. *Reach* simply means the number of people, at home or at work, exchanging information. *Richness* is defined by three aspects of the information itself. The first is bandwidth, or the amount of information that can be moved from sender to receiver in a given time. Stock quotes are narrowband, a film is broadband. The second is the degree to which the information can be customized. A TV ad is far less customized, but reaches far more people, for example, than a personal sales pitch. The third is interactivity. Dialogue is possible for a small group, but to reach millions of people the message must be a monologue.

In general, the communication of rich information has required proximity and dedicated channels whose costs or physical constraints have limited the size of the audience to which the information could be sent. Conversely, the communication of information to a large audience has required compromises in bandwidth, customization, and interactivity. (See the graph on page 104.) This pervasive tradeoff has shaped how companies communicate, collaborate, and conduct transactions internally and with customers, suppliers, and distributors.

A company's marketing mix, for example, is determined by apportioning resources according to this tradeoff. A company can embed its message in an advertisement, a piece of customized direct mail, or a personal sales pitch—alternatives increasing in richness but diminishing in reach.

The traditional economics of information.

Reach (connectivity)

When companies conduct business with each other, the number of parties they deal with is inversely proportional to the richness of the information they need to exchange: Citibank can trade currencies with hundreds of other banks each minute because the data exchange requires little richness; conversely, Wal-Mart has narrowed its reach by moving to fewer and larger long-term supplier contracts precisely because such contracts allow a richer coordination of marketing and logistical systems.

Within a corporation, traditional concepts of span of control and hierarchical reporting are predicated on the belief that communication cannot be rich and broad simultaneously. Jobs are structured to channel rich communication among a few people standing in a hierarchical relationship to one another (upward or downward), and broader communication is effected through the indirect routes of the organizational pyramid. Indeed, there is an entire economic theory (pioneered by Ronald H. Coase and Oliver E. Williamson*) that suggests the boundaries of the corporation are set by the economics of exchanging information: organizations enable the exchange of rich information among a narrow, internal group; markets enable the exchange of thinner information among a larger, external group. The point at which one mode becomes less cost-effective than the other determines the boundaries of the corporation.

The tradeoff between richness and reach, then, not only governs the old economics of information but is also fundamental to a whole

* Coase, R. 1937, "The Nature of the Firm" *Economica*, vol. 4, no. 4, pp. 386–405. Williamson, O. 1975, *Markets and Hierarchies: Analysis and Antitrust Implications*. Free Press, New York.

set of premises about how the business world works. And it is precisely this tradeoff that is now being blown up.

The rapid emergence of universal technical standards for communication, which is allowing everybody to communicate with everybody else at essentially zero cost, constitutes a sea change. And it is as much the agreement on standards as the technology itself that is making this change possible. It's easy to get lost in the technical jargon, but the important principle here is that the same technical standards underlie all the so-called net technologies—the Internet, which connects everyone; extranets, which connect companies to each other; and the intranets, which connect individuals within companies.

Those emerging open standards and the explosion in the number of people and organizations connected by networks are freeing information from the channels that have been required to exchange it, making those channels unnecessary or uneconomical. Although the standards may not be ideal for any one application, users are finding that they are good enough for most purposes today. And they are improving exponentially. Over time, corporations and individuals will be able to extend their reach by many orders of magnitude, with often a negligible sacrifice of richness.

Where once a sales force, a system of branches, a printing press, a chain of stores, or a delivery fleet served as formidable barriers to entry because it took years and heavy investment to build them, in this new world, they could suddenly become expensive liabilities. New competitors on the Internet will be able to come from nowhere to steal customers. Similarly, the replacement of expensive proprietary, legacy systems with inexpensive open extranets will make it easier and cheaper for companies to bid for supply contracts, join a virtual factory, or form a competing supply chain.

Inside large corporations, the emergence of universal, open standards for exchanging information over intranets encourages the emergence of cross-functional teams and accelerates the demise of hierarchical functions and their proprietary information systems.

The Deconstruction of the Value Chain

The changing economics of information threatens to undermine established value chains in many sectors of the economy, requiring virtually every company to rethink its strategy—not incrementally, but fundamentally. What will happen, for instance, to category killers such as Toys "R" Us and The Home Depot when a search engine on

The End of Channels and Hierarchies

In today's world, rich content passes through media with limited reach, which we call *channels*. The existence of channels creates *hierarchy*, both of choice (people have to gather rich information in an order dictated by the structure of the channels) and of power (some people have better access to rich information than do others). Hierarchy of choice is illustrated by the decision tree along which consumers are compelled to do their shopping in the physical world: They must choose a street, then a shop, then a department, then a shelf, then a product. They cannot select in any other sequence. They can return to the street and search along a different path, of course, but only by expending time and effort.

Hierarchy of power is illustrated by the traditional organization chart, where senior executives have a wider span of knowledge than do their subordinates.

Hierarchy enables richness, but constrains choice and creates asymmetries in information. The alternative to hierarchy is markets, which are symmetrical and open to the extent that they are perfect. But traditional markets trade only in less-rich information.

When the tradeoff between richness and reach is eliminated, channels are no longer necessary: Everyone communicates richly with everyone else on the basis of shared standards. This might be termed *hyperarchy*.

The World Wide Web is a hyperarchy. So are a deconstructed value chain within a business and a deconstructed supply chain within an industry. So are intranets. So are concepts of fluid, team-based collab-

Hierarchical decision tree.

Hierarchical organization.

oration at work. So, too, is the pattern of amorphous and permeable corporate boundaries characteristic of the companies in Silicon Valley. (So, too, incidentally, are the architectures of object-oriented programming in software and of packet switching in telecommunications.)

Hyperarchy challenges *all* hierarchies, whether of logic or of power, with the possibility (or the threat) of random access and information symmetry. It challenges all markets with the possibility of exchanging information far richer than the mere trading of products and certificates of ownership. The principles of hyperarchy will provide a better way to understand not just strategies for positioning within business and industry, but issues of corporate organization and even identity.

Hyperarchy.

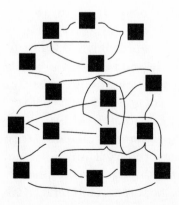

the Internet gives consumers more choice than any store? What will be the point of having a supplier relationship with General Electric when it posts its purchasing requirements on an Internet bulletin board and entertains bids from anybody inclined to respond? What will happen to health care providers and insurers if a uniform electronic format for patient records eliminates a major barrier that today discourages patients from switching hospitals or doctors?

Consider the future of newspapers that, like most businesses, are built on a vertically integrated value chain. Journalists and advertisers supply copy, editors lay it out, presses create the physical product, and an elaborate distribution system delivers it to the reader each morning.

Newspaper companies exist as intermediaries between the journalist and the reader because there are enormous economies of scale in printing and distribution. But when high-resolution electronic tablets advance to the point that readers consider them a viable alternative to newsprint, those traditional economies of scale will become irrelevant. Editors—or even journalists—will be able to e-mail content directly to readers.

Freed from the necessity of subscribing to entire physical newspapers, readers will be able to mix and match content from a virtually unlimited number of sources. News could be downloaded daily from different electronic news services. Movie reviews, recipes, and travel features could come just as easily from magazine or book publishers. Star columnists, cartoonists, or the U.S. Weather Service could send their work directly to subscribers. Intermediaries—search engines, alert services, formatting software, or editorial teams—could format and package the content to meet readers' individual interests. It does not follow that all readers will choose to unbundle all the current content of the physical newspaper, but the principal logic for that bundle—the economics of printing—will be gone.

This transformation is probably inevitable but distant. As newspaper executives correctly point out, the broadsheet is still an extraordinarily cheap and user-friendly way to distribute information. Little electronic tablets are not going to replace it very soon.

However, the timing of total deconstruction is not really the issue. Pieces of the newspaper can be unbundled today. Classified advertising is a natural on-line product. Think how much easier it would be to pay for, update, search through, and respond to classified ads. Stripping away classifieds, however, would remove 25 percent of the typical newspaper's revenues but less than 10 percent of its costs.

Newspaper companies have moved aggressively into the electronic classifieds business. They have exploited their incumbent advantage as makers of the original print marketplace to provide an integrated print and electronic offering that reaches the widest population of buyers and sellers, thus preserving the 60 percent to 80 percent margins they need from classifieds to cover their fixed printing costs.

But as more and more people use the electronic medium, companies focused on targeted segments of the electronic classifieds market (operating on, say, 15 percent margins) will gain share. The greater their share, by definition, the more attractive they will become to buyers and sellers. Eventually, the newspapers will either lose business, or (more likely) retain it by settling for much lower margins.

Either way, the subsidy that supports the fixed costs of the print product will be gone. So newspapers will cut content or raise prices to readers and advertisers, accelerating their defection. That, in turn, will create opportunities for another focused competitor to pick off another part of the value chain. Thus the greatest vulnerability for newspapers is not the total substitution of a new business model, but a steady erosion through a sequence of partial substitutions that will make the current business model unsustainable.

Retail banking is ripe for a similar upheaval. The current business model depends on a vertically integrated value chain through which multiple products are originated, packaged, sold, and cross-sold through proprietary distribution channels. The high costs of distribution drive economies of utilization and scale and thus govern strategy in retail banking as it works today.

Home electronic banking looks at first glance like another, but cheaper, distribution channel. Many banks see it that way, hoping that widespread adoption might enable them to scale down their higher-cost physical channels. Some are even offering proprietary software and electronic transactions for free. But something much deeper has happened than the emergence of a new distribution channel. Customers now can access information and make transactions in a variety of new ways.

Some 10 million people in the United States regularly use personal financial-management software such as Intuit's Quicken or Microsoft Money to manage their checkbooks and integrate their personal financial affairs. Current versions of these programs can use modems to access electronic switches operated by CheckFree or VISA Interactive, which in turn route instructions or queries to the customer's bank. Such a system lets customers pay bills, make transfers, receive electronic statements, and seamlessly integrate account data into their personal financial plan. In addition, almost all financial institutions supply information at their Web sites, which anybody on-line can access using a browser.

No single software program can achieve both richness and reach, yet. Quicken, Money, and proprietary bank software permit rich exchanges but only with the customer's own bank. Web browsers do much less but reach the entire universe of financial institutions. However, the software vendors and switch providers have the resources, and ultimately will have the motivation, to form alliances with financial institutions to eliminate this artificial tradeoff. Bridges between personal financial-management software and the Web, combined with imminent advances in reliability, security, digital signatures, and legally binding electronic contracts, will enable financial Web sites to provide the full range of banking services.

If that happens, the tradeoff between richness and reach will be broken. Customers will be able to contact any financial institution for any kind of service or information. They will be able to maintain a balance sheet on their desktop, drawing on data from multiple institutions. They will be able to compare alternative product offerings and to sweep funds automatically between accounts at different institutions. Bulletin boards or auctioning software will allow customers to announce their product requirements and accept bids. Chat rooms will permit customers to share information with each other or get advice from human experts.

The sheer breadth of choice will create the need for third parties to play the role of navigator or facilitating agent. For example, some companies will have an incentive to create (or simply make available) databases on interest rates, risk ratings, and service histories. Others will create insurance and mortgage calculators or intelligent-agent software that can search for and evaluate product offerings. Still other companies will authenticate the identity of counterparties or serve as guarantors of performance, confidentiality, or creditworthiness. (See the diagram on page 111.)

As it becomes easier for customers to switch from one supplier to another, the competitive value of one-stop shopping and established relationships will drop. Cross-selling will become more difficult.

The transformation of retail banking. In today's integrated business model, the retail bank stands between the customer and the full range of financial services. But soon, through internet technologies, customers will have direct access to product providers. As choices proliferate, totally new businesses will arise to help customers navigate through the expanded range of banking options.

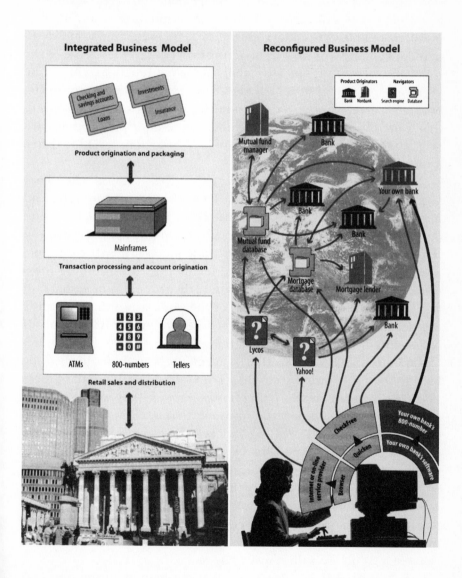

Information about the customer's needs or behavior will be harder for the provider to obtain. Competitive advantage will be determined product by product, and therefore providers with broad product lines will lose ground to focused specialists.

In this new world, distribution will be done by the phone company; statements by personal financial-management software, facilitation by different kinds of agent software, and origination by any number of different kinds of product specialists. The integrated value chain of retail banking will have been deconstructed.

Deconstructed, but not destroyed. All the old functions will still be performed, as well as some new ones. Banks will not become obsolete, but their current business definitions will—specifically, the concept that a bank is an integrated business where multiple products are originated, packaged, sold, and cross-sold through proprietary distribution channels.

Many bankers—like encyclopedia executives—deny all this. They argue that most customers do not have personal computers, and many who do are not choosing to use them for banking. They point out that people worry about the security of on-line transactions, and that consumers trust banks more than they trust software companies. All true. However, on-line technology is advancing inexorably. And because they generate a disproportionate share of deposits and fees, the 10 percent of the population that currently use personal financial-management software probably account for 75 percent of the profit of the banking system.

Market research suggests that Quicken users are more likely to be loyal to their software than to their banks. In one study, half of them said that if they were changing banks anyway, they would require their new bank to support the software, that is, allow them to transact their business on-line using Quicken. Now, bank accounts churn at the rate of about 10 percent a year. If a bank that doesn't support Quicken loses half the new Quicken-using customers it might otherwise attract every year, and such customers churn at the average rate, then it follows that the bank will lose 3 percent to 5 percent of its retail-customer margin per year. Refusal to support Quicken (or provide an acceptable alternative) could undermine the entire value of a franchise within just a few years.

The deconstruction of the value chain in banking is not unprecedented. Fifteen years ago, corporate banking was a spread business, that is, banks made money by charging a higher interest rate for loans than they paid for deposits. Their business model required them to form deep relationships with their corporate customers so that they could pump their own products through that distribution system. But then, thanks to technology, corporate customers got access to the same financial markets that the banks used. Today, corporate banking consists of small businesses that largely stand alone (even when they function under the umbrella of a big bank) and compete product by product. Credit flows directly from ultimate lender to ultimate borrower, facilitated by bankers who rate the risk, give advice, make markets, and serve as custodians. The bankers make money through the fees they charge for these individual services. Clients no longer bundle their purchases, and relationships are more volatile. Once critical, an advantage in distribution today counts for little.

Newspapers and banking are not special cases. The value chains of scores of other industries will become ripe for unbundling. The logic is most compelling—and therefore likely to strike soonest—in information businesses where the cost of physical distribution is high—newspapers, ticket sales, insurance, financial information, scientific publishing, software, and of course encyclopedias. But in any business where the physical value chain has been compromised for the sake of delivering information, there is an opportunity to unbundle the two, creating a separate information business and allowing (or compelling) the physical one to be streamlined. All it will take to deconstruct a business is a competitor that focuses on the vulnerable sliver of information in its value chain.

WHAT WILL HAPPEN TO YOUR BUSINESS?

All businesses will eventually be affected by the shifting economics of information, but not all at the same rate or in the same way. Answers to the following questions are a first step in determining how a business could be restructured:

1. How and where in the current value chain of this business is information a component of value?
2. Where are tradeoffs currently being made between richness and reach in this business?

(continued)

3. In what situations will these tradeoffs be eliminated?
4. Which critical activities—especially informational activities—could be peeled off as stand-alone businesses?
5. Could the underlying physical businesses be run more efficiently if the information functions were stripped away?
6. What new activities—especially facilitating-agent roles—might be required?
7. Among the successor businesses, how would risks and rewards be distributed?
8. How would losing control over key activities affect the profitability of the current business model?
9. Which current strategic assets could become liabilities?
10. What new capabilities are needed to dominate the new businesses that will emerge?

Implications for Competitive Advantage

Deconstructing a vertically integrated value chain does more than transform the structure of a business or an industry—it alters the sources of competitive advantage. The new economics of information therefore present threats to established businesses but also represent a new set of opportunities. Every industry will shift according to its own dynamics, and those shifts will occur at different speeds and with varying intensity. No single set of predictions can be applied across the board, but some fundamental strategic implications of the changing economics of information can be drawn.

Existing value chains will fragment into multiple businesses, each of which will have its own sources of competitive advantage. When individual functions having different economies of scale or scope are bundled together, the result is a compromise of each—an averaging of the effects. When the bundles of functions are free to re-form as separate businesses, however, each can exploit its own sources of competitive advantage to the fullest.

Take car retailing in the United States. Dealerships provide information about products in showrooms and through test-drives. They hold inventory and distribute cars. They broker financing. They make a market in secondhand cars. They operate maintenance and repair services. Although most of these activities are physical, the bundle of functions is held together by the classic informational logic of one-stop shopping. A dealer's competitive advantage is therefore based on a mixture of location, scale, cost, sales force management, quality of service, and affiliations with car manufacturers and banks.

Bundling these functions creates compromises. Each step in the value chain has different economies of scale. If the functions were unbundled, specialty companies that offer test-drives could take cars to prospective buyers' homes. Distributors of new cars could have fewer, larger sites in order to minimize inventory and transportation costs. Providers of after-sales service would be free to operate more and smaller local facilities to furnish better service. Auto manufacturers could provide product information via the Internet. And car purchasers could obtain financing by putting their business out for bid via an electronic broker. Eliminate the informational glue that combines all these functions in a single, compromised business model, and the multiple businesses that emerge will evolve in radically different directions.

Some new businesses will benefit from network economies of scale, which can give rise to monopolies. In a networked market, the greater the number of people connected, the greater the value of being connected, thus creating network economies of scale. There is no point, for example, in being the only person in the world who owns a telephone. As the number of people who own telephones rises, the value of hooking up for any one individual progressively increases.

This self-reinforcing dynamic builds powerful monopolies. Businesses that broker information, make markets, or set standards are all taking advantage of this dynamic. The implication: The first company to achieve a critical mass often will take all, or nearly all—although the continuing battle between first-mover Netscape and Microsoft in the market for network browsers illustrates that the lead of the first mover is not always insurmountable.

Reaching critical mass can be an enormous challenge. General Electric may have solved the problem of critical mass by using its own enormous purchasing power. GE has opened its internal electronic-procurement system to other buyers of industrial goods, turning its own sourcing system into a market-making business.

As value chains fragment and reconfigure, new opportunities will arise for purely physical businesses. In many businesses today, the efficiency of the physical value chain is compromised for the purposes of delivering information. Shops, for example, try to be efficient warehouses and effective merchandisers simultaneously and are often really neither.

The new economics of information will create opportunities to rationalize the physical value chain, often leading to businesses whose physically based sources of competitive advantage will be more sustainable.

Consider the current battle in bookselling. Amazon.com, an electronic retailer on the Web, has no physical stores and very little inventory. It offers an electronic list of 2.5 million books, ten times larger than that of the largest chain store, and customers can search through that list by just about any criterion. Amazon orders most of its books from two industry wholesalers in response to customers' requests. It then repacks and mails them from a central facility.

Amazon.com cannot offer instant delivery; nor can customers physically browse the shelves the way they can in a traditional bookstore. Its advantages are based on superior information and lower physical costs. Customers can, for example, access book reviews. They have greater choice and better searching capabilities. And Amazon.com saves money on inventory and retail space.

But Amazon's success is not a given. The discount chains are aggressively launching their own Web businesses. There is nothing defensible about Amazon's wide selection since it really comes from the publishers' and wholesalers' databases. By double-handling the books, Amazon still incurs unnecessary costs.

In fact, the wholesalers in the book industry could probably create the lowest-cost distribution system by filling customers' orders directly. If competition pushes the industry in that direction, electronic retailers would become mere search engines connected to somebody else's database—and that would not add much value or confer on them much of a competitive advantage. The wholesalers could be the big winners.

When a company focuses on different activities, the value proposition underlying its brand identity will change. Since a brand reflects its company's value chain, deconstruction will require new brand strategies. For instance, the importance of branches and automated teller machines today leads many banks to emphasize *ubiquity* in their brand image (Citibank, for example). However, the reconfiguration of financial services might lead a company to focus on being a product provider. For such a strategy, *performance* becomes the key message, as it is for Fidelity. Another brand strategy might focus on helping customers navigate the universe of third-party products. The key message would be *trust,* as it is for Charles Schwab.

New branding opportunities will emerge for third parties that neither produce a product nor deliver a primary service. Navigator or agent brands have been around for a long time. The *Zagat Survey* of restaurants and *Consumer Reports* are two obvious examples. It's the *Zagat Survey*'s own brand—its credibility in restaurant reviewing—that steers its readers toward a particular establishment.

Recently, the Platform for Internet Content Selection (PICS) was established. This is a way of embedding third-party ratings into searchable information about any Web site. It enables anybody to rate anything, and it makes those ratings ubiquitous, searchable, sortable, and costless.

The dramatic proliferation of networked markets increases the need for navigators and other facilitating agents, for example those that guarantee a product's performance or assume risk. Thus there will be many new opportunities to develop brands.

Bargaining power will shift as a result of a radical reduction in the ability to monopolize the control of information. Market power often comes from controlling a choke point in an information channel and extracting tolls from those dependent on the flow of information through it. For example, sellers to retail customers today use their control over the information available to buyers to minimize comparison shopping and maximize cross-selling. But when richness and reach extend to the point where such channels are unnecessary, that game will stop. Any choke point could then be circumvented. Buyers will know their alternatives as well as the seller does. Some new intermediaries—organizers of virtual markets—may even evolve into aggregators of buying power, playing suppliers off against one another for the benefit of the purchasers they represent.

WHERE THE NEW BUSINESSES WILL EMERGE

In a world of limited connectivity, choices at each point in the value chain are, by definition, finite. In contrast, broadband connectivity means infinite choice. But infinite choice also means infinite bewilderment. This navigation problem can be solved in all sorts of ways, and each solution is a potential business.

The navigator could be a database. The navigator could be a search engine. The navigator could be intelligent-agent software. The navigator

(continued)

could be somebody giving advice. The navigator could be a brand providing recommendations or endorsements.

The logic of navigation can be observed in a number of businesses in which choice has proliferated. People often react to clutter by going back to the tried and true. Customer research indicates that people faced with complex choices either gravitate toward dominant brands or confine their search to narrow formats, each offering a presorted set of alternatives. In the grocery store, for example, where the number of products has quadrupled over the last 15 years, hundreds of segmented specialty brands have gained market share in almost every category. But so have the one or two leading brands. The proliferation of choice has led to the fragmentation of the small brands and the simultaneous concentration of the large ones. The losers are the brands in the middle.

Similarly, television viewers seem to flock to the hit shows without caring which network those shows are on. But they select specialty programming, such as nature documentaries or music videos, by tuning in to a cable channel offering that format. In essence, the viewer selects the channel, and the channel selects the content. In the first case, the product's brand pulls volume through the channel; in the second, the channel's brand pushes content toward receptive viewers.

Those two approaches by the consumer yield different patterns of competitive advantage and profitability. Networks need hit shows more than the hit shows need any network: The producers have the bargaining power and therefore receive the higher return. Conversely, producers of low-budget nature documentaries need a distributor more than the distributor needs any program, and the profit pattern is, therefore, the reverse. In one year, the popular comedian Bill Cosby earned more than the entire CBS network; the Discovery Channel probably earns more than all of its content providers put together. Despite the fact that CBS's 1996 revenues were about six times those of the Discovery Channel, Discovery's 52 percent profit margin dwarfed CBS's 4 percent.

The economics playing out in the television industry are a model for what will likely emerge in the world of universal connectivity. Think of it as two different value propositions: one is a focus on popular content; the other, a focus on navigation.

Navigation might have been the right strategy for *Encyclopædia Britannica* in responding to the threat from CD-ROMs. Its greatest competitive asset, after all, was a brand that certified high-quality, objective information. Given the clutter of cyberspace, what could be more compelling than a *Britannica*-branded guide to valuable information on the Internet?

If *Britannica*'s executives had written off their sales force, if they had built alliances with libraries and scientific journals, if they had built a Web site that had hot links directly to original sources, if they had created a universal navigator to valuable and definitive information validated by the *Encyclopædia Britannica* brand, they would have been heroes. They might have established a monopoly, following the example of Bill Gates. In fact, he might have been forced to acquire them.

Customers' switching costs will drop, and companies will have to develop new ways of generating customer loyalty. Cmmon standards for exchanging and processing information and the growing numbers of individuals accessing networks will drastically reduce switching costs.

Proprietary electronic data interchange systems, for example, lock companies into their supply relationships. But extranets linking companies with their suppliers using the Internet's standard protocols make switching almost costless. The U.S. auto industry is creating such an extranet, called the Automotive Network eXchange (ANX). Linking together auto manufacturers and several thousand automotive suppliers, the system is expected to save its participants a billion dollars a year, dramatically reduce errors, and speed the flow of information to second- and third-tier suppliers. By reducing switching costs and creating greater symmetry of information, ANX will also intensify competition at every level of the supply chain.

Incumbents could easily become victims of their obsolete physical infrastructures and their own psychology. Assets that traditionally offered competitive advantages and served as barriers to entry will become liabilities. The most vulnerable companies are those currently providing information that could be delivered more effectively and inexpensively electronically—for example, the physical parts of sales and distribution systems, such as branches, shops, and sales forces. As with newspapers, even the loss of a small portion of customers to new distribution channels or the migration of a high-margin product to the electronic domain can throw a business with high fixed costs into a downward spiral.

It may be easy to grasp this point intellectually, but it is much harder for managers to act on its implications. In many businesses, the assets in question are integral to a company's core competence. It is not easy psychologically to withdraw from assets so central to a company's identity. It is not easy strategically to downsize assets that have high fixed costs when so many customers still prefer the current business model. It is not easy financially to cannibalize current profits. And it is certainly not easy to squeeze the profits of distributors to whom one is tied by long-standing customer relationships or by franchise laws.

Newcomers suffer from none of these inhibitions. They are unconstrained by management traditions, organizational structures, customer relationships, or fixed assets. Recall the cautionary tale of *Encyclopædia Britannica*. Executives must deconstruct their own businesses. If they don't, someone else will.

COLLABORATION RULES*

PHILIP EVANS AND BOB WOLF, 2005

Corporate leaders seeking growth, learning, and innovation may find the answer in a surprising place: the open-source software community. Unknowingly, perhaps, the folks who brought you Linux are virtuoso practitioners of new work principles that produce energized teams and lower costs. Nor are they alone.

By any measure, Linux is a powerfully competitive product. It is estimated that more servers run on Linux than on any other operating system. It has overwhelmed UNIX as a commercial offering. And its advantages extend beyond cost and quality to the speed with which it is enhanced and improved. While partisans debate its technical limitations and treatment of intellectual property, they agree that the product's success is inseparable from its distinctive mode of production. Specifically, Linux is the creation of an essentially voluntary, self-organizing community of thousands of programmers and companies. Most leaders would sell their grandmothers for workforces that collaborate as efficiently, frictionlessly, and creatively as the self-styled Linux "hackers."

But Linux is software, and software is kind of weird. Toyota, however, is a company like any other—any other consistently ranked among the world's top-performing organizations, that is. The automaker has long been a leader in quality and lean production, and the success of the hybrid Prius has established its reputation as an innovator. We have found that Toyota's managerial methods resemble, in a number of their fundamentals, the workings of the Linux community; the Toyota Production System (TPS) owes some of its vaunted responsiveness to open-source traits. In fact, Toyota itself is evolving into a hybrid between a conventional hierarchy and a Linux-like self-organizing network.

(Throughout this article, we use the term *Linux* as shorthand for the free/open-source software community that developed and continues to refine the operating system and other open-source programs. We use *Toyota* as shorthand for the Toyota Production System, which comprises Toyota and its direct—"tier one" in automotive parlance— suppliers in Japan and the United States.)

Toyota is remarkably similar to Linux in the way it blends key characteristics of both markets and hierarchies. Like markets, the Toyota and Linux communities can be self-organizing, but unlike markets, they don't use cash or contracts at critical junctures. Like hierarchies, Toyota and Linux enjoy low transaction costs, but unlike hierarchies, their members may belong to many different organizations (or to none at all) and are not corseted by specific, predefined roles and responsibilities. And like hierarchies, members share a common purpose, but that purpose emanates from self-motivation rather than from the external incentives or sanctions that hierarchies generally impose. In these respects, Toyota and Linux represent the best of both worlds. An analysis of their common characteristics suggests how high-performance organizations remain productive and inventive even under grueling conditions. We believe those lessons can significantly improve the way work in most organizations gets done.

Tuesday, December 2, 2003

Near midnight, Andrea Barisani, system administrator in the physics department of the University of Trieste, discovered that an attacker had struck his institution's Gentoo Linux server. He traced the breach to a vulnerable spot in the Linux kernel and another in rsync, a file transfer mechanism that automatically replicates data among computers. This was a serious attack: Any penetration of rsync could compromise files in thousands of servers worldwide.

Barisani woke some colleagues, who put him in touch with Mike Warfield, a senior researcher at Internet Security Systems in Atlanta, and with Andrew "Tridge" Tridgell, a well-known Linux programmer in Australia on whose doctoral thesis rsync was based. They directed Barisani's message (made anonymous for security reasons) to another Australian, Martin Pool, who worked for Hewlett-Packard in Canberra and had been a leader in rsync's development. Although Pool was no longer responsible for rsync (nobody was), he immediately hit the phones and e-mail, first quizzing Warfield and Dave Dykstra (another early contributor to rsync's development, who was based in California) about vulnerabilities and then helping Barisani trace the failure line by line.

By morning Trieste time, Pool and Barisani had found the precise location of the breach. Pool contacted the current rsync development group, while Barisani connected with the loose affiliation of amateurs and professionals that package Gentoo Linux, and he posted an early warning advisory to the Gentoo site. Pool and Paul "Rusty" Russell (a fellow Canberran who works for IBM) then labored through the Australian night to write a patch, and within five hours Gentoo user-developers started testing the first version. Meanwhile, Tridge crafted a description of the vulnerability and its fix, being sure (at Pool's urging) to credit Barisani and Warfield for their behind-the-scenes efforts. On Thursday afternoon Canberra time, the announcement and the patch were posted to the rsync Web site and thus distributed to Linux users worldwide.

A few days after the emergency, having caught up on his sleep, Barisani volunteered to collaborate with Warfield in setting up a system of deliberately vulnerable servers to lure the system cracker into revealing himself.

No one authorized or directed this effort. No one—amateur or professional—was paid for participating or would have been sanctioned for not doing so. No one's job hinged on stopping the attack. No one clammed up for fear of legal liability. Indeed, the larger user community was kept informed of all developments. Yet despite the need for the highest security, a group of some 20 people, scarcely any of whom had ever met, employed by a dozen different companies, living in as many time zones and straying far from their job descriptions, accomplished in about 29 hours what might have taken colleagues in adjacent cubicles weeks or months.

It's tempting to dismiss this as an example of hacker weirdness—admirable, yes, but nothing to do with real business. Consider, however, another story.

Saturday, February 1, 1997

At 4:18 A.M., a fire broke out in the Kariya Number 1 plant of Aisin Seiki, a major Japanese automotive parts supplier. Within minutes, the building and virtually all the specialized machinery inside were destroyed. Kariya Number 1 produces 99 percent of the brake fluid-proportioning valves, or P-valves, for Toyota's Japanese operations—parts required by every vehicle Toyota builds. And Toyota, true to its just-in-time principles, had less than a day's inventory. The Japanese Toyota Production System faced the possibility of a total shutdown lasting months.

Within hours, Aisin engineers met with their counterparts at Toyota and Toyota's other tier-one suppliers. The group agreed to improvise as much production as possible. As news spread through the supplier network, some tier twos volunteered to play leadership roles. Aisin sent blueprints for the valves to any supplier that requested them and distributed whatever undamaged tools, raw materials, and work in process could be salvaged. Aisin and Toyota engineers helped rig production lines in 62 locations—unused machine shops, Toyota's own prototyping shop, even a sewing machine facility owned by Brother. Denso, Toyota's largest supplier, volunteered to manage the messy logistics of shipping valves to Aisin for inspection and then on to Toyota's stalled assembly lines.

Everyone was surprised when a small tier-two supplier of welding electrodes, Kyoritsu Sangyo, was first to deliver production-quality valves to Toyota—1,000 of them, just 85 hours after the fire. Others followed rapidly, and Toyota started reopening assembly lines on Wednesday. Roughly two weeks after the halt, the entire supply chain was back to full production. Six months later, Aisin distributed an emergency response guide containing lessons drawn from the experience and recommending procedures for responding to such situations in the future.

No one individual or organization planned this effort: Rather, people and companies stepped in where they could. Competitors collaborated. No one at the time was paid for contributing. Months later, Aisin compensated the other companies for the direct costs of the valves they had delivered. Toyota gave each tier-one supplier an honorarium based on current sales to the automaker, encouraging—but not requiring—them to do likewise for their own tier twos.

Few communities appear more different than the anarchistic, caffeinated, hirsute world of hackers and the disciplined, tea-sipping, clean-cut world of Japanese auto engineering. But the parallels between these stories are striking. In both of them, individuals found one another and stepped into roles without a plan or an established command-and-control structure. An extended human network organized itself in hours and "swarmed" against a threat. People, teams, and companies worked together without legal contracts or negotiated payment. And despite the lack of any authoritarian stick or financial carrot, those people worked *like hell* to solve the problem.

Now, obviously, these were emergency responses. But a look at the day-to-day operations of the Linux community and the Toyota Production System reveals that those responses were merely intensifications of the way people were already working.

Obsession, Interaction, and a Light Touch

The rules of markets are about cash and contracts. The rules of hierarchies are about authority and accountability. But at the core of the Linux and Toyota communities are rules about three entirely different things: how individuals and small groups work together; how, and how widely, they communicate; and how leaders guide them toward a common goal.

A Common Work Discipline

The Linux and Toyota communities are both composed of engineers, so members have the same skills as their colleagues and speak the same language. But these groups are far more disciplined and rigorous in their approach to work than are other engineering communities. Both emphasize granularity: They pay attention to small details, eliminate problems at the source, and trim anything resembling excess, whether it be work, code, or material. Linux members, for example, share an obsession with writing minimal code, compiling each day's output before proceeding to the next and extirpating programming flaws as they go along. For their part, TPS engineers are relentless in applying short cycles of trial and error, focusing on just one thing at a time, and getting inside and observing actual processes. Both groups carry those principles to apparent extremes. Linux programmers whittle away at code in pursuit not of computational efficiency but of elegance. Toyota engineers reject stampings for the Lexus hood—while flawless and entirely within spec—because the sheen, to their eyes, lacks luster.

Widespread, Granular Communication

In both the Linux and Toyota communities, information about problems and solutions is shared widely, frequently, and in small increments. Most Linux hacker communication is not between individuals but by postings to open, searchable Listservs. Anyone can review the version history of the code and the Listserv debates—not executive summaries or abstracts but the raw activity itself. And every code contribution is stress tested by scores of people. As a famous open-source mixed metaphor puts it: "With a thousand eyes, all bugs are shallow." The median upload to the Linux kernel is a mere dozen lines of code. The working alpha version is recompiled every 24 hours, so hackers reconcile their efforts almost continuously. If someone worked in isolation for six months on even the most brilliant contribution, it would probably be rejected for lack of compatibility with the others' efforts.

The Toyota philosophy of continuous improvement likewise comprises a thousand small collaborations. Toyota engineers are famously drilled to "ask why five times" to follow a chain of causes and effects back to a problem's root. This is not a vapid cliché about thinking deeply. Quite the contrary, in fact. The precept's merit is precisely in its superficiality. Saying that B causes A is simplistic—all the complexities of multiple interactions boiled down to a single cause and effect. But the chain of thought required to discover that C causes B, and D causes C, quickly takes you into a new domain, probably someone else's. So rather than concoct complex solutions within their own domains, engineers must seek simple ones beyond them. "Doing your why-whys," as the practice is known, is not about depth at all—it's about breadth.

And as with Linux, Toyota's communication protocols enforce this discipline. Each meeting addresses just one topic and drives toward a specific outcome, even if that means the same people meet more than once in a day. Lessons are written in a standard format on a single sheet of A3 paper. And everyone learns how to craft these reports, down to the fold in the document that shows the main points and conceals the details.

Leaders as Connectors

At every level, Linux and TPS leaders play three critical roles. They instruct community members—often by example—in the disciplines we've just described. They articulate clear and simple goals for each project based on their strategic vision. And they connect people, by merit of being very well connected themselves. The top Linux programmers process upwards of 300 or 400 e-mails daily. Fujio Cho, the president of Toyota, manages by similarly numerous daily interactions that transcend the normal chain of command.

Neither community treats leading as a discipline distinct from doing. Rather, the credibility and, therefore, authority of leaders derives from their proficiency as practitioners. The content of leaders' staccato communications is less *about* work than it *is* work. (When Linux creator Linus Torvalds dashes off his scores of daily e-mails, he writes almost as much in the C programming language as he does in English.)

Occasionally, leaders do have to perform traditional leadership acts, such as arbitrating conflicts. That, however, is the exception and is viewed as a bit of a system failure. The default assumption is that, as far as possible, managers don't manage in a traditional sense: The human network manages itself. In Linux, development priorities are decided not by a CEO but by thousands of hackers voting with their feet by choosing what to work on. That kind of radical self-management does not happen at Toyota, except in emergencies. But even in daily operations, a single production worker who sees a quality problem can stop the line, and project teams have wide latitude to tap resources, make purchase decisions, and pursue priorities they set for themselves.

Taken together, these three principles seed a continuously adapting system. Over and over, ideas are formulated in tight, testable packets; they are communicated with minimal attenuation through established, direct, person-to-person connections; and where links are absent, widely connected leader-practitioners create them as needed. This is

BUILDING VIBRANT HUMAN NETWORKS

Companies laying the groundwork for high-performance collaboration should follow these principles:

- Deploy pervasive collaborative technology. Keep it simple and open: "small pieces loosely joined," in Cluetrain Manifesto coauthor David Weinberger's felicitous phrase. Tools should work together through common standards and be as compatible as possible with those of the rest of the world. Think options not integration, adaptability not static efficiency.

- Keep work visible. Unless there is a really good reason not to, let everybody see everybody's real work. Let people learn to filter and sort for themselves. Don't abstract, summarize, or channel. Fodder is good. Put it within everyone's reach.

- Build communities of trust. When people trust one another, they are more likely to collaborate freely and productively. When people trust their organizations, they are more likely to give of themselves now in anticipation of future reward. And when organizations trust each other, they are more likely to share intellectual property without choking on legalisms.

- Think modularly. Reengineering was about thinking linearly: managing the end-to-end process instead of discrete functions. That approach fosters focused efficiency but inhibits variety and adaptability. Modularity is the reverse: sacrificing static efficiency for the recombinant value of options. Think modular teams as well as processes. The finer, the better.

- Encourage teaming. Celebrate the sacrifices that teams make for the broader enterprise, including customers and suppliers. Dismantle individualized performance metrics and rewards that pit people against one another. Cheap transactions among the many fuel more innovation than expensive incentives aimed at the few. Reward the group, and the group will reward you.

discipline, but not the discipline of conformity produced by controls and incentives. Rather, it resembles the discipline of science. Like scientific communities, these systems rely on common procedures, common rules for communication and testing, and common goals clearly understood. Individual behavior is rigorously cautious, but collective achievement is marked by continuous, radical innovation.

What They Know and How They Know It

At the heart of Linux and the TPS, then, is a set of work, communication, and leadership practices that contributes to a new form of collaboration. This collaboration also relies on two infrastructure components: a shared pool of knowledge and universally available tools for moving knowledge around.

Common Intellectual Property

The General Public License under which Linux is published requires that all distributors make their source code freely available so that others can freely emend it. This viral principle prevents code from being stowed away in proprietary products. That transparency, in turn, breaks down the distinction between producer and user. A sophisticated "customer" like Andrea Barisani is really a user-developer, who fixes flaws and adds features for his own benefit, then shares those improvements with everyone else. Such a role is impossible when proprietary code is licensed from a commercial vendor. Similarly, Toyota's supply chain is predicated on the principle that while product knowledge (such as a blueprint) is someone's intellectual property, process knowledge is shared. That breaks down some distinctions among companies. Toyota's suppliers regularly share extensive process improvement lessons both vertically and laterally, even with their competitors. In Japan, suppliers are generally exclusive to a single OEM, so the collective benefit of that shared information stays within the Toyota supply chain. But even in the United States, where Toyota is just one of several customers for most of its tier ones, the carmaker does the same thing through its Bluegrass Automotive Manufacturers Association, which disseminates best practices to all members.

Simple, Pervasive Technology

Although information is the lifeblood of the Linux and TPS communities, their circulation systems are surprisingly rudimentary. Linux developers produce state-of-the-art software using communication technology no more sophisticated than e-mail and Listservs—but those mundane tools are used by everyone. Indeed, so great is the value placed on universality that plain-text, rather than formatted, e-mails are the norm, ensuring that messages will appear exactly the same to all recipients. Toyota, whose products are state-of-the-art as well, also prefers simple and pervasive internal technology. An empty kanban bin signals the need for parts replenishment; a length of duct tape on the assembly-line floor allots the completion times of tasks on a moving vehicle. Quality control problems on the assembly line are announced via pagers and television monitors. And everyone gets the alert. Even Ray Tanguay, head of Toyota Canada, is paged whenever a flaw is found in the latest Lexus consignment on the dock in Long Beach, California, or in a service bay anywhere in North America.

The Power of Trust and Applause

Such extremely rich, flexible collaborations have positive psychological consequences for participants and powerful competitive ones for their organizations. Those consequences are rich common knowledge, the ability to organize teams modularly, extraordinary motivation, and high levels of trust.

Rich Semantic Knowledge

A rigorous work discipline, common intellectual property, and constant sharing combine to distribute knowledge widely and relatively evenly across human networks. That knowledge includes not just the formal, syntactic information found in databases but also the semantically rich, ambiguous knowledge about content and process that is the currency of creative collaboration. What do we mean by the sheen of a body stamping having insufficient luster? What, precisely, must we discuss with the steel company to correct such an ill-defined problem? This kind of no-easy-answer question is continually discussed and resolved in a thousand small-team collaborations. The resulting nuanced thinking and richer common vocabulary on such matters are fed back into the knowledge pool, where they are available for further refinement by the whole community.

Modular Teaming

Modularity is a design principle by which a complex process or product is divided into simple parts connected by standard rules. In modular arrangements of teams, each team focuses on small, simple tasks that together make up a larger whole. Modularity allows an organization to run multiple, parallel experiments, making many small bets instead of a few large ones. The Toyota suppliers organized themselves this way to make P-valves, operating partly by direction but chiefly by volunteering to do what each knew best. The Gentoo group, Tridge's security experts, and Pool's circle of rsync alumni were preexisting and overlapping modules that mixed and matched roles as the emergency required.

When we mapped the patterns of day-to-day collaboration across the entire Linux kernel development effort, we found that such modular arrangements are pervasive and, to a degree, nest within one another. This creates a kind of dynamic organization chart—a chart that nobody wrote but one that enables the community to expand and adapt without collapsing into chaos.

Intrinsic Motivation

The Linux and TPS communities dissociate money from key transactions. Yet despite weak financial incentives, they command a level of motivation higher than that found in conventional environments. Monetary carrots and accountability sticks, psychologists have consistently found, motivate people to perform narrow, specified tasks but generally discourage people from going beyond them. Admiration and applause are far more effective stimulants of above-and-beyond behavior. "The personal reputation of the developer is attached to every release," Linus Torvalds explained to technology columnist Robert Cringely in 1998. "If you are making something to give away to the world, something that represents to millions of users your philosophy of computing, you will always make it the very best product you can."

Psychologists also emphasize the motivational importance of autonomy. Linux programmers decide for themselves how and where to contribute, and they enjoy the satisfaction of producing something whose quality is defined not by a marketing department nor by accountants but by their own exacting standards. Coauthor Bob Wolf and MIT's Karim Lakhani surveyed more than 800 user-developers, and over half said that their open-source work is the most valuable and creative endeavor in their professional lives.

The Toyota Production System doesn't offer such extreme autonomy, of course, and employees don't work for free. But compared with their counterparts in the rest of the auto industry, TPS workers enjoy fewer controls, greater encouragement of individual initiative, fewer metrics attached to individual performance, and louder peer applause. Professional and corporate pride, not Toyota's honorarium, was the payoff for the team at Kyoritsu Sangyo when it delivered the first batch of P-valves. That same pride is felt by a junior assembly-line worker when he is trusted by his peers to experiment with process improvements and to stop the line if something goes wrong.

High Levels of Trust

When information flows freely, reputation, more than reciprocity, becomes the basis for trust. Operating under constant scrutiny—which is challenging but not hostile—workers know their reputations are at risk, and that serves as a guarantor of good behavior, the equivalent of contracts in a market or audits in a hierarchy. Hence, the obsession in the Linux community with acknowledging code contributions and including personal e-mail addresses in the comment fields of Listservs. Hence the generous public credit bestowed on Barisani and Warfield. Hence the collective celebration of Kyoritsu Sangyo's heroic efforts.

With their reputations at stake, people are less likely to act opportunistically. With the same information available to everyone, there is less chance that one party will exploit another's ignorance. And with a common vocabulary and way of working, fewer misunderstandings occur. Those factors drive up trust, the fundamental social capital of these communities.

Trust would matter less if there were no cost to exiting these networks or if transactions were of radically different sizes (since that would tempt people or companies to break the rules when a big opportunity arose). But in both the Linux and Toyota communities, entry to the inner circle is a hard-earned privilege, and both operate on many small exchanges.

And, of course, where trust is the currency, reputation is a source of power. In a sparse network, such as most markets and hierarchies, power derives from controlling or brokering the flow of information and often, therefore, from restricting it. In a dense network, however, information simply flows around the would-be choke point. Under those circumstances, there is more power in being an information source than an information sink. Consequently, individuals are motivated to maximize both the visibility of their work and their connections to those who are themselves broadly connected. That, in turn, feeds the information density of the network.

Exploiting the Neglected 80 Percent

The Pareto Principle famously dictates that companies derive 80 percent of their value from just 20 percent of their products, customers, or ideas. Because of high transaction costs, the long tail of that curve—that 80 percent of uncertain value generators—cannot be explored. So in the name of company focus, the tail gets lopped off, segmented away, or reengineered out of existence. Potentially profitable innovations die with it.

Organizations that reduce transaction costs can embrace the rejected 80 percent. They can respond to weak market signals, tap small segments, and experiment with unlikely combinations of technologies. They can place a hundred small bets instead of a few big ones.

For example, Detroit considered hybrid vehicles to be an uninteresting intermediate product: U.S. auto executives preferred so-far-unfulfilled research on fuel cell technology. Meanwhile, Toyota was building the Prius. The hybrid is now in its second generation, and Toyota expects to sell 300,000 worldwide this year. Toyota's low transaction costs and penchant for small-scale collaborations helped it keep open 80 discrete options for the hybrid engine until just six months before delivering a final design. Conventional automakers would have needed to freeze those design variables at least two years earlier.

It is in the interstices of the human network—rather than in the minds of a few wunderkinder—that most real innovations are born. And so it is transaction costs that constrain innovation by constraining opportunities to share different and conflicting ideas, skills, and prejudices.

"Detroit people are far more talented than people at Toyota," remarks Toyota president Fujio Cho, with excessive modesty. "But we take averagely talented people and make them work as spectacular teams." The network, in other words, is the innovator.

Cheap Transactions and Plenty of Them

So far we have been discussing the content of work. But the TPS and Linux models change the economics of work as well, by driving down transaction costs. Low transaction costs make it profitable for organizations to perform more and smaller transactions—both internal and external—and so increase the pace and flexibility typical of high-performance organizations.

The classical sources of transaction costs are mutual vulnerability in the face of uncertainty, conflicting interests, and unequal access to information. We spend cash on negotiation, supervision, and restitution to reduce those imperfections. Both markets and hierarchies incur transaction costs (though hierarchies exist to economize on them, as Ronald Coase and Oliver Williamson have argued). Using a methodology developed by J. J. Wallis and Douglass North, we estimate that in the year 2000, cash transaction costs alone accounted for over half the nongovernmental U.S. GDP! We spend more money negotiating and enforcing transactions than we do fulfilling them.

In the Linux and Toyota communities, agreements are enforced not by the sanction of a legal contract, nor by the authority of a boss, but by mutual trust—lowering transaction costs dramatically. This is not new: Teams of people everywhere in the conventional workplace operate on the basis of trust.

What is new is how widely trust can extend, even to people who don't know each other—or even among those who have competing interests. Aisin trusted its rival suppliers with the P-valve blueprints. The rsync hackers swapped sensitive information with people they had never met. Toyota's component suppliers share process knowledge daily, trusting that Toyota will not use it to beat down prices. Linux hackers trust one another to make uncoordinated and simultaneous emendations in the code base.

Moreover, holding property in common—as certain kinds of intellectual property are held within these communities—lowers the monetary stakes among the joint owners. Transaction costs fall because there is simply less to negotiate over. In the Linux community, transaction costs approach zero. Hewlett-Packard paid Martin Pool to be a Linux engineer, but it does not follow that HP needed to be paid on the margin for Pool's nocturnal labors on rsync. In the Toyota community, transaction costs, while not zero, have been radically reduced. When the Aisin Seiki plant was destroyed, Toyota and its suppliers didn't sue one another or cobble together emergency supply contracts. They simply got on with the job, trusting that fair restitution would eventually be made. Jeffrey Dyer, a professor of strategy at Brigham Young University, estimates that transaction costs between Toyota and its tier one suppliers are just one-eighth those at General Motors, a disparity he attributes to different levels of trust.

A Model for Many

Bring together all these elements and you have a virtuous circle. A dense, self-organizing network creates the conditions for large-scale trust. Large-scale trust drives down transaction costs. Low transaction costs, in turn, enable lots of small transactions, which create a cumulatively deepening, self-organized network.

Once the system achieves critical mass, it feeds on itself. The larger the system, the more broadly shared the knowledge, language, and work style. The greater an individuals' reputational capital, the louder the applause and the stronger the motivation. The success of Linux is evidence of the power of that virtuous circle. Toyota's success is evidence that it is also powerful in conventional, profit-maximizing companies.

The Linux community and Toyota Production System are strikingly different. The fact that they achieve so much in such similar ways points to some principles others can follow:

- The discipline of science is surprisingly adaptable to the organization of corporate—and even intercorporate—work.

- Under some circumstances, trust is a viable substitute for market contracts and hierarchical authority, not just in small teams but also in very large communities.

- Across supply chains, organizations that are able to substitute trust for contracts gain more from the collaboration than they lose in bargaining power.

- Low transaction costs buy more innovation than do high monetary incentives.

These principles serve businesses' need for growth and innovation in ways that traditional organizational models do not. And perhaps the effectiveness of these collaborations suggests the ultimate emergence of something altogether new. Not markets. Not hierarchies. But a powerful combination of both—and a signature of the networked society.

GIVING CREDIT WHERE CREDIT IS DUE

The Linux community uses a particular format—a "credit file"—to acknowledge the contributions of its members. If we, for instance, were to acknowledge in the Linux format the contributions of individuals who helped shape our thinking for this article, here's how it would look:

n: Mark Blaxill
e: blaxill.mark@bcg.com
d: Exploration of economics of open source
s: Boston Consulting Group

n: Paul Carlile
e: carlile@bu.edu
d: Discussion of Linux/Toyota parallels
s: Boston University

n: Karim Lakhani
e: lakhani@mit.edu
d: Discussion of Linux/Toyota parallels
d: Survey of free/open source hackers
s: MIT

PART THREE

The Practice of Business Strategy

The Customer: Segmentation and Value Creation

THE PRACTICE OF business strategy must begin with the customer, for without customers with needs to be met, the business has no raison d'être. Strategy issues arise when customer groups with distinct needs emerge from what was previously thought of as a single, homogeneous group.

Business segments can be defined along several dimensions: by customer group (needs), by the economics of serving these groups (cost/price), and/or by the players who choose to serve them (competitive dynamics). Segments are like ecological niches, which some see as defined by the environment and others by the species that occupy them. The interplay of the dimensions makes segmentation an art.

BCG began exploring business segmentation with its clients in the early 1970s. The first insights were analytical. Different needs among customer groups entailed different costs to serve. We helped our clients deaverage their costs, identify the needs and economics of each segment, and align their value propositions with customer needs. We modeled the costs of the players serving each segment to identify potential competitive threats and opportunities. These analytical approaches, described in the first four *Perspectives* in this section, remain valid and useful.

The revolution in the economics of information added new dimensions to segmentation in the late 1980s. In consumer goods and services, information technology enables detailed tracking and analysis of transactions. In combination with flexible manufacturing, companies can now use information on buying behavior to customize both their communications and their product and service offerings to reach and serve segments as small as a single consumer. In industrial markets, information technology enables closer coordination and, ultimately, tighter relationships between venders and suppliers. The next four *Perspectives* in this section represent early contributions to the thinking on these trends.

Our thinking on segmentation continues to evolve. These days we are paying particular attention to pricing and to how organizational dynamics enhance or impede a company's ability to sustain a coherent pricing strategy. We are also noticing how traditional businesses are continuing to fragment into segments, as consumers trade up and trade down in price point, devastating what used to be the safe, rewarding mass middle market. There is no endgame in business!

SEGMENTATION AND STRATEGY

SEYMOUR TILLES, 1974

Segmentation problems often go unrecognized. Each of the managers quoted below focused on something else as the critical factor:

- "In this business the key to success is the broad product line. However, we are losing business to small producers who are cherry-picking at key accounts."

- "We are the Cadillac of our industry and recognized as the leader in quality. However, our competitors seem to be growing more rapidly than we are. Lately our profitability has been declining."

- "We seem to do a lot better in some regions than others. It's probably the result of differences in sales capability, although recently we shifted some sales assignments and our performance didn't change much."

Segmentation is a critical aspect of corporate strategy. It is essential in visualizing the competitive arena and analyzing the preferred strategic emphasis. The goal is to find a way to convert differences from competitors into a cost differential that can be maintained.

For commodity products the basic segment boundary is the cost differential for serving different classes of customers. Cost differences between customers often can be easily determined—differences in logistics or packaging are obvious. Other cost differences may be even more important but more difficult to measure. The cost of customization, the disadvantage of maintaining a broad product line, or the cost of technical service are examples.

For differentiated products, the basis of segmentation is the combination of the features built into the product and their cost/price ratio. For example, Cadillacs, Torinos, and Volkswagens are all very different in their price-feature relationships and for that reason do not compete directly with each other. The segmentation of markets for differentiated products rests on the relationship between the cost features to the producer and the value of features to the customer.

In considering differentiation, it is important to include all of the conditions of the transaction, as well as the product itself. Service, reliability of vendor, and delivery times are likely to be as important as inherent product characteristics. There are often highly differentiated suppliers in markets for commodity products.

A differentiated product remains a differentiated product only until the emergence of the first follower. After that it begins to behave as a commodity.

Over time, all products tend to become commodities. With the evolution of the market, pioneering companies face the choice of becoming limited-volume, high-priced, high-cost specialty producers or high-volume, low-cost producers of standard products. There is no obvious answer to which is best. The choice is dependent upon the predilections and financial resources of the individual company.

It is possible to serve both segments with great benefits in lowering average cost. However, to do this it must be possible to sell at different prices to each segment. Cost to the customer must match value in each segment. Different value requires different prices to cover different costs.

Powerful competitive strategies often can be constructed to force a competitor to choose one segment or the other. The alternative, in the absence of a price differential, is to sell below cost in one segment and be noncompetitive in the other, because a price must be charged based on average cost.

Measuring profitability by customer group is important. The inability to monitor profitability by customer group is extremely hazardous since it permits major changes in competitive position within a given group of customers to go undetected. Averages hide more than they disclose.

The base for a strategy is identification of products and customer groups that will achieve and sustain an economic advantage with respect to competitors. This requires:

- An assessment of the relationship between cost and value to the customer by both product group and customer group

- An assessment of cost on a comparative basis with selected competitors by product group and customer group

- An assessment of the eventual effects on cost and volume of changing the definition of the segment and consequently its potential market size

Competitive segmentation is a competitor-specific process. There is always a leading competitor in any area. The classic segmentation forces that specific competitor to choose between parts of the segment. If he chooses either alternative, he must abandon the rest or serve it at a loss. This choice is virtually unavoidable where a common price must be offered to customers who have quite different service or support costs. The same choice is forced where small-volume customers will pay high margins for special features but high-volume customers will pay nothing extra for such characteristics.

The infinite variety of factor combinations make segmentation an extremely difficult decision process to optimize. This is also why the competitive strategy rewards are potentially so great.

STRATEGIC SECTORS

Bruce D. Henderson, 1975

A strategic sector is one in which you can obtain a competitive advantage and exploit it. Strategic sectors are defined entirely in terms of competitive differences. Strategic-sector analysis performs the same function as cost-effectiveness analysis. Cost-effectiveness analysis optimizes value versus cost. Strategic-sector analysis optimizes margin relative to competition.

Strategic-sector analysis, like cost-effectiveness analysis, ignores the administrative unit until the objective and its feasibility have been evaluated. The resources and the program component are assigned as necessary to administrative units in order to accomplish the mission.

Strategic sectors cut across profit centers, strategic business units, groups, divisions, departments, markets, and all other administrative units. The boundary of a strategic sector is defined by the maximum rate of change of relative competitive margin as you cross that boundary.

Strategic sectors exist because the same product can be made in many variations and supplied with many related services. Each feature and each service has a cost. But the value added by such increments varies from customer to customer. It affects product design, manufacturing capability, and distribution practices. Every change in these affects both cost and value simultaneously.

Design requires focus on the strategic sector to be served. Yet every compromise of that focus either adds cost or reduces value.

Manufacture requires focus on the strategic sector to be served. Compromises and variety produce the same consequences on cost and value. No job shop can match the cost of a full-scale focused factory.

A given strategic sector can rarely use more than one distribution channel. Since different channels have different costs and provide different services, they appeal to different customers. Therefore, customers of one channel tend to be in a different strategic sector from those served by other channels. Competitors who try to serve both strategic sectors at the same price are handicapped by a too-high price in one sector and a too-high cost in the other sector.

Profit centers and strategic business units are self-defeating profitwise unless the whole company is the profit center. GM can be the most profitable competitor because the whole company is the business unit, while internal administrative units are tailored to focus on value added in strategic sectors in which they can be the largest factor.

Profit centers originated when companies became too big and complex to manage by individual function. Decentralization, however, led to suboptimization and loss of internal financial mobility that is critical to strategic concentration.

Strategic business units were devised to reverse the effects of overfragmentation into profit centers. So-called SBUs attempted to aggregate all the strategy decisions in an administrative unit. The critical factor, cash flow, cannot be delegated to any SBU. If it is, then the parent is merely a lockbox holding company without strategic options as a company except divestment or acquisition.

Strategic sectors are the key to strategy because the strategic sector's frame of reference is competition.

The very largest competitor in an industry can be unavoidably unprofitable if the individual strategic sectors are dominated by smaller competitors. Market share in the strategic sector, is what determines profitability not size of company.

SPECIALIZATION

RICHARD K. LOCHRIDGE, 1981

All competitors are specialists. No two competitors can serve exactly the same customers, at exactly the same time, in exactly the same way, at exactly the same cost. The differences between competitors are the measure of their specialization.

The greater the differences, the greater the specialization. Customers place a value on the differences through their purchasing behavior—how much they buy and at what price. In some markets specialization is highly valued. In others it is not.

When differentiation is costly, the specialist competitor will make adequate returns only if its customers are willing to pay a premium. If the costs of providing product or services are highly dependent on volume (because of either experience effects or scale economies, for example), the cost of differentiation may be doubly great. Not only the cost of differentiation but the cost of reduced volume must be added to the price customers must pay to provide adequate returns. In price-sensitive, commodity-type businesses this can be disastrous.

In other businesses, the reward for specialization is much greater. Both variety in customer preferences and lower cost of differentiation favor specialization. Not all customers want the same thing. Particularly in well-supplied markets, customers generally prefer products or services that are tailored to their needs. The variety can be expressed in terms of product or service features, service levels, quality levels, or something else. If the cost of serving the different needs of different customer groups is a large part of the value added, specialization is almost inevitable.

In a crude way, costs can be divided into two broad categories. The first is those costs required for basic participation in a business. These include, for example, the minimum level of ingredients or supplies, manufacturing or service, direct and variable costs, and sufficient overhead to manage the business.

The second category is discretionary costs. These costs are a function of the segments being served. They may be as specific as more expensive ingredients to add quality; advertising to reach specific customer groups; or service levels, sales support, and delivery systems valued highly by a portion of the market. The discretionary, or segment-specific, costs also include less obvious expenses, such as the cost of flexibility in manufacturing processes or the cost of complexity in overheads and other levels of value added to serve a variety of customer needs.

When the discretionary costs are a large part of the value added, opportunities for segment focus arise. One competitor can focus on a portion of the market and adjust its costs to meet the needs of that group and that group alone. Not only are the discretionary costs of flexibility and complexity reduced, but scale economies in segment-specific costs may be achieved. Thus the focused competitor achieves real advantage versus other competitors in serving the chosen segment's needs.

By corollary, when discretionary costs are a large part of the value added, basic costs will be a relatively small part. Thus the small penalty of higher basic costs due to lower volume, fewer scale economies, and less experience is outweighed by advantages in discretionary costs for the segment being served. If few cost differences exist between competitors in basic costs, then specialization-induced cost reduction in discretionary costs is even more valuable.

The competitor who can serve a segment at the lowest cost relative to other competitors will have a competitive advantage. If scale economies are important in segment-specific costs, the leader in each segment will be more profitable than the followers. Often, segment-specific costs are among the most scale-intensive. Advertising cost per unit, for example, is cut in half with each doubling of unit volume. When these costs are a large part of the value added, large differences in return by competitor by segment will result.

Superior specialization strategies should result in sufficient cost advantage so that a portion of that advantage can be passed on to consumers in either added quality/service or reduced price. This effectively raises the barriers to competitive attack. The specialist thrives, capturing a larger portion of the market, and expands the boundaries of the segment to encompass a larger area of competitive advantage.

For each dimension in which competitive advantage can be achieved, there will be a specialist supplier. It is the differences between competitors, not customers, that define segment boundaries. Customers merely place a value on the area of relative advantage. A competitor can be either a low-cost commodity specialist (with a minimum of discretionary costs) or a higher-priced specialist with higher levels of discretionary costs. Higher price realization in the latter segments will be valuable only if the added price more than covers the added cost. This is often true only for the leader in the segment.

Specialization is the result of both variety in customer needs and competitors' willingness to serve those needs. Specialization is a strategy to achieve competitive advantage in a portion of the market. Doing business outside the area of advantage will reduce the specialist's average returns. Worse, it may obscure the value of focus. Because accounting systems rarely capture discretionary costs by segment, they average costs and returns across segments. Thus even a successful specialist may not perceive its advantage or the segment boundaries. This misperception results in dispersion of effort and, eventually, eroded advantage as others with superior perceptions gain ground on the segment leader.

Specialization is a means of survival in a rich, but competitive, market. Competitive advantage cannot be achieved in all cases, with all customers, relative to all competitors. Where it is achieved, however, the rewards can be exceptional.

SPECIALIZATION: COST REDUCTION OR PRICE REALIZATION

ANTHONY J. HABGOOD, 1981

Specialization businesses are becoming increasingly significant. Fewer and fewer businesses can be run purely on the basis of overall volume. By specializing in particular areas, small companies can often coexist successfully with a much larger industry leader. Two quite different kinds of specialization are possible, each with its own strategies and risk profiles. Some specialist companies compete by reducing cost and cutting price, others by adding significant amounts of cost and achieving higher price realization.

Successful cost-reduction specialization is not achieved by reducing the level of important cost components but by totally eliminating one part of the industry leader's cost structure. Private-label producers do not owe their prosperity to lower costs of production but rather to the elimination of branding and distribution costs. Laker has not found a cheaper way to fly from London to New York; rather it has avoided all the costs associated with the IATA airlines' ticketing and full-route and customer coverage. Amdahl competes with IBM not by producing mainframe computers cheaply but by eliminating the operating system costs.

By eliminating a significant portion of the leader's cost structure, the specialist can often cut price between 20 and 40 percent. Theoretically, a vigorous response by the leader could drive out the specialist. In practice, organizational and structural constraints on the leader make many of these specialists quite secure. Market dynamics normally favor the specialists, although too rapid a shift toward the specialist's segment might force the market leader to react early, when the small company is most vulnerable.

Successful price-realization specialists, in contrast, compete by achieving a high price that is supported by additional costs that the leader may not incur at all. One often sees a wide range of price levels in these businesses. In cosmetics or automobiles, for example, there may be a tenfold cost difference between mass-market products and those designed, produced, packaged, distributed, and promoted for small, high-quality niches. The upmarket products are often produced by specialist companies like Daimler-Benz or BMW, which can compete successfully around the far larger producers of standard products.

Such specialists can achieve economic security against competition from the overall market leader by establishing an advantage in the significant scale-intensive cost elements specific to their high-quality niche. The risks lie in the market. A shift in consumer taste or user economics can change the size of a niche dramatically while hardly affecting the overall market. The customers almost always have the choice of shifting down-market.

Successful specialization may be based on either cost reduction or price realization. The two types of specialists face different risks and require different strategies. Cost-reduction specialists must concentrate on their areas of strength: focusing, keeping costs down, and resisting the temptation to enter other parts of the market less suited to their approach. Price-realization specialists must understand and optimize the relationship between the costs they incur to serve their segment and the price they can realize. They must monitor the market closely, for it is in market-segment dynamics that their risks and opportunities lie.

SEGMENT-OF-ONE® MARKETING

RICHARD WINGER AND DAVID EDELMAN, 1989

Remember back when predictions of the computer age conjured up an Orwellian landscape of impersonal robots dispensing mechanized service and standardized products? In fact, the opposite has happened.

Across a wide range of industries, computers have personalized, not standardized, the way companies serve their customers. For example, in a leading hotel chain personnel greet customers by name and remember special requirements. They are prompted by telephone consoles that flash up customers' names when a line rings, aided by a database that stores customers' personal requirements.

Ten years ago mass marketers discovered they could narrow their focus and create products for specific customer segments. Now a segment can be trimmed down to an individual.

Like most breakthroughs, Segment-of-One marketing brings together in a working relationship two formerly independent concepts: information retrieval and service delivery. On one side is a proprietary database of customers' preferences and purchase behavior; on the other is a disciplined, tightly engineered approach to service delivery that uses the information base to tailor a service package for individual customers.

Carriage-Trade Service

The advantage to the customer is straightforward and powerful. Increasingly, consumers are putting more value on being treated as individuals. They demand customized products and services delivered at the moment of need. They also value the reassurance and stability that comes from an enduring relationship with somebody who understands and can respond to their specific needs.

Of course these values aren't new—but until recently, only the very wealthy could afford them. Information technology has brought the services associated with the carriage trade within reach of the middle class.

At First Wachovia, an innovative and very successful North Carolina bank, the staff serves all of its customers the way it used to serve its best customer. The bank greets all customers by name, providing personalized information about their finances and how they relate to their long-term objectives. Based on this knowledge, Wachovia suggests new products. Commodity retail banking has been turned into a customized, personalized service. The result? More sales at lower marketing costs and powerful switching barriers relative to competition.

Three major investments are behind this seemingly effortless new service level: a comprehensive customer database, accessible wherever the customer makes contact with the bank; an extensive training program that teaches a personalized service approach; and an ongoing personal communications program with each customer.

Technology Surpasses Imagination

The foundation for Segment-of-One marketing is the ability to track and understand individual customer behavior. Thanks to the expansion of data-capture opportunities and lower storage costs, such databases are already cost-effective on a large scale. Indeed, technology is now far ahead of the imagination of many marketers.

But not all marketers. Citicorp is developing a massive database that will track the supermarket shopping behavior of 30 to 50 million households. This will enable packaged goods marketers to fine-tune their promotional efforts to an extent unimaginable today.

The major packaged goods companies will be able to know by name and address, by brand-loyal households and switchers, their own and their competitors' light and heavy users.

The second requirement of Segment-of-One marketing is the ability to use the information system to customize the product and personalize the service to the individual customer. In some cases, personalized service can be designed directly into the information system.

When Noxell introduced its Clarion line of mass-market cosmetics in drugstores, it looked for a way to differentiate the new line in a crowded market. The answer was the Clarion computer, where customers type in the characteristics of their skin and receive a regimen selected from the Clarion line. "Department store–type personal advice without sales pressure in the much more convenient drug channel" became the central customer value. The result? The only successful introduction of a broad line of mass-market cosmetics in recent years.

People and Systems

In most cases, the key to the personalized service bundle is the successful interaction of people and systems. But this interaction has to be carefully engineered. It requires user-friendly information systems and a tightly engineered service approach.

In the boutiques of Yves Rocher, the successful French cosmetics house, the customer shows an ID card and the salesperson flashes up her purchase history on a POS terminal. The salesperson is trained to use this information as the basis for a detailed conversation about the customer's individual experience with the company's products and what she should buy next. Compare that with the canned sales pitch used in many department stores. The result is higher sales and more customer loyalty. Shu Uemura, the large Japanese cosmetics firm, bases its U.S. market entry strategy on a similar concept.

Often, Segment-of-One breakthroughs will come from the ability to perform to exacting service standards at the customer's convenience.

D'Agostino, the large New York grocery retailer, builds shop-by-phone service by storing customers' shopping lists and updating them every time the customer calls in. With every call, ordering becomes more convenient because a standing order needs only to be modified. Over time, a denser and denser web of information ties the customer tighter and tighter to the store. Ultimately, the benefits of personalized convenience will, if not offset, at least mitigate the price signals of competitors and improve margin opportunities across the core customer base.

The ability to gather detailed information about a customer's purchasing behavior coupled with relationship-oriented delivery of services provides a tool and a context for the third element of Segment-of-One marketing: personalized communication.

Personalized Communication

Experience shows that even direct mail, not generally an attractive medium in today's cluttered environment, can work powerfully in the context of the intimate customer relationship of a successful Segment-of-One strategy.

Other media options for personalized communication are beginning to proliferate. Selective binding technology that makes it possible to customize magazines to individual subscribers is on the drawing boards. Videotext, point-of-purchase communication, and targeted co-op mailers are beginning to be available. Addressable cable TV is a technical, if not yet a commercial, reality.

These new options alone will force marketers to come to grips with personalized communications. But they will work most powerfully for

Organizational imperatives.

Approach:	Mass Marketing	Segment Marketing	Selling to Segments of one
Information needs	Limited	Periodic	Real time
Decision making	Highly centralized	Centralized	Decentralized
Organization	Functional	Functional and teams	Integrated system
Long-term planning	Product	Product/ Market	Capabilities

those who employ them in the context of an integrated Segment-of-One strategy.

A successful Segment-of-One strategy involves more than experiments with databases and direct mail—although these can be first steps. It requires a broad rethinking of the values a company provides to its customers and the way it approaches them. As the following chart indicates, it can also require significant investments in the infrastructure of service and information.

Because establishing this infrastructure represents a major broadening of a company's capabilities, it should blend with and build on existing strengths. But in every case, the constants will be service, information, and the marriage of the two.

From a competitive point of view, the implications will be dramatic. Economies of scale in production or product volume have eroded in many industries. Segment-of-One marketers will reestablish powerful scale economies in information, information management, service, and distribution. As a result, competitive advantage will tilt to those companies that simultaneously own the market and are able to satisfy individual customers' needs.

DISCOVERING YOUR CUSTOMER

MICHAEL J. SILVERSTEIN AND PHILIP SIEGEL, 1991

By now, everyone knows that giving the customer what he or she wants is critical to success. But if everyone is doing this, where is the competitive advantage? The answer is in going one step further and deeper. This means knowing your most important customers' business systems so well that you see opportunities before they do and are able to provide some useful ideas. When you serve your customers by helping them discover untapped potential in their businesses, you both reap the rewards.

Discovery is real work. It's not just asking your customers or their customers what they want. It entails learning the strategic and economic factors driving your customer's business and turning them into ideas, products, and services that benefit you and your customer. It's not just traditional marketing dressed up in help-your-customer clothes. It requires analytic skills, an open mind, curiosity, follow-through, and confidence in your company's adaptive and creative capabilities. Because it takes a lot of effort, you can afford to do it only for significant customers. The idea is to team with your customer to learn something of major value to him or her, then help make it happen.

How Does Discovery Work?

Discovery can be done in both consumer and industrial goods. One packaged-food producer worked with a supermarket chain to do in-store research on how browsing shoppers first notice, then select, particular items from the growing assortment of refrigerated food products. What they learned over two months led the store to radically change the way refrigerated items were displayed in the chilled case, including doing away with the glass door that deterred shoppers from examining the product packages. The changes triggered strong increases in sales of these high-margin items across the chain. All this was at the initiative of the producer, not the store.

This first round of discovery triggered more discoveries. The packaged-food company went on to tailor promotional programs to the unique demographics of each major store in the chain. The two parties now have an annual calendar of cooperative business-building activities where the benefits are monitored and shared.

A large commercial printer in the Middle West used discovery to create new value for major customers and for itself. Often, high-volume printing jobs, like catalogues and telephone books, are considered commodity businesses: The low-priced vendor wins. By understanding the business economics of a few key customers, however, this company uncovered a variety of revenue innovations and cost reductions for them. The company worked with one customer for three months in a five-step process:

- It analyzed the customer's core business practices—how it decides what products and services to offer consumers, how it merchandises these offerings, how it buys printing services, and so on.

- It discovered where the customer wasn't taking advantage of the extraordinary flexibility and speed of its printing process. More services to consumers at higher margins to the customer were possible.

- It tested and funded much of the R&D in the new-product development phase to become the only vendor that could deliver the full program.

- It monitored the sales response and customer satisfaction results of the new program and was the force behind execution.

- It used this success to reinforce the customer relationship and expand its base business as well. The new business revealed by the discovery was worth millions to both parties—more than 20 times the cost of the discovery effort.

In both these examples, the discovery team and the customer cooperated at several organizational levels—from field sales to top management. The work involved sharing sensitive internal information, including cost and profit data and customer-by-customer sales histories. You conduct deep discovery only for customers with whom there is mutual trust and respect.

Discovery is applicable in many settings. Good candidates will be large customers with varied needs. They must be strong enough in their markets to capture and keep the added business you are helping them get. Otherwise the benefits flow quickly to others.

The Rules of Discovery

To conduct a successful discovery process, you should:

- Make sure top management supports the partnership, but allow your salesperson to own the results. He or she is crucial to keeping the effort moving through the inevitable bumps in the road.

- Carefully select and train the teams of people that perform the discovery. Use only good people who are experienced in all the critical disciplines: reading customers for what they need but don't say, analyzing the economics of a business, knowing how to mobilize an organization to do something new.

- Follow through on the new ideas you and the customer decide to pursue with all the capabilities and resources of your company. You want to play this game only if you are thoroughly committed.

- Compensate those people in your organization who generate ideas from the discovery process and are able to make them work. Working with customers in new, unstructured ways will bring out the best in your people.

Simply listening to customers is not enough to sustain partnerships. You need to understand the structure and economics of their businesses and offer them a stream of creative ideas that tap their full capabilities. Discovery is a great opportunity to get more of your good people into direct contact with your customers' businesses. Discovery will unlock your organization and stimulate more rounds.

You can choose to be "just" a vendor. You can submit proposals to specifications. You can play golf and entertain. You can focus on friendships. You can win some, you can lose some.

Or you can learn about your customers' vulnerabilities, dreams, business-process blocks, decision-making weaknesses, and major growth targets. You can grow with luck or you can grow through knowledge and innovation.

TOTAL BRAND MANAGEMENT

DAVID C. EDELMAN AND MICHAEL J. SILVERSTEIN, 1993

A business revolution has come to brands. From every side, traditional brands appear to be under attack. Costs are escalating. Consumer loyalty is eroding. Retailers are competing through private label. Store brands are commandeering valuable niches. Some observers are even speculating about "the end of brands."

No, brands won't disappear. But what a brand is and how best to manage it are changing. Increasingly, a brand is far more than just a name on a product. Winning brands are carefully designed business systems. These systems stretch from the choice of raw materials to final service with the customer. And it is the total system that the customer purchases, not just the product.

When brands become business systems, brand management becomes far too important to leave to the marketing department. It cuts across functions and business processes. It requires decisions and actions at every point along the value chain. It is central to a company's overall business strategy. That's why we call it *total brand management.*

Escalating Investments, Increased Focus

Total brand management can take a variety of forms:

- In some cases, the brand extends beyond the actual product to include the infrastructure supporting it. For example, high-end brands such as Lexus or Infiniti, and even midmarket brands such as General Electric appliances, have invested heavily in information systems that support customer service and serve as marketing attributes enhancing the core product.

- In other cases, well-crafted umbrella brands like Gillette or Levi's stretch across many related products, enabling their owners to leverage materials innovations, marketing investments, and trade promotions more effectively.

- In still other cases, the entire retail system itself is the brand. At The Body Shop, for example, the way products are sourced (all-natural ingredients), developed (no animal testing), and sold (in distinctive Body Shop boutiques) is as important to the company's marketing image as the actual products.

Regardless of the particular form, total brand management has two fundamental imperatives. The first is a major escalation in the amount and kind of investments necessary to support a successful brand. It's no longer enough simply to increase the advertising budget. Companies have to invest in a broad range of costly capabilities— proprietary research methodologies for understanding subtle shifts in consumer attitudes, intertwined manufacturing and logistics networks providing superior retail service at lower cost, retail information processing capability to optimize inventory costs, and product development functions to speed innovative products.

But the total brand manager must also remember that such investments are only table stakes that allow entry into the game. It takes more than deep pockets to win. In particular, companies must concentrate on three key high-leverage activities.

Maximize synergies across a coherent brand portfolio. Financing a massive build-up in new capabilities requires spreading investments over many brands, cascading across price points and channels. Practitioners of total brand management, therefore, focus not on individual brands but on a coherent brand portfolio.

French cosmetics maker L'Oréal, for example, knew that increased R&D was essential to competing in the new brand environment. So over a five-year period, L'Oréal doubled its R&D budget. This major investment helped spark a key innovation: the company's new "anti-aging complex," a breakthrough in skin care that slows the onset and spread of wrinkles. But L'Oréal was able to afford this massive increase in R&D spending only because it could spread the costs over several brands in its portfolio at different price points and positions. The company introduced its anti-aging complex under the Lancôme brand, then moved it into the Vichy range and finally into broad distribution with Plénitude. It has been a tremendously successful innovation, yet couldn't have been done with one brand alone.

The key word in "coherent brand portfolio" is coherent. It's no good to cobble together a collection of unrelated brands. This only leads to higher overhead costs, fragmented business processes, and duplication of resources.

Not all brands contribute equally to enhancing the value of your brand portfolio. Brand managers must evaluate each existing brand along two dimensions: fit with core capability and potential for value generation. Such an assessment reshuffles the brands into four categories of investment priority, ranging from good fit/high value to low fit/low value.

Strengthen the brand portfolio through innovation. As the L'Oréal example suggests, innovation is now more important than ever. Other forms of growth, such as acquisitions and expanding margins, have been largely played out. Spending on retailers or consumers is becoming too expensive for all but the biggest budgets. What's more, consumers are becoming more sophisticated and harder to reach. Mere bells and whistles won't sell anymore.

But the kind of innovation that matters is not what managers might expect. It's not the creation of new brands, an increasingly expensive proposition. Rather, it is the reinvention of existing brands through three basic techniques: repositioning, extension, and transformation.

For example, SmithKline Beecham repositioned Lucozade, once considered a medicinal remedy, by directing it at anybody who cares about a healthy life, particularly athletes. Today, Lucozade is Britain's number one noncola drink. Unilever extended Flora, originally a "healthy fat" margarine low in polyunsaturates, across product categories to become an umbrella brand for a whole range of health-food oils and dairy products. And by moving quickly to exploit a technological breakthrough, Procter & Gamble transformed its traditional Pert Shampoo brand by launching a two-in-one shampoo/conditioner known as PertPlus.

Secure the brand through close relationships with customers and the trade. Increasingly, customers value the reassurance and stability that comes from an enduring relationship with someone who understands and can respond to their specific needs. But this requires a broad rethinking of the value a company provides for its customers, as well as of the specific products and services it provides.

Not long ago, for example, Japanese video game maker Nintendo found itself in a dying market with too many players and limited shelf space. The challenge: to discover a new way to hold its brand name with customers. So the company launched two new business initiatives: Nintendo Power, a $15-a-year magazine that receives 40,000 letters a month, and a 900-number line on game strategy that receives 10,000 calls a week. Both proved to be powerful customer-relationship vehicles that cut across hardware, software, education, product development, and customer service. But even more important, the magazine and 900 number have opened a direct line of communication from the customer back to new product development, which has enabled the company to forecast sales of a new product within 10 percent. Today, with annual sales of $5 billion, Nintendo is Japan's most profitable company.

For many brands, the most important customer is the trade. To fend off private-label growth, brand managers must find ways to create value for the trade without simply giving away more margin. A leading office products producer, for example, has been able to work with a superstore chain to create new packaging, replenishment, and stocking systems that provide more margin to the superstore than private-label products would. With its interlocking business systems, the manufacturer is now able to secure its brand franchise and to increase margins in a win-win relationship with a heavily deal-driven retailer.

The Role of the Total Brand Manager: Making Choices along the Entire Value Chain

As brand managers manage portfolios of brands, customer segments, and retailers across an entire business system, their role has become more cross-functional and strategic. Indeed, total brand management often involves redesigning the business through new partnerships, better cross-functional linkages, and innovation. To that end, brand managers must make choices at every point along the value chain, not just in marketing and sales.

This more strategic conception of brands means that the stakes involved in launching, maintaining, and evolving a brand are higher. But so are the potential payoffs. Companies that innovate new brand-building strategies will reap long-term rewards. Those that do not will slowly disappear.

PRICING MYOPIA

PHILIPPE MOREL, GEORGE STALK JR., PETER STANGER, AND PETER WETENHALL, 2003

Executives often suffer from pricing myopia. They underestimate their power to manage pricing, mistakenly believe that their customers are paying the amounts stipulated by their pricing guidelines, passively accept the prevailing approaches to pricing in their industries, or neglect to consider how they could use pricing to change the competitive game.

As a consequence, executives respond to today's challenges by trying harder to reduce costs, boost asset productivity, and pursue growth. But they overlook pricing opportunities. Instead they offer unnecessary discounts, miss chances to improve their competitive position through pricing innovations, and wage destructive price wars.

"I Don't Have the Power to Manage Pricing"

Many executives blame forces beyond their control—a sluggish world economy or increasing global competition—for their inability to manage pricing. They assert that pricing is a zero-sum game: If they raise prices, the lost volume will undermine the margin gain; if they lower prices, the additional volume won't make up for lost margin.

The reality is often not nearly so grim. Executives have this misperception because they are focused on cost rather than customer value, and set their prices on a cost-plus basis.

Customers are often willing to pay more than the current price. Different customers frequently place different values on products and services, as well as on specific components of an offering. In addition, perceptions of prices vary. This is true in virtually every market—even industrial and financial-services commodities. The keys to capturing such value are to:

- Deepen the understanding of demand elasticity and customers' behavior by analyzing existing data or conducting experiments.

- Segment customers more effectively along dimensions besides price sensitivity (such as current and lifetime cost to serve, delivery times, quality, and support).

- Communicate the value of the offering more effectively.

- Develop innovative pricing structures that elicit each segment's full willingness to pay.

One approach is to raise prices of those elements of the offering to which customers are less price-sensitive and lower them on the elements to which they are more price-sensitive.

"I'll Have to Change the Pricing and Discount Structure"

All too many executives are in a cloud when it comes to knowing the prices that their customers actually pay. Observe the pricing cloud an industrial goods company was under. It had a long-standing strategy that rewarded large accounts with lower net prices (higher discounts). But, in fact, there was little, if any, relationship between actual discounts and customers' volume. Discounts for many smaller accounts were much higher (and prices much lower) than those for bigger accounts.

Many people "touch" pricing, but nobody owns it. Pricing decisions, expertise, and information are fragmented and diffused across regions, business units, and functions. The information needed to control pricing is often hard to collect because so many people in so many parts of the organization are in a position to undercut the established price.

All too often, precise metrics and processes to monitor pricing are lacking. Thus, quantifying the true impact of incremental pricing actions is difficult. Another common problem is that incentives are frequently misaligned, creating disconnects between the overall pricing strategy and the actual tactics executed by the organization.

The result is "leakage." The average net price is much lower than it should be: The gap ranges from a few percentage points in some companies to half or more of the list price in others.

An industrial goods company was undisciplined in granting volume discounts.

SOURCE: BCG analysis.

The solution is to ensure that pricing strategies are defined, measured, executed, and managed. When companies focus on pricing and get disparate units to operate in sync, they typically deliver at least a three-percentage-point improvement in earnings before interest and taxes. In fact, the improvement can be as high as 10 points.

"I Can't Make It Happen in My Industry"

Many executives believe that the current approaches to pricing in their industries are unalterable. But pricing approaches are constantly changing. In some cases, the approaches are genuinely new ones; in many others, they are transfers of practices already been proven in other industries. American Airlines' pioneering use of pricing to maximize capacity utilization of its fleet was instrumental to its becoming a dominant force in the industry. Today, players in the fashion apparel industry are using yield management to optimize their use of markdowns.

"Pricing Is a Tactic, Not a Strategy"

Many executives assume that pricing is a tactical rather than a strategic variable. Because pricing decisions are made at fairly low levels in the organization and responsibility for pricing is fragmented, it doesn't get the strategic attention that other critical activities, such as sourcing and product development, receive.

History is replete with examples of companies that have proved that pricing is central to strategy: Wal-Mart's Every Day Low Prices, Microsoft's Office System (whose price is much lower than the collective prices of its component programs), and Capital One's offer of credit cards for every taste (more than 6,000 with different rates, credit limits, and payment terms). These companies' pricing approaches helped them upset the competitive balance of power in their industries. Moreover, advances in information technology are giving rise to new pricing strategies and increasing the potential power of familiar ones.

Examples of pricing strategies that can have a tremendous impact on the competitive landscape include the following.

Experience-Curve Pricing

Costs go down with accumulated experience. They always have and they always will. The competitor that prices ahead of the expected decline can drive purchases and accelerate the accumulation of experience and the creation of advantage.

De-Averaged Pricing

Pricing should reflect a matrix of relative competitive positions by location, segment, customer, or other factors. The company that understands its relative strengths and weaknesses can set prices differently in each market to maximize profits and thereby influence the dynamics of the industry. Instead of taking this approach, many companies average prices across customer segments. This practice, however, can open a window of opportunity for a focused competitor to lure away more profitable, low-cost-to-serve customers by offering them prices more closely matched to their needs.

Bundling

If one company has a much broader offering of products and services than others, it can meet customers' demand for a bundled alternative that puts competitors at a disadvantage. Industries in which companies are using bundling to steal a march on competitors include telecommunications, financial services, retailing, and software.

Loyalty-Based Pricing

Sophisticated IT is enabling companies to use customers' purchasing histories, including volume and mix, to make dramatic strides in how they tailor pricing. Such "rewards" systems encourage customers to buy more over time and, as they become invested in the continuing relationship, develop into a formidable barrier to switching. With the number and sophistication of these programs soaring, excellence in designing and implementing them has become crucial.

Dynamic Pricing

Setting prices closer to the moment when a customer needs a product or service is increasingly possible, but it requires a deep understanding of full and marginal costs and investments, and of the value proposition for the customer. Unfortunately, very few companies today are ready to exploit this opportunity.

What is the cure for pricing myopia? A good first step is to answer some fundamental questions about strategy and tactics:

- What would happen to the bottom line if you raised prices or lowered them by 1 percent?
- Which customers are—or are not—price sensitive and why?
- Where are the pricing leakages occurring in your company?

- What functions or departments control the final pricing decisions?
- How can pricing mechanisms be changed to build advantages?

Don't settle for one-time efforts to improve pricing. The return on developing a world-class pricing capability is much higher. Companies with such capabilities can continually design pricing mechanisms and set price levels that generate maximum sales and share growth, optimize company profits, and deliver sustained competitive advantage. Their rivals will have a hard time catching up to them.

TRADING UP*

MICHAEL J. SILVERSTEIN AND NEIL FISKE, 2003 AND 2005

America's middle-market consumers are *trading up*.

They are willing, even eager, to pay a premium price for remarkable kinds of goods that we call New Luxury—products and services that possess higher levels of quality, taste, and aspiration than other goods in the category but are not so expensive as to be out of reach.

Trading up spans so many categories and appeals to such a broad range of consumers that it has come to represent a major and growing segment of the economy. In twenty-three categories of U.S. consumer products and services worth $2 trillion in annual sales, New Luxury already accounts for 20 percent of the total, or about $400 billion per year—and it's growing 10 percent to 15 percent annually. It is about the same size in Europe and growing at a similar rate. We expect New Luxury to reach $2 trillion globally by the end of the decade.

So many middle-market consumers want to trade up, and so many can now afford to, that New Luxury goods sell at much higher prices than conventional goods and in much higher volumes than traditional luxury goods. As a result, they have transcended the prevailing price-volume demand curves. In multiple categories of consumer goods and

* From *Trading Up* by Michael Silverstein and Neil Fiske with John Butman, copyright © 2003, 2005, by Boston Consulting Group, Inc. Used by permission of Portfolio, an imprint of Penguin Group (USA) Inc.

services, New Luxury winners have emerged, traditional leaders have been dethroned, and the entire category has been transformed.

Characteristics of New Luxury

From our analysis of the most successful New Luxury goods in more than 30 categories, we have identified three major types.

Accessible Superpremium Products

Accessible superpremium products are priced at or near the top of their category, but still affordable to the middle-market consumer. For example, Belvedere vodka sells for about $28 a bottle, an 88 percent premium over Absolut at $16. Nutro pet food sells at $.71 per pound, a 58 percent premium to Alpo at $.45 per pound. Almost anyone can afford a bottle of Belvedere or a bag of Nutro if those categories are emotionally important to him or her.

Old Luxury Brand Extensions

Old Luxury brand extensions are lower-priced versions of goods that have traditionally been affordable only to the rich—households earning $200,000 and above. Mercedes-Benz, for example, has dramatically changed its product mix in the past 10 years, with continual reductions in the price of the entry-level C-class coupe—now about $26,000. At the same time, Mercedes-Benz has kept the brand aspirational by extending it upmarket. The Maybach sells for over $300,000. Such Old Luxury brands have mastered a neat trick: becoming simultaneously more accessible and more aspirational.

Mass Prestige Goods

Mass Prestige goods occupy a sweet spot between mass and class. While commanding a premium over conventional products, they are priced well below Superpremium or Old Luxury goods. Bath & Body Works body lotion, for example, sells at a premium of about 275 percent over Vaseline Intensive Care. But it is far from the highest-priced product in the category. Many Superpremium skin creams are even more expensive.

To qualify as New Luxury, a product must connect with the consumer on all three levels of a *ladder of benefits:*

- It must have technical differences in design, technology, or both. Subsumed within this technical level is an assumption of quality—that the product will be free from defects and perform as promised.

- Those technical differences must contribute to superior functional performance. It's not enough to incorporate "improvements" that are intended only to make the product look different or appear to be changed.

- The technical and functional benefits, along with other factors, such as brand values and company ethos, must engage the consumer emotionally. Emotional engagement separates New Luxury from other goods. Even relatively low-ticket items, such as premium vodkas, have a well-defined emotional appeal for their consumers. The engagement tends to get more dense and long-lasting with big-ticket items, such as home appliances and automobiles.

When a New Luxury brand solidly delivers the ladder of benefits, it can catch fire. It will take hold in the minds of consumers, quickly change the rules of its category, grow to market dominance—as Starbucks, Kendall-Jackson, and Victoria's Secret have—and force a redrawing of the demand curve. As that happens, the category tends to polarize. Consumers shop more selectively. They trade up to the premium New Luxury product if the category is important to them. If it isn't, they trade down to the low-cost or private-label brand, or even go without.

As consumers buy more selectively, trading up and trading down, they increasingly ignore the conventional, midprice product that fails to deliver the ladder of benefits. Why bother with a product that offers neither a price advantage nor a functional or emotional benefit? Companies that offer such products are in grave danger of "death in the middle." They will lose sales, profitability, market share, and consumer interest. To survive, they must lower prices, revitalize, and reposition their products, or exit the market.

The Forces behind New Luxury

Fundamental, long-term forces are driving the rise of New Luxury on both the demand and supply sides, forces that will propel trading up for years to come.

On the demand side, trading up is being driven by demographic and cultural shifts that have been building for decades:

- Higher real household incomes (especially at the high end) and higher wealth (especially in home equity) have translated into more money to spend.

- Mass retailers, like Wal-Mart and Costco, have passed on reduced costs to consumers, freeing an estimated $100 billion in annual spending.

- Not only are more women working, they are earning higher salaries than ever before—and they are spending more on themselves.

- Both men and women are getting married later in life and are having fewer children. Half of all marriages end in divorce, so there are more singles with more money to spend on themselves.

- The middle-market consumer is better educated, more sophisticated, better traveled, more adventurous, and more discerning than ever before.

- Middle-market consumers are more acutely aware of their emotions, and they are encouraged to indulge them. Lifestyle gurus endorse New Luxury products, celebrities display them, and specialty retailers make them available everywhere.

These factors have transformed the profile of the "average" middle-market American consumer from an unassuming and unsophisticated person of modest means and limited influence into a sophisticated and discerning consumer with high aspirations and substantial buying power and clout.

The supply-side forces have been just as important in producing the New Luxury business endeavor:

- New Luxury innovators and entrepreneurs are usually more knowledgeable, sophisticated and emotionally driven, and less willing to settle for creating conventional goods than established managers.

- Changes in retailing have increased the availability of New Luxury goods. The proliferation of malls has made it possible for premium specialty retailers, such as Williams-Sonoma and Victoria's Secret, to expand quickly. Mass merchandisers have been stocking more premium items as well.

- The easing of international trade barriers, the improving capabilities of global supply-chain-services providers, and the reduced costs of international shipping have enabled companies to access foreign labor markets and put together and manage complex global networks for sourcing, manufacturing, assembling, and distribution.

These factors have made it easier for New Luxury companies to attract capital, to develop products faster and produce them at lower cost, and to increase production volume quickly when consumer demand increases.

The Practices of New Luxury Leaders

New Luxury is a business strategy. It cannot be pursued with the methods traditionally used to develop products and bring them to market. We have found that, across categories and in very different kinds of organizations, New Luxury leaders follow eight practices:

1. *Never underestimate the customer.* Entrepreneurs believe the consumer has the desire, interest, intelligence, and capability to trade up—even absent data to prove his contention or a business model to follow.

2. *Shatter the price-volume demand curve.* They don't settle for incremental improvements or price increases. They go for higher prices and higher volume, earning disproportionate profits as a result.

3. *Create a ladder of genuine benefits.* They don't try to fool their customers with meaningless innovations, nor do they try to get by on brand image alone. They produce functional benefits that result in emotional engagement for the consumer. They don't try to pretend that better cosmetics are true innovations.

4. *Escalate innovation, elevate quality, and deliver a flawless experience.* The market for New Luxury is rich in opportunity, but unstable. Technical and functional advantages are increasingly short-lived as new competitors enter the market and as innovations cascade quickly from high-end products to lower-priced ones. What is luxurious and different today becomes the standard brand of tomorrow.

5. *Extend the brand's price range and positioning.* Many New Luxury brands extend the brand both upmarket to create aspirational appeal and down market to make it more accessible and competitive and to build demand. A traditional competitor's highest price may be three to four times its lowest; New Luxury players often have a fivefold to tenfold difference between their highest and lowest price points. They are careful, however, to create, define, and maintain a distinct character and meaning for each product at every level while articulating a common brand essence.

6. *Customize the value chain to deliver on the benefit ladder.* They emphasize controlling and orchestrating the value chain rather than owning it. Jim Koch, founder of The Boston Beer Company, specified the process—nineteenth-century brewing coupled with twentieth-century quality-control methods—for making Samuel Adams Boston Lager, selected the ingredients, and managed distribution. He did not grow hops or to build extensive production facilities.

7. *Use influence marketing and brand apostles.* In New Luxury goods, a small percentage of category consumers contribute the dominant share of value. New Luxury leaders do not rely solely on traditional consumer-research methods, such as polling and focus groups, to identify those customers; they work harder to define their core audience and spend more time interacting with customers, often one-on-one. In launching a product, they carefully manage initial sales to specific groups in specific venues, seek frequent feedback from early purchasers, and solicit word-of-mouth recommendations.

8. *Continually attack the category like an outsider.* They think like outsiders, act like mavericks, talk like iconoclasts, and strive never to think of themselves as insiders, even after they have become the leaders in their categories.

Potential of Trading Up

Americans have not finished trading up.

This movement to better goods and services is spreading to new categories and industries. In financial services, providers have identified the members of newly affluent households as a large potential market of consumers seeking advice, comfort, and protection. New Luxury is appearing in healthcare, driven by affluent, healthy consumers ages 50 to 60, who are willing to pay out of their own pocket for care they consider better and more personalized. New Luxury is also causing a transformation in grocery stores. Suppliers of gourmet foods, premium prepared dishes, and private-label products are squeezing traditional vendors.

There remains vast potential to reshape categories, create new winners, dethrone market leaders, simultaneously destroy and create immense value, and unleash growth and rebirth in mature industries.

TRADING DOWN: LIVING LARGE ON $150 A DAY*

LUCY BRADY AND MICHAEL J. SILVERSTEIN, 2005

Millions of people around the world are redefining what it means to be a middle-market consumer. By purchasing a mix of upscale and downscale products and services, they are creating a new standard of living. Thanks to the rise of the Internet and the popularity of big-box stores like Wal-Mart, they are using their discretionary buying power to reject mediocre products for the best at both ends of the price range. With their demand for quality *and* value, these consumers are fueling a new kind of market.

For several years now, we have been writing and talking about the New Luxury movement, in which consumers with annual incomes between $50,000 and $150,000 *trade up* to premium goods in selected categories. But there is another side to the equation. Those same consumers are also *trading down,* and this insight is just as complex and ripe with opportunities for businesses as trading up. Consumers are spending *less* on a variety of goods to acquire *more* of what they need and want.

Meanwhile, the middle is becoming a wasteland. The explosion of choices at both ends of the market is leaving run-of-the-mill products and services starving for consumers.

Premium entries are growing in number, and bargain brands are stealing share. For example, while the market for midpriced televisions declined by 40 percent over the past decade, high- and low-end models gained 33 percent and 7 percent, respectively. During the same period, as demand for midpriced hotels decreased by 15 percent, bargain lodging rose by 13 percent. In grocery stores, the middle lost a whopping 24 percent market share, while downscale retailers gained 23 percent. In women's apparel, the market for midpriced products fell by 18 percent, but the high and low ends both grew by 9 percent.

Our estimates indicate that the trading-down market accounts for more than $1 trillion of the $3.7 trillion in total consumer spending in the United States, and it will reach $1.5 trillion by the end of the

* An edited version of the original 2005 publication by Lucy Brady and Michael Silverstein.

decade. That's nearly twice the size of the trading-up market. Similarly, the increase in market value over the past decade of the top 10 trading-down companies was more than ten times larger than that of the top 10 trading-up companies.

The Thrill of the Hunt

Offshore manufacturing has contributed to the trading-down phenomenon by reducing the cost of value. Wal-Mart, The Home Depot, Costco, Target, and discount retailers known as *dollar stores,* such as Dollar General, are leading this revolution as both retailers and producers. As these businesses force costs out of entire industries, they make trading down an option in almost every category of consumer goods.

Dollar General's success has been particularly stunning. With some 4,000 SKUs, 60 percent of which are household necessities averaging $1.50 each, the retailer also offers the enticement of a treasure hunt—a retail version of the garage sale, where you can search out and land incredible bargains on everything from birdhouses to space heaters. Customers' satisfaction comes at least as much from hunting down a real deal as from the product itself. Interestingly, high-income households are dollar stores' fastest-growing consumer segment.

Similarly, in Germany the international hard discounter Aldi has become a powerful economic force, especially in markets where income growth has slowed. It offers only about 750 products, but almost all of them are private label. Such hard discounters now capture 40 percent of Germany's spending on groceries, with 19 percent going to Aldi. Today more than 90 percent of Germany's consumers shop at Aldi, an increase of almost 100 percent over the past 15 years.

Trading Down across All Segments

Emotional issues loom large in how consumers approach trading down, and that has resulted in a new math for balancing budgets and a new language for defining *luxury* and *value.* Today's consumers want to feel like experts in the "game" of shopping. What used to be seen as "getting by" is being reinterpreted as "spending smart" and "living large." Trading down is less about compromising than about looking for a good product at a lower price. It involves a shrewd weighing of the costs and benefits of trading up in one category and trading down in another, and consumers are scrutinizing their choices. Here's how trading down plays out in five demographic groups.

Young Singles

They are dazzled by the world, have few obligations, care little about saving, and see spending as an adventure. They may be going to school, working, traveling, or bouncing back and forth among these activities. Money is usually tight and income unreliable. They trade down in many categories in order to spend more freely in others. They like the brands that their friends admire.

Couples without Kids

They spend to enhance their identity, to strengthen their personal relationships, and to establish their professional image. They may save to buy a car or to get married. They trade down almost as if it were a cause—seeking out the best for less—and they often influence their partners' choices.

Young Parents

When children are born, spending patterns change dramatically. Working mothers, with so many demands on their time, are under intense pressure. Spending becomes a family preoccupation—how to spend, where to spend, when to spend. Young parents may trade down on almost everything—except when it comes to the new baby.

High-Commitment Families

For families with older children (and sometimes aging parents as well), managing spending consumes a large part of their busy lives. They worry about their homes, their investments and assets, their retirement income, and their children's education and inheritance. Children as young as four and five begin to influence the family's purchases and brand affiliations. Older children pressure their parents to buy the brands they believe will help them succeed socially and even academically. Meanwhile, their parents care less about buying a particular brand than about meeting everyone's needs without jeopardizing the family's financial future. Spending on small-ticket goods may decrease in favor of essential big-ticket items: a second or third car, a bigger house, a college education. Trading down becomes a way of life.

Empty Nesters and Secure Seniors

Many older couples and singles enjoy good health and have few financial obligations. They may be loyal to a handful of brands but aren't terribly interested in brand stories. For them, spending is a matter of values, such as quality and performance—and they have the time to

Exhibit 1   Consumers make smart choices to stretch their budgets.

The Top Ten Trading-Down Strategies

1. Know the market price to the penny
2. Buy on sale
3. Shop with coupons
4. Find the low-price retailer
5. Shop at discount stores like Costco
6. Go "treasure hunting" at Dollar General
7. Bargain with salespeople
8. Buy at end-of-season sales
9. Look long and hard for the best product at the lowest price
10. Do without

SOURCE: BCG research.

shop around. They are generally frugal, although price is not as important to them as it used to be. They may trade down when shopping for themselves but trade up for their children and grandchildren.

Life experiences can also determine how consumers spend. Patterns change, for instance, when people go through tough times, such as the loss of a job, the end of a relationship, or a period of bad health. Some try to compensate by going on a spending spree because buying things makes them feel better; others become fierce penny pinchers. But whatever their reasons, consumers wishing to trade down use a range of shopping techniques to help them stretch their dollars. (See Exhibit 1.)

Becoming a Trading-Down Winner

The implication of trading down for businesses is both profound and destabilizing. It's not as simple as stripping out costs or features to make a cheaper product. People want quality, and they have many choices. Trading-down consumers look closely at price, value, brand name, design, functionality, and longevity. Here are five principles for profiting from the trend:

- Escape the middle: move up, down, or in both directions.

- Keep searching for lower prices and higher quality because consumers will keep searching for better value.

- Attack the category like an outsider, taking out your weakest links.

- Listen, listen, listen to your best customers.

- Jump into the game and change how it is played.

Serving the large middle market of consumers can be exciting and rewarding. These people are looking up as well as out, to the future, to get what matters most to their families: a better car, a more comfortable home, a good education, more rewarding vacations, higher-quality food and clothing. And they attach a great deal of emotional significance to their ability to do so. Greed may be an element in the mix, but trading down is mainly about generosity. The choices consumers make are often agonizing. Yet, when they find a brand that gives them more time, greater convenience, better quality, and good value, they'll reward it with long-lasting loyalty.

Innovation and Growth

COMPANIES SEEM TO FALL in and out of love with growth. In the early 1990s, companies streamlined their infrastructures in the reengineering flurry, only to find that they had lost the capacity to innovate in the process. Growth pushed its way back onto the agenda in the late 1990s, only to see the resulting over-exuberance punished with the collapse of the internet bubble. Companies pulled in their horns as they regrouped, but recently, growth has reemerged at the top of most companies' agendas.

There are two sides to innovation and growth: generating creative ideas and translating them into viable businesses. The first three *Perspectives* in this section address the first of these. They are classics on how to find growth opportunities, and they validate BCG's belief that there is no such thing as a mature business.

The last three *Perspectives* in this section suggest processes that need to be put in place to turn ideas into reality. The first piece lays out the principles of rapid product development; the second identifies alternative routes to commercialization; and the third details how to navigate the intellectual property landscape as you grow.

FROM THE INSIGHT OUT

MICHAEL J. SILVERSTEIN, 1995

Behind every successful innovation is an unexpected insight. When it finds expression as a new business breakthrough, markets take off and competitors don't know what hit them. And yet, even at the best companies most attempts at innovation fail. Lacking a systematic process for developing new ideas, organizations rely too much on the random inspiration of individuals.

It doesn't have to be this way. Insight can be made to flourish. Genius isn't required; ordinary mortals can generate breakthrough ideas—systematically. What it takes is a rigorous methodology for conceiving new opportunities and a customer-driven discovery process for testing and refining them:

1. *Expand your business definition and map it exhaustively.* Focus may enable flawless execution, but it can impede insight. The way you see your market today can blind you to tomorrow's possibilities. Start by expanding your business definition—from "cellular phones" to "mobile communications," from "enamel paints" to "industrial coating systems," from "mutual funds" to "retirement services." The new definition may seem arbitrary. It may even sound a bit pretentious. It doesn't matter, as long as it jump-starts creative thinking. Focus can come later.

Exhaustively map the opportunity space described by these expanded boundaries. Visual representation helps. One company regularly charts opportunities on a cube whose axes list potential users of a product category, potential uses to which products might be put, and the range of benefits they might deliver. Each cell represents a possible opportunity. By identifying unoccupied cells and conceiving products that could fill them, the company uses the cube to give structure and direction to its innovation process.

Contrast this to traditional market-research techniques where, typically, a single idea is tested against the total user population. Mapping the terrain of diverse customer needs segment by segment allows you to explore a panoply of possibilities.

2. *Get inside the customer experience to tap core dissatisfactions.* Done properly, the mapping process will reveal more opportunities than most companies can pursue. How do you decide which ones to develop?

Don't rely on asking customers what they want. They almost never really know. It's the rare individual who can predict his or her own behavior or understand the inchoate emotions that motivate action. And few consumers can forecast the premium they'll be willing to pay for a unique new value proposition.

What they can do is articulate their dissatisfactions. Let these dissatisfactions guide you to the most promising cells of the opportunity cube. What matters most aren't so much the specific deficiencies of existing products as the broad customer disaffections—for example, frustrations born of time scarcity, inconvenience, or unfulfilled yearnings for affiliation.

Probe for how customers see current offerings in the context of these deeper dissatisfactions. They represent the grain of sand around which the pearl of a new innovation can grow.

You get to these dissatisfactions through intensive, face-to-face interactions with customers. Settle for nothing less than unfiltered, real-time contact. Watch how customers use your products where they live, work, or play. The goal isn't just getting close to the customer; it's getting inside the customer experience.

Doing so requires getting outside the cocoon of the executive suite. If you're a senior auto industry executive, for instance, pass up the perquisite of having your next new car ordered by your secretary, and experience firsthand what the typical buyer endures at the hands of your dealer sales-and-service organization. You will gain an invaluable stimulus to new insight.

Shop the way your customers shop. In fact, study the total buying and use process. In an industrial business, look at how a product is engineered, sourced, bought, received and stocked, installed and repaired, and recycled once it reaches the end of its useful life. In a consumer business, examine how consumers shop for the product, use it, and clean up or put it away afterward. Learn how customers really use your product, how they routinely ignore or modify instructions, how they discover unimagined uses for your product, and how they define quality and superior performance.

Understanding the customer's total experience offers clues for new ways to bundle products, shorten time requirements, or deliver a solution more directly. It's how you get behind taken-for-granted tradeoffs of quality, cost, and time to identify fundamentally new value propositions.

3. *Don't delegate responsibility for insight.* All this demands enormous personal energy. New ideas are hard to come by and easy to kill. The

obstacle course they must run to win approval too often reduces them to a sterile lowest common denominator. That's why companies that excel at innovation ensure that senior managers don't delegate responsibility for insight.

Those closest to the customer may have the most firsthand data to contribute, but too often it doesn't get through. Those at the top bring a perspective that comes with experience and a degree of distance from the trenches. It's often easier for them to help the organization hear what customers are really saying and draw the frame-breaking conclusion. And of course, senior executives are freer to take risks and to see their convictions through to reality.

Breakthrough innovators design top-management engagement into every stage of the idea-generation process. Senior executives continuously challenge the organization to expand business concepts; they spend time face-to-face with customers; and they actively participate in exploring the opportunity space.

When they take responsibility for insight, executives discover that there is no such thing as a mature business—you can grow any business from the insight out.

CAPITALIZING ON ANOMALIES

LAWRENCE E. SHULMAN, 1997

Sometimes the best opportunities lie hidden in something that, at first glance, makes no sense. Idiosyncratic customer preferences or employee behavior can lead to aberrations in business results. How do you deal with these anomalies?

One common response is to ignore them. Most organizations try to contain or suppress anomalies for fear they will draw attention to departures from standard operating practice. When senior managers learn of anomalies, they generally dismiss them as random, one-time events.

That's too bad. Anomalies can reveal what your customers really want—and what your organization is capable of delivering in response. Paying attention to them may point you to major opportunities to grow your business, by doing on a broad scale what some part of your company is already doing on a small scale.

Wise executives capitalize on anomalies. They dig into them and look for ways to exploit them, asking: What's really going on? How can we learn from this? Is there an insight buried here that can move the business to a whole new level?

Inadvertent Next-Day Delivery

At one broad-line manufacturer, the business-altering anomaly was in the behavior of its distributors in a single geographic market. In most manufacturing businesses, distributors tend to carry the products of only one or two suppliers, and suppliers tend to do business with only a few key distributors in any given market. But in Chicago, a large market with many distributors, the company found that it was selling its specialty products to nearly every distributor in town. This didn't make sense. Why were all these Chicago distributors willing to buy from the same manufacturer?

The initial answers—"Chicago is just different" and "We've got a great sales rep there"—weren't much help. But patient digging revealed the real explanation: The company's factory was located only 200 miles from Chicago, and Chicago was on the way to almost all of the company's other markets. The frequent shipping runs through the area had inadvertently created a system of next-day delivery in and around Chicago. Distributors could stock a broader range at dramatically higher inventory turns, simultaneously enhancing their economics and allowing them to be more responsive to their customers.

Once they saw it, company executives began thinking about their business differently. They realized they could replicate the pattern in other markets. They assigned pairs of drivers to each truck and increased the overnight service range to 600 miles. They added order-entry and logistics systems that allowed them to make overnight delivery of high-tonnage orders. They expanded product variety to exploit new opportunities for even wider market access. Over time, they tripled or quadrupled market share in a half dozen Midwest cities and improved the product mix. Profits increased eightfold. Recently, the company acquired a new factory in another part of the country and is rolling out the same strategy in this new region.

Traffic-Jam Sales and Service

At a maker of high-tech health care diagnostic machines, the key anomaly was in the unusual performance of a local sales-and-service unit. A curious manager noticed that in Manhattan, the company had an extremely high capture rate for lucrative service contracts to maintain and repair the complex technology. What's more, customers there were buying all their new equipment from the company, even in product lines where the company's market share was normally quite low.

Closer inspection revealed that the Manhattan sales-and-service unit was the only one in the company assigning full-time, on-site service engineers to customer locations. Constant contact bred close relationships with both the buyers and the users of the equipment, and an in-depth understanding of their needs. Master technicians had become the company's most productive salespeople. Was the decision to locate the service engineers on the customers' premises a brilliant strategic decision? Hardly. The local service manager was simply trying to avoid having highly paid service technicians waste time in Manhattan traffic jams going from site to site. But understanding the anomaly did lead to a winning strategy. By assigning on-site technicians to customers in other regions, the company added 8 points of market share and boosted margins by 25 percent. It also gained a first-mover advantage over its rivals.

From Serendipity to System

The innovations at these two companies were serendipitous. What does it take to capitalize on anomalies systematically?

For starters, you need to have metrics and information systems that are sufficiently refined to identify anomalies in the first place. Knowing the average margins and market share isn't enough; look at the entire range of outcomes—across customers, geographies, products, and the like. This allows you to surface out-of-the-ordinary results for closer inspection.

The next step is to separate wheat from chaff: those anomalies that signal a potential business opportunity from those that are merely one-time events. The key is to examine the pattern of unusual performance over time. The customer who consistently buys high volumes or the market that outperforms the average year after year are, by definition, not random. Is there an underlying cause that can be identified and then replicated elsewhere?

Finally, you need to understand the precise mechanisms that animate the anomalies you identify. Why is the unusual pattern of performance happening? What specific features of the product or the local environment or the customer experience are bringing it about? Don't accept the usual first-order explanations. It's not enough to know that a particular customer has been loyal for years; find out precisely why.

It's up to senior management to create the forum for asking why and to persist until the question is answered with genuine insight. Business-unit personnel may be closest to the details of the anomaly in question, but they are usually too caught up in the day-to-day demands of the business to recognize the strategic significance of unusual patterns and practices. It often takes someone one step removed—regularly scanning the business for unexpected results— to notice and act on anomalies. It also takes an appreciation of differences, a lively sense of curiosity, and a willingness to play with the taken-for-granted rules of the business.

Timing is important. The worst time to look for anomalies is during a budget review, when everyone is worried about control numbers. A much better time is in a strategic review, when everyone should be prepared to think creatively about the future. Companies that consistently exploit anomalies plan for their future by reflecting on their past. A retrospective look at their strategy and business results allows them to take advantage of the serendipitous in a highly systematic way. As one executive put it, "We innovate from our own accidents."

Taking advantage of anomalies is an opportunity to inject into your company some of the experimentation and vitality characteristic of start-ups. Every day, entrepreneurs are working to reinvent your business and carve out a piece of it for themselves. By capitalizing on anomalies, you can harness the same kind of creative energy and put growth back on your company's agenda.

BREAKING COMPROMISES

GEORGE STALK, JR., DAVID K. PECAUT,
AND BENJAMIN BURNETT, 1997

Many companies today are searching for growth. How and where should they look? One powerful way to grow is through innovations that break the fundamental compromises of a business. When a company successfully breaks a compromise, it releases enormous trapped value. Breakaway growth can be the result.

Compromises are concessions demanded of consumers by most of the companies in an industry. They occur when the industry imposes its own operating constraints on customers. Usually, customers accept these compromises as just the way the business works—inevitable tradeoffs that have to be endured.

But a compromise is different from a tradeoff. In choosing a hotel room, for instance, a customer can trade off luxury for economy by choosing between a Ritz-Carlton and a Best Western. Until recently, however, most hotels forced all customers to compromise by not permitting check-in before 4:00 P.M. No law of nature or economics decrees that hotel rooms can't be ready before late afternoon.

Uncompromising Opportunity

The idea of compromises can be a useful organizing principle to focus an entire company on growth. It provides a systematic way to search for growth opportunities that are logical extensions of a company's existing business system.

Take the example of Circuit City's recent foray into the used-car business through the creation of a network of used-car superstores under the brand name CarMax. Annual used-car sales in North America top $200 billion, making it the third-largest consumer spending category behind food and clothing. What's more, few experiences are more fraught with compromises. Shopping for a used car is extremely time-consuming. And the buyer is at a fundamental disadvantage, ignorant about the actual condition of the product and subject to high-pressure sales tactics.

Circuit City concluded that many of the distinguishing capabilities of its consumer-electronics business could be used to break the compromises imposed on used-car buyers. Circuit City is known for the wide variety of its merchandise. CarMax takes the same approach. The typical used-car dealer has only 30 vehicles in stock, CarMax sites have up to 1,500. That makes it easy for customers to compare makes and styles. CarMax further enhances customer choice and lowers search costs by harnessing Circuit City's considerable expertise in information systems. At CarMax, customers have access to easy-to-use computer kiosks that allow them to review the inventory of available cars at all the CarMax stores in the region.

CarMax hasn't hesitated to deviate from the Circuit City model when the strategic logic requires it. For instance, Circuit City pays percentage-of-sales commissions to its consumer electronics sales force, but CarMax does not. Because a key compromise in used cars is pressure selling, the unit has created a compensation system that encourages no-haggle pricing and no-hassle guarantees. The result:

an integrated business system that offers a fundamentally different experience to used-car buyers, and a business model that has allowed CarMax to capture roughly 15 points of share in the markets where it is active.

A Pathway to Growth

Compromises are inherent in any business. Even when a company breaks one compromise, it usually ends up creating another. By focusing on compromises, a company can continuously uncover fresh opportunities and thus sustain growth over time.

The financial services company Charles Schwab, for example, was founded on the breaking of a compromise. The company began as a discount brokerage in 1975, when the deregulation of U.S. security markets made it unnecessary for individual investors to pay high fees to full-service brokers.

But Schwab didn't stop there. Next, it broke the compromise set up by the discount brokerage houses themselves. Although these new firms offered low prices, most also provided unreliable service. By investing in computer technology that allowed almost immediate confirmation of orders over the telephone, Schwab was able to combine low prices with levels of responsiveness unusual for its industry. Subsequently, Schwab added convenience, flexibility, and ease of transferring funds to its value proposition through the provision of 24-hour-a-day, seven-day-a-week service, the Schwab One cash-management account, and automated phone and electronic trading.

Recently, Schwab has used its compromise-breaking capabilities to enter the mutual fund business. Most people invest in several fund families to achieve diversification. But diversification often comes at the price of frustration. It means dealing with a confusing variety of statements, rules, and sales representatives. In 1992, Schwab introduced OneSource, a single point of purchase for more than 350 no-load mutual funds. In the more than 20 years since its founding, Schwab has evolved from a simple discount broker to a comprehensive self-help financial supermarket, generating an annual growth rate of 20 to 25 percent.

Creativity, Flexibility, and Nerve

For a company to grow by breaking compromises, it must have the creativity to translate customer dissatisfactions into new value propositions, the flexibility to engage in constant reorientation of its business system, and the nerve to challenge business-as-usual in its industry. There are three basic steps:

1. *Get inside the customer experience.* Start by asking your managers and employees to immerse themselves in the customer's experience. It is critical to develop a visceral feel for the compromises consumers encounter when they do business with you.

A compromise often becomes visible when customers have to modify their behavior to use a company's product or service. So pay special attention to the compensatory behaviors customers engage in to get around the constraints that your product or service imposes on them. In the brokerage business, for instance, it was common knowledge that customers often called back a second or even a third time to confirm that their trade had gone through at the price requested. By paying careful attention to this behavior, Schwab realized that the ability to provide immediate confirmation when an order was taken would eliminate the extra calls, saving customers a lot of trouble and giving Schwab a significant advantage over its competitors.

2. *Travel up the hierarchy of compromises.* Once the organization is focused on the customer experience, learn to recognize three different types of compromises, each with increasing potential to create value.

Some of the most obvious can be found in your company's existing products or services. It was Chrysler's awareness of the compromises between station wagons (based on a car platform) and vans (based on a truck platform) that led to the minivan, a van based on a car platform. In the ten years after Chrysler introduced the minivan in 1984, minivan sales grew eight times as fast as industry sales overall.

Other, more powerful compromises can be found at the level of an entire product category. Witness how Nike has transformed the athletic footwear category by combining continuous innovation in shoe design with the proliferation of narrowly defined customer segments. Nike doesn't just make basketball shoes. It makes Air Jordans, Force, and Flight, each designed for a different playing style, with different design requirements and a different image.

The most powerful compromises are often the hardest to identify: broad social dissatisfactions that may have little to do with your product or industry but a lot to do with how your customers live their lives. For example, long-term social and economic trends are causing more and more people to manage their own investments. Yet lack of time and growing economic complexity can make this an immensely frustrating task. Schwab's ability to address that frustration is a big factor in its success.

3. *Reconstruct your value chain.* Defining new value propositions for the customer is necessary but not sufficient. You must also use the compromises you break to redefine the competitive dynamics of your industry to ensure that the economic value liberated by compromise breaking flows to you rather than to your competitors.

Think of compromises as an opportunity to reshape the value chain of your industry to your advantage. When Schwab entered the mutual fund business, its first thought was to create its own family of funds. Careful analysis of the industry value chain, however, revealed an even bigger opportunity: to become an intermediary between its own customer base and a large number of subscale mutual fund companies. Through OneSource, the firm serves the needs of the fund companies by providing them with economies of scale they could not achieve on their own. At the same time, Schwab interposes itself between the funds and the customer. Schwab's ownership of the direct customer relationship now provides a platform for growth in other financial services, such as insurance.

To break compromises, executives must first break with the conventional wisdom of their industry—about customers, about industry practices, and about the economics of the business. When they do, faster growth and improved profitability are the result.

A NEW PRODUCT EVERY WEEK? LESSONS FROM MAGAZINE PUBLISHING

Gary Reiner and Shikhar Ghosh, 1988

BCG's work with businesses that develop new products quickly, such as consumer electronics, autos, construction equipment, business equipment, and magazine publishing, suggests that, in a wide variety of industries, the most successful competitors have adopted many of the same principles that enable weekly magazine publishers to hit the newsstands like clockwork the same time every week.

First and foremost, new-product development is a way of life for a weekly magazine. The organization's structure, skills, and systems are all honed to deliver new products over and over, better and better, and closer and closer to real-time events (i.e., the news).

In fast organizations, new products are developed in a steady stream. No one program is make-or-break, and a feature or performance enhancement that is not available for one generation can be rapidly implemented in the next.

Lesson 1: Like a magazine, manage new-product development as a continuing process, not an isolated event.

Second, a weekly magazine never misses its deadline. In fact, time is the key management variable, and the organization is shaped around aggressive time targets.

Fast organizations differentiate themselves from slow ones by putting a high premium on time. Paradoxically, some of the fastest companies, such as Honda and Toyota in automobiles, Compaq in personal computers, and Panasonic in consumer electronics, also have the lowest costs and highest quality levels. Living with a tight and unchangeable schedule drives the organization to do the essentials well.

Lesson 2: To speed new-product development, make time the key variable. Acceptable levels of cost and quality must be maintained, but the clock is king.

Each weekly magazine issue dishes up timely, newsbreaking stories. This could not happen without powerful and highly tuned organizational machinery that makes it possible to move quality from concept to finished product. A shared computer system shows the current status of the magazine instantly. Runners bring layouts to the editors within 15 minutes. Editors give immediate feedback to writers—often by computer. A large, sophisticated library holds information on topics relevant to the publication.

Fast companies invest in capabilities to support rapid product development—for example, design libraries to use the experience gained in previous products, market research and technology development for future product families, and cost-estimation databases to minimize the time required to get a cost estimate. By investing ahead of a specific need, they remove these support functions from the critical path of product development, making it shorter and less risky. A primary role of senior management in fast companies is to build these capabilities so that each development cycle is faster and better than the previous one.

Lesson 3: Companies need to invest actively in the activities that support rapid product development so that they never slow down the process. Directing this investment is a key function of senior management.

Reporters, photographers, and artists work together in close-knit, cross-functional teams to deliver the magazine as quickly as possible, with senior editors empowered to make final decisions. For example, picture choices are made jointly by the picture editors and artists.

Honda, the fastest developer of new autos, incorporates the SED (Sales, Engineering, and Development) system, which calls for a small team consisting of members of each of these three departments whose joint task is to evaluate consumers' needs, design the auto, and plan the factory needs.

Lesson 4: A new-product development project should be managed by a team whose members bring skills from all relevant functions (e.g., product management, design, manufacture).

At a weekly magazine, the team works together and communicates intimately. The entire magazine staff is often on one floor. There are frequent team meetings and decisions are made orally, on the spot.

Successful teams typically have three characteristics. They are located close to each other—in the same room if possible. They are judged only by the overall success of the project—not by individual contributions. And they have the authority to make the key decisions that affect the product.

Lesson 5: Empower the team members to work as a team. They must have common goals and rewards, authority to make decisions, and an elbow-to-elbow environment.

At a weekly magazine, the doers are the decision makers, and they act quickly. Everyone who touches the product adds value directly.

Fast organizations typically minimize the role of staff in the development process. Decisions on the product are made by the people developing it. Senior management focuses on developing the organizational capabilities that will shorten the cycle for future products.

Lesson 6: Members of product teams must have the experience, expertise, training, and authority needed to make important decisions. The role of senior managers is primarily to create an environment that leverages the skills of the teams.

U.S. businesses are frequently exhorted to emulate their Asian competitors in order to reduce costs, increase speed, and improve quality. Mostly this is good advice—certainly with regard to speed. But good models can also be found right here at home. Companies hoping to bring products to market faster can learn a lot about process from some of their neighbors—the ones that have always managed time well, such as weekly magazine publishers.

INNOVATING FOR CASH

James P. Andrew and Harold L. Sirkin, 2003

There are several ways to take a new product to market. If a company isn't considering all of them, odds are it's leaving big money on the table.

We are not talking about strategies, such as first mover or fast follower, or processes, such as new-product development, but about broad managerial approaches, or models, for turning ideas into cash. There are three basic approaches. Most organizations instinctively act as *integrators*, managing all the steps involved in taking a product to market. However, organizations can also be *orchestrators*, which focus on some parts of the commercialization process and depend on partners to manage the rest. Finally, businesses can be *licensors:* they sell or license a new product or idea to another organization, which handles the commercialization process.

Each of the three approaches has a unique investment profile and profitability pattern, and requires a different set of capabilities. And each new commercialization opportunity presents unique challenges. Matching the right model to the right opportunity helps determine how much risk a business will assume and how much money it will make from an innovation. We find that the best approach for a specific innovation often yields two or three times the profits of the least appropriate approach.

Choosing the Right Approach

There is no secret formula that will help managers choose the most effective approach to commercialization. But managers can make a well-informed decision by conducting a systematic analysis of three dimensions of the opportunity: the industry, the innovation, and the risks. That may sound familiar, but we find that most companies base their commercialization decisions on fragmented and partial evaluations of these factors. Managers make assumptions—"We are as low-cost as any supplier can be," "We'll be the leader even if we're late to market"—and fail to explore the consequences. Only a rigorous three-pronged analysis captures what's unique and important about the innovation and points to the approach that will maximize profits.

The Industry

A company has to take into account the structure of the industry it's trying to enter, especially if the industry is unfamiliar. Four factors can be particularly revealing:

- The physical assets needed to enter the industry
- The nature of the supply chain
- The importance of brands
- The intensity of rivalry

The exact metrics that executives use for the analysis are often less important than the general direction those metrics suggest. If, for instance, a company needs to invest heavily in physical assets, if partners' maturity levels are low, and if rivals are likely to use standard weapons to fight back, the integrator approach may be a good fit. (For more on finding the best approach to commercialization, see the exhibit "Which Model Works for You?") However, if the supplier base is sophisticated, if rivalry is likely to be intense, and if the value attributed to brands is high, the orchestrator model may be best to help a company share risks and investments.

The Innovation

The characteristics of an innovation play a central role in the choice of an approach. Consider, for instance, the product's potential life cycle. If it's likely to be long, there will be more time to recoup the greater up-front investment that an integrator typically needs to make. Similarly, managers must factor into their decision whether an innovation requires infrastructures and complementary services or technologies.

If the product represents not an incremental innovation but a radical breakthrough, it will require additional resources for both educating the market and ramping up production when demand takes off.

Which model works for you?

Integrator	Orchestrator	Licensor
Manages all the steps necessary to generate profits from an idea	Focuses on some steps and relies on partners to carry out the rest	Licenses the innovation to another company, which takes it to market
Investment requirements: high Capital may be needed to set up new manufacturing facilities, for instance	**Investment requirements: medium** Capital may be needed only to market the product, for example	**Investment requirements: low** Manufacturing and marketing expenses are borne by other companies
Capability requirements • Strong cross-functional links within the organization • Product design skills • Manufacturing-process design skills • Technical talent sourcing	**Capability requirements** • Ability to collaborate with several partners simultaneously while not having direct control • Complex project-management skills • Insight into customers • Brand management skills • Culture that can let go of certain areas while focusing on core competencies • Ability to move quickly	**Capability requirements** • Intellectual-property-management skills • Basic research capabilities • Contracting skills • Ability to influence standards
Best used when • speed to market is not critical • technology is proven • customers' tastes are stable • innovation is incremental	**Best used when** • the supplier and partner base is mature • competition is intense • strong substitutes are available • technology is in the early stages	**Best used when** • there is strong intellectual-property protection • the importance of the innovator's brand is low • the market is new to the innovator • significant infrastructure is needed but not yet developed

SOURCE: BCG analysis.

In this case, the orchestrator approach might make sense. It's important to note, however, that as long as an innovation enjoys patent protection, a company will gravitate toward the integrator approach because competitive pressures won't seem as critical.

The Risks

Finally, managers will want to consider four risks when deciding which model to use. The first is that the new product may not deliver the improved performance it promises. The second is that consumers may not buy the product even if it works; the incremental improvement or even the breakthrough may not be exciting enough. The third risk comes from substitutes, whose availability shrinks margins. Finally, the risk profile will be influenced by the investment that the company must make to commercialize the innovation. Some products, clearly, are more expensive to develop than others (jet aircraft as opposed to industrial fasteners, for instance). By analyzing all four risk factors, managers can decide early on if the company should favor an approach that passes on some of the risks—and rewards—to other companies. In addition, because unwarranted optimism often interferes with the risk analysis process, managers must take great care to consider all four risks. A broad perspective will help align the innovation's requirements with marketplace conditions.

Breaking Habits

Because the commercialization approach can play a decisive role in how much cash an idea generates, the ability to choose the right one can be a significant competitive advantage. Too often, however, companies find themselves wedded to a single model, usually out of sheer habit: The old favorite always appears less risky. In addition, many companies don't know enough about all the approaches or how to weigh their advantages and disadvantages. Indeed, in many instances, choosing how to take a product to market isn't even built into companies' decision-making processes.

Yet, picking the right approach is not a mechanical process. Each business opportunity is different, and the decision is often a judgment call. Moreover, just getting a view of which model is best for a specific opportunity will not ensure success. Managers must also gauge which approach will fit best with the company's internal skills. The company's capabilities—those it has or can muster quickly—must match the requirements of the approach.

Managers, however, should match organizational skills with the demands of the innovation models only after they have evaluated all three. Otherwise, capabilities overtake the decision, and companies—once again—end up using their favorite approach to commercialization instead of the most effective one.

ACQUIRING YOUR FUTURE

Mark Blaxill and Kevin Rivette, 2004

"Assume that innovation will occur elsewhere." So says Joy's Law, a less famous cousin of Murphy's Law. But for many companies, Joy's is the far more important insight. Because at some point almost every one of them, wanting to grow, will be faced with the need to acquire the innovations of others.

What acquirers often discover, though, is that it can be far harder to pin down the value of innovation than other forms of property. Companies often buy a business for its technology and discover that it has limited ownership rights to the functions its inventions purport to provide. They may offer a premium for a "technology leader"—only to discover that the innovations of real value are developing in a different direction. And they may believe that they can rely on a target's patents to protect critical future product plans and cash flow streams—only to find that the company has deferred maintenance of its portfolio of intellectual property (IP) to "save costs" and has eliminated key protections that were the basis of the deal.

Acquirers make mistakes like these in part because they don't invest enough in the evaluation of the underlying intellectual property or rely too much on narrow legal assessments. But there are more fundamental reasons why companies miscalculate the value of intellectual assets. Innovation-driven acquisitions generate value only if the target's IP assets provide advantage in the marketplace. And advantage matters only when considered relative to a competitor. IP-based advantage takes this basic concept of relativity and multiplies it in some nonintuitive ways, making it that much harder to assess value:

- *Webs versus havens.* IP assets lack clear property lines. Every bit of intellectual property you can own comes with connections to other valuable innovations. The defensibility of property rights that rest in a connected web of ambiguous specifications and claims requires subjective, often legal, interpretation. So although relative position with respect to a cluster of patent rights is both real and important, it can be much more difficult to determine than a relative cost position in, say, a manufacturing process.

- *The past versus the future.* The value of innovation rights involves a mix of current claims and options on the future. Current claims provide a measure of security by ensuring the ability to stay in business and may even provide the ability to restrict the movement of competitors. But these current rights typically have little role in sustaining competitiveness unless a company can extend their function and utility, connect flanking inventions to an original position, and secure some kind of "value gate" in a particular market or layer of the value chain. Creating value through such extensions requires a subtle understanding of the web of connections among IP assets and a disciplined approach to extending protection that can secure an option's value in the future.

- *The unexpected versus the familiar.* Relative position in an IP competition is seldom a matter of competing with the "usual suspects." Key competitors for valuable innovation rights can take different forms. They might be *Rembrandt hunters,* who see your current cash flows as a target for licensing revenue. They might be preemptive *homesteaders,* forecasters with no plans to build a business but who have attempted to anticipate technology trends and stake out their claims before anyone else can get there. In most areas of innovation, an unexpected set of competitors lurks disturbingly close to the profit sources, often closer than the known competition. Unorthodox competitors can pose greater threats to your future than familiar ones, whose freedom to explore new avenues of innovation is typically more constrained. At the same time, observing the nature of their profit claims can give you considerable insight about new directions in both technology and market development.

The managerial challenge of all of this is to approach intellectual property as a business issue and not merely as a legal or technical question. That means you will need to formulate a view—literally a picture or landscape—that includes an IP dimension as well as competitive and market parameters. You will need to find effective ways to map your position, your target's position, and the positions of others. And here's the new part: You will need to consider the target's assets in the context of the web of connected claims. How often are these claims cited and by whom, how recent are the claims, how vulnerable are they to other asset webs, and how relevant are they to the desired product performance or your ability to master a layer of the value chain? Ultimately, the question is one of economics: How much does the IP web shape your economics, your industry, and your competitors' strategies?

Assembling such landscapes is a collaborative and ongoing exercise. Sure, it involves legal and technical experts. But your top team has to take ownership. What's more, the landscape needs to be complete. In addition to including the IP holdings of your target, it must also show the IP holdings of the target's key suppliers and customers. You will want to know not only the inventions at issue but also the names of the inventors, where they are now employed, and whether they have relationships with competitors or research institutions. This is hard work, but it can yield extraordinary insights. The amount of valuable competitive intelligence embedded in patent filings is phenomenal and largely untapped. This intelligence will help you make or save a great deal of money in three ways.

Selecting Better Targets

Not only is buying innovation rights different from integrating product and market positions, but the product and market positions of a given target are often unrelated to the IP protection positions. To assess the total competitive position of your target, you need to picture *both* the competitive landscape of the product and the market, *and* the IP terrain. Knowing where to invest and which of the players to buy can save you from major blunders. In some cases, due diligence can even show you that a deal is unnecessary, because there are ways to use the technology without buying the company. And quite often you may end up buying different companies in different areas of the IP landscape for different reasons—owning an interface or enhancing a potential spinoff, rather than securing a current product market or shoring up a weakness relative to suppliers.

Making Smarter Deals

You should know the competitive value of what you are buying and not simply apply an intuitive discount to the expected technology hype. Knowing more about the technology and intellectual property than your target does can dramatically increase your negotiating leverage and ensure that you make the best possible deal. More often than not, the closer you look, the less you find. Suppliers may be developing technologies around interfaces that box in the target and hurt your bargaining power. At the same time, customers may be aggressively exploring product substitutes through their own use of intellectual property.

Getting More Out of Your Investment

Getting to the next level of value creation (and, quite often, recouping a sizable acquisition premium) requires a deep integration plan that has several possible objectives. These goals include protecting your ability to deliver a distinctive brand or benefit, owning a key interface, controlling a future supply chain, and, in general, being closer to the value gates of the business as it evolves.

People will always be key, of course. Knowing how to identify the top innovation talent and taking the steps to keep that talent can make the difference between a one-shot boost and a future with even more upside potential. Sometimes you may not be getting the people you think you are getting. When conducting due diligence, put together a list of those who were responsible for the intellectual property you hold most valuable and make sure they are still at the target company—or have a plan for replacing them.

Making an acquisition is, after all, a strategic commitment to the future, and you should use the occasion to reinforce the advantage of the expanded enterprise and invest behind it to strengthen it further.

*   *   *

Developing effective strategies that create and sustain competitive advantage has always required top management to apply several lenses simultaneously. These lenses are the basis for points of view about the evolution of the market, your relative capability to serve customers in that market, and the pieces of the value chain that will earn the highest returns. If senior managers don't take a strategic perspective and continually synthesize the pictures these lenses reveal, then their companies are likely to make major mistakes and miss major opportunities. This is especially true when the challenge is to make the right acquisitions at the right price and then get maximum value from them.

Now we must add a new lens to the formulation and execution of strategy. And that is the lens of intellectual property. With this lens in place, due diligence can take on new vitality and offer new potential for adding value.

Deconstruction of
Value Chains

BCG PARTNERS BEGAN thinking in the mid-1980s about the impact on strategy of the two most powerful—and disruptive—technological developments of our times: cheap, pervasive computing power and high-bandwidth communication. The early implications for customer segmentation (discussed earlier in *Segment-of-One Marketing*) soon were matched by promising work on the benefits of using IT to better coordinate supply chains. Shortly thereafter, we began investigating the implications of media "convergence," as everyone was calling it then, for several entertainment and communications clients.

By the early 1990s, Philip Evans and Tom Wurster realized that we were onto something far more general and powerful than media convergence. They began trying out their ideas with clients at BCG CEO Conferences in the mid-1990s. They published their thinking first in their classic 1997 *Harvard Business Review* article, "Strategy and the New Economics of Information" (reprinted in the Milestones subpart) and then in their best-selling book, *Blown to Bits* (Harvard Business School Press, 2000). They and other partners also explored many of the implications in *Perspectives* written during the same period.

The thesis was—and still is—that these new technologies, plus the new standards that have accompanied them, eliminate the traditional trade-off between the richness and reach of communications. That, in turn, allows companies to deconstruct their value chains. The links can then become separate businesses, each with its own economics, and competitive advantage gets de-averaged as the value chain deconstructs. Some businesses become winner-take-all; others become stalemated. New forms of collaboration—and of competition—result. New sourcing—and outsourcing—arrangements flourish, as do more precisely tailored, responsive relationships with customers and employees.

That deconstruction—and reconstruction—of value chains is far from played out. We anticipate fluidity in their architecture for at least another decade. Enormous value has been created from the phenomenon over the past decade; even more will be created over the next.

THE NEW VERTICAL INTEGRATION

JOHN R. FRANTZ AND THOMAS M. HOUT, 1993

When Henry Ford set out to make the lowest-cost car in America, he integrated vertically. Turning iron ore into automobiles, Ford eliminated almost all inventories, reduced costs and prices, and was able to raise wages—until less-integrated competitors proved better at providing what customers wanted. Vertical integration as a business concept fell under a cloud from which it has not emerged.

Until now. Leading-edge companies are beginning to reinvent the vertically integrated enterprise. They are getting the same advantages of low cost and fast turns, but they are also giving customers more of what they want and sooner.

The new vertical integration does not involve ownership or exclusive relationships. Instead, it is about eliminating barriers and costs between independent companies.

The new integration starts by thinking of your business as part of a supply chain made up of several companies. But instead of the conventional view of separate companies transacting with each other, visualize one continuous business system. Most companies just manage their suppliers and serve their customers. But today's leaders consider their suppliers' suppliers and their customers' customers part of their business. And they understand that the only way to eliminate inventory is to coordinate actions across this system through the imaginative use of information.

Most overhead is incurred in dealing day to day with customers and suppliers—forecasting, placing and accepting orders, scheduling, stocking, shipping, warehousing, billing and collecting—and then changing it all daily to cope with surprises. The objective of the new integration is to collapse this cost structure.

To implement the new integration, companies generally progress through three stages. First, two companies decide to lower some of the barriers that separate them and begin to operate as one business. Second, they build a customized relationship, expanding on the new opportunities they have discovered. Third, they extend their new approach to the entire chain of companies surrounding their business and take some risks by dramatically changing the rules that govern how they all work with each other. The later the stages, the bigger the organizational challenge to make it happen, but the greater the total impact on the business.

Working as one usually starts with basics, such as paring the duplicate buffer inventories that have built up over time. The customer then starts to share product and point-of-sale information with the supplier. Together, these actions can cut inventories by at least 20 percent. Another variation finds a manufacturer running a full product mix through a flexible plant every day and shipping every night to a wholesaler or an end customer. This can triple the customer's inventory turn.

Logistics leaders in most industries are already getting these basics done, but even this is often not easy. Getting to this level takes trust and some new metrics. For example, when one manufacturer began to ship to its wholesalers every night regardless of the size of their orders, the transportation manager was not convinced that the policy made good business sense. He saw only that his departmental costs went up as trucks left half empty each night. He was not aware that overnight shipments were reducing inventory costs for both the manufacturer and the wholesaler and bringing down order-processing and scheduling costs as well.

Top management soon realized that opposition to daily shipments by the transportation manager and others stemmed from the company's failure to develop metrics that fit the strategy. The two missing metrics were total inventory turn for the manufacturer and wholesaler combined and total order-processing costs for the manufacturer, from order entry and scheduling through shipment. Once these metrics were in place and explained, everyone began to understand the big picture and could support the changes.

Companies like Helene Curtis have gone to the next level by customizing the delivery process, saving the customer costs that have always been thought of as fixed. With its ability to meet each customer's unique packing and delivery requirements without special handling, Helene Curtis has steadily gained share in the personal care business. Its warehouse data system manages the loading process right down to the order of cartons on the truck. All this costs no more at the sending end and saves money at the receiving end.

Customizing logistics between companies is organizationally demanding. It usually takes a permanent cross-functional team organized around a customer or customer group. Otherwise, there is too much reliance on standard solutions. The best customizing comes from hunches, idea fragments, and brave experiments. For these to go anywhere, everyone on the team has to have the same incentive, namely, "This is our baby and we had better make it work."

The ultimate form of partnership is when a supply chain of three or four companies recognizes the value of managing itself as a single logistics system. This is the third stage. One such group is Du Pont (fibers), Spring Mills (a fabric maker), Warren Featherbone (a children's apparel maker), and Mercantile Stores. They first got together to defend themselves against imported clothing and began by sharing point-of-sale information to reduce inventory and shorten lead times. Later they started to cooperate in planning product-line introductions.

The keys to the apparel business are keeping the retail shelf turning fast and avoiding markdowns. Domestic producers' only advantage against imports is logistics: the capability to quickly make more of what is selling and stop making what is not. The result of the cooperation among these companies has been spectacular. Markdowns are a third of the industry average, gross profit margins rose through the past recession, and share of market has increased.

Having learned to work with each other, these companies are now pushing the frontiers of cooperation. One possibility is that they will move together to execute one coordinated vertical order—whatever was sold off the shelf today would be replenished at each level in the chain at once. Each company would produce just the right amount and ship it to its customer immediately. Such coordination is now possible with fast information and flexible production. Current inventory turns in the system could double.

Going further, a well-integrated chain could eventually decide, for example, that no one gets paid until the final product is sold at retail. This is the ultimate discipline and test—but the rewards in overhead reduction would be great. Combining automatic replenishment with one-time payment for everyone would reduce costs across the board—billing, ordering, promotions, working capital, and so on—to a fraction of current levels.

Getting started is the hardest part, because so much of what is routine in companies must be overcome. Functional and company boundaries break the business into separate parts, each of which is managed by a person who is evaluated largely on the performance of that piece only. This discourages risk taking across the parts. Also, conventional accounting data hide rather than reveal radical logistics opportunities. ("Fixed cost" is one of the most misleading phrases in our language.)

The best place to start the integration process is at the top. However, it will take more than getting a group of people in a room together. The number of obstacles and setbacks you encounter rises sharply when multiple companies are involved. Trust is fragile in the early stages. You need continuous project management at senior levels across all the companies. And you need to create new sets of numbers and new language, like *total-system inventory* and *vertical cycle time*.

Vertically integrated supply chains can achieve extraordinary customer responsiveness with minimum inventories. We will see it accomplished in the 1990s by companies that buy and sell from each other as they push the frontiers of cooperation.

THE DECONSTRUCTION OF VALUE CHAINS

CARL W. STERN, 1998

The end of the last century saw the construction of the vertically integrated value chains that came to define modern business. The end of this century is witnessing their deconstruction. Markets are intruding on the web of proprietary arrangements that have held these chains together. As they do so, the boundaries defining businesses, companies, and industries are coming under attack—radically transforming the nature of competition. New concepts of strategy and organization are required in order to cope.

The Logic of Value Chains—Undermined

Integrated value chains have served business well. They enabled the sophisticated coordination that growing technical complexity required. They organized the dedicated assets, both human and physical, necessary for achieving economies of scale and scope. Expensive to create, they were a formidable barrier to competition once established. The vertically integrated value chain has been a potent competitive machine.

Not anymore. Powerful forces are undermining the logic and practice of traditional vertical integration. Eroding trade barriers and the resulting globalization of markets give businesses worldwide access to world-class capabilities. Modern manufacturing and distribution technologies make global sourcing and selling increasingly low cost. Deregulation and increasingly sophisticated capital markets allow the laws of economics to prevail at every step of the value chain.

But the most powerful force subverting conventional value chains—partly because it acts as a catalyst and accelerator for all the others—is a revolution in the economics of information. Information has always been the glue that held value chains together. The cost of getting sufficiently rich information to suppliers, channels, and customers made proprietary information systems and dedicated assets a necessity, and gave vertical integration its leverage.

That glue is now melting. Universal connectivity and common communications standards are enabling the open and virtually cost-free exchange of information of all kinds. Companies share product designs, CAD/CAM parameters, logistics information, and financial data with equal ease both inside and outside the corporation. New intermediaries are emerging to support interconnection, facilitate comparison, guarantee performance, and make markets. Searching and switching are vastly simpler and cheaper than they used to be.

These trends have two simultaneous effects. On the one hand, proprietary links give way to markets. Witness the outsourcing trend: Companies can now make use of key activities in the value chain without owning them. On the other hand, opportunities for rich communication and collaboration between customers and suppliers are greater than ever. Both these developments undermine vertical integration, replacing it with a highly flexible mix of new coordination mechanisms, ranging from the ruthlessness of the spot market at one extreme to the most strategic of partnerships at the other.

Patterns of Deconstruction

As traditional value chains deconstruct, fundamentally new business models begin to appear. In some cases, a start-up mounts a direct attack on the established business model by splitting information flows from physical flows. This is the essence of Amazon.com's challenge to conventional book selling.

A more common pattern begins when a vertically integrated incumbent recognizes the opportunity to outsource nonstrategic or particularly capital-intensive parts of the value chain—even as it continues to dominate the whole. In these cases, integration gives way to *orchestration*. Successful orchestrators possess powerful brands and use them to retain control of the lion's share of an industry's value added while minimizing their own assets. This is what Nike, Hewlett-Packard, and Sara Lee are trying to do.

But maintaining control of the value chain is not easy. The orchestrated—those who focus on a specific value-added step, or *layer*—have every incentive to drive for scale and scope themselves. If they succeed, they wrest control of the value chain from the orchestrator, as Intel and Microsoft did from IBM. The business then deconstructs entirely. Each layer becomes a distinct business with its own economics. Some of these layer businesses are highly scale sensitive; dominating them can be extraordinarily profitable. Others are naturally fragmented; after deconstruction, profits are hard to come by. The onset of fragmentation can, however, create opportunities for a new sort of player—*navigators* that help participants cope with the complexity of doing business in a deconstructed world.

The Implications of Deconstruction

The competitive implications of deconstruction are profound and wide ranging:

- The traditional definition of businesses and industries—and, therefore, the reference set of competitors, suppliers, and customers—becomes obsolete.

- Competitive advantage is de-averaged. Businesses in which the economics of one activity are compromised for the sake of the whole will be especially vulnerable.

- Advantage across the entire value chain no longer matters; it's advantage in each layer that counts. As a result, the new unit of strategic analysis is the layer.

- Horizontal strategies—those that leverage layer capabilities across previously distinct businesses—become serious alternatives to traditional strategies of vertical integration and customer franchise in a single industry.

- Managing resource allocation at the layer level requires new ways to evaluate investments and gives birth to a whole new concept of the portfolio. The finer parsing of risk permits imaginative new financial strategies.

- The boundaries of the corporation become fluid and permeable. Ownership is no longer a condition for effective coordination or control.

- Customers are empowered; brands become vulnerable. Traditional asymmetries of information are challenged by the rise of navigators that search and switch on the customer's behalf.

- Intermediaries that extract value from controlling a chokepoint in the flow of information are vulnerable to disintermediation.

In a competitive environment characterized by deconstruction, commitment to existing business models, however rational they may appear, becomes a liability. The attacker has the advantage. Incumbents are under threat from increasingly unfamiliar intruders—but they also have unprecedented opportunities to leverage their capabilities in new ways. In subsequent *Perspectives*, we will explore the new principles of strategy and organization that deconstruction requires.

HOW DECONSTRUCTION DRIVES DE-AVERAGING

PHILIP B. EVANS, 1998

In an economy of integrated value chains, competitive advantage is a game of averages. Take the simple example of costs. If a company's aggregate costs are competitive, then having a cost advantage at every step of the value chain isn't necessary: The steps are bundled together. But as value chains deconstruct into distinct segments, layers, and markets, average advantage loses its importance. What counts is advantage in each individual piece of the value chain. Deconstruction leads to *de-averaging*.

Whether de-averaging is good or bad, an opportunity or a threat, depends on your perspective. De-averaging means that companies no longer have the luxury of subsidizing poor performance in one activity by combining it with strength in others. But de-averaging also gives companies the opportunity to stop diluting strong performance in one activity by linking it to others that perform less well. Weakness in any particular activity can become a glaring liability, but strength can become a decisive competitive asset.

Companies have always been able to outsource activities they could not perform cost-effectively. Outsourcing for reasons of cost has been surging. But deconstruction goes beyond cost and beyond the support activities traditionally seen as candidates for outsourcing. Deconstruction permits an unprecedented separation of activities, including some that companies see as core pieces of their identity. It breaks down traditional industry structures, destroys old businesses, and creates new ones.

The Strategic Implications of De-Averaging

One strategic implication of de-averaging is the concentration of competitive advantage. When multiple sources of advantage are collected in a bundle, the impact of any single source is attenuated. That's why in most businesses so many competitors are able to survive and prosper. But within each of the new stand-alone, narrowly defined businesses of the deconstructed value chain, there are fewer bases of competitive advantage. With fewer ways to win, there are fewer winners.

In some segments, one dominant source of advantage prevails—scale, for instance. Monolithic advantage breeds monopoly, and the winner takes all. In other segments—for example, the manufacturing (as opposed to the marketing) of packaged consumer goods—there is no clear source of advantage, and its absence breeds stalemate.

But the logic of de-averaging applies not just to the separation of discrete steps on the value chain; it applies also to the information within each step. In most value chains, informational activities and physical activities are intertwined. Information technology—especially the advent of universal connectivity and standard protocols—allows the two to separate. When they do, information businesses and physical businesses will finally be free to pursue their different economics. The ensuing de-averaging is dramatic because the economics of information and the economics of things pull in diametrically opposite directions.

A retail store, for instance, is both a physical and an information business. On the physical side, it is a warehouse, holding inventory between factory and consumer. On the informational side, it is a billboard, providing the consumer with information and choice. Informational economics suggest that inventory should be maximized to give consumers the broadest choice. Physical economics dictate minimizing inventory in order to maximize the productivity of assets. A store is a necessary compromise between the two. Electronic retailing, however, renders this compromise unnecessary. A Web site can offer infinite choice with zero inventory. A fulfillment house can operate as an industrial warehouse with industrial efficiency.

De-Averaging as a Threat

The de-averaging of competitive advantage can transform a business beyond recognition and undermine its traditional sources of advantage. The typical auto dealership, for example, is a complex bundle of physical and informational services. As a physical distributor, it is less efficient than direct factory delivery or regional distribution centers. Its service is inferior to that of a specialized repair chain. As a provider of unbiased product information, its value added is negative. Its financing is overpriced. As a market maker in used cars, it exploits the ignorance and anxiety of consumers. What is it, then, that holds these activities together? And what makes them collectively advantaged when they are individually disadvantaged? Nothing but the consumer's economics of searching: the high cost of acquiring comparative information about price, service, delivery, quality, and interest rates.

Fortunately for consumers, the bundle is unraveling. OEMs are moving toward manufacture-to-order, using tighter information links between customers, factory, and suppliers to eliminate the need for retail inventory. Microsoft's CarPoint, Autobytel.com, and others are creating comprehensive car-shopping services on the Internet. Similarly, Quicken enables consumers to search for the cheapest credit and insurance across hundreds of institutions. Used-car rating systems, a vast array of electronic classifieds, and free Internet access to blue-book information are all improving the efficiency of the used-car market. The only potential source of advantage left to dealers is the test drive—for which they currently don't get paid.

At the very least, these trends mean that the dealer cannot continue to lose money on the new-car sale and make it up on warranties, service, and the trade-in. Every single activity will have to be competitive and profitable in its own right. Far more likely is that dozens of focused competitors will pick apart the dealer's business. Dealers will lose volume faster than they can shed overhead. Thousands will go out of business. The traditional auto dealership is being destroyed by the de-averaging of competitive advantage.

De-Averaging as an Opportunity

The same logic, with varying speed and intensity, applies to wide swaths of the economy. Deconstruction can occur wherever information economics hold a physical bundle together and wherever the informational activities themselves can evolve into separate businesses. Deconstruction will occur when de-averaging releases economic value—when activities cross-subsidize one another or when the economics of one activity are compromised for the sake of another.

But no company is required to sit by while its business is deconstructed. There are three initiatives companies can take to avert the threats and pursue the opportunities that deconstruction offers.

First, they can mentally de-average their own competitive advantage and that of their direct, indirect, and potential competitors. Which steps in the value chain would be most (or least) advantaged and profitable as separate businesses? How is information technology melting the "glue" that holds activities together as bundled businesses? Where can informational activities separate from physical ones into new kinds of businesses? What will be the sources of competitive advantage in each new business, and who is most likely to own them?

Second, each company can sort out its options. How vulnerable is its current business model? How do its "de-averaged" pieces compare with everyone else's? What, in each case, is the size of the prize? In light of its legacy assets, how fast can it achieve the necessary change? What, specifically, entitles it to win in the step or steps where it chooses to compete?

Third, and perhaps most difficult, companies can examine their own internal barriers to success. Many executives have only just begun to get comfortable with the idea of cannibalizing profitable product lines in order to speed the latest innovations to the marketplace. Winning in a deconstructing world will require cannibalizing entire business models and challenging a company's traditional sense of identity. To do so, an organization's leaders must not only build intellectual acceptance, they must overcome visceral resistance: Our customers won't shop this way. Our salesforce can't sell this way. Our organization will not operate this way. In short, the de-averaging of competitive advantage forces a company also to deconstruct its beliefs—starting with some of its most deeply held assumptions about the business.

THINKING STRATEGICALLY ABOUT E-COMMERCE

Philip B. Evans and Thomas S. Wurster, 1999

The first generation of electronic commerce has been a land grab. Strategy has ranked right below tactics—and tactics below experimentation. That phase is coming to an end. We are entering the second generation of e-commerce. The key players—branded goods suppliers, physical retailers, electronic retailers, pure navigators—must now shift their attention from claiming territory to defending or capturing it. In other words, they must focus on strategies to achieve competitive advantage.

The battlefield where competitive advantage will be won or lost is navigation—how customers search, compare, and decide what to buy. In the physical world, consumers have such a hard time finding and comparing goods that they seldom actually do it. They rely instead on product suppliers and retailers, who build advantage by creating navigational tools—branding, advertising, relationship building—to short-circuit a laborious and costly process.

On the Internet, however, people can exchange massive amounts of information directly, fast, and free. Product suppliers can sell directly to consumers. Electronic retailers can focus on navigation but outsource fulfillment. Pure navigators like Yahoo! or Quicken can organize information and help people make sense of it without being party to any physical transaction.

Product suppliers and bricks-and-mortar retailers have every reason to see the Internet as an arena for marketing and promotion—a new channel for doing old things. But if they persist in that view, they will handicap themselves in their struggle with new competitors who see navigation as a business in its own right. In most consumer businesses, far more profitability derives from influencing navigation than from any other activity. Companies have three basic ways to capture that profitability: reach, affiliation, and richness.

Competing on Reach

Reach is about access and connection: how many customers a business can access and how many products it can offer. Before e-commerce, retail superstores competed brilliantly on reach by offering broad selection and convenient locations. But they were limited by the economics of things. The largest physical bookstore in the United States carries about 250,000 titles. Amazon.com, by contrast, offers 4.5 million and is "located" on some 25 million computer screens.

Unconstrained by physical limitations, reach explodes. So do traditional industry boundaries. If consumers value comprehensive search, then the smart navigator moves from a comprehensive book domain to a comprehensive consumer domain. Although Amazon.com has unprecedented reach as an online bookseller, its true business is navigation. It is rapidly broadening its offering to include movies, drugs, toys, and perhaps much more. This strategy may help explain why stock market investors give Amazon.com a higher valuation than the entire traditional book-retailing and publishing industries put together.

Established players will have to match the reach of the pure navigators for the simple reason that buyers value it. Increasing a company's reach may mean establishing joint ventures with competitors. It may mean navigating to competing products and services. Incumbents will need to exploit synergies with their existing businesses wherever they can, but they must also expect the new business to cannibalize the old. Above all, they must learn to think of navigation as a business in its own right and not compromise its success in an effort to protect the traditional physical model.

Competing on Affiliation

Affiliation is about whose interests the new business represents. E-retailers tilt heavily toward the consumer. When salespeople have only one product to sell, they push it as aggressively as they can. Give them a universe of products, and they are much more likely to be neutral. Go further and equip consumers with the information they need to compare sales agents, and the odds are that sales agents will try harder to please the consumer than to please any single product supplier.

Take the example of Microsoft CarPoint, which enables buyers to compare new car models along 80 objective specifications. Dealers and automakers have never offered that kind of information. Microsoft does it because Internet technology lets it assemble rich information from multiple sites at negligible cost—and because doing so gives it an advantage over competing players.

Consumers don't need to pay Microsoft for this tilt in affiliation. The navigator's income can come from advertising, hyperlinks, and the sale of associated products and services. But for the most sophisticated consumers and the largest and most complex purchases, paid navigation is likely to emerge. When it does, the tilt will increase.

The players best positioned to exploit affiliation are the pure navigators. Worst off are the product suppliers. In some businesses—sports cars is one—consumers welcome blatant hype as part of the experience. But where data and affiliation matter, product suppliers have a problem.

There are several things they can do. One is to offer navigation services that solve problems instead of pushing products. Another is to provide objective information about their own and competing products—but slightly bias the presentation by means of ordering and emphasis. American Airlines did this long ago with SABRE. Dell provides broad and genuinely unbiased navigation to computer peripherals but continues to promote its own personal computers. The overall navigational proposition is consumer affiliated but preserves seller affiliation where it matters. This is the best defense in computer retailing against a potential cyber-Wal-Mart—be it Amazon.com, Microsoft, or, for that matter, Wal-Mart itself.

Competing on Richness

Richness is the depth and detail of information—about products and about customers. Although incumbents must struggle to keep up with e-retailers and pure navigators in terms of reach and affiliation, they have natural advantages when it comes to richness. Suppliers have deeper and more up-to-date product information than navigators, and it makes an especially powerful tool wherever consumers are open to product evangelism—entertainment, fashion, the next great product from Apple.

When it comes to information about consumers, traditional retailers have a definite edge. The Web gives e-retailers data-mining techniques they can apply to browsing behavior, purchasing history, and demographics. Yet the great advantage of physical retailers is the rich data they collect from other sources. Web-derived data are surprisingly thin compared with the information developed by grocery stores and credit card companies. Putting the two kinds of information together—then using the Web as a means of customizing ads, offers, and products—allows physical retailers to build powerful relationships and strong competitive advantage.

Because no single player is likely to have an ideal database and digital information can be bought and sold, there will probably be alliances and markets for information swapping. But the originators and primary aggregators of such information—stores, portals, credit agencies, or consumers themselves—will extract most of the value.

The Imperative of Reinvention

E-commerce presents incumbents with a serious dilemma. Their value chains are deconstructing. Their navigational functions are becoming businesses. To compete, they must identify the precise combination of reach, affiliation, and richness that works for them and then redefine their business strategies so that the e-business can grow beyond its physically defined origins. Every aspect of organization, incentive, and operating style will have to change.

These are enormous challenges for any organization. Traditional competencies, procedures, and power structures all stand in the way. How can an incumbent achieve the autonomy, motivation, and freshness of an Internet start-up and simultaneously make the most of its uniquely rich customer and product information?

The answer is some version of the corporate transformation and reinvention that Charles Schwab & Company recently undertook when it halved its brokerage fees, committed to navigation as its business definition, and started selling its competitors' products. But then Schwab has a history of reinventing itself. For many incumbents, the move into e-commerce will be their first chance at reinvention. They need to make certain that it isn't their last.

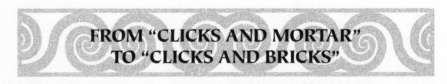

FROM "CLICKS AND MORTAR" TO "CLICKS AND BRICKS"

PHILIP B. EVANS AND THOMAS S. WURSTER, 2000

If ever there was a concept seeking an audience desperate to believe, it is "clicks and mortar." It's an answer to the incumbent's prayer. At last, something for the old-line corporation to bring to the Internet party.

No need to cannibalize departments. No need to start a civil war. Here's a ready-made competitive advantage straight from the status quo. Like cold fusion or the Laffer curve, clicks and mortar is an idea that a certain constituency simply craves. If clicks and mortar didn't exist, somebody would be working feverishly to invent it.

The fact that the buzzword is ideologically convenient makes it suspect, of course, but that doesn't make it wrong. There really is a point to physical synergies, as Schwab discovered when it found that a thin network of local branches would stimulate sales of telephone brokerage accounts. Physical demonstration and merchandising of a product, handling returns, service and repairs, signage—all of these issues matter to Internet businesses. Even Amazon.com, paragon of all things new, has been building warehouses.

Deconstructing the Core Business

The examples of Schwab and Amazon suggest that it may be far easier for online businesses to add physical capabilities than vice versa. It is organizationally cleaner to build a physical infrastructure from scratch than to shrink it down from something preexisting. Small, dedicated physical systems may actually be better than large, unfocused legacies. And certainly it's cheaper to build warehouses with Internet capital than to use money that expects a quarterly profit.

For traditional incumbents, so far the negative synergies seem to have outweighed the positive ones. Recall how Toys R Us crippled its online offering because the company couldn't bring itself to sanction an attack on its politically and financially dominant physical incarnation. Barnes & Noble effectively abandoned synergies between its physical stores and the Web and spun off its Internet bookstore.

The challenge for incumbents is to think about where to find valuable synergies. The smartest incumbents have stopped trying to redeem the legacy business and started deconstructing it. They look at each function or value-added step separately. They consider synergies piece by piece. They cast a cold eye on the outsourcing alternatives. Then they set up the minimal organization needed to support only those synergies that are really compelling.

This suggests a broader pattern. The defining characteristic of the Web is universal connectivity based on information standards. This rich connectivity blows up the need for closed information channels. It weakens the need for vertical or horizontal integration of any kind. Coordination that is supported internally by an intranet can be supported externally by an extranet since, after all, they're the same thing.

Before too long, we're likely to see the best online competitors teaming up with the best providers of physical services: Webvan handling returns for e-retailers; grocery stores taking small-business cash deposits for Internet banks; or Midas doing the warranty service on a dealer-free Ford.

Collaboration may still be easier within organizations than across them. So where alliances are not enough we will see restructuring. VerticalNet and Grainger could combine to build the Amazon of industrial procurement. Wal-Mart and Amazon could together build the mother of all retailers.

Clicks and Bricks

Businesses are made of bricks. Mortar is merely the glue that holds the bricks together. The glue is melting; the mortar is becoming obsolete. But the bricks are still needed for whatever new edifices will be built. The correct pairing isn't "clicks and mortar." It's "clicks and bricks."

There's nothing reassuring about clicks and bricks. If physical and informational resources are building blocks to be reassembled in whichever combinations yield advantage, that offers precious little comfort to traditional incumbents. If they have any brick worth reusing, it merely puts them in play.

THERMIDOR: THE INTERNET REVOLUTION AND AFTER

PHILIP B. EVANS, 2001

By the lights of the heady rhetoric of the last couple of years, the Internet revolution has been a failure. The NASDAQ lost half its value last year. Roughly 200 dot-com companies disappeared. It is increasingly clear that a new economy is not displacing the old one; instead, the old is transforming itself from within. The Internet is not proving to be a disruptive technology; instead, incumbents are using it to challenge their own business models. Information does not, in general, "want to be free"; instead, intellectual property rights are being extended.

So does this mean that the revolution is over and executives can safely return to running the traditional business? Not in the least.

This revolution is merely following the same bumpy path as that of all its predecessors.

Every revolution eats its own children. The Jacobins, who were in the vanguard of the French Revolution, were among the earliest victims of forces they themselves had unleashed. On July 28, 1794 (or the tenth of Thermidor in the revolutionary calendar), Jacobin leader Maximilien Robespierre was condemned to the guillotine. His execution marked the end of the Reign of Terror. But Thermidor, as the suppression of the Jacobins came to be known, was by no means the end of the French Revolution: The Directorate, the Consulate, the rise of Napoleon, and the conquest of Europe were all still to take place.

So too with economic revolutions. Between 1860 and 1890, almost every single railroad company in the United States went bankrupt. But that did not prevent the construction of the transcontinental railroads or the subsequent emergence of the United States as the world's dominant economy. In 1895, there were about 5,000 U.S. automotive manufacturers; by 1925, only a dozen survived. But that did not prevent the automobile from transforming the economy, cities, and lifestyles.

The Internet revolution will follow a similar course. Today many Internet entrepreneurs may be feeling as unappreciated as Robespierre. But executives at established companies shouldn't assume that the New Economy's recent Thermidor means a return to business as usual. Rather, it is merely the next step in the long-term evolution of powerful forces of economic transformation.

Tectonic Change

Paradoxically, these bigger, long-term shifts are easier to understand than the short-term prospects for stock prices and revenue models—just as geological fault lines are easier to map than the time and place of the next earthquake. Even though the timing of the next lurch is unknowable, the direction and strength of the tectonic forces driving the Internet revolution are relatively well understood:

- Computation speeds and bandwidth are still advancing by an order of magnitude every few years.

- As a result, connectivity is becoming pervasive and extending from computers to mobile devices, entertainment devices, and home appliances.

- The ability to deliver increasingly rich information to broader and broader audiences—already well established for textual information—will eventually extend into the full panoply of sight, sound, and motion.

- Increased connectivity is enabling radically new patterns of collaboration, control, and organization.

- As more and more information becomes digital, information flows are continuing to separate from the physical processes in which they were traditionally embedded, spinning off entire businesses that then can evolve according to their own logic.

- The informational glue that bonds together value chains, supply chains, and organizational relationships continues to weaken, driving the deconstruction of traditional business definitions.

- Asymmetries of information are steadily eroding. Power is inexorably shifting down supply chains from sellers to buyers and, ultimately, to the consumer.

The paradox in all these changes is that technologies are more likely to be disruptive—and companies more likely to be blindsided—when change penetrates slowly. Remember the oft-recited fable of the frog in the pot of water. Throw the frog into boiling water—scare a business leader into thinking that the Internet obliterates everything instantly—and the frog reacts in fright and jumps out. Heat the pot slowly, and he never feels his pain until it is too late.

Dot-coms may have lost their charm and their terror, but the forces driving the new economics of information continue to accumulate. The eternal verities of cost, cash, and compelling customer value matter more than ever, but not necessarily in the same ways as before. Learning how to harness the trends of the information economy in order to exploit legacy assets in fundamentally new ways is a far tougher managerial challenge than simply setting up a Web site or spinning off a dot-com subsidiary in the hopes of making a killing in the market.

The Return to Strategy

To meet this challenge, a company needs to identify the fault lines latent in its business. Try a thought experiment. Imagine that all the relevant fundamental forces have played themselves out: Computation is free, bandwidth infinite, information symmetrical and ubiquitous.

At that imaginary point, what would the economically efficient structure of the business and the industry be? How would value be added and profits earned?

Now ask, how can the business evolve from where it is today to that imaginary endpoint? Can it evolve through continuous adaptation, or are there necessary discontinuities? Will the business, at some point, deconstruct into its components? Will a basic technology have to be scrapped? Will the brand have to be reinvented or a product line cannibalized? Will distributors or retailers have to be disintermediated?

Every hypothetical discontinuity signals a point of vulnerability: a potential and unpredictable seismic shock. No one can know for sure when any particular shock will happen. It may be entirely rational to sustain the current business model for now. But eventually, the accumulation of technological and economic trends will make it impossible. At some point, the pressures will become too strong, the difference between practice and potential too great. Someone, somewhere (maybe two kids in a garage, but more likely another incumbent from a completely different industry) will find a way to blow the traditional business model to bits.

This is the starting point for strategy in the second phase of the Internet revolution.

Not a forecast, not a millennial vision, not a gold rush, but a cold and rational understanding of how information economics underpin the current business structure and will at some point undermine it. Armed with that insight, an organization can take control of its fate. It can reassemble legacy assets into new business configurations. It can achieve order-of-magnitude savings in costs. It can radically outsource to the point of redefining its core competencies. It can transform its internal methods of coordination and its external management of customer relationships. It can act to protect aspects of its current business. Or it can act to destroy another company that thinks the crisis has passed.

Competitive advantage in the information economy has little to do with pleasing the stock market or faking a hip dot-com sensibility. It has everything to do with the ruthless application of resources to a chosen end under conditions of high uncertainty: the classic definition of military strategy.

The Internet revolution awaits its Napoleons.

THE ONLINE EMPLOYEE

MICHAEL S. DEIMLER AND MORTEN T. HANSEN, 2001

The Internet has already transformed how companies relate to customers and suppliers. Now it is beginning to alter how companies relate to employees. A new generation of Internet-based business-to-employee systems is allowing companies not only to reduce costs and improve productivity but also to create a more satisfying work environment.

This development is not unexpected. As companies redesign their internal processes, they are applying some of the lessons they learned from the early phases of e-commerce—in particular, how to use Internet technologies to interact with customers and improve the customer's experience.

For those companies that succeed in this new phase, the payoff can be substantial. Executives at one organization have calculated that an initial two-year investment of $8 million would allow them to achieve annual cost savings of $75 million over the next five years and productivity gains in the neighborhood of 1 percent to 2 percent.

To build effective business-to-employee systems, companies need to take a comprehensive approach. They must focus on the benefits for both the company itself and its employees. They must also treat their employees as customers—developing an in-depth understanding of their needs and latent dissatisfactions, and then creating a compelling offering that encourages employees to use the new online tools.

What Are Business-to-Employee Systems?

Business-to-employee systems use Internet technologies to provide online delivery of employee-related processes—including recruiting, training, and knowledge management. Some of these new applications involve online people management—for example, benefits administration and healthcare information. Others focus on online business processes—for instance, providing access to knowledge management databases and moving online such work processes as scheduling employees. Still others take the form of online community services—for example, a private e-marketplace where a company offers employees discounts on products and services that it has negotiated with vendors.

Whatever the particular application, the benefits of such systems derive from three basic sources.

Reduced Interaction Costs

It's well known that the Internet has enormous potential to reduce transaction costs between sellers and buyers. It also has great potential to reduce the costs of interactions among employees by increasing their access to critical information and improving coordination among large groups of employees across time and space.

For example, an online manual and catalog system at a major airline has allowed maintenance engineers to cut in half the time it takes them to repair aircraft engines, which has significantly improved the productivity of the entire fleet. In addition, the airline's 30,000 pilots and flight attendants now bid online for slots on aircraft crews. This new system has increased the convenience of the scheduling process for employees and has greatly enhanced the capability of the airline to redeploy people and equipment rapidly in the event of unanticipated disruptions such as bad weather.

Employee Self-Service

Effective business-to-employee systems allow employees to take control of various administrative or job-related activities—for example, selecting benefits, finding and taking training courses, and scheduling work. Online self-service makes it easy for employees to handle such tasks quickly and efficiently. And companies realize major productivity and cost benefits. Cisco Systems, the company that has embraced employee self-service most aggressively, reported that putting its human resources services online resulted in a $2.8 million gain in productivity. The company also saved $9.6 million annually by reducing overhead and expenses. Similarly, IBM claimed that moving roughly one-third of its employee education online generated $350 million in savings.

Mass Customization

Just as the Internet has enabled companies to mass-customize relations with customers, business-to-employee systems allow for the mass customization of relations with employees. Take the example of health-care benefits. For years, companies have been offering cafeteria-style benefit plans in an effort both to save money and to be more responsive to individual employees' needs. But it can be difficult and time-consuming for employees to navigate their way through all the choices. For employees, online systems make it easy to choose the best benefits and providers; for companies, such systems make it possible to offer complex benefit programs cost-effectively.

A Comprehensive Approach

There are at least four steps that companies need to take in order to build comprehensive business-to-employee systems.

Understand What Employees Really Want

It's natural for executives, excited by the potential of new Internet technologies, to begin by focusing on those applications with the most significant cost savings. It's also a mistake: Frequently, a critical mass of employees end up not using the applications because they are not convinced the applications will benefit them.

For instance, one company tried to implement a commonly used online procurement system, expecting it to cut costs by reducing the need for purchasing personnel and ensuring compliance with contracts. But two years after implementation, barely one-fifth of its employees were actually using the system. Interviews revealed that it was easier to stick with the old method of picking up the phone and speaking to a procurement agent than to use the new system.

Managers should not assume that they know what employees want. They must research the needs and latent dissatisfactions of their employees, much as they do those of their customers. Then they can provide applications that are clearly valuable to employees—whether they initially provide substantial cost savings or not.

Identify a Killer App

Once companies know what their employees value, the next step is to identify the most promising killer app: the application or service so attractive to employees that it will compel them to spend a significant amount of time online. The most effective killer app will vary by company, industry, or even employee segment. It might be something as general as real-time stock quotes for employees with stock options at a high-tech company. Or it might be something as specific as the online scheduling system for pilots and flight attendants at the airline mentioned earlier.

Create an Integrated Corporate Portal

Once employees regularly spend time online, companies can build an integrated corporate portal that provides a wide array of tools and services. Unlike the standalone information systems and intranets common at most companies today, a portal allows employees to obtain a full suite of information tools and services in one place. The popularity of the killer app and the convenience of the portal encourage employees to use other online tools and services that they might not initially value.

The company with the underperforming online-procurement system ultimately took this approach. Recently, it launched a corporate communications portal that has been a hit with employees because it allows them to receive up-to-date information about the company. Recognizing that most employees were already logging on to the portal to get the latest company news, managers decided to add online procurement software to the portal. The impact on usage has been dramatic: In one month, adoption of the online procurement system jumped to 30 percent, and it has been growing steadily ever since.

Monetize the Human Asset

Pioneering companies have an opportunity to strike deals with vendors that want access to the online employee community. One company was able to trade privileged access to its large pool of employees for an attractive equity stake in an outside company that delivered discount deals through corporate portals.

* * *

Tapping the full potential of the Internet will require companies to overhaul their processes and organizational structures. Ultimately, business-to-employee systems may prove to be the most effective way to persuade employees to embrace such change. By treating employees as customers, companies have an opportunity to create not only more efficient operations but also more satisfying and rewarding work environments.

RICHER SOURCING

PHILIP B. EVANS AND BOB WOLF, 2004

Outsourcing is generally seen as a means by which to lower cost. But this is only half the story. The other half is about collaborative innovation. Companies therefore need two quite different modes of outsourcing. A failure to segment supplier relations accordingly results in a massive loss of competitive advantage.

The underlying logic is embedded in the economics of information. There is a near-universal trade-off between richness and reach. *Richness* is variously the amount, quality, specificity, recency, or trustworthiness of the information shared in a transaction; and *reach* is the number of people or entities involved. Typically, we can transact with lots of richness if we are willing to give up reach (a conversation) or with lots of reach if we are willing to give up richness (a newspaper ad). But we cannot have both at once.

The richness-reach trade-off is embedded in methods of transaction. Markets enable comparatively high-reach/low-richness transactions—hierarchies, the converse. In the past decade, technology has displaced the trade-off, but primarily for low-richness transactions: e-mail, Web publishing, electronic payments, and—prospectively—Web services. By favoring reach over richness, technology has favored markets over hierarchies, thus inserting market mechanisms into previously vertically integrated hierarchies and thereby shifting the boundaries of the corporation. (See Exhibit 1.)

Sourcing strategy reflects these general principles. Insourcing enables richness—of collaboration among colleagues with shared goals, common reporting relationships, and the ability to negotiate mutual expectations in a context of shared tacit knowledge and trust. But constrained, thereby, within the boundaries of the corporation. Outsourcing gives you reach—to the most innovative and lowest-cost specialists in the world. But constrained, thereby, within the narrow nexus of negotiated product specs and legal contracts. The make-versus-buy choice is thus a trade-off between richness and reach. By favoring reach in general, technology has favored outsourcing in particular.

Low-richness transactions are fine when the goal is cost reduction: Just write the spec, put it out to tender, find the lowest-cost global

Exhibit 1   Technology has displaced the richness–reach trade-off.

SOURCE: Adapted from Philip Evans and Thomas S. Wurster, *Blown to bits: How the New Economics of Information Transforms Strategy* (Harvard Business School Press, 1999).

supplier, keep the contract term short, and rebid whenever a cheaper source becomes available. Fine for commodity businesses. Fine for commodity inputs into noncommodity businesses. But overdo it, and you make your business into a commodity business. Remember IBM's decision to outsource the PC operating system? That put Microsoft on the map. Innovation, adaptability, variety, and quality-beyond-spec are the ways most companies earn superior returns. Relentless outsourcing must undermine those capabilities. That's the stuff that has to be kept in-house. Right?

Wrong.

Consider Toyota. Toyota emphasizes product variety and quality-beyond-spec far more than do its U.S. competitors. Its spectacular success with the hybrid Prius demonstrates a level of innovation and adaptability beyond anything achieved by Detroit. It is moving away from the "commodity" end of automobile manufacturing, as it must because of the strength of the yen. Yet, whereas U.S. OEMs outsource less than half of their component costs, Toyota outsources nearly three-quarters!

Achieving Richness and Reach

The resolution of the paradox is that Toyota outsources through a method of transaction that achieves *both* richness and reach: the richness of in-house collaboration and reach to a wide range of globally competitive suppliers. The elements of this method are:

- Long-term, open-ended relationships that commit both sides to mutual dependence but leave open many specifics

- Execution across the companies of a common work discipline, characterized by pervasive, quantified, and granular experimentation

- Development of a rich language, common to the entire supply chain, through which experimental results are communicated

- Investment in mechanisms to ensure the rapid dissemination of detailed learning—broadcast, small group, and hub and spoke—all based on pervasive IT

- Open sharing across the supply chain that treats process knowledge as common intellectual property while product knowledge remains largely proprietary

- A mutual understanding that the benefits of productivity gains will be shared equitably over the long term, and an acceptance that competitors may be incidental beneficiaries

This approach, applied consistently over a long period, generates trust, shared "semantics" (mental frameworks, vocabulary), and shared knowledge: forms of capital embedded in the network itself. Applied internally, it enables richer collaboration among coworkers. Applied externally, it allows elements of the supply chain to combine resources in whatever patterns make sense, unconstrained by corporate boundaries or contractual commitments. This focus on *network capital* accommodates both the flexibility of markets and the close collaboration and low transaction costs of hierarchies. This is *not* the Toyota Production System as conventionally understood (*kanban, kaizen*), though the latter is in many ways a manifestation of this managerial method. And it is *not* specific to Japan: Toyota operates the same way in Kentucky and Ontario, and Nissan operates quite differently in Japan.

The benefits of this approach are striking. Jeffrey H. Dyer, author of *Collaborative Advantage: Winning Through Extended Enterprise Supplier Networks*, estimates that Toyota's procurement costs are about one-third those of the average U.S. manufacturer. And whereas Toyota's suppliers have matched the productivity gains of Toyota itself (and Detroit has also matched those gains, albeit from a lower base), Detroit's suppliers have achieved negligible productivity improvements. (See Exhibit 2.) In Detroit's world, the low-richness

Exhibit 2   The benefits of investing in network capital: Japan versus Detroit.

SOURCE: BCG analysis, updating a time series developed by Marvin B. Lieberman and Shigeru Asaba in "Inventory Reduction and Productivity Growth: A Comparison of Japanese and U.S. Automotive Sectors," *Managerial and Decision Economics*, vol. 18, no. 2 (1977), pp. 73–85.

nexus of arm's length procurement has destroyed the capacity of the network to share learning. Affecting half the cost structure, this cumulative loss far outweighs the one-shot gains from aggressive price negotiation.

A Systematic Approach

There is still a richness-reach trade-off, of course. Toyota cannot deal with thousands of suppliers this way, only hundreds. But the resulting supply chain—neither traditional market nor traditional hierarchy—achieves a new combination of richness and reach. It displaces the traditional trade-off in that higher-richness zone where it *must* be displaced if new technologies and new organizational forms are to offer an escape from the relentless drive to commoditization. (For a comparison of the alternative sourcing strategies used by Toyota and Detroit, see Exhibit 3.)

The analysis required to adopt a network-capital strategy is rarely performed systematically. It comprises the following elements:

- Map the network of productive interactions by individuals and teams within and across organizational boundaries. "Richness" is embedded in the patterns of human networks, in the *connections* among activities, people, teams, modules, or functions. Information technology, for the first time, makes such mapping cheap

Exhibit 3   Alternative sourcing strategies: Japan versus Detroit.

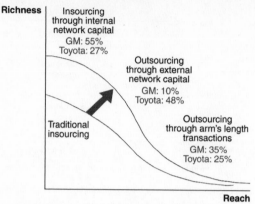

SOURCE: Sourcing data were estimated by Jeffery H. Dyer, *Collaborative Advantage: Winning through Extended Enterprise Supplier Networks* (Oxford University Press, 2000). NOTE: Percentages relate to the cost of components.

and accurate. Network analysis makes the richness-reach trade-off specific and quantifiable: It tells you, by activity, the value of richness.

- Benchmark the capabilities of alternative suppliers, both inside and out, current and potential. This is a conventional analysis (usually the only one done—hence the bias toward outsourcing). It tells you the value of reach.

- Segment the collaboration patterns by balancing the values of richness and reach. This approach would yield three types: those best supported by hierarchy (insourcing), by shared network capital (relationship outsourcing), and by markets (commodity outsourcing).

But the strategic analysis, as always, is merely preliminary. Implementation requires building networks and building network capital in entirely new ways. But that is another story.

THE REAL CONTEST BETWEEN AMERICA AND CHINA *

THOMAS HOUT AND JEAN LEBRETON, 2003

Shopping at Wal-Mart will give you the wrong idea about where China's threat to U.S. manufacturing lies. Most made-in-China consumer goods on those shelves represent industries that left the United States for Mexico and Southeast Asia years ago. Instead, the real contest between U.S. and Chinese factories is taking shape over industrial goods—a $2 trillion market of everything from small motors to oscilloscopes to locomotives, where fast-moving U.S. productivity and technology have kept production at home.

The problem is that China's rapidly growing capability and huge scale are turning these U.S. defenses on their head, creating astonishing cost advantages in moving to China. These can amount to savings of 20 to 35 percent with no loss of quality—opening the doors to moving even high-performance, highly automated product lines there.

Unlike Japan a generation ago, which reinvented manufacturing through quality and continuous improvement, China is *de*inventing it by removing capital and reintroducing manual skill and handling on the plant floor. China's far lower cost of not only production workers but also plant technicians, accountants, and managers allows U.S. companies to rethink everything from how the product and its parts are designed to how they are made and tested.

The result is more craft, less complexity in plant processes, and often a shorter time from design to production—all at a far lower total cost. Together with the improving quality of materials and reliability of supply chains inside China, this means some U.S. companies are moving whole core product lines there.

But many are not. China is still small fry in the U.S. industrial-goods market. Domestic production accounts for 70 percent of industrial goods sold, and imports from Japan and Western Europe account for another 20 percent. Only 10 percent comes from low-wage economies, and China has less than one-third of this—or 3 percent total penetration of the U.S. market, shipping fewer goods than Mexico.

Many U.S. companies find China's cost advantage elusive. Sending buying teams to China from their headquarters in the United States, armed with drawings and specs, to search for lower-cost sources often doesn't work—as U.S. auto companies have recently learned. Producers of small engines and low-end farm equipment, among others, have looked at taking production lines to China and found that uneven quality and unreliable supply lines back to their U.S. customers outweigh the advantage of lower production costs. The higher costs of technical and inventory support plus all the risks just aren't worth it.

Sourcing in China works best for companies that invest know-how and painstakingly nurture their China operations over sustained periods, and only a limited number of foreign manufacturers have done this so far. Our research shows that companies committed to large-scale manufacturing in China think differently in several important ways from competitors without such commitments.

First, committed companies accurately assess the labor and capital costs of their products. Accounting statements may tell a finished-equipment manufacturer that factory payroll is only 10 percent of its costs, but when the full payroll cost of the purchased components and company overheads is added in, the total labor costs are typically 40 to 60 percent of the final product cost. And those labor costs are lower across the board in China. Production workers typically cost 5 percent of their U.S. counterparts, while good engineers and plant managers may cost 35 percent.

But what about higher U.S. labor productivity? True, U.S. workers in capital-intensive factories can be several times more productive than their Chinese counterparts. That's because U.S. plants have replaced many factory workers with complex flexible-automation and material-handling systems. This has reduced labor costs but raised the costs of capital and support systems.

Chinese factories reverse this process by taking capital out of the production process and reintroducing a greater role for labor. Parts are designed to be made, handled, and assembled manually. This reduces the total capital required by as much as one-third. So output per worker is lower in Chinese factories, but the combination of lower wages and less capital typically raises the return on capital above U.S. factory levels.

U.S. companies like Kodak and Copeland, which develop several factories in China, will see more cost savings than a competitor taking its first steps. Several factors working together explain this. These companies develop and improve their local suppliers. Their Chinese engineers learn the quality disciplines. And they become smarter at hiring people and designing incentives. The costs and benefits of manufacturing in China increase with scale and experience there, meaning that the more you grow, the easier it is to continue to grow.

Second and counterintuitively, it usually makes more sense to send a distinctive new product line to China than an old, price-pressured one. The payoff from sending the latter to China is low. The many one-time expenses—product and process redesign, new local suppliers to sort out, and the need to requalify the finished product with U.S. customers—could wipe out any profit margin. But designing a new product for China makes sense for a company well down its experience curve there.

For instance, Tektronix's new oscilloscope was designed by U.S.-based engineers working virtually with their China-based tooling counterparts. Although some materials and components were imported, the product will have only one set of start-up costs and a lower capital investment to amortize.

Third, companies committed to production in China take a more realistic view of the risks involved. Supply chain risks are often exaggerated by outsiders. As for country risk, again China's resilience and production security tend to look better to insiders. That was recently demonstrated when the outbreak of severe acute respiratory syndrome earlier this year caused few supply disruptions from China. And Chinese authorities regard foreign-owned plants as valuable assets not to be disturbed.

But some risks are not exaggerated, such as the need to protect intellectual-property rights, which deters many companies from bringing highly proprietary processes to China. Armstrong, the world's leading manufacturer of floor and ceiling tiles, keeps some material formulas and processes in the United States. AMP, the world's leading producer of connectors, had no choice but to move to China because of the cost savings involved. So its proprietary inline-plating process in China is done in a special secure enclosure with specially licensed employees. U.S. auto companies know their technology is leaking to Chinese joint-venture partners, but in return they get a head start in China's exploding market.

There are limits to what can move to China. Product categories where customer-driven innovation is frequent and critical will not go. Nor will those requiring customization and intimate user contact with the factory. Some U.S. customers, especially publicly funded organizations, will insist on goods being produced in the United States. The most persuasive barriers to movement will be customer related, not technology related. Production technology is often surprisingly mobile and divisible between locations. Large portions of leading-edge medical diagnostic equipment are being made in China, and jet aircraft engines will follow.

While China today has only 3 percent of the U.S. industrial-goods business, its shipments are growing at 21 percent annually in a basically flat market. This penetration rate will be governed by the increasing capability of foreign-owned and operated plants in China, not by wage increases or exchange-rate revaluations. The cost differences are too great. In addition, China is becoming the world's largest market for some industrial goods—for example, machine tools and power equipment. There are many reasons to make more things in China. As more companies discover this, the impact on U.S. jobs will grow, making it an increasingly potent political issue.

Performance Measurement

NO BUSINESS STRATEGY, no matter how brilliant, can be brought to fruition unless the tactical support for its execution is in place. One of the primary tactical decisions a manager must make is how performance will be measured: individual, team, SBU, division, group, and company.

Bruce Henderson held a strong conviction that measurements linked only to the short-term profitability of a business would damage its long-term performance. He saw the profit center as the worst organizational offender—it forced a manager to sacrifice his career to the business, or (unfortunately more commonly) to sacrifice the business to his career. Judging performance on the basis of short-term profit alone caused managers to ignore investments to achieve long-term strategic goals.

The *Perspectives* in this section make the case that the metrics employed must be aligned with the strategy that the managers being measured are committed to execute. This requires, first, that information (costs, revenue, cash flow, market share, etc.) be collected in a way that allows progress toward strategic goals to be evaluated objectively. Second, the timing of performance evaluation must match the time horizon of the strategy. If a strategy is meant to play out over five years, managers must be measured against sensible milestones over the entire period. Finally, performance measures need to be evaluated regularly to ensure they are still creating incentives that buttress the strategy. All too frequently, performance measurements remain in place long after strategy or market demands have shifted.

What gets measured gets done—for better or worse. Recent developments have focused renewed attention on performance measures. A passion for process excellence has motivated a generation of managers to explore a whole new range of metrics that calibrate their businesses' responsiveness and operational effectiveness. A preoccupation with shareholder value has prompted a search for measures that motivate employees throughout the organization to seek the kind of results that enhance total shareholder return. The impact of "process excellence" has been unfailingly constructive; that of "shareholder value management" somewhat ambiguous. Some measures, like economic value added, highlight once again the dangers of mortgaging the future for short-term profitability, and the recent financial scandals underline how

227

elusive an alignment of interests between owners and managers can be. Still, it is an alignment to be sought.

The close of the 1990s saw a renewed focus on the importance of human, as opposed to financial, resources as the critical investment base of today's organizations. A number of BCG partners began thinking about how to manage this investment—and to measure returns on it. The final piece in this subpart introduces our emerging thinking, which we are calling Workonomics™.

PROFIT CENTER ETHICS

Bruce D. Henderson, 1971

Profit center managers are frequently caught in a cruel dilemma. They are often asked to carry out policies that they strongly feel to be unwise. Yet they know that they will be held responsible for failure, whatever the cause.

The ethics of dissent are a very real issue in profit center management. Is the good of the corporation the overriding concern? Or is it personal survival? How far should dissent be pushed if higher authority neither wants nor accepts advice? What is honorable when either protest or acquiescence lead to unacceptable consequences?

The situation is real even with the best of goodwill on all sides. Differences in perspective lead to far different projections of consequences. Clear-cut orders can be followed and must be followed. But orders to a profit center are rarely clear-cut just because it is a profit center. However, the manager of a profit center receives much advice that must be heeded.

By definition, a profit center is measured on results. In theory, future profit is the measure. In theory, the manager is free to follow his own judgment except within explicit, specific constraints. In theory, current performance is factored by the long-term benefits and the effect of corporate constraints. In fact, none of these conditions are ever wholly true.

Characteristically, profit center managers are measured over a quite moderate time span. The penalty for unsatisfactory absolute performance over the short term is severe. But the proper balance between the known performance and potential future benefits is never clear.

The executive stress is difficult to overstate when there is conflict between policy restrictions, near-term performance, the long-term good of the company, and personal survival.

Logically, a profit center should have a combination of all kinds of goals simultaneously. The management should be judged on the net results of this complex of goals. Yet if this is done, profit is merely a derivative of the interactions of the various goals and constraints over time. It is not a prime index of current performance. It would not be the conventional profit center if it were managed this way.

The manager's situation becomes more difficult when corporate staff becomes deeply involved. Should the manager do what is politically expedient and satisfy the preferences of staff advisers or optimize future performance for which he is held accountable? This can be an excruciating choice.

Corporate staff individually and collectively have their own ideas of how the business should be run. They are in a position to press those ideas hard. They can also significantly bias the evaluation of performance and the imposition of constraints. Failure to obtain their full support means being judged rigidly, even harshly, on near-term results. Yet the disagreement almost always concerns the longer-term consequences. *The most important decisions a manager makes tend to depress short-term reported performance in order to significantly improve long-term results.* The issue becomes, "Should I do what is expedient, or should I fulfill my responsibilities to the best of my ability?" Martyrs are rarely honored in business.

In most corporations the evaluation of the profit center manager is based on current reported profit. Managers know it. Incentive compensation schemes often tend to reinforce this specific measurement over all others.

The problems of ethics are inherently chronic. The manager's problem can be serious enough even in the absence of any constraints. The temptation is great to take the performance measurement at stated face value. It is all too easy to liquidate the future and thereby maximize apparent current performance. In all too many cases this leads to promotion, leaving the aftermath to the hapless successor.

When the overall interests of the company impose constraints or goals that conflict with short-term profit performance, the conflict of interest is compounded. Both count. A balance must be struck. Compliance with the conflicting constraints and contribution to corporate goals are apt to be evaluated in a subjective and often uncertain fashion. Political expediency becomes a necessity.

The problem becomes even more acute when corporate management has a short-term time horizon and profit center optimization requires long-term investments of expense as well as capital. No manager can expect to survive who has a longer time horizon than his superiors. But neither can the business survive if the time horizon is inadequate to encompass the actions required today in order to protect the business in the future.

The worst situation exists when corporate management has a different concept of the requirements for future success from the concepts of the profit center management. The differences in perspective and philosophy can apply both to the profit center itself and to the corporation as a whole.

When any of these conditions exist, then managerial ethics become a real issue.

There are often real tradeoffs between the personal career and the good of the company. There can be real dilemmas where only short-term survival seems possible because of the tradeoffs between long-term and short-term performance. The conflict between expediency and responsibility can become painful.

Regardless of ethics, everyone who aspires to responsibility in a complex organization must strike some balance. Those who are most realistic in their compromises inherit the responsibility and set the pattern for the future. That pattern may be far from the best interests of the company.

Resolution of this conflict can occur only if three conditions are met:

- There must be an explicit corporate strategy. To be useful, the strategy must relate administrative behavior to the allocation of resources over time. Action must be relatable to a value system that all members of management understand and accept.

- There must be an understanding and consensus on the strategy. The consensus must include essentially everyone who is in a position to make decisions and tradeoffs that would affect implementation.

- Profit center profit performance appraisal must encompass a time horizon equal to the strategy time horizon.

Few multidivision corporations have a strategy that is adequate enough to spare their profit center managers the stress implicit in the ethics of dissent.

THE STORY OF JOE
(A FABLE)

BRUCE D. HENDERSON, 1977

Joe made himself quite a reputation as a "turnaround" manager. It began when he was put in charge of a very sick division of his very large and diversified company. Within a couple of years he changed it from a big loser to a modest profit maker.

He turned around sick divisions not once, but several times, one after the other. His staff thought he was the best. The corporate management eulogized him. Morale in his operations was high. But Joe's reputation began to tarnish.

After Joe left these divisions and turned them over to someone else, they seemed to go sour. They seemed to drop back slowly and inexorably into their former unprofitability. The managers who succeeded Joe, one by one, convinced top management that major new investment was necessary if their sick operations were ever to be built into something really worthwhile. The suspicion grew that Joe had not really "turned around" those operations.

By then Joe was a high-ranking officer of this great company. Joe was put in charge of one of the company's very large divisions, which over many years failed to realize its promise. Under Joe nothing changed. He tried hard. But nothing changed. He tightened budgets. He cut overhead. He looked for every penny he could save. All this had been done before. Joe failed. This operation continued to slowly sink into mediocrity.

So Joe was fired. It wasn't done lightly. Joe had been a hard-working and loyal employee. No one could find fault with what he had done. He had seemed to be a first-class manager. Yet the facts were clear for all to see. Every operation that Joe managed looked good for awhile but became a disaster eventually. Joe was really bad news.

Some of the younger managers in the company were greatly disturbed. How could Joe look so good and turn out like that? Joe had seemed to be a good man, a good manager, a good businessman, a leader. Why . . . ? So the young men sought out a retired old-timer wise in the ways of people and corporations. They asked him why. And this is what he told them.

"Business is complex. Nobody is really sure what determines success. The only thing that seems sure is results. The bottom right-hand corner of the P&L statement seems real. But it is not real either. It is based on a whole series of assumptions about the future that have been stylized as accounting.

"Joe's company believed its own accounting. It set Joe's goals in short-term budgets. It asked Joe to make those accounts show a profit and do it quickly. Joe did it.

"Joe cut out every expense that didn't have an immediate payback. He cut back on advertising, product development, maintenance, personnel development, training, and all support activities not absolutely essential.

"Joe liquidated every asset he could that had a depreciation charge in excess of current contribution. This not only improved the return on the remaining assets but reduced his excess capacity and left mostly assets with low book values. This was done very early when Joe took charge, since early writeoffs can always be attributed to your predecessor.

"Joe then held prices firm and perhaps a little on the high side. This tended to slowly lose market share, but then, customers do not ordinarily shift suppliers very fast. Meantime, a few percentage points in margin looked very good in a marginal operation.

"Joe did exactly what he should have done. He did exactly what the company's control system asked him to do. He did exactly what the company's incentive plans rewarded.

"Far beyond that in importance, Joe did exactly what the company should have wanted him to do. Joe initiated an orderly liquidation of those businesses that should have been liquidated because they were too poorly situated to really compete."

So why did Joe get fired?

"Joe did what he was told to do, but the results were neither what the company expected nor wanted. The company wanted a weak and poorly positioned operation to be turned around immediately into a profitable one. Joe did that."

But the company wanted and expected this and much more. The company expected the immediate turnaround to be the first step in a long and steady increase in profitability ending in industry leadership. This, of course, was utterly unrealistic.

In fact, there was no way for any of these businesses to be converted into long-term profitable leaders without very substantial long-term investment, which would necessarily be very heavy in the beginning. The risk would have been high. The end result would have been completely dependent on the established leaders already in place as competitors.

The company had no strategy and confused short-term operating goals with long-term investment decisions and investment evaluation. Neither Joe nor the company knew what they were really doing or what they should have done.

A REQUIEM FOR JOE

His company wanted the impossible and expected Joe to get it.

Joe gave his company what they asked for but not what they expected.

Poor Joe, he did the right thing for the wrong reason and was fired for the wrong thing for the wrong reason.

CONTROLLING FOR GROWTH IN A MULTIDIVISION BUSINESS

PATRICK CONLEY, 1968

Profit centers and return on investment have been equally popular concepts for evaluating the performance of a division in a multidivision business. As concepts taken at face value, however, both are inappropriate when a division is engaged in a growth business. ROI and profit centers both imply an absolute current measure of performance: "Profit is good, loss is bad." In a rapidly growing business, this is simply not true unless important—and universally overlooked—riders are attached; as a measure of optimum performance current profit or return are usually downright wrong.

To optimize performance in a growth business, a manager must use, and be measured on, a long-time perspective. Traditional control systems discourage this. Conventional control systems emphasize profits reported now. This is in direct conflict with appropriation evaluation systems that measure discounted cash flow. Cash flows may be far out of phase with reported profits. This becomes critical when dealing with more intangible relationships such as organization development, R&D, or the value of market share.

For example, long-term profitability appears to be a direct function of sustainable relative market share. Growth in market share proceeds fundamentally from better values for the customer than competitors are willing or able to offer. Therefore, improving market share requires a commitment of resources and expense that depresses current reported profits for the sake of the future. It is a fact, though, that the greater the market share over time, the lower the relative costs can be compared to competition: The more you produce, the faster your costs can go down; the greater your total production experience, the greater your cost advantage can be over less-experienced competitors. The more market share you can get, the more market share you can afford to buy—because your costs are going down faster than your competitors'. Your increasing market share represents foreclosed cost-reduction opportunities for competitors.

In this context current profit could be bad and could reflect *poor* performance on the part of a division manager. Maximizing current profit here would require prices and margins higher than the optimum for capturing market share. It would mean funds withheld from investment in market growth and future cost reductions. On the other hand, loss could reflect, instead, investment in a sustainable cost advantage and thus substantial future profits. These future profits can have a discounted present value far higher than the current profits being sacrificed. Investments can be in expenses as well as in capitalizable assets. Investments can also be made in relationships that are created by forgone revenues.

For every product there is an optimum achievable and sustainable market share. Top management should make explicit the appropriate market share for each product. This should be calculated on the long-term value to the company of attaining and keeping the target share. This can be done if there is a characteristic relationship between accumulated experience, cost, price, margin, and market position. If the value of the appropriate share for a product can be determined, then management can determine how much it can afford to spend in forgone current profits in order to invest in market-share growth. Management can also establish some schedule for achieving the target share.

Divisional control can then be effected by computing the cost-decline schedule that corresponds to market projections. Performance can be monitored by cross-checking cost levels achieved and market share achieved to date. By treating changes in short-term profits as changes in investment, it is possible to construct a strategy of competitive behavior that will have the probability of the highest return on investment in terms of present values.

In the long run, all that counts is "cash in versus cash out discounted to present value." Evaluating the changes in the present value of the cash-flow profile is not as easy as accepting conventional "good accounting practice." Yet it is clear that it is worth the effort. It seems obvious that profit centers and return on investment based on conventional accounting practice can lead to gross misinterpretations of current performance.

A multidivision business runs a peculiar and characteristic risk. It is quite likely to rely on primarily financial performance measures in controlling its business. These controls by definition discount any performance or policies that are not reflected in the books of account. If the controls are effective, then other considerations are downgraded.

The result of this can often be that multidivision companies are effective in operating mature businesses but singularly inept in capitalizing on the opportunity of the growth product. In such a situation, the manager of a growth division is vying for corporate funds against appropriation requests for short-term projects and investments in mature businesses with established annual returns. He obviously cannot compete for funds on these terms without there being a completely different frame of reference than the financial controls used in operations.

The only time a multidivision company seems able to fully accommodate both mature and growth businesses is when the growth opportunity becomes so big and so visible that the policy and strategy is set by top management and the financial controls are adjusted to fit—*instead of vice versa.*

For the large multidivision company, explicit strategies and long-term plans would seem to be a prerequisite for growth. This means that nonfinancial goals and performance checkpoints must be established in parallel to the financial controls. These in turn must be the result of optimizing *long-term* financial performance, not current performance necessarily. "Cash in versus cash out discounted to present value" may show quite different plans and policies than maximization of current reported profit and current apparent return on assets invested.

It is becoming increasingly clear that multidivision, multiproduct companies can be extremely efficient competitors if they are able to direct and redirect the flow of capital internally into the *best long-term* returns. The conglomerate is potentially far more efficient at this than the public capital market.

For this potential to be realized, however, a far more sophisticated set of control concepts is required than those that are implicit in the conventional profit center.

MAKING PERFORMANCE MEASUREMENTS PERFORM

ROBERT MALCHIONE, 1991

Performance measurements at most companies are out of step with the business environment. What matters today is meeting rising customer expectations by emphasizing time and quality. Let's look at the characteristics of traditional performance measurements to see why they no longer work.

Traditional performance measurements focus more on internal goals of cost and efficiency than on external realities of customer satisfaction and competitive capabilities.

Company A's customers almost always received their orders when the shipping department promised. Yet the company was losing customers to higher-priced competitors. The problem was that the internal measurement of "ship-to-promise" failed to detect the external reality that customers wanted the product even sooner and would pay a premium to get it. A "ship-to-customer want" measurement would have captured this.

An automotive component company achieved its key customer's highest-quality classification, yet its competitor was gaining market share. It turned out that the competitor was supplying other customers with twice the quality at lower cost. While focusing on one customer's quality criteria, this company neglected to look at what its competitor could do for other customers.

Traditional performance measurements emphasize control at the expense of customer response.

Company C's distribution outlets were measured on their fill rate, that is, how many orders they could fill off the shelf. When the product wasn't in stock, however, some customers went elsewhere. Because the distribution department's measurement tracked only customers who placed orders, the number of orders lost went undetected. In fact, it was to the distribution center manager's disadvantage to persuade the customer to order and wait for delivery because that would count as a stock-out for the distribution center.

Traditional performance measurements focus on the end product and overlook the importance of the process.

Market share and profitability are results. They measure how effectively and efficiently a company has met its customers' needs after the fact. Additionally, a company could focus on the process employed to meet these needs. Such measurements as the percentage of transactions handled in one phone call, time from customer order to delivery, or percentage delivered when customer wanted it would highlight how well an organization's business system was performing against customers' needs.

Traditional performance measurements focus on particular departments or aspects of a business, often at the expense of overall business goals.

When Company D's distribution center ordered parts from the factory, the factory would make more than ordered because it could never be sure of the yield. Because the distribution center was measured on product turns, however, it would take only the number ordered, even if the factory yielded more. If demand was greater than expected and the distribution center ran out of inventory, orders were lost even though the organization had already committed time and money to producing the product.

A specialty material producer, believing its business to be capital-intensive, measured and focused on asset utilization. This resulted in large product backlogs to ensure that machines were kept busy. A smaller competitor observed that many customers needed product quickly and chose to measure time. It put in "excess" capacity to achieve its time objectives. The result: a complete reversal of market shares and profitability for the two.

These four characteristics of typical performance measurements can result in an organization's spending significant effort without making much progress toward its goals.

Measurements That Work

Every business is different, so each should have its own set of performance measurements. But there are some common rules to follow in designing effective measurements.

Start on the outside of your business, not inside the company. Ask yourself: "What do customers really want and when?" "What do our best competitors give customers that we do not?" For example, customers almost always welcome recommendations on how they might make better use of their suppliers. They also want personal relationships to help build commitment from suppliers. But these items aren't high on the agendas of most departments. If you value them, measure them.

Responsiveness to customers overshadows all other marketing goals. Make sure control measures don't get in the way. You have to dismantle control measures that work against customer responsiveness. For example, backlog is a time-honored measurement of a company's strength. Companies are comfortable when backlog is high. Department heads use it to justify hiring more people. But high backlog means slow response to customers. If you're serious about responsiveness, don't reward backlog. Reward throughput.

Think of process and product as equals. Focusing on the end product can cause you to lose sight of the process unless measurements make both equally visible to your people. Most employees think in terms of fixing the product as it goes by. This is because it's easier to spot a flawed product than a flawed process. Make your process explicit. Map and measure it. Reward people who fix the process.

You compete as a company. Don't let overall business goals get lost among the many operating measures. In measuring more processes and more variables, it's easy to lose sight of the overall goal. Beware of losing track of the larger measures that tell you how the customer views you against competitors. Watch customer retention, customer gains, and customer losses. Share this information with your people. If you measure them only on their own piece of the company, they may not look beyond to the larger picture. Train your people to think of the company as one integrated delivery system for the customer's benefit.

Establishing New Measurements

Externally focused, process-oriented, and systemwide performance measurements are essential for encouraging the actions that create competitive advantage today, but they won't happen without strong management support.

The process starts with communication. Convincing an organization to rethink measurements that have been part of its business mindset for years is not an easy undertaking. Rules give people security and a sense of purpose. Changing them arouses anxiety. Some employees will worry about having to work too hard; others will wonder if the company isn't neglecting the bottom line.

Therefore, management has to give the rationale behind the new measurements. Too often, people are told the "what" without the "why." The more employees know about why customer satisfaction, time, and quality really matter, the more they can support the new goals. Once the rationale is clear, give your people a chance to design the new measurements. Let them wrestle with the various options to figure out which make sense and which will just get in the way.

Management also needs to show commitment to the new rules by monitoring them to make sure they are keeping pace with the rapidly changing competitive environment and by sticking to them even if results are slow to materialize.

The purpose of performance measurements is to focus the energy of the organization on its strategic goals, to track progress toward the goals, and to provide feedback. If performance measurements haven't been realigned with the new priorities of the business, they will keep the organization from achieving advantage. When in conflict, the old performance measurements will win out over new goals because measurements, not goals, determine promotions and compensation. Changing the goals without changing the measurements is no change at all.

ECONOMIC VALUE ADDED

ERIC E. OLSEN, 1996

What gets measured gets done—for better or worse. Too many companies chase growth in earnings per share, only to find themselves employing too much capital at too low a rate of return and thereby eroding shareholder value. Economic value added* offers a beguiling solution: an easy-to-understand measure that recognizes improvements in earnings only to the extent that they exceed the cost of the capital employed to secure them.

Eminently sensible but for one critical flaw: EVA discourages growth. The conceptual problems have been there all along; the empirical evidence is beginning to mount. At a time when renewing growth represents the major competitive challenge facing most com-

---

* Economic Value Added—which we will abbreviate as EVA—is generally calculated as net operating profit (before interest, but after tax) minus a charge for capital employed.

panies, dependence on EVA can become a major obstacle to building shareholder value. Fortunately, there are better alternatives.

Evaluating EVA

The value financial markets assign to a company reflects its prospects for profitability and growth. A change in value is driven by a change in expectations for one or both. CEOs naturally seek to influence shareholder value. The trick is to pick the right metric—one that tracks the market valuation process closely, yet is fairly simple and intuitive—and then drive the management of that metric down through the organization.

EVA is easy to understand and to calculate, but at a cost: It tracks actual market valuations rather poorly (see figure) and introduces three fundamental distortions into managers' decisions:

1. *EVA is biased against new assets.* EVA shares the same bias against new assets as do all conventional accounting-based measures. When an investment is made, its full cost hits the capital charge, and EVA shows artificially low. As the investment depreciates, the capital charge declines proportionally. At maturity, EVA shows artificially high. Inflation exacerbates the tendency, since EVA recognizes its impact on earnings but ignores its impact on the replacement cost of assets.

This has the perverse effect of penalizing managers who bet on growth by investing. Except for the rare case where an investment has an immediate payback, growth-oriented managers take a short-term EVA hit.

2. *EVA encourages managers to milk the business.* Even worse than punishing progrowth behavior, EVA rewards antigrowth behavior. Investing aggressively at rates of return exceeding the cost of capital may be the preferred way to move the EVA needle. But managers quickly learn that the easier way, at least in the short term, is to reduce assets faster than earnings—to milk the business.

Pursued long enough, say three to five years, this strategy creates an EVA trap. Lack of investment can leave managers with such a depreciated asset base that any new investment will have a huge negative impact on EVA. The disincentive—whether to grow or to renew with more productive assets—compounds over time.

Little surprise, then, that the record of longtime EVA converts is one of delivering enhanced returns but not long-term growth in the

EVA has a low correlation to shareholder value. Total shareholder return (TSR) versus percent change in economic value added 1994–1995.

capital base. Indeed, several have experienced growth rates in their asset bases close to zero and well below those of their peers.

3. *EVA is biased in favor of large, low-return businesses.* EVA is a marginal measure: It represents the incremental earnings above a base level set by the cost of capital employed. This makes EVA heavily biased by size. Large businesses that earn returns only slightly above the cost of capital can have bigger EVAs than smaller businesses earning much higher returns. What's more, the rate of change in EVA is accentuated for businesses whose historical performance hovers around the cost of capital. Small improvements in the performance of a marginal business generate large percentage gains in EVA.

This makes EVA a poor metric for comparing businesses, whether to benchmark performance against peers or to allocate resources across a company's portfolio. Because EVA sends misleading signals about the relative attractiveness of businesses, companies that rely on it run the risk of growing the wrong ones.

Moving beyond EVA

Companies that want to grow must move beyond EVA. There are two viable alternatives. The simpler approach is to adjust the measure to a cash basis by adding depreciation and amortization back to net operating profit and accumulated depreciation back to book capital. You might term this measure *cash value added* (CVA). Because it eliminates the worst of EVA's antigrowth or reinvestment bias, CVA takes an important step beyond EVA. It remains inadequate, however, as a means to compare businesses.

For that reason, more and more companies are going even further. They are evaluating business-unit performance in the same way that investors look at a company's stock or executives size up a potential acquisition. Call this approach *total business return* (TBR). By comparing the beginning value of a business with its ending value, plus free cash flow, TBR effectively replicates total shareholder return inside the company at the level of the individual business unit. (For a more detailed treatment of TBR, see "Meeting the Value Challenge," The Boston Consulting Group, Inc., 1995, and "Shareholder Value Metrics," The Boston Consulting Group, Inc., 1996.)

As one might expect, TBR displays a much more satisfying correlation with observed total shareholder return: 40 percent over one-year periods and 57 percent over three years, roughly double the correlations for EVA. The results are sufficiently convincing that some companies are using TBR directly to peg planning and executive compensation targets. Others are using TBR at the corporate level to set objectives, which they then translate into more familiar accounting-based measures for the operating units. The result is to reward executives for expanding businesses that create value for shareholders.

Aligning your managers' interests with those of the company and its shareholders is critical, especially at a time when the chief imperative—to grow—runs counter to the behavior encouraged by accounting-based measures. Recognize the limits of these measures and move beyond them.

NEW DIRECTIONS IN VALUE MANAGEMENT

ERIC E. OLSEN, 2002

Every CEO of a public company runs the risk of getting caught between two powerful constituencies: On one side, increasingly demanding investors, determined to maximize their returns relative to the risk they take; on the other, the organization and its managers, largely insulated from shareholders and typically focused on what's achievable given the constraints of industry, competitive position, and corporate culture. The CEO's constant challenge is to manage the tension between the two: to get the organization to act in ways that will lead to success in the capital markets.

Value management was supposed to help CEOs meet this challenge. By instituting new metrics that better capture improvements in intrinsic value, the thinking went, value management would focus a company's executives on improving business fundamentals. And since capital markets were efficient, improvements in intrinsic value would translate automatically into improvements in a company's stock price—thus rewarding investors.

It hasn't entirely worked out that way. To be sure, value management has helped many companies focus internal decision making on increasing intrinsic value. In many instances, it has improved the management of existing capital employed and brought a more explicit value-creation focus to incremental investment decisions.

But increasing the intrinsic value of a business is one thing; realizing that value in the capital markets can often be quite another. One of the lessons of recent years is just how much investor expectations can drive shareholder value—either above or below the level that the intrinsic value of a company would suggest. (For a more complete treatment of this subject, see "The Continuing Relevance of Investor Expectations," *BCG Perspectives*, December 2001.) Traditional value management largely ignores the gap between intrinsic value and realized value. Fortunately, some companies are developing techniques to address that shortcoming. Consider the following two examples.

Eliminating Valuation Gaps

There are two ways for a company to improve its total shareholder return (TSR). One way is by generating improvements in the fundamental indicators of intrinsic value. In this approach, traditional measures for determining intrinsic value (such as earnings per share) are complemented with a set of more sophisticated metrics— for example, free cash flow, economic value added (EVA), or cash flow return on investment (CFROI).

But it is also possible to increase TSR by improving how the market actually values those fundamental indicators, as measured by a company's *valuation multiple* (usually quantified as the price-to-earnings ratio). A company's multiple is a snapshot of how investors view both current performance and future growth prospects. Many factors influence it: the company's cost of capital, the relative riskiness of its businesses, its sources and uses of free cash flow, its outlook for revenue growth, its financial policies, its management vision and credibility, and its portfolio strategy, to name just a few.

Traditional value management doesn't have much to say about multiples, despite their importance. As a result, most executives manage as if their company's multiple were outside their control. They're wrong. Although it is true that the *absolute* level of a company's multiple is influenced by macroeconomic or industrywide factors, there is a lot that managers can do to analyze what drives their *relative* multiple within their peer group—and to improve their relative valuation over time.

The experience of one industrial-goods company provides a good example of both the limits of traditional value management and what managers can do to overcome them. In terms of intrinsic value, the company's performance looked great. The company consistently delivering a higher return on capital employed (ROCE) than its most direct competitor. And yet, its multiple was 25 percent below that of its rival. How to explain this valuation gap?

By analyzing the economic characteristics of the two companies and using regression analysis to isolate the factors determining multiples for their entire peer group, managers were able to identify and quantify four key sources of the gap. (See the exhibit "Quantifying the sources of a valuation gap.") For one thing, the company's high ROCE was accompanied by above-average volatility. As a result, value investors, who constituted the company's dominant investor group,

Quantifying the sources of a valuation gap.

SOURCE: BCG analysis.

perceived the stock as a relatively risky investment and discounted it accordingly.

What's more, the company's chief competitor was far more disciplined in its use of free cash flow. Our example company was replacing its assets at a rate 20 percent faster than that of its competitor. As a result, investors weren't fully benefiting from the high ROCE—whether in dividends returned to shareholders or in more cash to reinvest in profitable growth.

The company also had a much higher debt-to-capital ratio than its competitor, which exacerbated volatility and added default risk. Finally, diversification gave the company an overly complex portfolio, which caused investors to discount the company's stock even more.

Once corporate executives realized the true sources of their relatively low multiple, they were able to design a series of moves to address the key problems. The company reshaped its portfolio to increase focus and minimize volatility (even at the price of sacrificing some high-margin but relatively risky businesses). It used the proceeds from these divestitures to pay down debt. Finally, it revised its capital-allocation process to lengthen investment cycles and depreciation periods. Within six months, these moves contributed to closing the valuation gap, resulting in a $2 billion increase in the market value of equity.

Getting Managers to Think and Act Like Owners

Another promise of value management was to get line managers to "think and act like owners" by linking compensation and incentives to some measure of intrinsic value, such as EVA and CFROI. However, this approach had the unintended consequence of insulating line managers from the signals of the capital markets.

The reality is that incentive targets are usually the result of negotiation about what's achievable—not about what would be required if the business units in question were standalone, publicly traded entities. Over time, this practice only perpetuates the climate of negotiation, gaming, and tensions between the corporate center and the line that existed before value-based measures were introduced.

Business unit managers need to be directly exposed to the demands of investors in the capital markets. They need to manage to goals that can deliver superior TSR, and they need to understand how their local priorities and trade-offs affect the company's overall valuation multiple. This approach holds everyone accountable for delivering realized value creation.

Here's how one manufacturing company did it. Management set itself the goal of delivering a top-quartile TSR within a large group of diversified manufacturing companies. To reach that goal, the company calculated it would have to deliver an annual TSR of about 16 percent (assuming there was no change in its relative multiple).

The incentive plan used that target to set bonus levels for corporate, sector, and division executives. If a business unit contributed less than 6 percent to TSR, its executives received no bonus at all. A 10 percent contribution (equivalent to average performance in the peer group) amounted to an average bonus. A contribution of 16 percent triggered the maximum bonus.

To measure each business unit's contribution to TSR, the company employed a simple internal measure of capital gains and dividend yield at each operating level. The proxy for capital gains was the business unit's percentage change in earnings before interest, taxes, depreciation, and amortization (EBITDA). The proxy for dividend yield was the net free-cash flow to (or from) corporate by the end of each year. This measure provided a simple way to link business unit results to capital market targets. It also clearly positioned each line executive to act as if he were CEO of his own publicly traded company—with direct accountability for meeting or exceeding the returns required by investors and full freedom to manage priorities and trade-offs in order to do so. Because the bonus-award schedule was preset, there was no need to negotiate with the business units. (After all, companies can't negotiate targets with investors.)

Before adopting the new approach, the company ran it as a shadow exercise. Unsurprisingly, the exercise revealed that under the old system, the best negotiators (those with the most modest plans) got the biggest bonuses, even though they contributed less to TSR than managers of other businesses. Meanwhile, executives who fell short of what were often ambitious plans for improvement got little or no bonus—even though they made very high contributions to TSR. Aligning internal measures and incentives with TSR can go a long way towards both empowering and disciplining value creation efforts at the operating level.

Both these examples demonstrate how companies can begin to transcend the limits of traditional value management. Employing the new generation of approaches helps CEOs anticipate the likely impact of strategic moves on TSR performance and align manager accountability with investor expectations.

WORKONOMICS*

FELIX BARBER, JEFF KOTZEN, ERIC OLSEN, AND RAINER STRACK, 2002

Today's performance measures focus on yesterday's success factors.

Over the past decade, companies have become increasingly sophisticated in the ways they measure the performance of their capital investment. Yet, as business shifts from manufacturing to service- and knowledge-based industries, capital itself is becoming relatively less important as a determinant of competitive success. By just about any measure, people are increasingly central to business performance.

Even in asset-intensive businesses, improvements in asset productivity are getting harder to achieve. Shareholder value management systems have helped companies pick the low-hanging fruit, and for many, particularly in an economic downturn, the emphasis is shifting from investing in the right new plant and equipment to getting the most value from past investments. Employees make this happen.

* Abridgment of *Quantifying Employee Contribution*, Felix Barber, Jeff Kotzen, Eric Olsen, and Rainer Strack, 2002 (excerpted from *Shareholder Value*, May–June 2002).

So the challenge for most businesses today is not asset productivity but employee productivity. Few companies, however, measure the performance of their employees in any systematic way. Our traditional capital-oriented measures, which we use to manage the business, tell us very little about employees. In fact, they can often be quite misleading. A software company's balance sheet, for example, may appear healthy, despite the company losing half of its top engineers.

HR departments sometimes collect lots of data, but often even the most basic employee information can be hard to come by. The connections between changes in the composition of the workforce, changes in employee performance, and changes in business performance are poorly understood. Companies lack the measures, and thus the capability, to manage their human capital for greater shareholder value.

The idea of measuring employee productivity is nothing new. So why have employee-oriented performance measurement systems not caught on? Most companies already have some measures of employee productivity, but few pay great attention to them. That is probably because the most common employee productivity measures, such as sales-per-employee and profit-per-employee, are easily distorted. They aren't comparable between different businesses, or for one business over time. Sales-per-employee, for instance, still the most common measure of employee productivity, is strongly influenced by the level of out-sourcing and capital investment in the business. If a business outsources activities carried out by half its employees and the cost of outsourcing is the same as the previous cost of carrying out the activity internally, productivity doesn't increase, but sales-per employee doubles.

A New Approach

Our approach to employee-oriented performance measurement, Workonomics™, uses a measure of employee productivity that eliminates these distortions and represents true value creation per employee. Common measures of shareholder value creation in a traditional capital-oriented system, such as economic value added or cash value added, differ in their measurement technicalities but are all variants on the same theme. They all measure shareholder value creation by determining how much a company's actual return on invested capital exceeds investors' required return.

Workonomics considers the value created by each employee (employee productivity) to be the amount a company could, in principle, afford to pay for an average employee and still achieve the required return on investment for shareholders. With this approach, the relationship between the traditional capital-oriented system and the employee-oriented Workonomics system is very simple. (See Exhibit 1.)

From a capital-oriented perspective, value creation for shareholders, measured either by economic value added or cash value added, is the amount of capital invested, multiplied by the difference between the actual return on capital (including employee costs) and the required return on capital. From an employee-oriented perspective, value creation for shareholders is the number of employees multiplied by the difference between employee productivity and cost per employee (including capital costs). From either perspective, the measure of shareholder value is the same, but the variables that would influence performance in each perspective are quite different. Workonomics focuses the spotlight on an employee's contribution to value creation and suggests employee-oriented levers to improve it.

Workonomics productivity is just one measure in the more extensive set of employee-oriented measures shown in Exhibit 2. These measures answer the same questions about employees that a tradi-

Exhibit 1   An employee perspective on value creation.

Exhibit 2   Employee measures to mirror capital measures.

Traditional Measures: Capital-Driven		Workonomics: People-Driven
Return on assets	⟷	Employee productivity
Cost of capital	⟷	Employee cost
Balance sheet structure	⟷	Workforce competencies & capacity
Balance sheet changes	⟷	New hires/attrition
Plant and equipment utilization	⟷	Workforce utilization
Capital investment plan	⟷	Workforce development plan
Capital gearing (debt/equity ratio)	⟷	Employee gearing (fixed/variable comp
Capital gains	⟷	Long-term contingent compensation
Long-/short-term financing	⟷	Employee contracts (golden handcuffs)

tional performance measurement and management system answers about capital.

To evaluate performance from an employee perspective, we first look at the shareholder value created by the company and by each business unit, just as we always have. But then, instead of looking at the drivers of performance in terms of the amount of capital invested, the productivity of the capital, and it's cost, we look at the number of employees working in the business, their productivity, and their cost. Instead of asking whether we have made the right capital investments in the right plant and equipment, we ask if we have the right workforce with the right competencies and capacity. We don't ask if our equipment is well utilized, we ask if our employees are well utilized. And so on.

One question, however, is different. It doesn't make sense, so far at any rate, to ask if a machine tool or delivery truck is motivated to perform. But asking how motivated employees are makes a great deal of sense.

Evaluating Employee Performance Measures

Employee performance is probably the most important driver of shareholder value creation, if:

- Your company or business unit is employee-intensive.

- Its sales, services, and/or R&D are becoming more important.

- Your competitors' employees are substantially more or less productive than your own.
- You are facing shortages or major changes in needed skills in critical job families.

Measuring it better is the first step to managing it better.

In the most employee-intensive industries—contracting, software, retailing, temporary help, or catering—employees can cost four or more times as much as capital. In these situations, very small changes in employee performance or costs lead to large changes in capital performance.

Capital-oriented measures, such as return on net assets, are highly volatile and not very helpful. Software companies often achieve returns on assets above 100 percent—not because they are performing spectacularly, but because they need few assets. In these industries, employee-oriented measures offer clearly superior insights. Our studies show that in software, the difference in productivity between a top-performing project leader and an average project leader is worth several million dollars a year. When that is the case, a company needs to be sure of who its top performers are, where it can find more like them, and, once they are on board, how it can motivate them to excel.

Indeed, most large, highly-capital-intensive companies, such as banks, oil companies, and automotive manufacturers, have major employee-intensive business segments. Large companies often find that their most profitable business units require little capital. That has historically been the case, for example, with the large Swiss banks UBS and Credit Suisse. They have earned their most attractive returns in private banking, a business that requires very little capital.

In fact, large, capital-intensive corporations that are moving into knowledge and service businesses often will benefit the most from an employee-oriented perspective. Workonomics metrics are particularly attractive because they provide new insights, yet translate back into traditional capital-oriented measures. Each business segment can use the measures that are most appropriate for it and still be able to make comparisons between different parts of the corporation.

In businesses where the balance between people and capital is more even, capital investments may be high, but people often make the greater difference. For example, commercial airplanes come mostly from two manufacturers, Boeing and Airbus, making it difficult for any airline to make advantaged capital investments. But performance differences are nevertheless substantial. Southwest Airlines' distinctive people management and service processes achieved productivity of $76,000 per employee, compared to American Airlines' $62,000 and United Airlines' $69,000 in 2000.

Building Superior Capability for Managing Human Capital

Employee-oriented measures can generate powerful insights, foster more efficient behavior, and create more value for investors. They are the basis for building a new, defensible competitive advantage. Companies using a full set of employee-oriented Workonomics measures to manage human capital as a strategic asset improve their performance in several ways:

- They give higher priority and more effective time to people-oriented issues.

- They put the performance of their people at the center of management discussions and improve the quality of human capital through better recruitment, hiring, and career development.

- They make better portfolio decisions, balancing the mix of capital- and employee-intensive businesses.

- They diagnose performance problems more quickly and effectively by benchmarking employees against competitors.

- They make smarter decisions on incentives, optimizing the mix of fixed and variable compensation and the type of variable compensation, thereby reducing capital costs and taxes.

- They make better investment decisions and execute them more effectively by planning for needed employee capabilities.

- They use superior human resources management capabilities to achieve additional PMI benefits.

A company's top management team needs tools that will help it unleash the potential of human capital in the organization. It needs to know if employees are as productive as competitors' employees. It needs hard data on how much and where value is created. The Workonomics metrics represent one way to get at hard answers.

Resource Allocation

BRUCE HENDERSON WROTE a group of *Perspectives* in the 1970s that are now considered to be a classic body of work on corporate resource allocation and investment. Bruce attempted to distill the art of financial decision making into a few simple rules. At the core of these rules is the importance of cash flow in measuring performance.

Bruce observed that many product lines and businesses are cash traps. Companies evaluate performance on near-term reported profit, but this measure understates the cash required to sustain the business. In most cases, only a small number of products and businesses generate cash in excess of the working capital and reinvestment required to fund operations. The net cash that they throw off is too precious to squander—it is the primary source of funding for businesses that represent the company's future. Generally, only a few of a corporation's cash-consuming businesses have the potential to achieve a competitive position that will result in net cash generation when their growth slows. All the others are—or will be—cash traps.

The dynamics of cash flow make diversification a viable corporate strategy. Businesses have life cycles, just as products do. Mature businesses generate much more cash than they can reinvest productively. This excess cash is best used to support new or growth businesses, which have a voracious appetite for cash during their sprint for market leadership. A corporation with a diversified portfolio can balance cash generation and cash use among its businesses most efficiently.

Bruce Henderson's bold writings on corporate portfolio strategy have been both lauded and assailed. How do they hold up today? First, the core of portfolio theory remains valid, though admittedly it has been widely misapplied over the years. Resources must be allocated with steadfast discipline only to those businesses whose competitive positions, current or potential, promise real returns. Second, the diversification thesis is gaining renewed respectability. After years of fixation on conglomerate discounts and breakup values, new research is showing that well-managed diversified companies enjoy real advantages over—and frequently outperform in shareholder value creation—their more focused peers. The portfolio lives.

CASH TRAPS

Bruce D. Henderson, 1972

The majority of the products in most companies are cash traps. They will absorb more money forever than they will generate. This is true even though they may show a profit according to the books of account. Continued investment sends good money after bad. Escape from the trap requires extreme measures. Either stop investing and manage solely to maximize cash withdrawal, or invest so heavily that a leading position is reached in the market.

Reported profit always exceeds payout to owners in any business over time. Much of the reported profit must necessarily be reinvested just to maintain competitive position and finance inflation. If the required reinvestment, including increased working capital, exceeds reported profit plus increase in permanent debt capacity, then it is a cash trap. Cash is rarely ever recovered from a cash trap unless relative competitive performance is improved by obtaining a superior market share.

Historically, the typical manufacturing company with typical growth rates and asset turnover had to have a pretax profit of about 7 percent on sales, or the entire company became a cash trap. Fast-growth sectors of the economy required even higher margins. So did capital-intensive businesses. At any lesser margin, the required increase in assets exceeded the reported profit. This cannot continue unless the permanent debt also increases in the same proportion or new equity is constantly added.

With higher rates of inflation, the minimum required return is increased in proportion. Inflation of assets must be financed and will never be recovered in dividends or liquidation.

Real cash traps are worthless because the owners will never receive a payout. Instead, the owners will put in cash. Reported profit is not payout. Even if you escape from such a cash trap eventually, you have still lost. The longer it takes to escape, the greater the loss in present value of your investment.

It is a fact that most of the net cash generation of virtually all companies comes from a very few products that have a clearly dominant share of their relevant product-market segment. This is inevitable.

Pareto, an Italian economist, discovered this effect many years ago while trying to determine why most of the wealth was concentrated in a few families. It is a familiar pattern: Approximately 20 percent of the items produce approximately 80 percent of the margin. However, when a constant reinvestment requirement is subtracted from all margins, then that 20 percent may well represent 120 percent or more of the actual net cash generation.

Pareto's law alone would lead to most of the net cash generation coming from only a small number of products. The experience curve effect compounds the relationship and couples cash generation to market share. The experience curve effect causes your relative cost to decrease about 20 to 25 percent each time your market share doubles. Both margin and volume increase with increase in market share. The converse is true also, of course. That is why there are many cash traps, and most of them are low-market-share products.

Reported profit is really irrelevant to the shareholder who actually holds the shares. All he will ever receive is a cash payout of either dividends or liquidation value. This is all a corporation receives internally from a product: either net cash throw-off or net liquidation proceeds. Regardless of reported profit, a business or product is worthless unless it compounds and returns the cash invested in it.

In a dynamic economy, almost every business, even slow-growth ones, require reinvestment of a substantial proportion of reported profit. Inflation alone requires financial growth to compensate for inflation in asset values as they turn over. Additional growth in assets employed is required in order to maintain market share as the industry grows with the economy. Consequently, only a portion of the reported profit can ever be available for distribution unless the business is liquidated. If it is liquidated, many assets will prove to be unconvertible into cash at book value.

When profit margins are low, the required reinvestment will often exceed the reported profit indefinitely, even in mature, stable businesses. Do nothing, and such businesses trap cash forever. The longer the delay until liquidation, the greater the loss. If eventual liquidation will produce only a portion of book value, then the reported profit until then is being overstated in proportion. If the company's required threshold on investment return is higher than this deflated profit, then the difference represents the company's annual opportunity cost.

Fast-growth products are even more dangerous cash traps than slow-growth products. Growth compounds the cash input required. But growth alone does not improve relative cost or profit compared to competition. Yet the eventual payout depends on a superior cost compared to competition whose margin is just sufficient to finance growth needed to maintain their own market share. Superior margin is rarely achieved without superior market share. Consequently, growth just compounds the cash drain unless it also leads to superior market share.

The only advantage of a growth product is that share can be shifted more rapidly from one competitor to another by preempting the share of the growth itself. The disadvantage of a growth product is that it usually requires a large negative cash flow just to hold position in the market. Yet failure to achieve a leading position before the growth slows can be fatal to any hope of a cash payout later.

The critical market share seems to be a level about twice that of the largest competitor. At about that point, debt capacity increases with market share even faster than the assets required. The cost level that can be achieved makes it possible to service debt equal to total net assets employed even though competition is selling at cost or below. When this condition is reached, the entire reported profit and more can be withdrawn as cash and reinvested elsewhere or paid out. It is a highly desirable position. This leads to a competitive rule of thumb.

Take at least twice as much of the growth as your leading competitor in any relevant product-market segment. If you cannot, then plan the process of extricating your investment as expeditiously as possible.

Only the largest two or three competitors in any product-market segment can reasonably expect to avoid being a cash trap. However, there are usually several times that many active competitors. *Therefore, the majority of the products in the average company must be cash traps. This means that a majority of the products in the average company are not only worthless but a perpetual drain on corporate resources.*

Prices could be lower to customers and profit could be higher at the same time if all competitors would recognize their cash traps and stop wasting money on them. Anytime there are more than two or three active competitors in a given product-market segment, then someone is making a mistake. The leader may be failing to compete by holding an umbrella over higher-cost competition at his own expense. Or it may be that competitors are caught in cash traps. Either way, there are major opportunities being lost.

THE STAR OF
THE PORTFOLIO

Bruce D. Henderson, 1976

The high-growth market leader is a star. Its P&L statement scintillates. But cash is all that counts. Profit is a promise. The star of the portfolio must keep twice the market share of its next competitor or its apparent performance is an illusion.

Cash-flow generation is a function of the differential in cost from competitors. The cost differential should be and usually is a function of market share. The differential can be approximated or predicted by the experience curve on value added. High relative share means high relative cash generation. But high growth also means high required reinvestment. If the financial growth rate exceeds the return on net assets employed, then even the star will not be self-financing.

Growth requires more of everything, but particularly assets. Assets added equal cash investment added. If a star is to be self-financed, then its after-tax return on assets employed must equal physical growth plus inflation. That is a high return where growth is high too in an inflationary environment. It is so high that many competitors will be tempted to settle for less profit if they can finance the required growth by any means. Even the debt capacity of other businesses may be used as long as it increases reported profit.

Reported profit is not net cash throw-off. It may never be. But reported profit is the frame of reference for decision making for many potential competitors. That is why the high-growth, high-share star of the portfolio is rarely allowed the opportunity to both hold market share and be self-financing. Stars are not cash generators.

Challengers of the star must have deep pockets full of cash. Differences of two to one in market share typically result in differentials in cost equal to 5 to 8 percent of value added. This times asset turnover times financial growth in revenue is equal to the added cash input per unit of sales required by a follower to keep the pace of a star in a growth business. Yet many do. Growth and reported earnings attract many competitors who can never hope to recoup their gross cash input, much less the present value.

With the passage of time all stars set. Growth above average is not forever. Cash input requirements subside with growth. But cash-generation capability does not change if the cost differential from competitors remains unchanged. However, if competition is real, the number of competitors becomes fewer and fewer as the higher-cost and underfinanced competitors fall behind. The survivors gain that share. The leader can lose relative market share even if absolute market share is maintained.

The ultimate value of any product or service must be the value of the stream of cash it generates net of its own reinvestment. For the star, that stream of cash will be in the future, sometimes the distant future. For real value, that stream of cash must be discounted back to the present at a rate equal to the return on alternative opportunities. It is the future payoff of the star that counts, not the present reported profit.

For a future worth the wait and the cost, the market share differential must be preserved. The star of the portfolio that loses its market-share differential is a costly investment that will not pay off regardless of its interim reported profit.

ANATOMY OF THE CASH COW

BRUCE D. HENDERSON, 1976

The first objective of corporate strategy is protection of the cash generators. In almost every company a few products and market sectors are the principal source of net cash generated. These are the cash cows.

The cash cows fund their own growth. They pay the corporate dividend. They pay the corporate overhead. They pay the corporate interest charges. They supply the funds for R&D. They supply the investment resource for other products. They justify the debt capacity for the whole company. Protect them.

By definition a cash cow has a return on assets that exceeds the growth rate. Only if that is true will it generate more cash than it uses.

This requires high return and slow growth if the cash generation is to be high. Almost invariably, the cash cow has a high market share relative to the next two or three competitors. The experience curve relationships would predict that.

The debt capacity of the cash cow standing alone is always high. The net cash generation provides high interest coverage and debt repayment assurance. Increased market share for the cash cow frequently increases the debt capacity much more than it increases the total assets employed. This makes possible a leveraging of shareholder investment that can be converted either into higher return on net assets or into lower prices in order to buy more market share. Or the leverage can be converted into increased cash generated for use of other businesses.

There is a limit to the market share of the cash cow. The total cost of buying market share gets greater and greater as the share increases, since the margin on total volume is affected. The total value of market share available becomes less and less as the remaining share becomes small. When market share exceeds twice that of the next-largest competitor and four times that of the second-largest competitor, there is rarely any incentive to gain more.

Conversely, market share of a cash cow can be sold off for a very high price in near-term cash flow. A price umbrella converts all the higher price into cash flow and profit multiplied by total volume. However, the competition can increase their growth under a price shelter. The result is a continuing loss of both volume and relative cost potential for the cash cow. Eventually, the growing capability of competitors removes the value of the remaining market share until the cash cow goes dry.

The value of the cash cow's market share is almost always higher than the value of any competitor's market share, point for point. This is because the higher market share can and should produce a lower cost than competitors' on equivalent investment.

If it is properly leveraged to equate risk with higher-cost competitors, the cash cow can be a very high generator of cash and profit on the net investment. Yet the decision to invest or disinvest in a cash cow's market share depends on the alternative opportunities for investment in other parts of the corporate portfolio.

The real value of a cash cow is the discounted present value of the projected cash generated. A high discount rate will almost invariably favor liquidation because of the emphasis on near-term cash flow. The reported profit and net cash flow tend to be parallel and near equal in a low-growth business. Consequently, many cash cows are unwillingly liquidated by short-time-horizon profit budgets even though there is no alternative investment that would yield the same net return on net assets.

The real test of value of a cash cow is the net return on net investment when the cash cow has been leveraged with debt to the point at which its break-even cost as a percent of revenue is the same as the break-even cost of the largest-share alternative competitor. To be valid, this comparison must be made after the competitor has also been leveraged to his optimum debt usage.

This test will frequently show that both competitors have high potential returns on net investment. But if extended to each successively smaller competitor, it will eventually reach the one whose net return is no greater than the GNP growth including inflation. It is then possible to determine the true return for each competitor. Rarely will more than three or four competitors be involved if the market is both stable and competitive.

The marginal competitor whose net cash flow just finances the investment required to maintain his market position is worthless except in liquidation. Yet such a competitor is the ultimate reference. All competitors with superior costs and margins can convert that margin differential into a net cash throw-off. That is how you determine the output of a cash cow.

The value of a cash cow is determined by the rate of return on alternative corporate portfolio investments that must be used as the basic discount rate on the cash cow's output.

Do you wish to buy or sell market share for your cash cow? If you buy share, where will the money come from? If you sell, where will the money that you receive be reinvested?

THE CORPORATE PORTFOLIO

BRUCE D. HENDERSON, 1977

Diversified company portfolios are the normal and natural business form for efficiently channeling investment into the most productive use. All diversified companies, as distinct from holding companies of any kind, have one major characteristic in common. They are able to control the internal allocation of financial resources. In a holding company, each business must be self-financing and independent. In a corporation, cash flow and investment can be rechanneled from one business to another. This is a critical capability.

A diversified business portfolio enables a company to carry the process of business evolution to a higher level of complexity. Instead of developing a family of products, it is able to develop a family of businesses.

All products go through a life cycle. In the beginning they need far more cash input than they can generate. If they succeed, they generate far more cash than they can productively reinvest. Successive, overlapping generations of products smooth out this cash flow to some degree, but even the product family has the same life cycle. Cash input is needed when they are succeeding. Cash generation cannot be reinvested when they have matured successfully. This is what drives many companies to diversify into a family of businesses as well as products.

But businesses as a whole go through the same cycle. They tend to be unprofitable when very new, profitable but undercapitalized when their growth is the fastest, and then generators of cash when they become successful, mature, and slow growing. The problems change with maturity. The young, fast-growing business needs capital to take advantage of its potential growth and exploit its opportunity. The mature business has real problems in finding suitable investments for its cash flow.

The diversified company with a portfolio of businesses is exceedingly well positioned to discharge the function of directing capital investment into the most productive areas. It can be far more efficient and effective than the public capital market is likely ever to be.

Top management of even a far-flung diversified company is better equipped to appraise the potential and characteristics of a growing business than an outside investor. Such a company has staff research capability and access to data that even the most detailed prospectus cannot provide to the general public.

This ability to divert and reinvest the cash flows of a mature business is very important. There is no reason to reinvest the profits of a business in further expansion of the same business merely because it has been successful in the past. General Motors is not the only successful company that would find it difficult to expand faster than its industry.

The U.S. tax structure severely curtails investment funds available for reinvestment, first when they appear as reported profits, and again when they pass through the hands of shareholders as dividends. The value of this advantage is not small. Income taxes would take away about half the reinvestable funds if the cash flow is reported as profit. If paid out in dividends before reinvestment, then only a fraction of this is left for reinvestment.

Any company that can treat its investments in growing businesses as an expense to be offset against other profit has a great advantage in terms of its cost of capital. Also, any company that can obtain its equity from internally generated funds has a far lower effective cost of capital than if it obtained those funds outside from stockholders who can retain only a fraction of the proceeds they eventually receive in dividends.

The diversified company with a portfolio of businesses is in an unexcelled position to obtain capital at the lowest possible cost and to put it to the best possible use. The question, of course, is: Will it?

Any company that treats each of its divisions or units as separate and independent businesses fails to take advantage of its own strength. The traditional profit center concept of management has a fatal defect. It concentrates attention on near-term reported earnings rather than investment potential. This is why many successful diversified companies have been composed of mature businesses and have been notably inconspicuous for their success in incubating new businesses. A company must behave as an investor, not as an operator, if it is to achieve its potential.

Experience curve theory dramatizes how great the potential really is. This theory says that costs are a direct function of accumulated market share. It further says that investment in market share can have extremely high returns during the rapid-growth phases of a product. As long as the growth rate exceeds the cost of capital, then every year in the future is worth more in present value than the current year. Today's losses therefore may be very high return investments, provided those losses protect or increase market share. If market share correlates with cost differential, then it can be translated into investment value.

If this is true, then the logical consequence of competition will be low prices initially on new products. These prices will tend to be so low as to be preemptive. They will also be stable. The result will be negative cash flows for a considerable period until costs decline to below the low initial price. This will be followed by even larger positive cash flows as costs continue their decline and volume continues to increase. This produces the return of investment and the return on that investment.

The diversified company is eminently well suited for this kind of "expense investment." Only the diversified company can match positive and negative cash flows. Only the diversified company can pair off the tax consequences of expense investment. Only the diversified company can accumulate and analyze the detailed information required to make a wise investment involving a sequence of initial negative cash flows.

Everything favors diversified companies: tax laws, capital costs, sources of funds, breadth of business opportunity. Their inherent advantage lies in their ability to manage a set of portfolio tradeoffs. If the flexibility is not used, diversified companies are under a handicap. The individual business has no advantage except uncertain financial backing, which is hardly to be called an advantage! The corporate overhead structure can be a real burden with no offsetting advantage. There are quite a few lackluster diversified companies. It can be quite different if the company is managed as a portfolio.

If a company is to realize its potential, it must have investment and strategy development skills that go well beyond the characteristic needs of the independent business. Some corporations are going to do this. Those that do are quite likely to be the preeminent and dominant firms of the future. They will manage their cash-flow portfolios to continually increase the present value of future cash flows.

RENAISSANCE OF THE PORTFOLIO

ANTHONY W. MILES, 1986

The current wave of corporate restructuring is bringing about radical changes in many companies' business portfolios. For most, this is a positive action, the recognition of a need for focus on areas of competitive strength and greatest opportunity for future growth. For a few it is a retreat to a focus on businesses with secure net cash flow, the aftermath of the Pyrrhic victory of successful takeover defense. In either case, it is compelling witness to the power of the portfolio concept.

This set of ideas was developed in the late sixties, proved immensely popular and powerful during the seventies, and then drifted out of the limelight for a variety of reasons in the late seventies and early eighties. It is time to retrieve these ideas before they are lost to the wastebasket of business fads and to reconsider seriously what they still have to contribute.

What the Portfolio Concept Says

The basic message is very simple. It begins with the fact that most companies participate in a number of different "businesses," even if all fall within one general industry category. These businesses were not created equal, are not equal at any point in time, and will never offer equal opportunities to earn high and sustained returns.

The portfolio concept asserts that one of the primary responsibilities of the chief executive is to make decisive investment choices for the benefit of shareholders. To make choices there must be alternatives. For some companies there are too many, and the challenge is finding a sound rationale for discrimination. For others there are too few, and the challenge for them is creating opportunity. For all there is a need to ensure that every major alternative for a given business has been uncovered and considered before a course of action is chosen.

Companies must choose on the basis of the closely linked combination of sustainable competitive advantage and potential financial contribution to the company. The former yields the high profits that convert to high net cash flow as growth slows and investment requirements moderate. This in turn creates the high returns and high valuations that satisfy shareholders and protect against takeovers. More

Business performance and portfolio position.

	Competitive Advantage	Competitive Disadvantage
High Market Growth	Moderate returns High investment Neutral-to-positive cash flow	Low returns High investment Negative net cash flow
Low Market Growth	High returns Moderate investment Positive net cash flow	Low returns Moderate investment Neutral-to-negative cash flow

positively, high returns and high valuation make raising new capital relatively easy and cheap. They make acquisitions possible. The company has superior ability to repeat the process and invest to grow in pursuit of competitive advantage in new businesses.

The portfolio concept stresses the critical need to keep resources fully employed in the areas where they have the highest yield or potential yield. This means focusing technical and human resources where the company can gain and hold an edge over competitors that is valued by customers. It means concentrating physical assets where they can be used to create or support unique or at least scarce capability. And it means using equity capital only where there is no safely cheaper alternative.

Imagine a company following these guidelines, and you have a company that grows, is profitable, earns high returns, has a high valuation, is in full command of its fate, and is very well protected. One of the two basic justifications of potential acquirers—the ability to use existing resources more efficiently or effectively than current management is doing—is all but eliminated.

All enduring and continuously successful corporations follow this pattern, whether they think of it as a portfolio strategy or not.

Real Advantage

Like all great ideas, the portfolio concept is simple—but the application is not. The portfolio concept is a guide to action, a summary of thinking, and not a substitute for detailed analysis and judgment.

First there is the problem of sustainable competitive advantage. The portfolio concept builds on the observation that superior profitability depends first and foremost on competitive advantage and that growth is easiest where the market itself is growing. Often, superior market share carries with it competitive advantage—often, but by no means always. Advantage may be based on superior technology, speed of response, quality, attention to specific customer needs, location—many factors that may or may not translate into overall market share leadership.

What matters is not whether advantage fits some preconception or general rule, but that the company pursues advantages that are truly available to the business, are valued by customers, provide a basis for competitive differentiation, and have lasting power. This almost always requires focus within the marketplace. Thus the search for advantage must be serious, detailed, imaginative, and rigorous. The bigger the company and the further removed the strategist from the business, the more likely it is that opportunity will be overlooked and the greater the risk of oversimplifying what it will take to succeed.

The fact is that some markets yield more opportunities for advantage than others, and some none at all. Some companies invest heavily in pursuit of the mirage of a secure future competitive edge. Nowhere is this more likely to end in disappointment than where there is blind faith in the value of market share or in the rewards of technological superiority. The portfolio concept works only when competitive advantage is real, when all the homework has been done, and when the competitive nature and likely future evolution of the market have been ascertained.

Leveraged buyouts, raiders, and low-labor-cost foreign competition have gone a long way toward taking care of another problem: the disadvantaged business, performing poorly and relatively stable, but with no realistic hope of much improvement in its market, competitive fundamentals, or performance. While these have not disappeared, they have in many cases become freestanding special cases, highly leveraged and managed for cash flow—very much along the lines the portfolio concept indicated. Marketplace forces have brought about an appropriate solution where corporate managements were reluctant to act decisively.

Discovering Growth

Second, there is the issue of growth. The long period of across-the-board expansion through the sixties and into the seventies spoiled us, and we now think of growth as more elusive. The easy conditions of broad market growth have given way to more localized patterns of growth. These often involve substitution—not just product-for-product substitution, but the substitution of one (better) way of doing business for another. Latent customer needs must be uncovered before they become obvious. Creating and exploiting growth opportunities in these conditions calls for more insight, better preparation, and greater risk taking than before. Growth is often where you make it. Growth opportunities often lie dormant within what at first sight appear to be low-growth, "mature" markets. This only heightens the importance of first-class, forward-thinking staff working closely with vigorous and decisive management. Building and sustaining a strong portfolio is more difficult now, but more necessary than ever.

From Strength to Strength

It has been easy to pick at the portfolio concept as being too simplistic or difficult to interpret in action, or to cavil with one aspect or another of the way it has been discussed or displayed. This is to miss the essential point.

All exceptional rewards in business derive from that scarce commodity, competitive advantage. To have the right to stay in business, a company must earn these rewards and then keep doing so. Building new positions of advantage on top of old calls for focus of effort and intensity of application. That is what the portfolio teaches and experience confirms.

Each new turn in the business cycle only strengthens the message.

PREMIUM CONGLOMERATES

DIETER HEUSKEL, 1996

In the 30 years since they first gained broad notoriety, conglomerates have mostly been dismissed as a failed experiment. Focus has become the order of the day.

It's time for a fresh look. As traditional boundaries between businesses erode, simple business definitions are becoming increasingly untenable. Even the most focused companies are finding that they may need to adopt a multibusiness perspective.

Two myths about conglomerates, in particular, need to be revisited. The first is that conglomerates are penalized systematically in the capital markets. In fact, analysis of the recent empirical evidence reveals the following:

- Although some conglomerates sell at a discount, others sell at a premium. On average, they generate returns equivalent to those of the market as a whole.

- Breaking up a successful conglomerate does not create value— and may well destroy it.

The second myth is that business complexity should be minimized at all cost. In fact, the best multibusiness companies—we call them *premium conglomerates*—exploit complexity to enhance and extend their competitive advantage. As complexity explodes in nearly every business, even companies that pride themselves on their focus would do well to emulate them.

Discounting the Conglomerate Discount

The case against conglomerates is compellingly simple. Markets are too specialized, business competition is too complex, and the rate of economic change is too rapid for even the most astute corporate managers to stay on top of a collection of unrelated businesses. And with today's efficient capital markets, it is no longer imperative to ensure internal funding for growth businesses. Better to divide the company into its constituent parts. Managers are better able to focus on the specifics of their individual businesses, and investors get the pure plays they prefer. An increase in shareholder value can often result.

Twenty years ago, this may well have been true, a necessary correction to the excesses of the 1960s and 1970s. But today, there is no apparent correlation between a company's industrial diversity and its performance. From 1985 to 1995, the 40 largest U.S., European, and Australian conglomerates generated total shareholder returns virtually identical to the averages of their respective markets. Half outperformed their markets; half underperformed them. More significantly, the top quartile turned in annual returns almost 5 points above the market averages. Capital markets seem to reward business value creation, whatever the source.

But might the individual businesses of these companies have performed even better on their own? An analysis of 16 recent breakups suggests not necessarily. Ten of the conglomerates in the sample had historically underperformed the market; of these, nine garnered breakup premiums. The six that had historically delivered above-average returns, however, saw the market valuations of their businesses remain level or decline. Breakup seems to create new value only when a conglomerate has consistently underperformed the market.

The conglomerate discount is not automatic. Valuation rests ultimately on underlying business performance. Yes, there are conglomerates that destroy value. But there are also quite a number that consistently create value. Their management practices contribute importantly to their ability to sustain a market premium.

How Conglomerates Create Value

What underlies the deep-seated suspicion of conglomerates? A healthy skepticism about complexity. The more complex the managerial task, the less certain the results. And yet, operating executives know that complexity is increasingly a given in today's global environment. What distinguishes premium conglomerates is their executives' skill in managing this complexity. They excel at three key managerial tasks.

First, premium conglomerates are active, but highly disciplined, business portfolio managers. They make acquisitions only when the competitive logic is compelling, and they don't hesitate to divest businesses that are competitively disadvantaged or a poor fit. General Electric is the classic example. In the early 1980s, GE divested hundreds of operations that had poor prospects for achieving the company's stated goal of being "number one or number two" in its industries. An even more consummate move was the company's 1987 swap with Thomson: GE traded a marginal position in consumer electronics for a key piece of a globally dominant position in medical equipment. Although not every acquisition has been successful, GE's total shareholder return under CEO Jack Welch has been 20.8 percent, a comfortable 6.4 percentage points ahead of the U.S. market average.

Second, premium conglomerates manage portfolios not just of businesses, but also of people and ideas. Companies like ABB engineer the career development of their most promising managers from the corporate center. This ensures that they get a broad range of experience across businesses and functions and that the best talent is assigned to the biggest challenges. Enterprisewide initiatives—to speed product development, to improve quality, or to sharpen asset management—replicate best practices across the company's many businesses and help each to move up the learning curve more quickly than stand-alone competitors.

Finally, perhaps the most distinctive characteristic of premium conglomerates is the way they mobilize and deploy advantaged capabilities to breach competitive barriers and enter new businesses—in effect, making complexity their ally. GE Capital, for example, has invaded sector after sector in financial services. The German conglomerate Veba has parlayed infrastructure from businesses as diverse as nuclear power generation, electricity distribution, gasoline retailing, and real estate to configure a unique entry into the German telecommunications business. And the Korean conglomerate Samsung is drawing on its capabilities in aerodynamic engineering, electronics, heavy manufacturing, and global logistics to drive its foray into automobiles. Premium conglomerates can pop up where they are least expected, and when they do, they are a good bet to upset the competitive status quo.

As they do, other companies are forced to compete in multiple industries as a defensive measure, to secure their claim on the value chain. British Petroleum, for example, has had to turn itself into a world-class retailer to defend its gasoline business from attack by grocery chains in the United Kingdom. It's getting harder to find true single-business companies.

As the boundaries between traditional businesses blur, the distinction between conglomerates and their more focused brethren is blurring as well. To survive and flourish, every company will have to master the complexity-management skills of the premium conglomerates.

THE END OF THE PUBLIC COMPANY— AS WE KNOW IT

LARRY SHULMAN, 2000

The avalanche of initial public offerings in recent years has obscured an intriguing—and potentially significant—countertrend. Even as many new start-up businesses are going public, many traditional publicly held companies are moving in precisely the opposite direction. They are going private, replacing public equity with private equity and debt, often in alliance with private equity firms.

Private buyouts, as measured by number and dollar volume, are at their highest levels since the LBO heyday of the late 1980s. According to one recent estimate, 49 deals valued at $6.88 billion were announced in the first quarter of 2000—almost four times the dollar amount of deals announced in the first quarter of 1999.*

Many of these deals involve small and midsize companies. According to recent press reports, however, much bigger and better-known companies—the Borders bookstore chain, the printing company R.R. Donnelley & Sons, and Continental Airlines, to name just a few—are exploring the buyout option, too. In addition, Seagate Technology, the world's largest disk-drive maker, recently announced that it would go private in a $20 billion transaction.

Most observers interpret the trend as a natural reaction of low-technology companies that have lost out in the recent bull market. Although this explanation is accurate as far as it goes, the real story is much more interesting. Long-term changes in the structure of financial markets are presenting traditional companies—those that make or sell tangible products, whether for other businesses or for consumers—with new choices and the opportunity to pursue new kinds of financial strategies. These changes will continue even after the current bull market cools down.

The New Cash Cows

The companies taking advantage of privatization tend to have three things in common. First, they are highly productive and generate significant amounts of cash. More than a decade of investments in information technology and capital-goods spending in the manufacturing sector has finally paid off. These investments are allowing companies to post continual productivity gains equal to or greater than the rate of price attrition in their markets. As a result, real margins are increasing, and average cash-flow return on investment (CFROI) is at a 50-year high. Although this trend is well under way, it is far from over.

It will receive a major boost as business-to-business e-commerce allows companies to wring improvements from not just individual factories but the entire supply chain.

Second, these companies have modest growth prospects—generally equal to GNP or, at most, to GNP plus 2 percent. As a result, there is an imbalance between the cash they are generating and the opportunities they have to plow that cash back into the business as new invest-

* See Steven Lipin, Nikhil Deogun, and Kara Scannell, "Raiders of the Lost Decade: 1980s-Style Mergers Return," *Wall Street Journal*, March 29, 2000, pp. C1 and C24.

ments. In fact, these companies have grown so productive that their markets can no longer absorb the de facto increases in capacity that continual productivity improvement creates.

Third, as these companies pile up cash, they are penalized with low price-to-earnings ratios. This fact reflects a major shift in what public equity markets value—specifically, a greater emphasis on future growth prospects as a contributor to total shareholder return. It also demonstrates the growing understanding on the part of investors that a public corporation is a relatively risky and inefficient vehicle for accumulating cash.

The New Private Equity

In the past, a company facing such a combination of circumstances would have diversified in search of new growth. And yet today, few traditional modest-growth companies can get away with aggressive diversification. Active investors dislike corporate diversification, preferring to make their portfolio decisions themselves. Typically, public markets pummel any company that announces a major diversification strategy.

An alternative approach is to acquire other companies in the same business—for instance, buying an analogous company operating in another part of the world. Indeed, the globalization wave in many traditional businesses is driven more by this specific financial logic than by any compelling strategic imperative. In effect, companies are using their excess cash to take other companies private, thus liquidating the shareholders of the acquired company rather than their own.

But more and more companies are choosing to go private themselves. When they do, they discover that they can take advantage of large private-equity pools that amount to hundreds of billions of dollars in investable funds. Private equity firms, such as Clayton, Dubilier & Rice, Texas Pacific, and Berkshire Partners, and the private equity divisions of investment banks, such as Goldman Sachs and Donaldson, Lufkin & Jenrette, are awash in liquidity. What's more, although many trace their origins to the LBO wave of the 1980s, these firms have evolved from being predators to becoming masters of the friendly takeover.

These firms no longer buy companies in order to gut them and immediately sell the pieces back to the public markets. Indeed, many are convinced that they can outmanage the market and create value even above the 20 percent acquisition premium they often have to pay. They can do so because they have the freedom to manage aggressively the financing, tax payments, and reinvestments of these companies in ways that would not be acceptable to a major publicly traded corporation. In short, private equity has become an efficient, profitable, and permanent alternative to the public equity markets.

Financial Deconstruction

The rise of private equity has broad implications for senior executives. Managers need to recognize that they now have a choice in equity markets. Creating the right fit between assets and owners has become a critical strategic challenge.

Many companies that currently are traded publicly do not need the public equity markets to raise cash. And their business economics do not match the preferences of public investors. For such companies, remaining public may mean chaining themselves to an inappropriate capital structure that forces management to waste energy and, eventually, lose frustrated senior executives. Conversely, going private may be an opportunity to align the business to financial structures and ownership models that are more appropriate to the dynamics of their business.

But in some situations, the choice may not be a simple either/or. Different parts of a company may require different equity models. If so, there is an opportunity to deconstruct the business financially. Some units—say, an e-commerce venture with great potential for future growth—may thrive in the public markets, whereas other, more traditional units may have the financial structure, tax base, and cash flows more suited to private equity.

Seagate's recent announcement is one version of this financial-deconstruction strategy. The company's privatization deal includes a complex transaction in which Seagate shareholders will be paid in the stock of a software company in which Seagate owns a 33 percent share. Although the software company has revenue equal to only one-tenth that of Seagate, its market value is many times that of Seagate's core business. The deal is a way for Seagate to unlock the value of its ownership stake in the software company, "pay" its shareholders in a way that minimizes both their tax burden and that of the company, and allow executives to focus on the core business.

As more and more traditional companies invest aggressively in building dot-com businesses, this kind of financial deconstruction may become a trend. For example, the industrial wholesaler W.W.

Grainger could take its traditional MRO supply business private even as it takes its parallel dot-com business public. Or thinking more radically, a major auto company such as Ford could take its highly productive manufacturing assets private, while leaving its brand, marketing-and-sales, and product-development organizations public.

No one knows just how far the privatization trend will go. But it's clear that public ownership is no longer a given. What's more, the privatization trend is only one aspect of an even broader transformation of the traditional public company. The rules of ownership are being rewritten. As the forces of deconstruction redraw industry boundaries, they are restructuring how different types of economic activity are owned and managed, by whom, and to what end.

ADVANTAGE, RETURNS, AND GROWTH—IN THAT ORDER

GERRY HANSELL, 2005

Short-term market pressures make it tempting for managers to play a game of growing volume, beating plan, or exceeding analysts' estimates for the quarter. But sustained value creation requires disciplined portfolio choices that drive performance along three critical dimensions: competitive advantage, returns (on capital), and growth. The sequence is important: Without advantage, returns decrease; and without adequate returns, growth destroys value. Although these principles sound deceptively simple, the wishful funding of me-too strategies and chasing after growth in low-return business positions annually extinguish immense amounts of shareholder value.

Market Valuations: Providing a Feedback Loop on Performance Priorities

Exhibit 1 compares how investors value businesses with different returns on capital. Each dot shows a particular company's valuation multiple, or entity price-to-book ratio, versus the profitability of the business, measured as the five-year-average after-tax return on gross invested capital (ROI), excluding goodwill. The exhibit indicates an overall positive relationship between ROI and the valuation multiple.

Exhibit 1 Investors price stocks based in part on demonstrated ROI performance.

Example: Consumer products and industrial goods companies, 1985–2003.

SOURCES: Compustat, BCG ValueScience Center analysis.

One dollar of cash flow reinvested in a high-return business creates $1 of new book capital and often $2 or $3 of net present value, while the same dollar reinvested in a low-return business will usually be worth less than $1.

Looking more closely at the left-hand side of the exhibit, we see dots representing 75-cents-on-the-dollar businesses. These businesses earn ROIs of less than 8 percent (roughly at or below the cost of capital), and their valuation multiples cluster between 0.7x and 0.9x. There is a small but steady upward drift in the valuation multiple as ROI increases from left to right.

These businesses on the left are usually low-margin and asset intensive, with little competitive advantage. And the market values these low-return companies on the basis of assets (not earnings): The flat slope of the trend line suggests that there is a relatively weak link between valuation and current period profits. These companies consistently trade at a discount to book value because the capital reinvested to sustain the assets doesn't earn back the cost of capital. In other words, each $1 reinvested and on the books is worth only about 75 cents.

As ROI increases above the cost of capital, investors seem to price companies differently. An upward "kink" in the exhibit's trend line indicates that the slope of the relationship between ROI and the valuation multiple becomes much steeper. The story behind this steeper slope is competitive advantage: High ROIs reflect competitive advantage, and higher ROIs signal more advantage. Investors, in short, are willing to pay a premium for advantaged assets.

At the same time, however, the goodness of fit seems to decrease for these high-ROI businesses. Turning again to the exhibit, we can see that the vertical scatter in the valuation multiples increases with increasing ROI. Competitive advantage, then, doesn't tell the whole story. A key variable is missing, and that additional variable is growth. High-ROI businesses with more growth potential are above the trend line, and high-ROI businesses with low growth potential are below the trend line.

Portfolio Priorities: Differentiating Goals and Skewing Capital Allocation

So what does all this mean for managing the corporate portfolio?

First, senior managers must frame decisions about portfolio choices at the business level—not just at the project level. That may sound simple, but many companies destroy value through a bottom-up process of funding all "good" projects as they appear or setting one-size-fits-all performance goals across all units (such as increasing volume growth, market share, or operating income margins). Managers of low-return businesses constantly fund incremental investments whose high (forecast) project-level returns fail to raise the business as a whole to attractive levels.

Portfolio choices do not emerge magically from a mechanical review of historical returns. But the business economics are simple: If you don't understand and address the underlying competitive realities that are causing sustained low ROIs, you should expect investments in those businesses to continue to return 75 cents on the reinvested dollar. Often, these value-destroying investments are funded or subsidized with cash flows from higher-ROI sister units. Such cross-subsidies destroy value and are a common cause of the so-called conglomerate discount. Despite the name, such a discount can plague any company that averages reinvestment across a mix of high- and low-return business positions. Even focused companies, such as single-format restaurant chains or retailers, can earn a conglomerate discount by deploying cash flow from their high-ROI legacy locations to fund the opening of marginal new locations.

Second, senior managers need to segment the portfolio and adopt business-specific goals across competing performance priorities. Each company—each dot in the exhibit—is in fact an aggregation of underlying business positions with different competitive positions and business economics. A one-size-fits-all goal-setting approach treats businesses with different starting positions as if they had the same value-creation priorities. But they don't. In framing the relative merits of investing for growth, focusing on raising returns, or decapitalizing the business, managers need to start with a fact-based review of the long-term return patterns in the peer group of each business unit:

- Are long-term industry returns attractive overall? In other words, are ROIs above the cost of capital?

- Which companies earn high returns and what is their source of competitive advantage? Does that advantage show up in relative cost, relative price (and mix), or relative asset intensity?

- How do your businesses and business subsegments perform relative to industry leaders in terms of ROI level and consistency?

By segmenting the portfolio in this way, you will usually uncover three groups of businesses: those with low returns, those with high returns, and those with erratic returns.

For businesses with sustained low returns and therefore little competitive advantage, you must probe to discover root causes and think as an owner would. "Value" investors who specialize in making money from low-return assets focus their efforts on the restructuring (not growth) implications of low returns:

- If there is a structural problem with the industry—for example, depressed returns for all participants—can you consolidate (either as a seller or as a buyer) to improve industry returns?

- If the strategy is misguided, can you identify the segments and activities that would provide customer value and profits? And can you refocus your efforts, and shrink or exit the remaining segments and activities?

- If the issue is one of bad execution, how quickly can you prioritize the problem areas and close the gaps?

- In all cases, how does the return from selling the business compare with the value, risk, and achievability of the "keep and fix" program?

For businesses with sustained high returns, and therefore meaning-ful competitive advantage, growth is the obvious priority. Paradoxi-cally, the portfolio management choices can become substantially trickier when you begin from such a strong position:

- An easy choice, if you are lucky enough to be presented with it, is to fund a high-return business facing growth opportunities that reinforce the core business and preserve or raise relative market share.

- A more common—and difficult—challenge is to assess growth investments in a high-return business with few close-in growth opportunities (those to the right and below the trend line in Exhibit 2). Growing successful but mature positions often entails taking a leap to new business models or constructing a bridge to "adjacent" markets, where the company's current capabilities and drivers of advantage often apply weakly or not at all. But if the economic linkages between adjacent markets and the core are real, such incremental investment can create significant new

Exhibit 2   Companies with high returns confront different challenges than those with low returns.
Example: Consumer products and industrial goods companies, 1985–2003.

SOURCES: Compustat, BCG ValueScience Center analysis.

businesses, raise the sustainable growth rate, and trigger a positive rerating. (See B→A in the exhibit.)

- In either case, growing through acquisition can be rewarding but requires the discipline to pay a reasonable price and capture substantial net synergies after the acquisition. You will pay market value (plus a control premium) for the assets, resetting the ROI equation.

Finally, for businesses with erratic (not just cyclical) returns, one of two things is likely:

- There may be a temporary industry instability, usually related to competitive or technological dislocation. In these cases, it's especially useful to think creatively about the future—who is likely to win and why.
- The sources of competitive advantage (and returns) may be inherently fleeting or unstable. These businesses are usually not very good candidates as significant portfolio positions for publicly owned companies.

*   *   *

Portfolio strategy can be a huge lever in driving sustained shareholder value. But managers need to pull up from a purely executional focus and skew their goal setting and capital bets aggressively, finding and funding strategies with competitive advantage and high returns, and fixing or disinvesting disadvantaged businesses. Growth without advantage buys size but creates no value. And beating plan and making the quarter are not enough.

Organizational Design

ORGANIZATION STRUCTURE HAS always been a vexing issue for corporate leaders. Models—functional, divisional, SBU, and matrix—seem to come in and out of fashion. Companies find they need to adapt their structures periodically. No design seems to work very well for long.

There is a good reason for this. Every organization scheme makes some things easier and others harder. Each scheme's primary impact is on the organization's communication patterns. Some interactions are hardwired; others are relegated to informal status or allowed to languish, affecting time and accuracy. When the environment changes—and the change is major enough to call for a change in the company's priorities—structure frequently has to change to facilitate the personal connections necessary to effect a change in strategy.

BCG pursues several threads in its thinking about organizational design in this section's *Perspectives*. First, strategy should drive structure. Because of the impact on communication patterns, the optimal design depends crucially on what you are trying to accomplish. Second, certain mechanisms and interactions can be built into an organization to increase its creativity and serve as platforms for growth. Finally, with growth, and especially global growth, comes a high degree of complexity. Organizations need both to delayer and to explore new, sometimes radical, ways of thinking about organizational design if they are to cope.

PROFIT CENTERS AND DECENTRALIZED MANAGEMENT

BRUCE D. HENDERSON, 1968

The idea of profit centers and decentralization often gets in the way of good management if the idea is taken very seriously. Such ideas are often not what they seem.

Many companies that profess decentralization do not really have it. Profit centers are not necessarily so—if overall corporate profit performance is being optimized. Independent profit centers are by definition neither independent nor profit centers if, in fact, there is any significant mutual interaction or synergy between cost centers.

There are several ambiguities involved. They grow out of the underlying assumptions and implications in the concepts of *profit center* and *decentralization:*

1. There is the implication that absolute level of profit is a measure of management's current performance. It may be nothing of the kind. The near-term absolute level of profit may reflect a long series of previous management decisions. It may also represent a conscious decision either to increase heavy "expense investment" for the future or, conversely, to liquidate past "expense investment." All investment and deferred benefits cannot be capitalized.

2. There is the implication that profit can be the measure of divisional performance in a multiunit company. This is seldom the case. If there is any mutual support between divisions, then the resulting benefits are necessarily windfalls to one division or the other, when compared to an independent operation, and are largely beyond the influence of divisional management.

3. There is the implication that each profit center should optimize its own profit when obviously it is the total profit of the corporation that should be optimized. Most unit managers are faced sooner or later with the conflict between improving their own unit's reported performance and improving overall corporate performance. Often there are many circumstances that require the apparent unit performance to be depressed in order to optimize the corporate overall performance.

4. There is the implication that profit centers can be measured and evaluated as if they were separate companies. This is hardly

defensible if there is in fact good reason for the separate units to be grouped together.

Profit centers and decentralized management have become almost a hallmark of American business organization. The underlying philosophy is that authority and responsibility should be in parallel. Further, there is the implication that in a complex business the authority, and therefore responsibility, must inevitably be delegated. These principles are valid—but only up to the point that there is a conflict with the principle that overall management should optimize overall performance.

The justification for any central management in a diversified company must always be that it can produce results superior to those that a decentralized organization would produce if left completely alone. By definition, this means that a central management must impose constraints on the direction of decentralized operations.

The best balance between centralization and decentralization must be far more effective than either extreme. At the same time this balance requires a level of management sophistication much more demanding than the simpler modes. The required conditions are easily stated although hard to achieve.

To achieve this balance, the goals and potential of the organization as a whole must be clearly and explicitly understood by the corporate management. This means that the corporation as a whole must have a well-defined and explicit strategy. Those who make decisions of consequence must either understand this overall corporate strategy in all of its complexity or be subject to policy constraints that effectively limit choice to decisions compatible with the overall strategy. When this has been done, then each decision should be delegated to that part of the organization that is in the fullest possession of all the relevant information.

Corporate strategy, corporate policy, and corporate organization are inseparable. They are mutually dependent.

Left alone, each profit center should be expected to maximize its own value system. It is the central authority's responsibility to optimize the combination of profit centers. However, it can do this only by one of two approaches. The first, and obvious one, is to closely supervise the operation and internal policy of the profit center. By definition, this is not decentralization. It also implies a centralization of wisdom. The other alternative is to optimize the system by depressing one profit center's performance in order to achieve an even greater improvement in other profit centers. This is highly desirable and laudable, but it distorts the performance measurement of all the profit centers. The direct use of profitability as a performance measure is immediately undermined. Thus, overall optimization also implies a quite restricted definition of decentralization.

There is a wide range of degrees of freedom possible within the concept of decentralization. Listed here in descending degrees of freedom are some typical levels:

1. Parent company is essentially an investment portfolio custodian (regardless of corporate form).

2. Parent company is in effect a holding company that serves as a board of directors would in setting policy for the individual operations.

3. Parent company in addition provides common financial resources to each operation in accordance with overall corporate policy.

4. Parent company actively participates in strategy development and policy formulation for operating units.

5. Parent company coordinates activity in some key activity or activities—for example, in a common sales organization.

6. Parent company provides detailed policy direction of operations in all major activities.

7. Parent company makes key operating decisions, in addition.

These various parent-division roles require differing degrees of internal communication and of specialization in the decision-making process. This is another way of describing internal organization form.

All practical basic organization forms for complex operations have certain common characteristics:

- Centralized policy direction based on explicit strategy concepts
- Decentralized operation administration based on complex, not simple, operating standards and expectations
- Mechanisms of communication and review that keep both strategy and operating objectives realistically related to each other
- A quality of leadership that achieves consensus on both strategy implementation and operating standards

Profit centers and decentralization are a too-simplified description of this set of organization relationships.

Some form of decentralized operation is essential and always will be necessary for any business of substantial size. This is because there are many reasons that multiproduct organizations are more efficient in the use of their resources than a single-product organization. In fact, virtually all corporations of any consequence sell more than one product. However, as the variety and breadth of product time increases, the degree of relatedness or synergy between products decreases.

It is obvious that management techniques, style, and organization must be modified as products and markets become more numerous, more diverse, and less related. If this is not done, then diversity and size eventually become handicaps instead of advantages. The management organization and policies must be tailored to the individual combination of products, markets, and people.

For each company there is an optimum organization and set of policies that are superior to centralized management, with its inflexibility, bureaucracy, slow response, and insensitivity, and yet superior to fully decentralized profit centers that act independently of their potential for mutual reinforcement.

UNLEASH INTUITION

RICHARD K. LOCHRIDGE, 1984

Every organization can become more intuitive. For this to happen, the leadership of the organization must recognize that intuition operates best when the creative people have a chance to recognize patterns that others cannot see. The ability to see new patterns is greatly enhanced when the collective knowledge and experience of the organization are tapped.

The solution is not to hire people with, one hopes, more intuition, but to use the inherent skills of the organization. This requires consistently maintaining the building blocks of required knowledge in a fashion that allows key people from different functional areas to understand what is evolving elsewhere in the organization.

Organizational processes must be in place to produce a reasonable forecast of the evolution of the market, customers' values, costs, and bases of competitive advantage. These predictions open the way to seeing new patterns, and thus to inventing new options. This is, ultimately, a creative process, but it has no chance of developing a critical momentum unless the building blocks are in place.

If the goal is broad ("Let's be more innovative"), but an individual's perspective is narrow, little insight can develop. The goal and the breadth of perspective must be roughly comparable. This is where management direction and organizational processes are critical in determining the level of organizational intuition.

Creating Organizational Intuition: The Flow

Each person and organizational unit designated to help must play a role in providing the basic data from which the insight or new patterns can be derived. Each can stimulate a broader perspective among colleagues with different biases, databases, or functions. When management sets appropriate intermediate goals and creates effective organizational processes, even those who are ordinarily less than intuitive geniuses can add to the scope and fabric of the pattern. When a critical mass of information is available, intuitive insight will often emerge.

Too many companies do not do an adequate job of maintaining the basic building blocks. Even the required raw data may not exist. If they do, they are rarely shared across functional boundaries. Yet to discover new insights, creative people must share the building blocks of innovation in a way that allows them to see new patterns, challenge old assumptions, and put together new combinations of ideas in a better synthesis.

Communication

This is the great advantage of the successful small entrepreneurship over the large corporation. It inherently has short lines of communication. By necessity, all boundaries mean little. Relationships between people are determined by respect for proven expertise, not rank or status. But the large corporation cannot afford the chaos implied in such an organization. In a firm of several thousand employees, it is physically impossible for everyone to talk regularly to everyone else. Thus, to unleash the intuition of the large corporation, management must go beyond merely identifying the individuals with creative skills and develop ways for them to interact.

Organizational intuition.

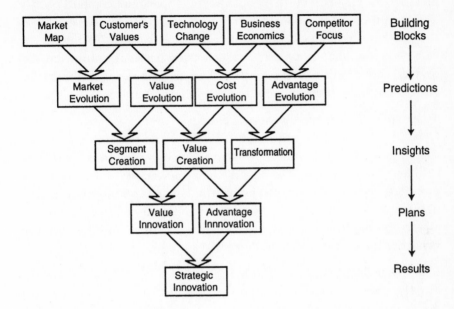

The Five Building Blocks

The intuitive organization encourages teams of people to understand each of the five building blocks and share them across functional boundaries. This can be accomplished organizationally by combining teams of functional experts from neighboring areas to produce valuable intermediate forecasts. When management really invests in a process to produce such predictions, the results themselves can be insightful.

Market Map

The goal of combining the market map and a good description of customer values should be to get a much better idea of how the market will evolve. This is more than a growth forecast. At its core must be a description of segmentation of user groups, the logic that supports the scheme, and a prediction of how the basic forces that determine segment size will influence the growth of each segment over time.

Customer Values

The purpose of combining people who understand customer values and those who know about the potential for technology changes is to forecast how the customers' values will evolve. Users can purchase only what is available. In addition, rarely can a consumer tell an innovator specifically what product or service he or she really wants. For example, the vast majority of the people buying a personal computer today know nothing about the insides of an integrated circuit. Nevertheless, they do have basic needs and value certain attributes. Technologists can estimate what is possible. The basic customer values can be defined. Tools exist to combine these knowledge bases to allow predictions about the evolution of consumers' values.

Technology Change and Business Economics

Combining an understanding of technology and business economics should give a forecast of cost evolution. The potential to relax technical barriers to increase the size of the scale facility, substitution of new materials for old, reduction of the cost of complexity through new manufacturing technologies, and application of electronics can all change the fundamental cost structure of a business and thus the resulting value of investment alternatives.

Competitor Focus

Finally, combining an educated guess about what competitors are doing with a real understanding of the business economics describes how the basis of advantage might evolve. It is the relative advantage versus competition that determines the long-run profitability of a business. Forecasting both changes in relative position and the basic potential of the industry describes both the need for and the value of a change in strategy.

Creating Value through Intuition

Meeting these goals requires not only cross-functional communication, but also cross-functional work. It requires a commitment to putting together the building blocks and making predictions. It can be done reasonably regularly and in an organized (not merely serendipitous) fashion. It may not even need esoteric leaps of creativity.

Combining the predictions about the future with a broad perspective will lead to new strategic insights. This is where the really creative managerial task is demanded. The goal of such an effort should be to produce an inventory of options available to the corporation. Can new segments be created? Is it possible to transform the basis of advantage and the nature of the industry?

Too many companies try to start their innovation efforts with these questions. Without the building blocks and resulting predictions, these questions will remain unanswered and lead to frustration unless exceptional genius is at hand.

Most organizations can unleash an enormous amount of their creative capacity. The fact that too many organizations are not sufficiently innovative means that the creative energies are spent in an inefficient and expensive fashion, relying totally on individual rather than organizational intuition.

Yet one need not fail. The essential insights of Apple Computer, McDonald's, Club Med, Federal Express, and Sony in developing the Walkman are the type one should expect from using the organization's intuition. By combining an understanding of trends across a number of functional areas, each of these companies created new segments, created new value, and transformed an industry.

NETWORK ORGANIZATIONS

TODD L. HIXON, 1989

Today's business problems—shortfalls in quality, innovation, and cost-effectiveness—defy solutions offered by traditional organizational concepts.

These problems will intensify as customers expect ever greater levels of variety and customization. Products are becoming more design-intensive and more service-intensive. Examples range from cars (increased engineering content of four-valve/cylinder engines) to computers (value-added shifting from standard hardware to software) to sweaters (Benetton's infinite variety).

Design and service tasks are best accomplished by small, multidisciplinary teams that are created specifically for the immediate problem, positioned to interact intensely with the customer and each other, and then left alone to do the job. Senior management provides the vision and capability. It can also establish incentives and measure progress. But it can't manage the team process closely, and it shouldn't try. The impatient, independent, and talented person who, for truly creative tasks, outperforms ten well-qualified drones can thrive only in a lightly managed environment.

Such an organization works like a computer network: many autonomous, intelligent work units interacting rapidly with the outside world and each other, and quickly rearranging themselves to solve new problems. The corporate center supervises the network, but it does not pace the work or filter the information moving from one working unit to another. Instead, the center focuses on building the capabilities of the work units, setting overall goals and strategy, and monitoring progress.

The Traditional Organization

Traditional organizational thinking seeks the structure that works best for the company's business and strategy, with resource coordination and decision making coming from the top. In the 1950s and 1960s, for example, many companies followed GE's lead to profit centers, an effective response to increasing company size and product lines. In the 1980s we shifted again to greater functionalization as a way to consolidate staffs and take advantage of scale.

Two assumptions underlie the traditional approach:

- The business strategy determines the organization's structure. Every strategy has its optimal organizational structure, which in turn dictates optimal decision systems, staff composition, and so on. Once discovered and implemented, this structure is expected to function over a number of years.

- Whatever the structure, a management hierarchy must aggregate and screen decisions, funneling the key ones to the senior officers at the top. Hence the typical diagram of an organization is an upside-down tree, or a matrix, which is two trees entangled together.

The Network Organization

Designing and managing a network organization requires overturning the old assumptions:

- You can't reason linearly from strategy to structure and on to systems, staff, and so forth. Instead, the process is iterative: A team is formed to meet a strategic need; it sizes up the situation, develops a specific strategy, and reorganizes itself as necessary. What's more, the structure is temporary. The organization needs to be ready to change its configuration quickly to respond to new needs and circumstances.

- The organization's purpose is not to control from the top; it is to empower a group of people to get a job done. Management occurs through training, incentives, and strongly articulated goals, strategies, and standards.

Network organizations are found most often in businesses that are driven by product development and customer service—electronics and software companies in particular—and often in smaller, younger organizations where traditional boundaries are weaker. Some large-scale models exist: parts of Honda and Panasonic in Japan, 3M in the United States, and, in some ways, GE, which has shown extraordinary flexibility in recent years in reshaping its organization and pushing authority down to frontline managers.

Network organizations have obvious drawbacks: they lack tight controls; they're ill-suited to exploit scale or accomplish massive tasks in large organizations; and they depend on capable and motivated people at the working level. However, companies that cannot use the full network model can appropriate aspects of it, like new-product-development teams.

Some large companies (such as IBM, Digital Equipment, and Dow Chemical), with the need for both innovation and coordination of resources among markets, product lines, and technologies, often use the network concept in modified form. They frequently change the focus of resources and control by reshuffling product groups—shifting power among the parts of the organization—or using ad hoc teams. IBM is quite close to the network concept in the fluidity of its approach—reorganization is the norm, with frequent shifts keeping the organization focused on current problems (such as the recent changes that put strategic decision making closer to the market in the United States).

Western economies are moving toward industries based on product innovation and services. Success will require creative reasoning, quick reflexes, and constant communication with the customer. Managers have to empower their people and live with less control to make this happen. A high-tech CEO recently put it this way: "The less you sign, the more you achieve."

THE MYTH OF THE HORIZONTAL ORGANIZATION

PHILIPPE J. AMOUYAL AND JILL E. BLACK, 1994

One of the messages of reengineering is that companies, once structured as hierarchical pyramids, now need to be "turned on their sides" and restructured as horizontal organizations. The logic for this restructuring flows from the logic for reengineering: if processes, not functions, are the correct way to organize work, then horizontally must be the correct way to organize a company.

It seems obvious. And it is wrong.

There are no great horizontal organizations, nor are there likely to be any. One company has experimented with this new organization, but is now unwinding it. This two-billion-dollar heavy-equipment manufacturer reorganized around its product lines, pulling engineering, marketing, and manufacturing people together into customer-centered units, one for each product line. The payback to the company was immediate—its people, cut loose from old department loyalties, began to work much better together, and customers noticed the difference.

But when the next generation of equipment was needed, there was no one to design it. The best design engineers were busy coming up with incremental new applications that current customers wanted. In addition to breaking up the core engineering group, the reengineering effort had redesigned performance evaluation measures and incentives to reward engineering and marketing people for today's customer satisfaction. For the first time, engineers were getting good bonuses and could relate them to the work they were doing. In this environment, with both customers and employees so happy, the president found it hard to mobilize his organization around the future.

Processes and Disciplines

Horizontal organizations won't survive because they address only half of a company's needs—its processes: managing transactions with the customer from order to delivery, giving better service, developing new products. Today, companies are spending millions on reengineering these processes—and they do need to be fixed. For most companies, breaking old habits and power structures takes a big push. But, ultimately, good enough in horizontal processes is good enough. Like quality in the 1980s, "best practice" processes are table stakes for doing business today. A company can't simply declare victory once it puts its horizontal processes in place.

The reason is simple: great horizontal processes don't make companies great. In telecom transmission equipment, NEC is extremely customer-responsive—with typical Japanese process excellence. But AT&T poured greater effort into creating new technology and is gaining market share against NEC with more truly innovative products. In pharmaceuticals, other competitors have spent more on processes, but it's Glaxo that is envied for its cleverness in defining research priorities and deploying its scientists.

The other half of what companies need is a set of core disciplines: the engineering skill to design state-of-the-art products; the technical expertise to invent out-of-the-box information systems; financial brains, like those at GE Capital, who create the accompanying financial services that differentiate the equipment GE sells. These vertical disciplines replenish the horizontal processes. They provide the professional excellence that elevates a company's processes from best practices to competitive breakthroughs.

In fact, the disciplines are the company's seed corn for its future. While the processes focus on today's customers, the disciplines are inventing the products—and the customers—of tomorrow. You always need people working for the future who aren't absorbed by today's customers. And, despite the brave vocabulary of reengineering, there will always be handoffs—from creators to implementers and from the center to the field.

Horizontal organization isn't the answer because it tries to create what every general manager wants today—the fast-moving, responsive company—through organizational structure. Structure alone cannot do it. In the past, matrix organizations didn't solve the problem. Nor will a horizontal one do so today. The real challenge of building better companies is to intertwine and reinforce the horizontal and vertical dimensions. Achieving this new organization isn't really about structure. It's about infrastructure. Infrastructure is what your people see and feel every day that tells them what really matters. Role models. Location of people. Distribution of rewards. Flow of information. Sense of membership.

Creating the Infrastructure

Companies that build both thriving processes and disciplines do not make it simple for their key people; instead they make it rich. They go beyond structure to infrastructure. They ask their business-unit heads, senior functional people, and key program and process managers to lead the way in integrating the horizontal and vertical dimensions. They follow five ground rules:

- *Build tension into objectives.* Having the industry's fastest customer-delivery lead time will contribute to growth for a couple of years. But beyond that, only innovation will continue the growth. All your key people need to be driven by both objectives.

- *Give senior executives dual roles.* Each functional vice president should either be responsible for one product line's new-product-development process or the health of a business. Our conventional organization charts have made too many key, able people too one-dimensional. Let each senior person wrestle with both dimensions of the organization rather than sit comfortably on just one side of a matrix organization.

- *Emphasize roles along with positions for every manager.* Positions are what you are directly and formally accountable for. Roles cover what you can influence—one steps up to roles.

- *Visibly reward people who contribute in both dimensions.* Don't let rewards be driven wholly by formula incentives. The notion that "you get what you pay for" is one of reengineering's more sterile maxims. It's not that simple. Your best people want to contribute in both dimensions and in uncharted ways. So reward people who step up to new roles for which there are no measures or incentive formulas, and more people will step forward.

- *Remove the one-dimensional barons.* Some want to stay inside their old functional domain. Others get so hooked on the new horizontal world they lose touch with their home base. Both need to get the message they are jeopardizing the company's performance.

American companies are improving their horizontal business performance dramatically. The phone company is getting repairs right the first time. Reengineering is paying dividends by removing obstacles and highlighting interfaces between functions. But it shouldn't try to dominate or eliminate functions. Reengineering is spawning some well-intentioned but simplistic ideas—the horizontal organization, pay people on what you can measure, eliminate all handoffs, and more. If reengineering doesn't recognize what it can and can't do, it will become just another adventure in short-term performance boosting.

THE ACTIVIST CENTER

DENNIS N. RHEAULT AND SIMON P. TRUSSLER, 1995

Is the corporate center dead? An emerging consensus would suggest so. The sentiment goes deeper than the natural impulse—intensified by perennial pressure from Wall Street—to trim bloated bureaucracies. More and more executives are convinced that the traditional functions of the center no longer add value.

Central planning and oversight, the argument goes, make less sense in an era of fast-changing technologies and markets. And information technology and outsourcing have made many centralized support functions unnecessary. Since no one knows the individual businesses as well as the people who run them, better to have a minimalist corporate center that sees to corporate governance, provides a few essential shared services, sets the right objectives, measures, and rewards—and then gets out of the way.

Actually, minimalism may be less the logical consequence of decentralization than a failure of managerial imagination. Some of today's most respected organizations—companies like GE, PepsiCo, and Hewlett-Packard—make strong centers a cornerstone of their managerial practice. These centers are lean, but they aren't minimalist—they're activist.

The Case for Activism

The purpose of the new-style center is to leverage innovation and growth, not to enforce command and control. The very trends that seem to call for a hands-off, minimalist center—fragmenting markets, rapidly changing technologies, faster innovation cycles—probably require the opposite: a corporate center that engages otherwise autonomous business units, stimulating them to transcend the limits of established business-unit boundaries.

Even good managers, running top-performing business units, sometimes let game-changing opportunities pass. They tend, quite naturally, to focus on their own industry and their traditional competitors, missing broader market trends or new competitive threats. An activist center helps ensure that business-unit managers develop and maintain a broad strategic perspective. The center is, after all, the guardian of the company's future. Its job is to encourage, cajole, and sometimes push line managers to look beyond their natural horizons both longer term and across businesses.

In doing so, it contrasts markedly with the old-style center. Rather than imposing a process and an agenda, a few experienced people engage the business units in a dialogue of exploration. At PepsiCo, for example, a small, high-caliber corporate planning staff works with business units to make sure they don't sacrifice long-term strategic thinking for short-term financial goals. And at Hitachi, a central group focuses on the interfaces between business units by identifying new opportunities the business units might miss, thus acting as a catalyst for innovation and organizational evolution.

Even more fundamentally, activist centers are broadening the classic concept of portfolio management. To be sure, these centers take on the traditional—and still necessary—task of allocating cash among the businesses. But they are going much further, applying the same principles to new kinds of resources.

One such resource is the distinctive organizational capabilities that are increasingly central to long-term competitive advantage. An intelligent center can assemble the right portfolio of capabilities and then drive them across the company's businesses. Asea Brown Boveri, for example, has used a small central team to initiate time-based process-improvement programs at all its worldwide companies, as well as to coordinate sharing of the emerging best practices.

Some companies have gone so far as to build an entire business model around the role of aggressively managing the capabilities portfolio. The Newell Corporation, for instance, has developed systems that excel in satisfying the unique and highly demanding requirements for supplying Wal-Mart. Over the past decade, Newell has sustained impressive growth rates by acquiring a series of product-focused companies and then "Newellizing" them by systematically instilling these capabilities.

Another key resource that activist centers manage is the company's portfolio of human talent. Most companies now have the financial measures in place to ensure that business units don't hoard capital, but too few have comparable processes to ensure that business units don't hoard the best people. By actively managing their careers, the center can ensure that the corporation develops leaders with a breadth of experience while at the same time promoting cross-business capabilities transfer.

Building an Activist Center

If activist corporate centers are so important, why do so few companies have them? Many senior executives worry that once they start adding new roles and new people to corporate, they will have taken the first step down a slippery slope and end up losing all the hard-won cost savings of recent years.

That's why the first step in saving corporate is often to destroy it. The process: strip corporate down to the basic governance and compliance functions; take the rest and either streamline it into a shared services arrangement or outsource it; and all the while purge old-style corporate managers. Once bureaucracy and cost are rolled back, companies can rebuild their centers on activist lines.

The next step is to redefine the social contract between the center and the line businesses and to identify the new skills, roles, and career tracks of activist corporate managers. Activism is a tough balancing act. Executives need to know how to support, but also challenge, business unit managers—without undermining either their own credibility or the authority and responsibility of the line.

Getting this balance right requires repopulating the activist center with a small group of the company's most talented individuals. Only accomplished managers with extensive line experience will have the credibility to get senior line executives to buy in and treat the center as a resource rather than as an imposition. Generally, the assignment to corporate is temporary—one stop in a continuous rotation between the center and the business units. And instead of having a fixed brief, these new-style corporate managers focus their attention and energies on a few key priorities at a time. Witness the evolution of GE's strategic planning group, whose composition and focus have shifted repeatedly to support the changing priorities articulated by CEO Jack Welch.

If you are unwilling to routinely cycle a few of your top people into the center, better stick to minimalism. But be prepared to pay the price in timid strategies and underleveraged capabilities and people.

SHAPING UP: THE DELAYERED LOOK

RON NICOL, 2004

Even after all the job cuts of the last few years, many organizations are still out of shape—literally. They have too many layers; there are too many pay levels within those layers, and, not surprisingly, spans of control are too narrow. Companies are too lean in some places and too fat in others.

By layers, we mean the hierarchy of reporting relationships. Levels refer to pay grades. And spans refer to the number of direct reports. The costs to companies of being out of shape are enormous, particularly in terms of reaction time and decision making.

Why, then, are so many companies still out of shape? One reason is that belt-tightening (across-the-board layoffs and department closings), while fast and uncomplicated, is often a blunt and unfair instrument that does little to fix an organization's basic structure. At the other extreme, process redesign, which seeks to change the detail of organizational interactions, is a lengthy approach that often doesn't question whether something really should exist. "Value-based" cost reduction, which also focuses on process activities rather than the interaction of people, is another alternative, but it can miss the big opportunities and still doesn't improve decision making or responsiveness.

Focusing exclusively on delayering at the management level, on the other hand, speeds up both information flows and decision making. Moreover, with leaner managerial ranks and the focus on work rather than coordination, activities that don't deliver value get eliminated.

Jack Welch understood this when he took over at General Electric. He inherited an organization that had at least 12 layers and an average span of control between three and four. Imagine: On average, each manager had only three or four direct reports. Within a few years, there were only six layers at GE, and the average span of control was more than 10. It's clear now that Welch's "strategy" was focused on organization and human resources. Managers may be tired of hearing about the lessons they can learn from GE, but this is one they should remember.

Nonetheless, they would rather forget it. Delayering is certainly not a new idea, but it has been shelved for more complicated schemes because it is hard to let people go when you work directly with them or they are your friends' friends. It is much easier, or at least less personal, to order the elimination of frontline employees. Taking out layers of management, particularly middle management, requires discipline, a willingness to confront sacred cows, and a clear sense of where you want your company, division, or unit to go. Outsiders hesitate to offer help because flattening a steep organizational pyramid is an emotionally bruising process for everyone involved. If it is conducted mechanically or in a way that seems unfair or inconsistent, the delayering process can damage relationships across an organization.

Mapping the Problem

So, how do you do this right? First, find out if you really have a problem. Conduct a detailed analysis of the layers, levels, and spans in your organization. The data exist in your company to help you assemble—within a few weeks—a picture like the one shown in the exhibit below. You may be surprised by what you see.

The exhibit—before and after snapshots of a large company—shows that before delayering, no fewer than 18 officers were separated from the CEO by 4 reporting layers, almost 40 percent of the company's managers were 8 or more layers deep, and more than 800 people were in reporting chains of 11 or 12 layers. (Imagine how fast decisions got made in this company.) What's more, middle management had the narrowest spans of control, not the top or bottom layers. This is typical. In most cases, the CEO is well aware of the top few layers, so the spans are usually good. And the bottom of the organization is lean as a result of traditional cost cutting. But the middle ranks of management seem to remain immune to shape-up efforts.

Assembling a picture like this allows you to see what kind of organizational challenge you face and the value of reshaping the pyramid. In the company illustrated in the exhibit, management decreased the layers from 12 to 8 and achieved savings of roughly 30 percent. If flattening the organization will produce savings of 10 percent or less, you don't have a big problem—at least not one worth solving with delayering. Just assign your managers to reduce costs in the course of their budget execution. But if your excess structure represents more than 10 percent of excess costs, then you need to consider a more formal process that will maintain morale and retain the right people.

Keep this reality in mind: Any process that aims to restructure an organization by taking out significant numbers of people can't be executed without an iron will. That means CEO ownership of and commitment to a fact-based and transparent approach. There is no

One company's changing profile: Reducing layers and increasing spans.

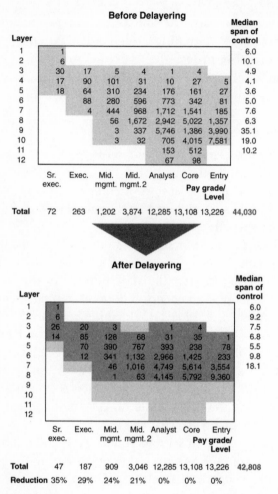

Before Delayering

Layer	Sr. exec.	Exec.	Mid. mgmt.	Mid. mgmt.2	Analyst	Core	Entry	Median span of control
1	1							6.0
2	6							10.1
3	30	17	5	4	1	4		4.9
4	17	90	101	31	10	27	5	4.1
5	18	64	310	234	176	161	27	3.6
6		88	280	596	773	342	81	5.0
7		4	444	968	1,712	1,541	185	7.6
8			56	1,672	2,942	5,022	1,357	6.3
9			3	337	5,746	1,386	3,990	35.1
10			3	32	705	4,015	7,581	19.0
11					153	512		10.2
12					67	98		
Total	72	263	1,202	3,874	12,285	13,108	13,226	44,030

Pay grade/Level

After Delayering

Layer	Sr. exec.	Exec.	Mid. mgmt.	Mid. mgmt.2	Analyst	Core	Entry	Median span of control
1	1							6.0
2	6							9.2
3	26	20	3		1	4		7.5
4	14	85	128	68	31	35	1	6.8
5		70	390	767	393	238	78	5.5
6		12	341	1,132	2,966	1,425	233	9.8
7			46	1,016	4,749	5,614	3,554	18.1
8			1	63	4,145	5,792	9,360	
9								
10								
11								
12								
Total	47	187	909	3,046	12,285	13,108	13,226	42,808
Reduction	35%	29%	24%	21%	0%	0%	0%	

Pay grade/Level

SOURCE: BCG analysis.

such thing as a covert reorganization. Treat your employees like adults and be clear about the what, the why, and the how of the delayering process.

Debate the issue with your top team and then establish some principles such as the following to guide the process:

1. We are not a democracy—all decisions are subject to senior management's approval.

2. Our commitments, once we agree on them, are set in stone.

3. We will deal in an open and direct fashion on all issues.

4. We will restructure to create competitive advantage.

5. We will complete all organizational changes by a certain date.

6. We will count cost reductions only when the costs are off the books.

7. We will put together the best team (the lowest performers will have to leave).

8. We will execute quickly without taking shortcuts that undermine success.

9. We will use the same process and timing throughout the company.

10. If we violate any of our principles, we will be required to change them.

A Cascading Process

Organizations are geometric structures and therefore require a geometrically scalable process to redesign them. Senior executives who think they can redesign a major corporation over a weekend are fooling themselves, considering that everything two layers below them recedes into a fog. The best way to delayer an organization is for managers to participate in a cascading process. The people who are closest to the problems are best able to solve them, and when senior management sets the right example, others will follow. All this means that you start the delayering process at the top, not at the bottom.

One objection we hear to this approach is that it will take too long and reduce productivity because it increases uncertainty. On the contrary, well-communicated processes result in less disruption and better execution than blitzkrieg reorganizations, which rarely work.

Delayering is an honest, effective, and empowering way of reducing costs while speeding up decision making. The goal is to put the right people in place and let them make decisions about what is important. Delayering looks to the future, not just at the present. After getting the structure right, there are fewer "jump balls," less confusion over who follows up, increased responsiveness to customers, and, in general, cleaner ways of doing business.

Delayering's success rests on a couple of hypotheses. The first is that increased spans of control force managers to do their jobs differently. If you have just three or four direct reports, you will be tempted to meddle and micromanage. But if you have 15 reports, you have time to do only two things: Communicate your goals and manage exceptions. Effective management requires trust in your reports and an ability to focus on the trouble spots. The second hypothesis is that breaking down hierarchy sets the stage for the formation of networks that cut across processes and functions, and that these networks, properly engaged and motivated, are the key to superior performance.

Flattening the pyramid is just the first step, but arguably the toughest one, toward leaving a legacy of organizational readiness and agility—a legacy far more important than any particular strategy or market position.

A SURVIVOR'S GUIDE TO ORGANIZATION REDESIGN *

Felix Barber, D. Grant Freeland, and David Brownell, 2002

Few people associate redesigning organizations with survival. But the fate of companies and their employees can hinge on how a redesign is approached. All too often, major organization redesigns create little, if any, value. In many cases, they actually rob value, frustrate managers, and lower employee morale.

How does a company not just survive an organization redesign but flourish? Four building blocks will ensure success. (See Exhibit 1.)

Identify the Right Business Issues

Too often, executives despair midway through a redesign. What are we really trying to achieve, they ask, and why did we choose this approach? These executives have skipped the crucial first step in a redesign: identifying the business issues and translating them into goals.

Good design springs from good strategy. You need to understand how you want to compete, where you make money, and what organiza-

---

* An edited version of the original 2002 publication.

Exhibit 1   Getting organization design right.

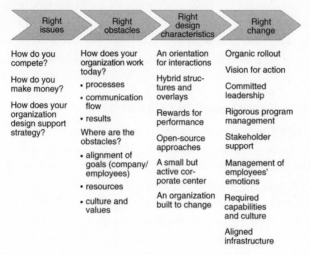

Right issues	Right obstacles	Right design characteristics	Right change
How do you compete? How do you make money? How does your organization design support strategy?	How does your organization work today? • processes • communication flow • results Where are the obstacles? • alignment of goals (company/ employees) • resources • culture and values	An orientation for interactions Hybrid structures and overlays Rewards for performance Open-source approaches A small but active corporate center An organization built to change	Organic rollout Vision for action Committed leadership Rigorous program management Stakeholder support Management of employees' emotions Required capabilities and culture Aligned infrastructure

SOURCE: BCG analysis.

tional levers will enhance performance. You might ask, for example, How important is leveraging global opportunities? How critical is cost to shareholder value? Where are the synergies across the business portfolio? The questions raised by a functional redesign are equally strategic. When it comes to redesigning a salesforce, for instance, you need to understand where customers get value from your company, how they buy, and what opportunities are not being fully exploited.

Consider what a leading industrial company uncovered during a strategy review preceding an organizational change. The company was already one of the world's leading shareholder-value creators. The existing business-unit organization was working well, and management was reluctant to change it. However, opportunities to improve performance within the units had hit a plateau. The strategy review identified three opportunities to improve profits that cut across business unit boundaries: cross-selling to existing customers, increasing asset utilization by sharing production facilities, and lowering costs by more effectively transferring best practices. How could the opportunities be exploited without disrupting the existing, highly effective business-unit structure?

The company concluded that so-called network overlays, which wouldn't require changes in the existing structure, could address both cross-selling and best-practice transfers. Moreover, these overlays would benefit all business units. Sharing production facilities, by contrast, would be painful for those units that would lose control over their own production. So rather than attempt a wholesale reform of the production organization, the company decided to mandate them from the center. It also resolved to give the center an activist role in identifying and implementing critical synergy opportunities in the future.

Pinpoint the Right Underlying Obstacles

Once you have identified the right business issues, how do you know what it will take to address them? Sometimes the problem is a misalignment of goals and performance measures—in effect, people do what is inspected, not what is expected. It may be that there are insufficient resources or that the company's values and culture are getting in the way. Unless you look at the combined impact of incentives, culture, resource allocation, and information flows, recommendations will often address symptoms instead of causes.

A major pharmaceutical company recently observed that the marketing units did not work well together. The initial thinking was that the marketing teams simply lacked an adequate common mechanism for coordination. In fact, the underlying problem was worse: The teams had objectives and incentives that encouraged them to compete with one another. Until the company changed those objectives and incentives, coordination mechanisms would fail. (See Exhibit 2.)

Exhibit 2   Identifying causes, not just symptoms.

A Case of Competition, Not Cooperation

Questions	Marketing's Answers
Why don't the marketing teams work together?	We don't have time.
But when you do have time?	Our products are not related.
But you sell to a common set of customers?	We are all structured differently.
So if you were structured in the same way, you would work together?	Well, no, because we all sell through the same sales force, so I need to maximize my share of voice.
So if you win, others lose?	Yes. I'm interested in getting my products sold, even at the expense of others.

SOURCE: BCG analysis.

Adopt the Right Design Characteristics

There is no such thing as a "perfect" organization design. But some designs clearly won't work. Successful redesigns manage the trade-offs inherent in any choice as well as the people affected by that choice. They also respond to three powerful forces driving today's economy. First, the basic nature of business is evolving: Industries are becoming increasingly global, companies are depending increasingly on information gathering and exchange, and value chains are deconstructing at an accelerated pace. Second, the workforce is evolving: Employees are more qualified, more mobile, and have greater career expectations. Third, the route to competitive advantage has changed, hinging now on achieving greater speed, leveraging capabilities, and capturing scale both in corporate knowledge and in costs. (See Exhibit 3.) These forces have produced a common set of characteristics that can guide any organization redesign.

An Orientation for Interactions

While structure is necessary in any organization, a redesign should focus on other aspects of how people work together—their objectives, capabilities, roles and responsibilities, and the information flows and incentives that support them. Managers need to work together within their own function or business unit *and* across organizational boundaries. This work is more difficult and time-consuming—and provides

Exhibit 3   Organization design characteristics.

SOURCE: BCG analysis.

less instant gratification—than redrawing lines and boxes on white-boards. But you neglect the forces that drive employee behavior at your own peril.

Hybrid Structures and Overlays

Forget about rigid, symmetrical structures. Companies require a variety of forms to reflect economic and organizational reality. (See Exhibit 4.)

Consider the global redesign of a supply chain. The business economics vary depending on the stage of the value chain—and so should the form. In the example in Exhibit 4, sales forecasting requires deep local knowledge and a strong commitment from the local organization, and should be relatively decentralized. And since speed to market is important, distribution should also be organized locally. By contrast, production planning and manufacturing, given their scale and reach, should be organized more globally. A hybrid structure would work best, with sales forecasting and distribution reporting to country managers and production reporting to heads of European, U.S., and Asian production.

Exhibit 4   Economics and organizational realities often support a supply chain's hybrid structure.

SOURCE: BCG analysis.

Hybrid structures also help companies cope with organizational realities that go beyond business economics. For global companies that derive most of their sales from the United States, the heads of some business units may realistically need more control and power than others.

Organizational structure tends to channel and constrain value creation. Structures exist to provide formal decision-making authority, a function that is both necessary and valuable. But increasingly, value creation crosses structural boundaries through network overlays and hybrid structures. Some examples include shared-service centers for otherwise independent businesses, cross-customer sales teams, and best-practice-sharing groups. Whatever the form, success depends on aligned goals and incentives, a culture of cooperation, an effective infrastructure for knowledge sharing, and clarity about decision-making.

Rewards for Performance

Individuals and business units need to be rewarded for performance. Accordingly, many companies have successfully adopted highly variable incentive programs for individuals throughout the organization. These programs are not confined to such special cases as investment banking and biotech start-ups but also exist in basic industries such as steel minimills and fashion retailing, where shop floor workers and sales personnel, respectively, receive incentives.

To introduce performance incentives, you must measure performance. Companies are now linking prices to the outside market. Such systems now permit these new business units to measure performance when supplying goods and services to one another.

Open-Source Approaches

As corporate walls fall, companies are exploring novel, "open" approaches to organization. Customers and supplier integration is a key to adding business value. Such integration can take the form of traditional supply-chain linkages between, say, inventory data and production. Conversely, once a company is divided into many small business units, it is easy to redefine boundaries and outsource certain activities by spinning off business units and buying back their services. Some companies are combining the benefits of both closer supplier links and outsourcing by building a common industry supply-chain platform with competitors to lower costs. The joint purchasing and design exchange of the major automobile manufacturers is one such successful effort.

A Small but Active Corporate Center

In many companies, the corporate center is drowning in "administrivia," overseeing everything from tax, legal, and finance functions to the synthesizing of business activities. Many of these tasks would be better performed either at the business unit level or in a shared-service operation. The most effective centers are those with the resources and capabilities to manage senior talent, disseminate best practices, drive major change efforts, and define and drive strategy.

An Organization Built to Change

Given the evolutionary forces at play, change is now a constant—and a company has to institutionalize the capacity to remake itself. Business units can manage some change efforts, but there often is a need for mechanisms that are linked to but outside of the nuts-and-bolts operational structure. This is especially true of the need to foster ideas critical for future growth but potentially disruptive to the existing business. Some examples include temporarily establishing incubators for hatching such ideas and assigning the task of directing long-term change to certain top executives. Approaches that are more radical include separating the roles of chairman and CEO, deliberately duplicating R&D activities to create internal competition, and empowering internal-audit and business-development functions to ensure a second opinion on key quality and strategy issues.

Implement Change the Right Way

Successful organization redesigns—particularly those that seek dramatic, long-term change—tend to be implemented more organically than mechanically. A test-and-learn mentality often prevails. For example, a global automotive company pioneered shared services in finance, human resources, and other support functions by first piloting the new organization. It did not change formal reporting lines until employees were confident that the new processes could deliver.

A successful redesign requires clear vision, committed leadership, and exacting project management. That is just for openers. The company also must ensure that key stakeholders are involved in and support the process. It must also monitor the emotional response of its employees from the outset of the redesign. If they are consulted too late, employees will almost certainly react negatively, and the redesign effort may not survive. The price of such a failure will be high in financial terms but its cost on people will be even higher.

Leadership and Change

CHANGE IS THE very essence of the business leader's job. Sensing the need, identifying the direction and magnitude of change required, convincing and inspiring the organization, blowing away the obstacles—this is what real leaders do. Most find it excruciatingly difficult.

The *Perspectives* in this section explore two themes. The first is the tension between the conflicting organizational needs for stability and change. On the one hand, for companies of any size, some degree of stability is essential to the effective execution of strategy. On the other hand, competitive environments are notoriously fluid, and organizations must adapt or face extinction. But to do that, they must change the way they operate and, even more fundamentally, their very self-concept. The first four pieces in this section explore how leaders do this.

The second theme is the evolving nature of the relationship between leaders and their organizations. Command and control just doesn't work anymore. Getting change to occur is as urgent as it ever was, but requires greater subtlety.

The last seven pieces in this subpart explore how leaders instill organizational learning, and how they orchestrate the interactions necessary to effect change. John Clarkeson's "Jazz vs. Symphony" and Jeanie Duck's *The Change Monster* (Crown Business, 2001), in particular, are pioneering classics.

WHY CHANGE IS SO DIFFICULT

BRUCE D. HENDERSON, 1967

Success in the past always becomes enshrined in the present by the over-valuation of the policies and attitudes that accompanied that success. As long as the environment and competitive behavior do not change, these beliefs and policies contribute to the stability of the firm.

However, with time these attitudes become embedded in a system of beliefs, traditions, taboos, habits, customs, and inhibitions that constitute the distinctive culture of that firm. Such cultures are as distinctive as the cultural differences between nationalities or the personality differences between individuals. They do not adapt to change very easily.

These characteristics are deep-seated and difficult to change. Frequently, this means that the organization becomes the prisoner of its own past success. Such individual characteristics become so much a part of the firm that any effort to change them is quite likely to be viewed as an attack upon the organization itself.

Examples of these observations are a matter of common experience:

- The sharp and painful adjustments when two comparable organizations merge are the inevitable consequences of the differences in corporate style and culture.

- When a new chief executive is appointed from outside the organization, one of two actions will follow. There will either be a substantial period with little change while he gets to know the organization, or there will be a period of considerable stress and perhaps personnel turnover while a new corporate culture is being evolved.

These problems of change cannot be avoided, however. All organizations, like all organisms, must adapt to changes in their environment or die. All organizations *do* change when put under sufficient pressure. This pressure must either be external to the organization or be the result of very strong leadership.

It is rare for any organization to generate sufficient pressure internally from the ranks to produce significant change in direction. To do so is likely to be regarded as a form of dissatisfaction with the organization's leadership. To change by evolution rather than revolution, the change must not only be tolerated, but actively guided and directed in very explicit terms by the leadership of the firm.

In this process the corporate leadership faces major dilemmas. The organization's investment in the status quo is always a heavy one. This is almost inherent in the definition of a culture. Changes in policy and strategy are inherently threatening, producing a whole series of changes in objectives, values, status values, and hierarchy arrangements. Jobs, rank, and many cherished beliefs are put in jeopardy.

Most of the organization is not in a position to see the needs for policy and organization change until long after the optimum time for action has passed. Corporate culture tends to blind an organization to a need for change until the organization as a whole can accept the reality of the need. But when the need is so obvious that the whole organization can recognize it, competitive advantage in flexibility and speed of response has been lost.

On the other hand, if an effort is made before there is a general awareness of the need, it endangers the very ability to lead. Any fundamental change in corporate policy is almost certain to be regarded by a significant part of the organization as irrational. No matter how sound the change may be, it is at some point rooted in a nonprovable, intuitive concept of the relative values of a complex of factors affecting the future. There will always be a large part of the organization that does not perceive these values in the same way and therefore considers the change unwarranted and a reflection on the leadership's ability to make reasonable decisions.

It is obvious, as well, that major changes in policy have far-reaching consequences that dictate caution and conservatism. The attitude toward change is always conservative or reactionary until both the reasons for the change and the consequences are clearly defined. This is an impossible set of preconditions for most policy changes. Any significant change produces a train of interrelated and often unanticipated corollary changes. Each policy has been keyed to others, and changes in one require a reevaluation of the related policies. Too much readiness to change policies leads to a complete restructuring of the corporate edifice, with all the cost and confusion incident to any major reconstruction.

Not only the organization, but the leadership itself, incurs considerable risk by changing policy. By definition, a policy is applied to decisions in the future. To be valid the policies must be based on assumptions about the conditions and competition in the future.

These assumptions in turn are based on other assumptions. At some point, the needed information becomes so problematical and conditional that further fact finding and analysis is unrewarding, and the decision becomes intuitive.

Such decisions on major issues constitute a severe exposure risk. The apparent verities of the past successes must be abandoned for unproven policies based on uncertain data. And to the risk of failure from incorrect choice must be added the risk of failure in leadership because the organization just does not see the need for the change. Even the best-chosen risks may prove to be fatal to the current leadership if the consequences are unprovable in fact.

All the forces of corporate culture are set against change. Yet the rewards can be substantial for those managements who have strong enough leadership to both anticipate the change required and manage the evolution. The competitive advantages of superior strategy will be available only to those managements that can make major shifts in policy *before* the need or the purpose becomes obvious to their organization as a whole or to their competitors.

There are at least three major requirements of management who expect to outperform their competition. The first is to conceive and make explicit a superior strategy. The second is to provide the leadership required to overcome the obstacles to change. The third, and often critical one, is to provide that leadership at a time when the organization as a whole would ordinarily oppose the changes required.

LEADERSHIP

BRUCE D. HENDERSON, 1966

There are three fundamentally different executive functions. The first is preservation of the organization. The second is control of organization response to deviations from expectations. The third is planning future expectations. All of these are made possible by the personal qualities of leadership.

The essence of leadership is the ability to change the organization's conception of ideal performance. The strength of leadership can be measured by the rate at which these ideals are changed. The quality of leadership is reflected by the wisdom used in choosing the new ideals. The initial test of leadership skill is in the choice of the inescapable compromise between speed of change and security of the leader's ability to lead.

Management can be distinguished from leadership. The management function deals with what the organization ought to do. The leadership function deals with motivation of the organization to do that which it ought to do. Normally, the two functions are so interrelated that the differences are not recognized even by the leader-manager himself. However, in very strong manager-leader combinations, the difference may become clearly apparent to the manager-leader because of the obvious compromise required between what good management dictates and what continued leadership will permit.

Both good management and strong leadership require clearly defined goals and objectives. Good management will produce worthy goals, and good leadership will rapidly obtain organization acceptance and motivation toward these goals.

In a business organization, good and strong leaders will do these things:

1. Gain complete and willing acceptance of their leadership.

2. Determine business goals, objectives, and standards of behavior that are as ambitious as the potential abilities of the organization will permit.

3. Introduce and motivate the organization to accept as its own these privately established objectives. The rate of introduction will be the maximum consistent with maintenance of the acceptance of the leadership. This need for acceptance is why the new manager must always go slowly except in emergencies. In emergencies, the boss must not go slowly if he is to maintain leadership.

4. Change the organization relationships internally as necessary to facilitate both the acceptance and accomplishment of the new objectives.

The strengths and weaknesses of different types of managers can be observed with reference to these things.

Some managers are unable to get past the first hurdle to become accepted as leaders of their organizations. They may be managers in title but not leaders. Their organizations fight them on every change.

They are told only that which they ask. Their followers feel "the boss doesn't understand."

Before a leader can lead he must first belong. He, more than anyone else, must live up to the ideals and standards the group has already previously accepted. If he cannot do this, he cannot lead, no matter what his ability or power. For these reasons, leaders are strong or weak only with reference to specific groups. The leader leads only with respect to the group that will accept him first as a member and then as first among them.

Other managers fail even though they are fully and willingly accepted as the leader. They fail because they do not lead anywhere. They conform to the group's norms and standards; in fact, they defend and preserve the status quo. Their leadership can remain secure provided the group standards do not call for the leader to promote or initiate change. With such a manager the leadership survives but the organization eventually dies because of its failure to adapt to a changing world.

Some managers fail even though they are accepted as leaders and actively lead their organizations. They fail because of faulty or inadequate goals and objectives. This is an intellectual failure, not a spiritual one. This is lack of managerial vision, not lack of courage or willingness, and is one of the most difficult of all managerial failures to detect because the strength of leadership hides its own weakness.

Partial failure is still common where leadership is accepted, where goals are wisely chosen, and where leadership is vigorous. The cause is a less-than-optimum choice between rate of progress and leadership security. This failure is not absolute; it is a comparative failure. It is a failure to do as well as it is possible to do. The leader who leads too rapidly loses his leadership; the one who leads too slowly just does not get there as fast. Like driving on a mountain road, the penalty is extreme for loss of control. As in racing, the stress on the driver is very great at maximum speeds. Most leaders just do not take the risks required for maximum results. Many do not attempt anything like maximum performance because of the stress and strain they experience.

Even when a leader has done everything else, he may fall short of the best possible performance by failure to adapt his organization relationships to the current objectives, needs, and resources. This again is a technical handicap in a comparative sense rather than an absolute failure. It is a removable limitation on performance. However, the correct decision is a highly intuitive and subjective decision. The ideal organization, even in a static situation with idealized people, would be difficult enough to formulate; with flesh-and-blood people in a dynamic situation, the optimum organization relationships are virtually unknowable. The inevitable cost of change and the temporary loss in effectiveness must be balanced against the hoped-for benefits. The disturbance in the informal relationships will certainly reduce the leader's acceptance and control, at least temporarily. The hoped-for benefits are based on projected behavior of people, which can never be fully predictable. The benefits will be effective at a time in the future when the situation may be quite different from that now visualized. The net advantage of organization change is most difficult to determine, and the known costs are usually great. Therefore, many leaders cling to the known versus the unknown at the risk of their potential performance.

Being an effective leader and manager has some of the same requirements as being a winning poker player. A knowledge of the odds is indispensable. Ability to intuitively sense others' attitudes is also indispensable. Adequate working capital must first be acquired before any major risks can be taken. Properly choosing balance in calculating risk versus reward is essential.

Good management sees the opportunity and what must be done to grasp it. Good leadership chooses the right timing and speed of implementation while developing an organization that not only can but wants to achieve those objectives.

HOW TO RECOGNIZE THE NEED FOR CHANGE

CARL W. STERN, 1983

Change is a fact of business life. Organizations, like organisms, must adapt or die. Neither course is comfortable. In its operations, an organization evolves a way of thinking about itself, its competitors, and the environment with which it and they must cope. It conceives of itself as playing a game under well-defined rules against a set of easily identifiable opponents, each pursuing well-understood strategies. Since this model has the effect of imposing order on chaos, it first rationalizes and ultimately governs behavior within the organization. The internal culture will tend to resist any challenge to the model or the assumptions underlying it, even when conditions change. Yet adaptation requires that an organization be weaned from outdated conceptions.

The stakes are high. Take, for example, the personal financial services industry. Few days seem to pass in which the *Wall Street Journal* fails to announce a new product, a new competitor, an arrangement among competitors to offer a new package of services, or a merger. How is a bank to view Merrill Lynch's Cash Management Account? How is Merrill Lynch to view Charles Schwab? How is a mutual life insurance company to view a host of new offerings, from ever cheaper term insurance to E.F. Hutton's universal life? How are any of the participants to view the many mergers, consummated or proposed? And how are they to view the widely anticipated changes in the regulatory structure of the industry? It is difficult for the traditional competitor to know how to think about these developments, much less to formulate a response.

Wholesale rethinking of strategy in response to every minor competitive or environmental perturbation robs an organization of its sense of direction and its operational effectiveness. Failure to adapt at critical turning points threatens its viability. Distinguishing the latter from the former is easy after the fact: Failure to adapt leads to deterioration in financial results. By that time, however, it is generally too late to take effective remedial action. Management needs an early warning system that highlights those fundamental threats to which the organization must respond.

Competitive Stability

A useful approach is to characterize the conditions that make for stability, and then to identify potential destabilizing influences. Competitive conditions will tend to be relatively stable in businesses where:

- Barriers around the business and between segments are well defined and high.

- Relative competitive positions within segments are well established and defensible.

While competition is almost by definition never totally stable—there are always skirmishes among competitors, often across segment boundaries—these conditions allow competitors to play the game they know under the established ground rules without fear of intrusion.

Destabilizing Influences

A useful early warning system is one that will identify nascent threats to these conditions for competitive stability. Because the attendant

self-examination is painful, disruptive, and therefore generally coun-
tercultural, the organization's operating systems rarely prove equal to
the task. A combination of vigilance and vision is requisite. It thus
falls to top management to be alert to the critical warning signals:

From the marketplace

- Have you lost control over your pricing? Have you recently led a
  price increase and been unable to make it stick? Have you
  recently been unable to sustain your customary price premium?
- Have you experienced swings in volume beyond those explain-
  able by cyclical demand fluctuations?
- Is part of your market under pressure from substitute products or services?
- Have you recently lost major accounts? With particular characteristics or needs? To particular competitors? To backward
  or forward integration?

From the channels

- Have your distributors' margins deteriorated? Have the
  channels' economics changed in such a way as to threaten their
  viability?
- Have they had to broaden their lines to defend their competitive position or to supplement their income?
- Have you experienced an abnormal incidence of defection?

From competitors

- Has a traditional competitor been gaining market share? Across
  the board or through a particular focus? Using what tactics?
- Have new competitors entered? Where do they come from: a
  complementary industry? overseas? On what part of the market are they focusing, and what tactics are they employing?

From your financials

- Does the historical relationship between volume and profitability no longer hold?
- Have you experienced a cost/price squeeze?

From your organization

- Are your systems no longer capable of answering the questions
  you deem most relevant? Or do they give you misleading or
  erroneous signals?

- Do you sense that your organization has lost a measure of its responsiveness? Its morale?
- Have you experienced an unusual defection of key personnel? Is it concentrated on those closest to the marketplace?

From your intuition

- Have you lost confidence in its reliability?
- Have many of your recent intuitive decisions proven wrong?

These signals—some subtle and some obvious—should alert management to the possibility that a threat to competitive stability may be impending.

At minimum, these signals should motivate a diagnosis of the underlying destabilizing influences. A number of areas will bear investigation. On the one hand, the signals may herald a fundamental shift in demand patterns due, for example, to demographic or macroeconomic factors, the emergence of new market segments, or the introduction of substitute products. On the other hand, they may denote a shift in the value-added structure of the business, perhaps as a result of technology affecting the economics of production or delivery.

Such developments generally erode the barriers that have traditionally protected the business and its segment structure. They almost inevitably alter the established balance among competitors. They therefore require a response: often a change in the organization's very basis of competition.

SUSTAINED SUCCESS

ALAN J. ZAKON AND RICHARD K. LOCHRIDGE, 1984

We all need to progress, to achieve, to seek a greater goal. Yet the more successful we are, the harder it is to find the "what next."

Earnings and return on investment are the scorecards of past success. A portfolio of strong and advantaged competitive positions that translate into strong financial performance is the base of current success. But what of the future? What signs are there that success will be repeated?

The Lure of Growth

The most visible sign of future success is market growth. The opportunities are clear, and the only question is whether competitive advantage can be gained—and held. For this reason, managers and shareholders alike seek growing markets. Yet we know that few competitors win, and that pure growth markets are the exception, not the rule, in mature economies.

Sustained success appears easiest, therefore, for companies in large, growing markets. But progress is necessary for all of us, not just those in growth markets. We must build, manage, and gain advantage. Having done so once, we must do it all over again. But this does not necessarily require an all-out assault on new (or unfamiliar high-technology) markets.

A recent study of the 500 fastest-growing private U.S. companies provides dramatic insight. Thirty-one of these companies reached $25 million in revenues by 1982, and all have grown at least 50 percent per year since 1978. Only seven are in high technology. Twenty-four are transforming mature businesses, ranging from shoe manufacturing to agriculture to financial services. They are innovating by approaching old businesses in new ways.

Organize for Success

Sustained success requires most organizations to continually find new opportunities in mature markets. We must find new organizational vehicles that will focus our attention on sustained success, as well as manage what we have today. Unfortunately, it is axiomatic that organization structure is developed to execute current business strategies, not to seek new strategic opportunities.

Corporate strategy is more than the summation of individual business strategies. Corporate strategy must provide for tomorrow's success as well as today's. For this reason the corporate organization is different from each business organization. Corporate organization requires a unifying theme that highlights where the overall company is and what the next strategic challenge will be. It must recognize the management needs of each business unit, the skills required for success in it, and the need for transitions.

Successful business units pass through four phases in their development toward maturity. Each phase is most fundamentally different from the others in orientation.

Phase	Goal
Creation	Finding the opportunity
Growth	Making it real
Advantage	Gaining competitive position
Efficiency	Tying it down

Each of these phases—and orientations—requires a different set of management skills, imperatives, and focus. Success within one phase is necessary for survival, but does not guarantee transition to the next.

Sustained success requires managing the transitions between phases. Competitors who do not see the transitions fall by the wayside. This is, in part, a question of skills and attention. It is also a question of orientation, goals, and values, as reflected in organization.

Low-calorie beer was a brilliant insight in the creation phase, but did not succeed until Miller added the skills and attention needed for growth. Xerox built a worldwide business, but Ricoh found a cost-effective strategy to attack a segment with efficiency.

Creation of opportunity rests on entrepreneurial skills—and people. Successful businesses are founded by entrepreneurs, grown by marketers, made great by strategists, and fine-tuned by administrators. The complex of orientations, goals, and success skills becomes the organizational values. The more powerful the values in each orientation phase, the more difficult the transition. In part, this is "the way we do things" in the culture.

In a more concrete sense, corporate culture is the information collected and acted upon for each orientation, the quantitative measure of achievement for each goal, the skills rewarded in money and promotion for each phase, as well as "the way we do things" for each value.

	Phase			
	Creation	*Growth*	*Advantage*	*Efficiency*
Orientation	World	Market	Competition	Internal
Goal	Find the opportunity	Make it real	Gain competitive position	Tie it down
Skills	Inventor	Marketer	Strategist	Administrator
Measures	New business	Growth	Relative position	Return on investment
Transition skills	→	Building →	Strategy →	Operations

Orientation phases and transition skills.

Manage Transitions

Of all the ideas presented, only a few are built into businesses. This explains why successful entrepreneurs are so highly rewarded and praised. But business can be grown into bankruptcy unless competitive advantage is gained and maintained. This explains why so many businesses fail. The transition skill required from growth to advantage is strategy, and the change from building to strategy is difficult for most organizations.

Once advantage is captured, the next transition is often much easier—perhaps too easy. Organization structure moves from loose to increasingly hierarchical and rigid. The internalization of "the way we do things" becomes even stronger:

Action plans become rules of thumb.

Rules of thumb become beliefs.

Beliefs become norms.

Each business—and the corporation—becomes larger as ideas become businesses and businesses grow and mature. Transitions then become not only harder, but more risky. Efficiency has a way of depressing innovation. The fourth transition skill is innovation.

The Adaptive Organization

Managing an adaptive organization is far more than managing a business within each phase. Managing within a phase is structured by clear orientation, goals, success skills, and measurements of success. Managing adaptation is attending to the transitions from phase to phase.

Managing adaptation requires understanding that all four phases must exist simultaneously in a vital corporation. Whenever the orientation, goals, skills, and measurements of any one phase become the dominant corporate values, change will cease to occur. Thus we see the great tension between efficiency and innovation in many companies today. Innovations come too often from outside the company, even in our strongest businesses. Perhaps they especially come from outside in our strongest businesses.

Great businesses should come from great corporations. Large companies can and will innovate. All it requires is:

- Managing transitions as well as businesses

- Making the culture tangible to see what it is, what it should be, and what to change

- Internalizing the fact that vitality depends on finding and acting on opportunities in all of our businesses, even if the ideas come from the outside

- A willingness to compete with ourselves, for if we don't, someone else will

Change is never easy, but we need not make it harder by locking ourselves into the success pattern of one phase. We all want to be professionals and do things right and better. At the same time we must remind ourselves that management means vision as well as professionalism. While we manage today's business, we must see the next phase clearly and build a road map for transition.

This is sustained success.

STRATEGY AND LEARNING

SEYMOUR TILLES, 1985

In a fast-changing industry, learning and strategy are so tightly linked that they are virtually synonymous. Effective strategy cannot be determined unless the senior executive group understands in detail the changes taking place in the competitive system and their implications for future competitive advantage.

The most difficult aspects of learning in connection with strategy are:

- Letting go of obsolete concepts
- Creating the relationships between people that make learning feasible
- Appreciating rates of change
- Developing a systems perspective

Letting Go of Obsolete Concepts

Old concepts are very sticky. It is hard to let go of them, which effectively inhibits new learning.

Will Rogers is reported to have said, "It ain't what you don't know that hurts—it's what you know that ain't so." That summarizes well a common deterrent to adaptation: a set of beliefs that is no longer appropriate to the company's reality.

All companies operate with a set of assumptions about how the business works. It is this set of assumptions, typically the result of long years of experience in the industry, that determines corporate behavior. These beliefs, once rooted, are persistent, and they lead to manifestations of the classic symptoms of prejudice: rejection of data not consistent with prior beliefs and a strong reluctance to experiment. As a result, previously successful strategies have a high probability of being pursued long after they have ceased to be appropriate. For example:

- As the proportion of standard cars in the U.S. market continued to decline, the U.S. automotive industry resisted a major thrust toward small cars because, "The American public likes a large car."
- Howard Johnson created a successful formula for a highway-oriented family restaurant that was not changed until long after

the demographics and the travel patterns of U.S. families indicated that it was no longer appropriate. As a result, it has been totally eclipsed by more aggressive and innovative competitors.

- With rapid growth in world trade over the past 40 years, many U.S. companies have been seriously disadvantaged by their inability to shift soon enough from a domestic system to a worldwide system. Particularly glaring examples are the major rust bowl industries, including steel, auto parts, and machine tools.

- Even the formidable IBM has been late in responding to the transition from centralized data processing to an office environment characterized by networking and compatible equipment. The greater the past success, the greater the challenge of potential change.

The basic step in promoting corporate adaptation is to recognize that the old belief system is no longer working and that a new one is required. For this to occur, senior executives need to be encouraged to make the old belief system explicit, so that its continued utility can be appraised.

Our experience suggests that when the old beliefs are replaced with new ones, effective adaptive behavior quickly follows.

Creating the Relationships That Make Learning Feasible

Whether learning is feasible within a company is critically sensitive to the character of existing relationships between people. Effective organizational learning is necessarily a joint activity. It can take place only if those who normally work together can contemplate a joint exploratory activity. Necessarily, this will include:

- The relationship between the chief executive and his immediate subordinates
- The relationship between peer senior executives
- The relationship between executive groups and potential sources of support

The relationship between the chief executive and his subordinates: If real executive learning is to take place, the chief executive must set the pace.

There is a Gresham's law of executive behavior that causes the urgent to drive out the important. Without a strong executive example to lend some urgency to the learning effort, it will inevitably be crowded out of executive calendars. We have never been part of a major learning effort that was not personally sponsored by the chief executive or by a division manager within his own division.

Some time ago, the chief executive of one of our client companies, an old organization in a mature industry, said to his six key subordinates: "We are jointly going to spend one-third of our time creating a corporate strategy. You have three months to make the arrangements necessary to allow you to do this."

Within a year, the group had created a major new business that remains an important part of the company's overall position.

The relationship between peers: If effective strategy is to be developed, it must encompass the whole firm. Consequently, an important challenge is to produce cross-functional learning, so that each function can improve not only its own activity, but also the way it interacts with others.

It is important to understand not only how to do better from the perspective of each function, but also how that connects to the relevant system: the company as a whole. The key to overall company performance is the relationship between peers. When there is tension between peers, systematic learning is not feasible.

The relationship between executive groups and sources of support: As important as the role of the chief executive in legitimizing the learning process is the task of providing staff services to this process.

This is commonly the role of external resources. It would be possible for the strategic planning function to be an important agent in the process. In many companies, however, it has disqualified itself, either by being simply a compiler of results or by being concerned primarily with issues outside the current operations, such as acquisition.

Appreciating Rates of Change

One of the most severe tests of learning is whether something is so well understood that rates of change can be predicted.

In a recent interview, Jack Welch, chairman of General Electric, observed: "I make the argument that 80 to 90 percent of the things that fail are not because people don't execute or implement—it's because they don't read how fast our competition is moving or how fast the market is changing."*

---

* "At G.E., More Planning Means Less Planning," *Washington Post,* Sept., 30, 1984, p. B8.

One of the most powerful devices for helping senior executives understand rates of change is to require them to develop an explicit forecast of their industry as a basis for assessing their company's future performance. We would expect this forecast to be wrong initially, given the way industries change. We would also expect, however, that effective companies would spend a significant amount of time looking for and trying to understand what was missed, what strategies would be required to deal with the uncertainties, and what might be considered to make future forecasts more reliable. We would expect ineffective companies to make the same errors repeatedly, without deriving any learning benefit from their expensive experience.

As change has accelerated, forecasting has become more difficult, but also more and more important.

Developing a Systems Perspective

Strategy is inherently a systemic issue. To deal with it effectively, people responsible for major components of the system have to learn how their activities mesh with those of others in the system to create an overall direction. Unless this perspective is learned, it will be difficult to create consistent behavior. Few things are as disruptive to the long-term interests of a large company as a strong function narrowly pursuing its own interest.

One of the most powerful ways to promote systems learning is to require people to become knowledgeable about external events before they develop a joint strategic response. Among the more important external events to be used for this purpose are competitive initiatives and other changes in the evolution of the competitive system.

As part of this activity, it is important that senior management support an analytical effort that has two basic purposes. One is to develop, pool, and integrate information about competitors' actions, capabilities, and intentions. We are struck by how seldom this is done adequately. The second is to model the evolution of the competitive system.

For example, after a recent discussion with a major U.S. company that had completed an analysis of what was happening within its industry in Japan, the observation we heard was, "We knew most of that information, in the sense that someone within our company had observed most of the individual activities described. But we had not put it together to form the picture displayed, nor had we considered its implications."

Conclusion

Learning is a major requirement for corporate survival. Executive turnover is a fact of life—and sometimes a fact of death. The combination of a rapidly changing external world and substantial internal mobility makes learning a necessarily high priority.

How this priority is pursued is greatly influenced by the chief executive, who determines both the time committed to learning and the agenda. It is also strongly influenced by the willingness of senior managers to open existing practices to challenge and to support the CEO's effort to carefully examine sacred cows.

A prerequisite for learning is to continue to develop comprehensive data that are externally relevant and to see that these data are shared across organizational boundaries. This requires group activity, which can be effective only if there is leadership to make it effective and a time commitment to make it possible, and if there are support services to make it efficient.

Executive learning is hard. Among the major difficulties are letting go of obsolete concepts, developing the relationships that make learning possible, and creating a systems perspective. Such learning is essential, however. When companies stop learning, they begin to pursue relentlessly what used to be appropriate behavior. How long they then survive is a function of how rapidly their industries change.

LET MIDDLE MANAGERS MANAGE

JEANIE DANIEL DUCK, 1991

In the annals of corporate reorganization, the eighties might well go down as the decade when CEOs rediscovered their workers. Walking the plant floor and the front lines, CEOs found that employees knew a lot about how the business worked and had suggestions worth following. This revelation, together with a competitive environment that demands quality, flexibility, and customer satisfaction, has paved the way for such concepts as the delayered organization, flattened hierarchies, empowered employees, and self-managed work groups.

The results are now coming in from these brave new reorganization programs, and they are mixed. After months of drafting vision statements and rearranging organizational boxes, many companies have bogged down in the muddy terrain that separates theory from implementation, change on paper from change in reality. What went wrong? In their eagerness to unlock the creativity of the worker, some companies neglected a most valuable and necessary player in any change process—the middle manager.

The Management Vacuum

Stationed between the executives who shape the new vision and the employees who are to carry it out, middle managers are in the ideal position to bridge the gap between vision and implementation. With their years of experience and knowledge about the business, they are the people who can show newly empowered teams what to do and how to work effectively.

Japanese companies are noted for building on the experience and knowledge of their middle managers, but American companies have often undervalued them. Now they may be confusing them as well. Told they should relinquish their former roles of directing and enforcing, some managers are at a loss to know what they should be doing instead.

Empowerment can be abandonment when employees are given responsibility without guidance or training. A vice president who suddenly shows up one day and tells his plant manager that he will have sign-off authority for $1 million instead of the $5,000 he formerly had isn't empowering his employee, he's setting him up to fail.

Many companies are now struggling with the consequences of moving too quickly from authoritarian management to little or no management. Given new power and responsibility but little guidance and instruction, employees can become confused and demoralized, programs can get slowed down, and the skeptics of change seem justified.

Managers Are Essential

Of course, we prefer to think that employees will happily rise to meet any new challenge, and that given the opportunity, they will exhibit the necessary initiative and ability. This can happen. But it is not realistic or fair to expect people to acquire the experience, skills, and information they need overnight. Nor should they be expected to show unbounded enthusiasm for something they haven't done before and that looks like more work and responsibility with little likelihood of success.

Here's an example from a Fortune 100 company that shows the value a strong middle manager can add. This middle manager had run up against a problem common to companies undergoing organizational change: Her people were taking too long to establish viable cross-functional teams. She suspected that their often-voiced skepticism about the new process was a contributing factor.

The usual approach to this problem would be to call the group together for a series of pep talks on the new vision, its goals, and its purpose and to remind them that it's up to them to make it happen. Instead, the manager drew up a list of detailed activities and requirements (number and length of group meetings, who would attend, a list of prioritized problems for each group to address, the required deliverables, etc.) and insisted each team accomplish its assignment by a deadline and report back. She also arranged a training program for people who lacked skills for facilitating cross-functional teams and agreed to meet with any team whenever asked. What's more, she made it clear that she was available to help.

Forced to perform the required activities, the group learned that the change did, in fact, lead to impressive improvements. By determining what activities were necessary to get teams working cross-functionally and requiring that they perform them in spite of their skepticism, the manager gave them the experience of success, which led to a change in attitude.

Reactivate the Middle Manager

Ask yourself the following questions to determine whether you are getting the full value from your middle managers:

- Do my managers have a clear vision of how our business works as a whole, not just in their functions? Have they ever met a customer? Do they know the business from the outside in?

- Do they understand that their role is not only to communicate the company vision, but also to determine which processes and activities will make it a success? Do they know how to focus people on processes and the appropriate activities? Do they know how to coordinate these processes horizontally and vertically?

- Are my middle managers spread too thinly? Have I given them the adequate time, training, and resources needed to succeed?

- In the attempt to empower the workers, have I undermined the managers? Do my managers have to direct the workers in performing the necessary activities?

- Do my managers feel that they are part of the solution, not part of the problem?

Eager as we are to unleash the initiative and creativity of our workforce, we must remember that employee empowerment is a goal to work toward. The transformation from authoritarian to participative management cannot be accomplished in a single leap, and it should not bypass the middle managers. Rather, it must evolve over time and with help from all levels of the organization. No one can help to speed this evolution along more than middle managers. Employee empowerment may mean fewer managers, but the role those managers play will be even more crucial to the company's success.

JAZZ VERSUS SYMPHONY

JOHN S. CLARKESON, 1990

Is there a leadership crisis? Are we really lacking executives to lead our organizations into the twenty-first century? Or are the specifications for the job changing: Should we reexamine what kinds of leaders our organizations need?

The critical function in today's organization is the creative function. As change accelerates, organizations that are not continuously re-creating their reason for existence will not survive for very long.

Whether a business is driven by the need to increase variety, to segment the market more finely, to cope with shortening life cycles, to harness the possibilities of new process technologies, or to reposition against new competitors, the key task is to lead the organization to create products, processes, and services that have not existed before.

Routine work can eventually be broken down into individual, repetitive, and ultimately unchallenging tasks. Creative work requires harnessing the knowledge and thinking abilities of many people with different and highly specialized skills—in other words, professionals.

Most of our organizations today derive from a model whose original purpose was to control creativity. The Ford assembly line's virtue was that each man did one job the same way every time, without distractions, interactions, or self-expression. Today's organization follows a similar blueprint in maintaining walls between its specialized functions: marketing, manufacturing, engineering, finance.

This suits many professionals just fine. Professionals of all types share a number of preferences: commitment to their specialty, insistence on autonomy and the right to choose their work methods, and resistance to direction and evaluation by anyone other than their professional peers. Our modern organizations often encourage specialists to pursue the goals of their specialties at the expense of the other functions, the firm, and the customer.

As a result, the biggest leadership challenge in business today may be leading specialized professionals from various functions to achieve the overall aims of the firm in a rapidly changing environment.

What kind of leaders are able to do this? Where might we look for examples?

In the world of classical music, the symphony is regarded by many as its most complex creation, requiring the integration of a large assembly of highly talented individuals for its performance. It has been suggested that the CEOs of the future may resemble the great conductors.

There is one major flaw in this analogy: No one gives a CEO the music he should play. But American music suggests another possible answer.

Duke Ellington was not an unusually gifted individual or musical theorist. It is disputed how well he could read musical notation. But measured by his output of original compositions, he may be the dominant figure in twentieth-century music.

How is his prodigious creativity to be explained? From people who worked with him, it appears he learned how to forge the divergent personalities of his jazz group into a single, highly creative instrument.

Members of his band have described how he learned to create on the run: he would offer up a scrap of an idea, suggest in general what he wanted, and then rely on his players to take cues from each other and to fill in their parts as they thought best.

His players were good but not without equal. He knew their quirks, their gifts, their problems, and he encouraged them to learn to do things they didn't think they could do. Some players came and went, but many stayed for years. They developed through their membership in the group, and they learned from each other. Most of all, their capacity for innovation grew as they built on their cumulative experience.

Finally, by performing live in the close atmosphere of a jazz club, audience reaction was immediately visible to all, and refinement of new ideas came fast. On piano, Ellington was in the middle of the process, and communication was instantaneous. The results were astonishing.

The winning organization of the future will look more like a collection of jazz ensembles than a symphony orchestra. Functional barriers will be reduced. Different specialties will work in more permanent teams around specific customer opportunities. Customer contact will be continuous. Information will be current, rich, and available to all.

Leaders will be in the flow, not remote. Teamwork and cooperation will increase at the expense of individual competition. Cooperative support will moderate anxiety and encourage risk taking. Talented people will be attracted by the ability to see and influence the whole process, to learn from other knowledgeable people, and by the opportunity to create and grow.

The leaders who emerge from this environment will not look exactly like the old models. They will not necessarily excel at any one specialty. They will not have all the ideas. They will not be able to rely on exclusive decision-making authority, on the overwhelming force of personality, or on a monopoly of information.

Leadership will flow to those whose vision can inspire the members of the team to put their best abilities at the service of the team. These leaders will create rather than demand loyalty; the best people will want to work with them. They will communicate effectively with a variety of people and use the conflict among diverse points of view to reach new insights. They will exert influence by the values they choose to reinforce. They will make leaders of their team members.

There are no set pieces anymore. The distinctions between composer/conductor/performer are eroding. The new leaders are all around us.

THE CHANGE CURVE*

JEANIE DANIEL DUCK, 2001

Traveling into new territory is a good metaphor for the experience of major change. No matter how much you prepare and no matter how experienced a traveler you are, you will run into unexpected situations and weird incidents. Things will go wrong and fabulous things will happen. Plus, traveling to new destinations intensifies emotions. Your senses are on alert, your mind is fully engaged, you seem more alive. Everything seems more amazing, exciting, exhausting, frustrating or painful than it would otherwise.

The Change Curve is a kind of map of the territory of change, and a guide to the tricks and habits of the lurking change monsters. Like kids on a long road trip, organizations can constantly ask, "Are we there yet?" Knowing what to expect—of the territory and of what does and doesn't work along the way—can help leaders and their followers stay the course and calibrate their progress. The Change Curve is a map that's been battle tested.

Stagnation: Monsters in Hibernation

You might think that Stagnation is not a problem in today's successful, fast-growing economy. It is. Stagnation can be caused by several factors including poor strategy, lack of leadership, a shift in the market, a product failure, lack of new products or services, too few resources (including, most important, human capital), outdated technology or processes, or poor execution.

Stagnation can befall any organization. IBM suffered badly in the 80s, because it became culturally rigid and too reliant on legacy technologies. America Online suffered a bout in the early 1990s, a victim of faltering strategy. Hewlett-Packard found itself languishing in the late 90s, primarily due to a confused product line in its nonprinter businesses. Gillette, the world's largest maker of shaving products, took a dive at the turn of the millennium. It, too, became rigid and inflexible and depended on what had worked in the past. Even start-up firms and tiny boutique software shops suffer periods of micro-Stagnation

* From *The Change Monster* by Jeanie Duck, copyright © 2001 by Jeanie Daniel Duck. Used by permission of Crown Publishers, a division of Random House, Inc.

Change curve created by Jeanie Daniel Duck, from *The Change Monster*, © 2001.

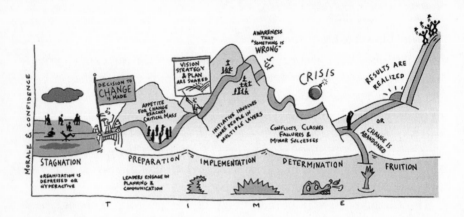

when they find themselves out of sync with the market, or unable to come up with new working ideas.

The external signs of Stagnation are quite obvious: outdated products or services, falling sales and share price, customer desertion and talent drain. In technology companies and start-ups, however, it is entirely possible to be in Stagnation and show none of these signs. Stagnation can show up as a lack of "buzz" in the press, the inability to attract new capital or to sign up the hottest talent.

In some stagnating companies, change monsters are in a kind of hibernation. There is so little change that people feel comfortable and safe; they may be working hard, or not, but they feel unthreatened. They keep on nursing and pruning the same flowering plants that have been producing for ages; they know what to do and how to do it. This is especially true for profitable companies with legacy products. There is an implicit faith that the corporation—and the jobs it provides—will exist forever. If there is a threat, it is seen as a phantom—not a danger.

In other stagnating organizations, the management may know that change is needed, but can't figure out what or how to change.

Ending Stagnation

Stagnation can only conclude when somebody in a position of power and authority—the CEO, board of directors, a big shareholder or possibly an internal operating committee—demands it. There are two routes out of Stagnation: through external action or internal action.

The external category includes takeovers, mergers and acquisitions, leveraged buy-outs, and restructuring caused by deregulation and privatization. The internal kind includes divestitures, transformations, reorganizations, cost-cutting exercises, reengineering, and initial public offerings. A merger is a powerful method for shaking up a hide-bound corporation and forcing radical change. In a merger, nobody in either company—no matter how delusional—can escape the realization that everything is up for grabs.

Preparation: The Phase Leaders Like to Skip

In a merger or acquisition, the Preparation phase begins with the public announcement of an acquisition bid or accept a buyout offer. Although there may have been rumors, the actual announcement usually comes as a shock because the negotiations have been conducted— as they must be—in secret. The majority of employees will learn that their company is in play when they hear about it in the news.

In the case of an internal initiative, the time between announcement and implementation can and should be much shorter. Preparation starts with the announcement of the decision to change—at an all-employee meeting, a special CEO announcement, or some other wide-ranging communiqué. The Preparation phase can last for months, and sometimes—when approvals are required from government agencies—a year or more.

A huge amount of operational work must be done during the Preparation phase: designing the new organization structure, defining roles and responsibilities, determining which products, services and capabilities will be critical, and redesigning core processes, to name just a few. The leaders must flesh out the change plan so that their managers and employees can add the details that will be necessary during Implementation.

The Monsters Awake

In Preparation, the change monster is rudely awakened from hibernation, causing emotional tremors throughout the organization. When a change is externally initiated, everyone within the company (and friends and relatives) begins to speculate on what the initiative means. People feel anxious, jittery, hopeful, threatened, excited, betrayed and distracted. Everybody knows something big is going to happen but no one yet knows exactly what. The senior executives are not immune to the monster: They worry about their security, start jockeying for position and defending their turf. In internally initiated change efforts, the monster may not awaken immediately. Often, people assume that the announcement of a new initiative is just another in a long series of programs or projects. They may feel annoyance and irritation, cynicism and disbelief. In either type of change, when the rush of emotions occurs, it is sure to cause some distraction from the work at hand. Productivity often goes down.

Action-oriented executives would prefer to skip the Preparation phase because it is an in-between stage, filled with anxiety and uncertainty—and difficult and often tedious work. They have an overwhelming urge to "get on with it!"—to start doing things. If they give in to the urge, senior managers generally zoom off in a dozen different directions with only superficial alignment of purpose or agreement about actions or outcomes.

Leading Cause of Failure

The most common cause of failure for major change efforts is lack of alignment of the leaders, according to a major study of change initiatives conducted by The Boston Consulting Group. The sample included companies in every major industry—as well as some government agencies—in North America, continental Europe, the U.K., Scandinavia, and the Asia-Pacific region. We examined all kinds of change efforts, including postmerger integrations, new strategies, deregulation, privatization, reengineering, and streamlining for speed. Middle managers often take the rap for lack of success in change efforts, but the study showed that, in all regions and in all types of initiatives, the leaders are generally to blame. I firmly believe that when middle managers are "acting out" they are only slightly exaggerating behaviors at the top.

When they are misaligned, top executive can react in several ways. One is to tolerate a lack of unity among the operating team, reasoning that they can overcome the resistance of one or two executives. The study showed, however, that even one recalcitrant and resourceful executive can subvert and derail change. These executives act like resistance fighters—building rebel forces, defending turf and even seeking to win new territory; they rarely think of themselves as subversives or see their destructive course. Other resisters will acknowledge that they are engaged in subterfuge, but of a virtuous sort—they feel honorable in defending the right course and resisting misguided, forces of change.

When leaders are misaligned, it disastrously ripples through the rest of the organization. People quickly break into factions and subgroups, aligning themselves behind a leader. The top executive then spends too much time playing policeman, arbiter, and peacemaker within his own team, and among the rival groups. The longer this lack of alignment at the top continues, our study found, the less likely the change initiative is to succeed.

Preparation Unravels When It Goes on Too Long

Even when senior executives are in alignment and have done a good job of communicating the need for change, things can start to unravel if the Preparation phase lasts too long. In the merger of two telecommunications firms, preparation became a new form of Stagnation when the regulatory hurdles took two years to clear. During those two years, the majority of the workforce did not know what would become of their functions and divisions. Would they have to relocate? What products would they sell? Who would stay and who would go? Who would report to whom?

Both organizations went into free fall. Nothing seemed to matter because no one could be sure which activities would survive. No one had much formal authority because no one knew who would survive. Budgets didn't seem to matter either, because no one knew who would review them. Besides, once the deal was done and Implementation had begun, there would be new budgets and measurements. In the meantime, people grabbed influence and funding, costs rose, and customers came and went. From the outside, the companies looked strong because demand was robust and sales continued to rise. Internally, it felt quite different. The company was actually losing money. People were up one day and down the next. As the uncertainty wore on, many felt a combination of hilarity and weariness.

Implementation: The Journey Begins

Implementation can be like embarking on a big trip to an exotic place you've only read about—Africa or New Guinea or Iceland. During Preparation, you spend weeks working on the itinerary, getting your shots, booking hotels and transportation, reading about the politics, exchanging money, and sending contact information to relatives. Even when you start to fold your undies into the suitcase, the destination and expected adventure can still seem unreal. It only really hits you when you step off the plane that your journey has actually begun. It's called Implementation.

Implementation begins when the leaders announce the overall plan and assignments and institute new reporting lines, and processes. When those things happen, the change monster stomps out of its hiding place, and there's a virtual free-for-all of reactions. The emotions of threat, fear, exhaustion, and uncertainty that appeared in Preparation are now joined by feelings of confusion, apathy, resentment, inadequacy, volatility—and relief, exhilaration, excitement, and recognition. Often people feel a sense of unreality. Everything has changed, but nothing has—yet. Most important, no one is 100 percent sure about his or her ability to function or be successful in the new order. People are hedging their bets.

Operational Changes Are Not Enough

During Implementation, leaders must help people understand the overall plan, convince them it will work, motivate them to participate in fleshing it out, and then work with them to be sure it is executed. Unfortunately, many executives and managers believe that having a clear plan is the final deliverable. They assume that the operational changes will occur and then beget the full transformation. They take their eye off the ball and are surprised months later when things aren't working as intended. Change is not just a blueprint for a new structure; it requires changing people's mindsets and work practices.

Communications is always critical but never more so than when you're trying to get others to see and do things differently. Formal communications often focus on telling folks what to do—assignments and required actions—rather than on explaining the decisions. People need to understand the thinking that went into the decisions. What principles and goals did you use in making trade-offs? What alternatives did you consider, and why were they discarded? If leaders want to change the thinking and actions of others, they must explain their own. If people within the organization don't understand the new thinking or don't agree with it, they will be unable to change their beliefs and to make decisions that are in alignment with what's desired.

Companies can get hopelessly lost in the Implementation phase. There seem to be so many tasks with so many details, with so little direction or hierarchy of priorities, that it's easy to feel overwhelmed. The organization seems to be going a million miles per hour but not moving. People wonder if they can keep pace and if this activity will matter.

Determination: Monsters Roam the Hallways

Now comes the most critical phase of the change process, when the initiative is in most danger of failing. If the other phases have been successful, management may turn their attention elsewhere rather than reinforce the need for change. If the organization is still feeling confused, people are likely to revert to their old ways, leave or, worse, "quit and stay." In most companies when Implementation has gone badly, no one wants to discuss it, let alone make a public show of diagnosing the failures and missteps. Rather, the change initiative is allowed to slip quietly into the corporate graveyard of failed programs and the monsters settle down, knowing that they've won.

The Determination phase is critical because results start to appear and the organization starts to experience change fatigue. People get exhausted from the energy needed to rethink their daily work and change their ways. If they feel signs point to success, they will maintain momentum even when exhausted. If it looks like "this too shall pass" then they will throw in the towel even as they go through the motions.

One middle manager reflected on his journey, "Trying to figure out what works in this New World that we're trying to create keeps you constantly guessing and experimenting. You have to think deeply about what you're trying to do. It's not like being given orders by your boss, saluting and then executing the plan. You keep trying to figure out how to make new ideas come to life. Sometimes something works and you feel fulfilled, but most of the time you feel unsatisfied and frustrated."

During Determination people at last begin to realize the change is for real, that they have to work differently. They have to report to the new boss, or work with new colleagues. Pet projects are scrapped in favor of ones with higher potential. Offices have been moved. Headquarters may be relocated from Sexy City to Podunk. Past relationships and processes (even those that had not worked well) now are remembered with "euphoric recall." They seem, in retrospect, so much more effective than they actually were and so much clearer than the current chaos. People long for an excuse to quit the hard path of transformation.

If the extraordinary focus on change continues and problems are addressed honestly, then progress and commitment can survive the

most trying of circumstances. But if management does not pay attention and acknowledge problems, then the overall feeling will be,
"There's something seriously wrong here." You can almost hear the
funeral dirge.

The Many Guises of Retreat

The most insidious monster of them all, however, is also the most
common—retreat. Retreat disguises itself as something else: apathy,
hopelessness or cynicism. Even worse, it can put on a positive face.
The change leaders will declare a halt in the march toward change,
and offer reasonable sounding rationalization for the pause. "We
need a little breathing space, before we start up again." Or, "We just
need a little period of normalcy." Innocuous sounding, those explanations send a clear signal that that change is dead. It's okay to stop
pushing. Suddenly, there are no consequences for people who abandon the new processes or violate the agreed-on rules. Leaders make
no attempt to stop people who revert to "the way things were."
Accountability and follow-through become scarce. Because the halt is
supposedly temporary, it doesn't look or seem like failure. The organization refuses to acknowledge the failure of projects that have
made it through Implementation but die quietly during Determination. The monster is sitting in the hallway, but no one will talk about
it or point it out. In a merger, people give up trying to get the much-
ballyhooed strategic synergies to materialize. Old processes exist
alongside the new as if in parallel worlds, or, one company's ways are
allowed to dominate by default. After a while, the failure of change
becomes a bad corporate memory seldom mentioned, or mentioned
only in corporate code—"I think we tried something like that once
before, didn't we?"

To manage change during Determination, the leaders must manage
people's expectations, energy, and experience. Acknowledging and
addressing setbacks can do wonders to credibility and morale. When
people band together to confront and conquer the change monster,
they are usually victorious and find their way through to the final
phase, Fruition.

Fruition: People Reveal Themselves as Monster Slayers

Fruition is the payoff for months and years of hard work. The activities and changes that have occurred throughout the organization now
combine and fuel one another to make the enterprise seem new. The

place feels different. People who have fought the monsters now see them as benign. People feel confident in themselves; they're optimistic and energized. They're able to get their work done with less hassle in less time with better results. Signs of proof are everywhere: The stock price goes up, sales rise, profits improve, costs go down, talented people join, and the company wins more customers and brings out a great new product or service.

A friend of mine is a natural cook. She can open any refrigerator, pull out what seems like random ingredients and within a few minutes—voila!—serve a delicious dish. Her salads are particularly splendid, magical combinations that transform the individual ingredients into a delightful new and unexpected whole. When I try the same, I end up with a bowl of torn-up lettuce punctuated by chunks of other stuff. There is no "synergy." The experience of Fruition is similar. Like salad ingredients, all the individual efforts, projects, and initiatives come together to create a new way that works. It is magical. The magic makes the effort worthwhile and inspires those to go for it again and again.

When you reach Fruition, it's important to stop and relish the moment, to acknowledge that hard work is paying off and that people have successfully transformed the organization. Put the spotlight on the achievements—big and small—and broadly share the rewards. Take time to distill and assimilate the benefits and learning that have occurred during the journey.

The success of Fruition brings the organization full circle, because the territory on the far side of Fruition is a new period of Stagnation. It won't look the same as the old Stagnation, but it will be just as paralyzing and perilous. The primary danger of Fruition is a lulling sense of satisfaction. The organization feels proud of its accomplishments and wants to bask in the limelight of success. But the limelight fades fast, and the basking can quickly give way to napping. Before you know it, the new thinking—so hard-won—turns into dogma. Meanwhile, the market continues to evolve and the customers increase their demands.

Exceptional change leaders realize that their most important legacy is not creating a single transformation, but teaching the organization how to perpetually change and adapt, and helping it muster the will to do so. When an organization sees itself as a hearty band of monster slayers, change becomes a challenge they're ready to meet rather than a threat that signals retreat.

LEADERSHIP IN A TIME OF UNCERTAINTY

BOLKO VON OETINGER, 2002

> If the mind is to survive this constant battle with the unexpected, two qualities are indispensable: first, an intellect that even in this moment of intense darkness retains some trace of the inner light that will lead to truth, and second, the courage to go where that faint light leads.
> —Carl von Clausewitz

The events of September 11 and the ongoing economic downturn have created a business environment of nearly paralyzing uncertainty. As a result, there will be greater demands on the capacity of senior executives to lead than in any recent period in business history. Some of the best insights into meeting this leadership challenge come from a book written nearly 170 years ago: the classic text of military strategy, *On War,* by the nineteenth-century Prussian general Carl von Clausewitz.

Clausewitz lived through the unprecedented social and political upheaval inaugurated by the French Revolution and spread throughout Europe by the Napoleonic Wars. His experience in those conflicts led him to develop a view of war as the archetypal "realm of uncertainty." Deeply influenced by the example of Napoleon, Clausewitz believed that in times of extreme uncertainty, great leaders emerge.

In his book, Clausewitz describes three basic challenges of leadership in a time of uncertainty. They are as relevant for business executives today as they are for military and political leaders.

Piercing the Fog

The first challenge is intellectual: developing the habits of mind that allow the leader to pierce what has come to be known, since Clausewitz, as the fog of war.

Many business executives thrive on clear solutions. They value analysis, compelling logic, the "right" answer. Confronted with uncertainty, their natural tendency is to narrow down what seems like an overwhelming range of possibilities and to drive quickly to a conclusion. Clausewitz urges precisely the opposite. Rather than being an obstacle, uncertainty is the very engine of transformation in a business, a continuous source of new opportunities.

So instead of reacting defensively to uncertainty, embrace it. Expand radically the range of alternatives, possibilities, and scenarios to consider. Think in what Clausewitz calls polarities; in other words, systematically consider contradictory courses of action.

The purpose of exploring polarities is not to arrive at a synthesis, compromise, or right answer but rather to avoid resolution and explore the extremes in depth. Systematically examining the range of forces that could lead to radically different outcomes allows the leader to sharpen his or her capacity to observe a foggy reality. This is partly a matter of data—expanding one's understanding of which data are relevant and considering information one might not have considered before. But it is mainly a matter of judgment—taking a second look at the same data and considering what one thinks one already knows from a variety of diverse and even contradictory perspectives.

Thinking in polarities allows the leader to develop what Clausewitz describes as the "skill in discerning, from a mass of countless objects and relations, what is most important and decisive." As such, it is an essential preparation for action. When great leaders act, their actions, from the outside, may appear sudden, even arbitrary. In fact, they are built on an intuitive understanding of likely options and outcomes—what Clausewitz calls "the rapid recognition of a truth that is utterly invisible to the ordinary view."

Acting with Courage

Exploring polarities can prepare executives to act, even when they don't have all the information. But in the end, decisive action is not purely a function of intellectual understanding. It is also a product of courage, a personal act of will. The leader, writes Clausewitz, must have "deep confidence in himself." Otherwise, he will be vulnerable to "the pressure of the moment."

Frequently, leaders can have a strong grasp of the intellectual issues, only to be tripped up by hesitancy and indecision. "Although they are aware of the need to make a decision," writes Clausewitz, "they also see the dangers lurking in a wrong decision." As a result, "their intelligence loses its original strength."

This is the moment when personal courage must come to the fore. When insight is joined with courage, the product is what Clausewitz terms "the determination that wins out over a doubtful situation." For the true leader, "the fear of hesitation and delay overrides all other human fears."

Engaging with Details

"In war," writes Clausewitz, "everything is very simple, but the simplest thing is difficult. . . . countless minor events . . . conspire to decrease efficiency, and one always falls short of the goal." The third leadership challenge is neither intellectual nor psychological but practical: knowing how to orchestrate action, despite uncertainty, across the broad range of people and activities in a complex organization.

This is what managers call execution. In periods of uncertainty, effective execution becomes a leadership challenge in its own right. Often the smallest details can make the greatest difference. So the leader has to be engaged with the details, in touch with people on the front line, aware of the complexities confronting the organization. Like New York Mayor Rudolph Giuliani in the aftermath of the Word Trade Center attack, the leader must be everywhere.

Staying close to the details of execution is essential not so much to avoid the "countless minor events" that can go wrong but to adapt to them quickly when they occur. "In war, more than anywhere else in the world," writes Clausewitz, "things turn out differently from what we expected, and look differently up close from how they looked at a distance." When the leader is engaged with the details of execution, he or she can respond quickly to unintended consequences and adjust to new facts on the ground.

Such engagement is also an important means for tapping the energy of the entire organization. According to Clausewitz, the power of the French Revolution came from its ability to mobilize the French nation, a mobilization of people and resources so total that it allowed France to dominate Europe. So, too, the leader's ability to unleash local energies and build morale can be a powerful mechanism for an organization coping with uncertainty and change.

The Wellspring of Strategy

The intellectual imagination to embrace polarities, the personal courage to act decisively even in the presence of imperfect information, a practical engagement with the details of execution that unleashes energy—these three dimensions of leadership in a time of uncertainty are also three key dimensions of strategy. If war is the realm of uncertainty, then uncertainty is the wellspring of strategy.

In the months ahead, the true leaders in your organization will emerge from the mass of managers and employees. Make sure you have a strategy for recognizing them. Make sure you are one of them.

LEADING IN EMOTIONAL TIMES

JEANIE DANIEL DUCK, 2002

Emotions and values drive behavior. They are the fuel of human performance. In these tumultuous times, spiraling emotions and a hunger for values are providing leaders with the opportunity of a lifetime to create change—whether that change is to chart new directions, establish new priorities and work practices, or inspire their organizations to achieve unprecedented levels of performance.

Since September 11, the longing for community and purpose has been intense. The job losses and insecurity generated by the current recession have only magnified those feelings. People in all walks of life yearn for leaders to provide context, meaning, and direction—as well as opportunities to make positive contributions. Now it's up to business leaders to step up and provide their followers with a sense of purpose and a chance to make a difference.

The Personal Touch

As always, the right strategy for change is critical. Equally important, however, is the way the organization is led to embrace and then to execute that change. In a period of uncertainty and high anxiety, six fundamental tenets of leadership are particularly crucial.

Be Highly Visible

In times of stress, the more available and approachable leaders are the better. You need to be out and about. You need to interact constantly with employees, customers, and suppliers. Avoid communicating solely by memo—remoteness is not reassuring.

Provide Relevant Information

Everyone knows we're in a recession. But they don't know, and desperately need to hear, what their leaders think it means for them. People will not expect you to have definitive answers. But they will expect you to have contingency plans for different scenarios and to be able to explain what the different plans will require of them.

By telling employees and suppliers what you know, what you don't know, and how you will make decisions—and by communicating that information frequently and in a personal manner—you will provide comfort while helping people feel in control of their own lives.

Ask for Help and Share the Credit

Many leaders find themselves in unfamiliar territory: having to lead during a major recession and a new kind of war. No one expects a single person to have all the answers, but your employees and suppliers do hope you will have the wisdom to know when to ask for help from people inside and outside the company in order to get through these tough times. And, of course, share the credit. Making space for others to contribute and be recognized has enormous payoffs.

Be Human

People want to think their leader is in control and in charge, but they won't go the extra mile for someone who is all logic and no emotion. Especially in times like these, that kind of behavior is a turnoff. It makes people wonder, Doesn't he care about what has happened or what we're facing? In other words, it's not just the information that you share that matters; it's also how you communicate that information.

Speeches at large group meetings or videotaped addresses will not suffice. You should also talk individually to as many people as you can. Take the time to listen—to show that you genuinely care about how your employees, suppliers, and customers feel. Just as important is conveying how you feel. Authenticity, connection, and humanity are powerful aspects of leadership—and ones that cannot be faked. A major reason why Mayor Rudolph Giuliani was so effective in the wake of the terrorist attacks was his demeanor: He was calm and strong, while also being human and vulnerable.

Offer Hope and a Renewed Sense of Purpose

Business leaders need to put a stake in the ground for the future, to show the way to a better tomorrow. People can endure a lot when they believe that there will be an end to the turmoil and that the hardships and demanding initiatives are part of a credible strategy for creating a brighter future.

Encourage People to Get Excited

The events of recent months have been so depressing that people often feel shallow, disconnected, or even guilty if they are in a good mood. What people need now is permission to feel good, to be excited about their work, and confident about the future. The challenge for leaders is not only to give direction and goals worth striving for but also to exemplify the energy and enthusiasm needed to get there.

Connecting Emotionally

The yearning for leadership has never been greater. Companies led by leaders who can connect emotionally to their employees, suppliers, and customers—and who can satisfy the hunger for direction and purpose—will emerge vastly stronger from these tumultuous times than they entered them.

THE FORGOTTEN HALF OF CHANGE *

LUC DE BRABANDERE, 2005

In the country, I had a dog that used to take sly pleasure in jumping over the garden fence and escaping into the neighboring fields. So one day I decided to remove the ugly wire netting, which no longer served any useful purpose. Imagine my surprise the next day when I saw my dog jumping up at the exact point where that fence had been—and with the same sly pleasure.

But before you laugh at him, think a moment. Maybe he's laughing at us—incapable of getting out of the boxes that we make for ourselves, squatting inside fences that disappeared long ago, and shut inside imaginary walls.

There is a clear lesson here for business leaders: Sometimes, in order to lead, you need to change perceptions, not reality. Indeed, your business is one thing, but the way you look at it is another—and

---

* Adapted from, *The Forgotten Half of Change: Achieving Greater Creativity Through Changes in Perception,* © 2005 Dearborn Trade Publishing. Quantity discounts available. For more information, call (800) 621-9621, ext. 444.

too many people forget this sometimes crucial second half of the change process.

Consider the couple who always arrive late. They could use an appointment book or wake up earlier or schedule more time between meetings. But change is not just a matter of better organization. If they limit their change to action only, they will arrive late again within weeks, back to their old bad habits. To make a permanent change, they need to change the way they look at punctuality.

In fact, they will need to change twice. And that is a task faced by many business leaders. Running a company is a task that straddles two distinct dimensions. There is, of course, the daily management role, which entails making decisions to improve processes and the like. This is where the CEO acts for the benefit of the company. But there is another dimension that is parallel to this one and just as essential. This is where the CEO imagines change, seeks out new ideas, invents the future. This is where the CEO thinks for the benefit of the company. In the end, successful companies evolve up a steady slope and a stepped staircase, both at the same time.

You can visualize this continuous and discontinuous evolution with the help of the following geometric metaphor. Slowly turn the drawing upside down. When the rotation is modest, your perception of the drawing doesn't change. But turn it a little more, and what you see is totally different—even though the "reality" of the drawing hasn't changed at all.

Now, back to the slope and the staircase. The trick is to know when the staircase needs more of your attention, to anticipate the day when strategic vision is exhausted and contributes less and less to keeping things moving. This is the moment at which to turn from innovation to creativity. (To understand the key differences between the two, see the exhibit on the next page.)

Change comes in two ways: Through innovation and creativity.

Innovation Changes Reality	Creativity Changes Perception
Innovation requires *action*	Creativity requires *thinking*
It is a challenge for a team	It is a challenge for an individual
The process is continuous	The process is discontinuous
It takes a long time	It takes an instant
It delivers something new to the system	It envisions a new system
Its impact is measurable	Its impact cannot be measured
Project management is required	Brainstorming is required
The fuel is practical ideas and useful suggestions	The fuel is questions, surprises, and strange and incomplete ideas
The role of a consultant is to cause action	The role of a consultant is to encourage reflection

SOURCE: Luc de Brabandere, *The Forgotten Half of Change: Achieving Greater Creativity through Changes in Perception* (Dearborn Trade Publishing, 2005).

Navigating a Different World

Being creative isn't easy. It requires more than a quick course in "thinking," because our minds insist on seeing the world as it was. Yet for most of us, the world that existed when we were born, and that shaped us, has changed completely. The fences are down. Can you still trace the borderline between professional and private life? Where do cosmetics stop in the drugstore and start in the pharmacy?

The disappearance of barriers is just one of many changes. Another is what Michelangelo might have called *non finito*. Many of Michelangelo's statues are unfinished. The four naked slaves, for example, give the impression that the figures are emerging from the marble. The heads and torsos have been drawn out, as if to allow the statues to breathe, while the rest of the body is trapped within the marble, waiting.

The idea of *non finito* is strangely modern. It's an attitude that consists of just being ready, since we no longer know how to make forecasts. It is in opposition to the sinister approach that says, "We don't move so long as we don't know where we're going." Instead, *non finito* would say, "Let's in any case do what has to be done," even if it can't be finished. Non finito is humility in the face of one sole certainty: We don't know what's going to happen. Non finito is the will to act while leaving the future open, the habit of writing in pencil rather than ink, of actively participating in a world that is becoming, without knowing what it's going to become. In the end, *non finito* is respect for others and the liberty we grant them to finish in their own way.

Leaders will need to ask many more people in their organizations to be *non finito*. Creativity was once defined as a revolution in the way we look at things. But this revolution should not be limited to future Nobel Prize winners; the insurrection has to appeal to everyone, because every individual's eye can contribute to the imagination of us all. You have to be the scientist of your own life and be astonished four times: at what is, what always has been, what once was, and what could be.

Creating a New Strategic Vision

But how can we ask people in our organizations to be *non finito* in a world that increasingly demands and extols flawless execution? How can we ask them not only to execute but also to think and, when necessary, to transform? What does this mean for the leader who must change minds as well as matters? It means coming to grips with the challenge of creating a new strategic vision. Here are some points to remember:

1. Developing a strategic vision is above all an intellectual process. It is located in the world of thought and not in the world of action. Its objective is to change the way we see things and not the things themselves.

2. All reflection is based on a system of values that we construct from what we believe is desirable. It is essential to express these values clearly. Sticking to them is a sine qua non for strategic vision.

3. Thought has its own laws. If we want to create a strategic vision, we have to defer to it. As ideas develop more like a stepped staircase than a steady slope, a new vision implies that there is a break with the old one. What is broken is a stereotype—at least one—that supported the previous vision.

4. A strategic vision has to be easy to understand and coherent. At its start, it must not contain any contradictions or ambiguities; if it does, it is doomed to confuse people and fail.

5. The first challenge the vision will have to face is that of credibility. Whoever develops the vision will immediately have to be able to show that it is feasible—in particular, through a clear demonstration of what the available resources are.

6. A strategic vision exists only if it can be shared among those it concerns. It exists only if they take ownership of it. It has to motivate. It gives everyone involved room to be creative and space for personal development.

7. Good communication is essential; a strategic vision has to appeal to the emotions. So why don't you put it in pictures and communicate with both sides of the brain?

8. A strategic vision has to be visible from the outside—to clients, suppliers, and the public, among other constituencies—and it has to provide information on the specific characteristics of the company, on the project itself, and on the difference it will make. It can be crystallized in a strong phrase, but the temptation to create a slogan must be resisted.

9. A strategic vision is limited in space and time. It is defined by limits that are set down in advance, and it "knows" it is not eternal and that—just like its predecessor—it is based on a certain number of hypotheses that will one day no longer be verifiable. In short, it knows that it, too, will end with a break.

10. A strategic vision contains qualitative elements that can't be tracked with traditional metrics. There are no figures that allow us to evaluate how things are progressing. Nonquantifiable objectives should therefore be accompanied by criteria, if they are not to become wishful thinking. These criteria will allow permanent comparison of what is with what was supposed to be.

11. Growing uncertainty is a fact, so strategic vision is necessarily incomplete. Because the unknown cannot be taken into account, it will be fitted out with correction mechanisms. While we can "preview" what is certain, we can "prepare" for the uncertain.

The points set out here say nothing about the quality of the vision being created. There comes a time for validation. Is it ethically acceptable, practically feasible, economically tenable? Moreover, quite simply, is this the right moment? A positive response leads to a decision to "freeze" the vision, and that decision leads to action.

To make a long story short, a strategic vision is a representation—an ambitious image of a future state that is radically preferable to the current state. It becomes a reference and thereby provides a set of concepts that allow all employees to approach their work thoughtfully and effectively.

If you keep this definition in mind, the forgotten half of change will be forgotten no more.

PART FOUR

Business Thinking

BRUCE HENDERSON DEDICATED his life to learning and ideas. The preface cites Jay Forrester's observation that "virtually everything interesting in business lies in fourth-order effects and beyond." Bruce pushed beyond fourth-order effects as a common practice, and he expected his colleagues to do the same. Intellectual curiosity was one of the main characteristics he looked for in people he sought to attract to The Boston Consulting Group. Thinking insightfully and defending conclusions were rites of passage—and often intimidating ones—for new consultants. One recounts that on his first day of work at BCG, Bruce trapped him in the corridor with the question, "How would you price a new jet fighter aircraft?"

The intellectual energy Bruce brought to BCG has driven high standards for analysis and higher aspirations to creativity. Both are reflected in this group of *Perspectives*. These essays do not posit concrete maxims on strategy. Rather they muse on the essential nature of strategy and competition—very simply, business thinking.

353

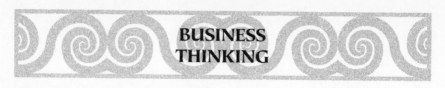

BUSINESS THINKING

BRUCE D. HENDERSON, 1977

Business thinking starts with an intuitive choice of assumptions. Its progress as analysis is intertwined with intuition. The final choice is always intuitive. If that were not true, all problems of almost any kind would be solved by mathematicians with nonquantitative data.

The final choice in all business decision is, of course, intuitive. It must be. Otherwise it is not a decision, just a conclusion, a printout.

The tradeoff of subjective, nonquantifiable values is by definition a subjective and intuitive choice. Intuition can be awesome in its value at times. It is known as good judgment in everyday affairs. Intuition is in fact the subconscious integration of all the experiences, conditioning, and knowledge of a lifetime, including the emotional and cultural biases of that lifetime.

But intuition alone is never enough. Alone, it can be disastrously wrong. Analysis, too, can be disastrously wrong. Analysis depends on keeping the required data to manageable proportions. It also means keeping the nonquantifiable data to a minimum. Thus analysis by its very nature requires initial oversimplification and intuitive choice of starting assumptions with exclusion of certain data. All of these choices are intuitive. A mistake in any one can be fatal to the analysis.

Any complex problem has a near infinite combination of facts and relationships. Business in particular is affected by everything, including the past, the nonlogical, and the unknowable. This complexity is compounded by multiple objectives to serve multiple constituencies, many of whose objectives must be traded off. Problem solving with such complexity requires an orderly, systematic approach in order to even hope to optimize the final decision.

When the results of analysis and intuition coincide, there is little gained except confidence. When the analysis reaches conclusions that are counterintuitive, then more rigorous analysis and reexamination of underlying assumptions are always called for. The expansion of the frame of reference and the increased rigor of analysis may be fruitful.

But in nearly all problem solving there is a universe of alternative choices, most of which must be discarded without more than cursory attention. To do otherwise is to incur costs beyond the value of any solution and defer decision to beyond the time horizon. A frame of reference is needed to screen the intuitive selection of assumptions, relevance of data, methodology, and implicit value judgments. That frame of reference is the *concept*.

Conceptual thinking is the skeleton or the framework on which all the other choices are sorted out. A concept is by its nature an over-simplification. Yet its fundamental relationships are so powerful and important that they will tend to override all except the most extreme exceptions. Such exceptions are usually obvious in their importance. A concept defines a system of interactions in terms of the relative values that produce stable equilibrium of the system. Consequently, a concept defines the initial assumptions, the data required, and the relationships between the data inputs. In this way it permits analysis of the consequences of change in input data.

Concepts are simple in statement but complex in practice. Outputs are almost always part of the input by means of feedback. The feedback itself is consequently a subsystem interconnected with other subsystems.

Theoretically, such conceptual business systems can be solved by a series of simultaneous equations. In practice, computer simulation is the only practical way to deal with the characteristic multiple inputs, feedback loops, and higher-order effects in a reasonable time at reasonable cost with all the underlying assumptions made explicit. Pure mathematics becomes far too ponderous.

Concepts are developed in hard science and business alike from an approximation of the scientific method. They start with a generalization of an observed pattern of experience. They are stated first as a hypothesis, then postulated as a theory, then defined as a decision rule. They are validated by their ability to predict. Such decision rules are often crystallized as policies. Rarely does a business concept permit definitive proof enough to be called a law, except facetiously.

Intuition disguised as status, seniority, and rank is the underlying normative mode of all business decisions. It could not be otherwise. Too many choices must be made too often. Data are expensive to collect and often of uncertain quality or relevance. Analysis is laborious and often far too expensive even though imprecise or superficial.

Yet two kinds of decisions justify rigorous and painstaking analysis guided by intuition derived from accumulated experience. The irrevocable commitment of major reserves of resources deserves such treatment. So do the major policies that guide and control the implementation of such commitments.

All rigorous analysis is inherently an iterative process. It starts with an intuitive choice and ends with an intuitive decision. The first definition of a problem is inescapably intuitive. It must be in order to be recognized as a problem at all. The final decision is also intuitive. It must be or there is no choice and therefore no need for decision.

Between those two points of beginning and ending, the rigorous process must take place. The sequence is analysis, problem redefinition, reanalysis, and then even more rigorous problem redefinition, and so on, until the law of diminishing returns dictates a halt—intuitively.

The methodology and sequence of business thinking can be stated or at least approximated:

- State the problem as clearly and fully as possible.

- Search for and identify the basic concepts that relate to the perceived critical elements.

- Define the data inputs this conceptual reference will require. Check off and identify any major factors that are not implicitly included in the conceptual base.

- Redefine the problem and broaden the concept as necessary to include any such required inputs.

- Gather the data and analyze the problem.

- Find out to which data inputs the analysis is sensitive. Reexamine the range of options with respect to those factors and the resulting range of outputs.

- Based on the insights developed by the analysis, redefine the problem and repeat the process.

- Reiterate until there is a consensus that the possible incremental improvement in insight is no longer worth the incremental cost. That consensus will be intuitive. It must be. There is no way to know the value of the unknown.

It is a matter of observation that much of the value of a rigorous and objective examination of a problem will be found in one of three areas:

- First, the previously accepted underlying assumptions may prove to be invalid or inadequate as the problem definition is changed.

- Second, the interaction between component functions may have been neglected, resulting in suboptimization by function.

- Third, a previously unknown or unaccepted or misunderstood conceptual framework may be postulated that both permits prediction of the consequence of change and partially explains these consequences.

It is also a matter of common observation that the wisest of intuitive judgments come after full exploration and consensus on the nature of the problem by peers of nearly equal but diverse experience.

Finally, it is also a matter of general experience that implementation of the optimum decision will prove difficult if that discussion and consensus have not been continued long enough to make the relationship between the overall objective and the specific action seem clear to all who must interpret and implement the required policies. Otherwise, the intuition of those who do the implementation will be used to redefine the policies that emerged from analysis. This is one reason planned organization change is so difficult and random drift is so common.

Here are some fundamental procedural suggestions. Define the problem and hypothesize the approach to a solution intuitively before wasting time on data collection and analysis. Do the first analysis lightly. Then and only then redefine the problem more rigorously and reanalyze in depth. (Don't go to the library and read all the books before you know what you want to learn.) Use mixed project research teams composed of some people with finely honed intuitions from experience and others with highly developed analytical skills but too little experience to know what cannot be done. Perhaps in this way you can achieve the best of both analysis and intuition in combination and offset the weaknesses of both.

BRINKMANSHIP IN BUSINESS

Bruce D. Henderson, 1967

A businessman often convinces himself that he is completely logical in his behavior when in fact the critical factor is his emotional bias compared to the emotional bias of his opposition. Unfortunately, some businessmen and students take the attitude that competition is some kind of impersonal, objective, colorless affair, with a company competing against the field as a golfer does in medal play. A better case can be made that business competition is a battle royal in which there are many contenders, each of whom must be dealt with individually. Victory, if achieved, is more often won in the mind of a competitor than in the economic arena.

I shall emphasize two points. The first is that the management of a company must persuade each competitor to voluntarily stop short of his maximum effort to acquire customers and profits. The second point is that persuasion depends on emotional and intuitive factors rather than on analysis or deduction.

The negotiator's skill lies in being as arbitrary as necessary to obtain the best possible compromise without actually destroying the basis for voluntary mutual cooperation or self-restraint. There are some commonsense rules for success in such an endeavor:

1. Be sure that your rival is fully aware of what he can gain if he cooperates and what it will cost him if he does not.

2. Avoid any action that will arouse his emotions, since it is essential that he behave in a logical, reasonable fashion.

3. Convince your opponent that you are emotionally dedicated to your position and are completely convinced that it is reasonable.

It is worth emphasizing that your competitor is under the maximum handicap if he acts in a completely rational, objective, and logical fashion. For then he will cooperate as long as he thinks he benefits at all. In fact, if he is completely logical, he will not forgo the profit of cooperation as long as there is any net benefit.

It may strike most businessmen as strange to talk about cooperation with competitors. But it is hard to visualize a situation in which it would be worthwhile to pursue competition to the utter destruction of a competitor. In every case there is a greater advantage to reducing the competition on the condition that the competitor does likewise. Such mutual restraint is cooperation, whether recognized as such or not.

Without cooperation on the part of competitors, there can be no stability. We see this most clearly in international relationships during times of peace. There are constant encroachments and aggressive acts. Without mutual self-restraint, these acts would rapidly escalate into all-out war. Constant confrontations occur. And the eventual consequence is always either voluntarily imposed self-restraint or all-out mutual destruction. Thus international diplomacy has only one purpose: to stabilize cooperation between independent nations on the most favorable basis possible. Diplomacy can be described as the art of being stubborn, arbitrary, and unreasonable without arousing emotional responses.

Businessmen should notice the similarity of their economic competition to the peacetime behavior of nations. The object in both cases is to achieve a voluntary, cooperative restraint on the aggressiveness of competitors. Complete elimination of competition is almost inconceivable. The goal of the hottest economic war is an agreement for coexistence, not annihilation. The competition and mutual encroachment do not stop; they go on forever. But they do so under some measure of mutual restraint.

A breakdown in negotiations is inevitable if both parties persist in arbitrary positions that are incompatible. Yet we have identified major areas in business where some degree of arbitrary behavior is essential for protecting a company's self-interest.

In effect, a type of brinkmanship is necessary. The term was coined to describe cold war international diplomacy, but it describes a normal pattern in business, too.

In a confrontation between parties who are part competitors and part cooperators, the decision as to what to accept is essentially emotional or arbitrary. The decision as to what is attainable is essentially an evaluation of the other party's degree of intransigence. The purpose is to convince him that you are arbitrary and emotionally committed while trying to discover what he would really accept in settlement. The competitor known to be coldly logical is at a great disadvantage. Logically, he can afford to compromise until there is no advantage left in cooperation. If, instead, he is emotional, irrational, and arbitrary, he has a great advantage.

The heart of business strategy for a company is the creation of attitudes on the part of its competitors that will cause them either to restrain themselves or to act in a fashion that management deems advantageous. In diplomacy and military strategy the key to success is very much the same.

The most easily recognized way of enforcing cooperation is to exhibit obvious willingness to use irresistible or overwhelming force. This requires little strategic skill, but there is the problem of producing conviction in the competing organization that the force will be used without actually resorting to it (which is expensive and inconvenient).

In industry, however, the available force is usually not overwhelming, although one company may be able to inflict major punishment on another. If each party can inflict such punishment on the other, we have the classic case. If there is open conflict in such a case, then both parties lose. In the event of cooperation, both parties are better off, but not necessarily equally so—particularly if one is trying to change the status quo.

When each party can punish the other, the prospects of agreement depend on three things:

1. Their respective willingness to accept the risk of punishment

2. Their beliefs about each other's willingness to accept the risk of punishment

3. Their degree of rationality in behavior

If these conclusions are correct, what can we deduce about how advantages are gained and lost in business competition?

First, management's lack of willingness to accept the risk of punishment is almost certain to produce either the punishment or progressively more onerous conditions for cooperation—provided the competition recognized the attitude.

Second, beliefs about a competitor's future behavior or response are all that determine competitive cooperation. In other words, it is the judgment not of actual capability but of probable use of capability that counts.

Third, the less rational or less predictable the behavior of a competitor appears to be, the greater the advantage he possesses in establishing a favorable competitive balance. This advantage is limited only by his need to avoid forcing his competitors into an untenable position or by creating an emotional antagonism that will lead them to be unreasonable and irrational (as he is).

If I were asked to distill the conditions and forces described into advice for the businessman-strategist, I would suggest five rules:

1. You must know as accurately as possible just what your competition has at stake in his contact with you. It is not what you gain or lose, but what he gains or loses, that sets the limit on his ability to compromise with you.

2. The less the competition knows about your stakes, the less advantage he has. Without a reference point, he does not even know whether you are being unreasonable.

3. It is absolutely essential to know the character, attitudes, motives, and habitual behavior of a competitor if you wish to have a negotiating advantage.

4. The more arbitrary your demands are, the better your relative competitive position—provided you do not arouse an emotional reaction.

5. The less arbitrary you can seem to be, the more arbitrary you can in fact act.

These rules make up the art of business brinkmanship. They will guide a businessman to winning a strategic victory in the minds of competitors. Once he has won it there, he can convert it into a competitive victory in terms of sales volume, costs, and profits.

BUSINESS CHESS

Rudyard L. Istvan, 1984

Profound parallels exist between business and chess. Both are complex forms of competition. Both have been studied for centuries, and both depend on strategy.

Chess is a simplified, stylized representation of ancient conflict. Two forces of 16 pieces, each in six types representing different rules of maneuver and engagement, are arrayed in perfect view of each other on an eight-by-eight playing field. The game lasts at most a few hours.

Yet even for this simplified representation of competition, the most powerful computer is unable to devise a winning strategy on the basis of analysis alone. Rather, sophisticated chess computers depend on rules of thumb and experience-based policies and procedures to develop strategies and direct tactics.

These rules to simplify a complex world are the parallels to the mental maps successful managers develop to determine a corporation's strategy and tactics. Like chess programs, these maps become implicit decision rules based on experience. Learning organizations build success on success as they revise and update their maps. Others continue to follow old maps and gradually become ineffective. Making maps explicit and continually reflective of reality separates grand masters from computer programs and successful businesses from bureaucracies.

The immense sophistication of business compared to chess makes us even more dependent on our experience and less aware of how much our maps guide behavior. Business is an infinitely more complex form of competition. The number of players is almost always more than two. The variety of pieces and the extent of the playing field are limitless. Nothing is ever fully in view. The rules of business maneuver and engagement can be changed by any competitor at any time. And for corporations, the competition never ends.

Despite their dramatic differences in complexity, chess and business share two essentials:

- They are systems of competition.
- The competition involves indirect consequences.

Basic competitive lessons are more readily understood in chess. Yet they are paralleled in business.

Strategy over Tactics: The Japanese Gambit

In chess, a good strategist excels over a good tactician. Good individual moves do not add up to good play. The strategist sees and manipulates patterns and positions. Certain offensive and defensive chess sequences have become so familiar and predictable that knowledge of appropriate responses is mandatory for skilled players. Truly innovative responses to the Queen's gambit or the Sicilian defense have a high probability of failure, no matter how well played.

In business, the Japanese gambit has become equally familiar. Take a complex product, but one for which the technology is fairly mature. Begin with simple goods catering principally to domestic or Southeast Asian markets. Build very high volumes to drive costs down and get quality up. Then attack the North American market at the lower end with these low costs. Roll up the market as domestic manufacturers execute a segment retreat to higher-margined, lower-volume specialties suitable only for their market. Add high-end complexity only at superior total volume and cost. Finally, mop up Europe with the full line of higher-quality, lower-cost goods.

The Japanese gambit became a familiar pattern in transistor radios and televisions. The pattern is being repeated in autos, machine tools, trucks, farm implements, engines, and forklifts. Yet some domestic competitors appear to be executing segment retreats as if the gambit had not been recognized. The best defense against the gambit is strategic offense, not tactical retreat. One response is confrontation in as many markets as possible to choke the volume growth that facilitates the roll-up. A second is to form alliances of complementary strengths. In the automobile industry, Ford seems to be doing the former with the world car and GM the latter with Toyota in California. Both may be more strategic responses to the Japanese gambit than segment retreat.

Competitive Evolution

The strategic value of chess pieces changes during the course of the game. On a crowded early-game board the knight, although limited in range to three squares, is essential because it can skip over pieces to drop behind enemy lines. At that time, the rook, able to strike anywhere on the board along its rank and file, is virtually useless because it has no ability to exercise its inherent range. Later in the game, their utilities are reversed. Pieces fall in battle, enhancing the rook's ability to strike while placing much action out of the knight's range.

The strategic value of various economic competitive advantages also changes as a business evolves. Early on, production experience and cost position may be essential. Later, as markets mature and basic needs are satisfied, differentiated segments can emerge. Marketing may become more important than production. Henry Ford's unassailable cost position with the volume-based Model T strategy was devastated by General Motors during the 1920s with a marketing-oriented strategy of model variation and style change.

Win, Lose, or Draw

Many chess games do not result in a win or a loss, but rather in a stale-mated draw. This occurs when neither side has sufficient forces left to checkmate the opposition. Inexperienced players frequently fail to recognize these conditions. They continue pointlessly to maneuver. Masters foresee an impending stalemate and either change strategy or agree to stop play.

Impending stalemate can be recognized in business. If a product is relatively undifferentiated and costs are essential, and if the market is large, with many capacity units at maximum scale and with comparable technology, then the industry will have a significant flat section on its supply curve. Stalemate threatens when growth slows. Portions of the forest products, chemicals, metals, and financial-services industries failed to recognize impending stalemate. They continued to invest in unchanged strategies long after such investment was pointless.

Strategy and Complexity

Direct lessons from chess are applicable in business. More applicable still is the intellectual process by which the game can be mastered. This process describes how an organization plays the business game—and how its performance can be improved.

Many attempts to understand chess have been made by computer scientists and artificial-intelligence researchers. If a computer could play chess well, then perhaps it was intelligent. All early attempts failed miserably.

The problem is permutations. Given rules and positions, it is easy to calculate all possible next moves and select the best. There are always fewer than 1,024 possibilities. It is more than just difficult to do this for the move after next, for that requires calculating all possible responses to the position that results from the best of all possible opposing reactions to one's own best of all possible moves—where the next move may not be clearly best until later, and where the opponent may not choose its best move!

Nevertheless, there are computer programs that play passable chess. Such programs depend on two devices to circumvent the multiplying combinational permutations required to devise a winning strategy. These devices are equally useful in the formulation of business strategies.

Pattern Recognition

One device is recognizing patterns. This is the art of making useful abstractions. Rather than analyzing square by square and piece by piece, a pattern of play becomes the unit of analysis. Strategies rather than tactics are evaluated.

Failure to seek patterns in business results in either analysis paralysis or firefighting. The forest becomes lost in the trees. Patterns filter extraneous information, reduce complexity, focus on the essential. Only key patterns of competitive behavior are evaluated. Chess gambits are patterns of moves. Stalemate is a pattern of low growth in a large commodity market with multiple units of similar cost and capacity and high operating leverage.

Rules of Thumb

The other device is guidelines, rules of thumb. Rules of thumb are guiding principles that, while never strictly true because oversimplified, point reliably to the probable direction of action. Experience builds rules by remembered results of trial and error.

All good chess programs depend on rules of thumb to simplify calculations. Some moves are not examined because they almost never pay. Very possibly, the brilliantly innovative winning move will be excluded by such a process. But the frustrations of novice players matched against the simplest chess programs demonstrate their power.

Most of the major ideas in business strategy are conceptual rules of thumb about economic competition. The experience curve, the growth-share matrix, average costing, and the environments matrix are all rules of thumb. They help to pattern competitive behavior. They point toward the relevant and away from the extraneous, and they suggest probable courses of action. They simplify, but cannot substitute for, the thought process.

Learning

In chess, the ability to learn and adapt still gives grand masters an edge over computer rules. Rules are fixed. Even modern "learning" programs merely readjust the probabilities attached to a predetermined set of rules as their experience accumulates. They cannot rewrite their basic logic.

Most organizations behave like such chess programs. They become bureaucratized. Their decision processes become fixed and difficult to revise.

A learning organization can both refine its pattern recognition and revise its rules of thumb as business competition evolves. The failure of most major businesses does not involve bad initial play; at one time they grew and prospered. Rather, it is a failure to learn and adapt as the business changes.

The effort to create successful chess programs parallels the effort of top management to form successful business organizations. Strategic success requires:

- *Appropriate pattern recognition.* The organization must seek out all relevant information but not be overwhelmed by trivial detail.

- *Appropriate rules of thumb.* Decision rules must reflect competitive reality at several levels of complexity. Too simple, and decisions will be erroneous; too elaborate, and they will be made late or never.

- *Learning.* No intelligence networks, reporting systems, filters, or decision rules can be appropriate always, everywhere. Learning when rules do not apply, and when exceptions justify new ones, is the essence of adaptive strategy.

Business is infinitely more complex than chess. It is played continuously, in earnest, for real and significant consequences. Good strategies, flexible responses, and recognition of end games are valuable lessons. Pattern recognition, rules of thumb, and learning are needed to cope with the infinite diversity and indirect consequences of business decisions. The grand masters of business may never truly master it. But they do win consistently over the competition.

PROBING

JONATHAN L. ISAACS, 1985

The single most important word in strategy formulation is *why*.

Asking why is the basic act of probing. Searching for root causes takes strategy formulation away from the unconscious repetition of past patterns and mimicry of competitors. Asking why leads to new insights and innovations that sometimes yield important competitive advantages.

Asking why repeatedly is a source of continuous self-renewal, but the act of inquiry itself is an art. It can evoke strong reactions from the questioned. It is only rarely welcomed. It is sometimes met with defensiveness and hostility, on the one hand, or, on the other, the patronizing patience reserved by the knowledgeable for the uninformed.

To ask why—and why not—about basics is to violate the social convention that expertise is to be respected, not challenged. Functional organizations in mature industries have a particular problem in this regard. One risks a lot to challenge the lord in his fiefdom.

Questioning the basics—the assumptions that "knowledgeable" people don't question—is disruptive. Probing slows things down, but often to good effect. It can yield revolutionary new thoughts in quite unexpected places.

Few new thoughts have been as revolutionary as the so-called Japanese manufacturing technique. Toyota was a leader in its development, and over more than 20 years slowly learned to turn upside down the most basic assumptions about how manufacturing must be conceived and organized. Central to this rethinking was tireless probing. In his book on the Toyota production system, Taiichi Ohno, vice president of manufacturing for Toyota, cites the practice of "the five whys." He gives an example of how asking "why" five times (or more) led him through all the explanations to find the most important root cause.

CAN YOU REPEAT "WHY" FIVE TIMES?*

It's easy to say, but difficult to practice.
   Suppose a machine stopped functioning.

   1. *"Why did the machine stop functioning?"*

"There was an overload, and the fuse blew."

   2. *"Why was there an overload?"*

"It was because lubrication of the bearing was not sufficient."

   3. *"Why was the lubrication not sufficient?"*

"Because the lubrication pump was not pumping sufficiently."

   4. *"Why was it not pumping sufficiently?"*

"The shaft of the pump was worn, and it was rattling."

   5. *"Why was the shaft worn out?"*

"There was no strainer attached, and this caused metal scrap to get in."

   To have stopped anywhere along the way would have ended the search before the root cause was found. To probe to the limits is to simplify the problem to its essentials and solve one problem rather than five.
   To pursue such probing takes a special, strongly motivated person, unless one makes it the norm for the organization. Asking why five times is easy to say, but hard to do. It challenges people's knowledge and even self-respect. It can call into question their diligence and the basis of their expertise. It requires fresh thinking on all sides. Yet it's so basic to learning, to seeing new things from the familiar. In the early nineteenth century, doctors routinely went, without washing, from autopsies to the treatment of patients—with disastrous results. Ignaz Semmelweis is the man who first hypothesized the basic relationship and proposed and tested a change to clean hands—yet in his own time he had to struggle with his peers because he questioned the accepted practice.

* Source: *Toyota Seisan Hoshiki—Datsu-Kibo no Keiyei o Mezashite* (*Toyota Production System—Aiming at an Off-Scale Management*) by Taiichi Ohno, published by Diamond Inc., Tokyo. May 25, 1978.

Probing Takes Us beyond Data Analysis

Good strategy depends critically on knowing the root causes. Finding them is often a task beyond quantitative analysis. One must look to broader frames of reference and bring basic judgment and common sense to bear. Probing—asking why—is the often intuitive search for the logic that heavy data analysis can miss or bury.

Asking why is a qualitative act. It is different from quantitative analysis, but the one gains power from the other. It propels analysis forward by raising new questions to be subjected to rigorous analysis. It takes us beyond the numbers to new answers, new solutions, and new opportunities. Quantitative analysis should not become both the means and the end.

Asking why can raise the questions that are fundamental, but not necessarily answerable through rigorous analysis itself. These are the basic questions of leadership and common sense. They are the search for "the point." For example:

- Why do we continue in this business?

- Why should anyone buy this product?

- What will prevent competitors from matching us? What will we do then?

- Why are we making so much money? Why won't it eventually come to an end? What must we do now to prepare for or moderate that change?

These sorts of probes search for the bedrock reasons for value and advantages to test how enduring they may be. They ask whether the shape and character of the business and its strategy make sense.

Asking why five times is easy in concept, but harder in practice. It can be very rewarding. Why not do it?

CREATIVE ANALYSIS

ANTHONY W. MILES, 1987

We think of successful entrepreneurs—those who have not only started a business, but steered it successfully through the shoals of expansion—as people primarily gifted with remarkable enterprise and get-up-and-go. Surprisingly, though, classic entrepreneurs are as characterized by a high order of creative analytical ability as they are by dynamism.

Entrepreneurs have tremendous drive and energy. They are endlessly creative and imaginative about their business and its opportunities. They have strong people skills, and they know their operations inside and out. They know their competitors so well they can anticipate, out-guess, and outsmart them consistently. They at once respond to and lead their customers, with whom they spend a lot of time. And they are constantly analyzing and reanalyzing the business—although their intense familiarity with it, and their depth of experience, are such that much of this goes on inside their heads or on the backs of envelopes.

They would probably be surprised to be told they were superb analysts. Yet without a tremendous command of the details and of the relationships within the details, and an unusual if not unique insight into the meaning of the details, they would not have been so successful for so long.

The power of creative analysis usually is not made much of when the virtues of successful entrepreneurship are being extolled. It is masked by terms like *savvy* or *street-smart* or *feel for the business*. It is, however, central. If a primary goal for companies in our time is to recapture as far as possible the instincts and abilities of the entrepreneur on a larger scale—and it should be—then developing powerful creative analytical skills must be close to the top of the agenda.

Analysis slid into some disfavor in much of the business world a few years ago. "Analysis paralysis" was a catchy tag used to describe obsessive and pedestrian staff work, the indiscriminate regurgitation of information by mainframes, and the use of a ready delaying tactic by bureaucracies reluctant to face and make decisions. There had been a period in which too many managers saw numbers as all of reality, rather than as an illumination of reality.

The reaction was to stress immediate experience, face-to-face motivation, direct involvement in operations, and time in the field with customers—no question a necessary and beneficial shift. But as often seems to be the case, this risks becoming its own overexploited panacea. Numbers may make nothing happen, but action for its own sake can quickly become perilous. Many senior executives have been saying for some time that things have gone too far, that the reaction to excessive abstraction has become an excuse in their organizations for not thinking very thoroughly at all. Analysis—efficient, directed, incisive—is definitely back in fashion.

What distinguishes this analysis is that it feeds directly off an imaginative interpretation of experience and feeds directly back into more effective action. Like the most fruitful scientific research (as great scientists describe the experience), it requires excellent notions of what might be revealed before the analysis begins, expects and quickly recognizes better ideas while it is proceeding, foresees the profound practical consequences of what is being revealed as this happens, and is enthusiastic about exploiting the possibilities.

This is the creative analytical process of the outstanding entrepreneur. It is the right and left sides of the brain in harness, thinker and doer in one. In a large organization, it comes with close-knit teams of first-class thinkers and first-class doers.

Both groups are in short supply.

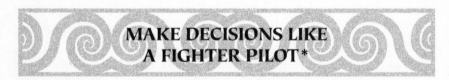

MAKE DECISIONS LIKE A FIGHTER PILOT*

MARK F. BLAXILL AND THOMAS M. HOUT, 1987

Real advantage requires of management something uniquely active and not easily achieved. Consistently greater speed in making management decisions, in developing new products and in delivering orders to customers ahead of the competitor creates that advantage. Fast-response companies are also likely to have lower costs and be more innovative than their competitors.

The best analogy for this kind of highly competitive management comes from the Air Force, which studied why certain pilots consistently won dogfights in wartime. Their findings were that winners complete the so-called O.O.D.A. loop—the cycle of observation, orientation, decision and then action—faster than losers.

The outcome between comparable planes was decided by which pilot could size up the situation and read opportunities in each encounter and then decide and act before the enemy. By preempting an adversary's move, the winner throws the loser into confusion and into a reactive cycle. After gaining this insight the Air Force designed aircraft and trained pilots to process sensory data into decisions faster.

The business world moves faster today. Business competition has become more like an encounter between fighter planes than a chess game, which had been our prevailing analogy. Product life cycles are much shorter. New products that utilize hybrid technologies are more frequent. Mass markets are dissolving into smaller customer segments, making competition messy. New materials and technology are multiplying company choices in how to design, make and distribute a product.

Fast-response companies manage their O.O.D.A. loops, starting with timely observation and orientation. For example, they collect today's sales data at the retail level because wholesale data are too late and distorted. They visit advanced university labs as research is taking shape and do not just read the papers. They study their customers thoroughly from several different points of view. Reactive companies suffer late recognition and disparate views, then incur the extra cost of studies and dispute resolution to fix them.

Fast-response companies accelerate decisions by better preparing the participants. They move senior executives around temporarily, forming new teams to vary the interaction patterns and fracture old assumptions. They move decisions down the corporate ladder and make the small decisions continually, without putting them off. No organizational habit is more insidious than constant formal, upward review and the need to wait for the big decision.

Speed in the action stage of the O.O.D.A. loop requires a particular operations architecture and a lot of high-quality work. The company's operations architecture—how the elements in its value-added chain are designed and interconnected—must be rooted in systems thinking. If each working part of the company is closely linked with others and work is done right the first time, the company will do everything faster than its competitors. When manufacturing people join the product development team, the new product and the process to make it can match, eliminating later redesign and retooling. When new orders enter the plant's production schedule directly, customers get their shipments faster.

Typically, less than 10 percent of the total time devoted to any work in an organization is truly value-added. The rest is wasted because of unnecessary steps or unbalanced operations. A few multifunctional working teams perform better than many departments that separately handle and slow down information. New product development is usually authorized by top management in big, discrete projects, but is done better in a continuous flow.

Fast-response companies not only have marketing advantages, but also tend to have lower costs because when production materials and information move through a company's operation quickly, they collect less overhead and do not accumulate as inventory. Also, the company can innovate more effectively because more new products can be conceived and engineered in a given period, giving customers more choices.

Management's focus on O.O.D.A. loop improvement will heavily influence our concept of business strategy. Competitive strategy has to be dynamic and recognize the systemlike nature of a company. But the planning lexicon has become too reliant on static and positional notions. Our concept of competitive advantage must shift to more of an operations and real-time orientation.

To accomplish this, the analytic questions become: How can my company build faster capability? Where does my current operations architecture and mindset slow the company? What is the performance of my competitor's O.O.D.A. loop?

Governments carefully design aircraft/pilot systems for superior O.O.D.A. loop performance, and companies are starting to follow. The basic building blocks are the flow of information, the organization of work and the perceptual range of people. Building such an organization is not hard science, it is rigorous craft.

The focus of the O.O.D.A. loop will ultimately influence the nation's competitiveness and trade balance. American companies with fast response time and high-quality products will close the gap against imports. But highly competitive foreign companies seeking greater shares of the American market will also be establishing self-sufficient operations in the United States. They will be removing the delays that long distances impose on their own performance in order to quicken their response time in today's fast-changing environment.

THE SEDUCTION
OF REDUCTIONIST THINKING

JEANIE DANIEL DUCK, 1992

There's hardly a company today that isn't grappling with the difficulty of change. The problem isn't so much figuring out what to change—everyone knows that business has to become faster and better—it's how to get from here to there. Unfortunately, the approach to managing change that seems most reasonable and least arduous also turns out to be wrong.

For example, one general manager of a $500 million business unit took the seemingly rational approach and came up empty. He summed up his experience this way: "We tackled the change process the same way we would approach any other project: divide it up into specific tasks to be executed by the appropriate functional heads and put it together at the end. We monitored the various pieces as we went along, and it seemed everything was pretty much on target. But as we got closer to the goal, everything started to unravel. We were worse off than when we had started and everyone was demoralized."

What went wrong? The problem, as is often the case, was the seduction of reductionist thinking.

Reductionist thinking teaches managers how to respond to complex problems: break them down into simple parts and then attack them separately. It's a method that works fine for solving problems of algebra; it even worked in the early days of industrialization, as Adam Smith demonstrated with his pin factory and Frederick Winslow Taylor illustrated with his pig-iron workers. But it doesn't work very well in complex organizations where the whole really is greater than the sum of its parts.

A reductionist approach reduces a change process to a nice, neat checklist of tasks. But it doesn't account for how the separate pieces fit together or how they should go on fitting together in the future. It mistakenly treats change as a series of isolated episodic events—not as the continuously evolving process that change really is. Too many managers approach the change process as if it were a series of stepping-stones to negotiate across a rushing river. If they can only get across without slipping, they tell themselves, they'll be home free. In fact, change is more like the river—it keeps coming and it doesn't stop. The only answer that will work is to jump in and learn to swim.

So if the reductionist approach doesn't work for managing the change process, why do so many organizations persist in following it? What makes it so seductive? There are a number of reasons. First, it appears to do away with the ambiguity and complexity that are implicit in change. Managers can reassure themselves: "If everyone will just concentrate on improving his or her own piece of the problem, we'll have 100 percent improvement." Second, it allows managers to spread responsibility around, thereby creating the sense that a lot of organizational effort is going into the process. And third, since the checklist does contain items that will actually help, legitimate improvements do occur—although they're often not profound or long-lasting.

But the strongest appeal of the reductionist approach is that it plays into an all-too-common response to change: skepticism. It provides a rationale for failure, an easy out. If results don't materialize, it's because someone failed to execute his or her part of the formula: "Corporate wouldn't let us guarantee jobs and that was one of the required steps." If it's someone else's fault, you're off the hook. But if the fault is in the formula, or even more profoundly, in the whole approach to change, then you've got to go back to the drawing board.

In that naive belief in the simplicity and surety of a formula, the change process runs aground. People become wedded to their separate tasks and ignore the overall goal. When change is continuous and complex, like the river instead of the stones across it, managers need to focus on the dynamics of the system, not the checklist. That means making sure not just that tasks get done, but when and how they get done and how the performance affects everything else in the system. In a large company the process is too extensive for one person to keep track of and too complex to be delegated in pieces. It calls for the full attention of a dedicated cross-functional team. It requires fast feedback loops that permit the team to monitor what's working and what's not. And when something isn't working, the team has to have the flexibility and imagination to make the necessary adjustments, rather than adhering blindly to a checklist or a "foolproof" formula.

Here's how a major high-tech equipment manufacturer describes learning this lesson:

A few years ago when we reorganized to streamline our interface with customers, each vice president was in charge of the changes in his area. We had come up with a radical new design to drive synergies, but each VP listened only to his part of the organization and then narrowed it to suit his management purposes. By the time implementation was done, the changes weren't radical and the necessary synergies couldn't occur. The VPs lost touch with each other and the compelling rationale of the original idea.

We learned that our piece-parts formula didn't work. In fact, we were dealing with a dynamic system and we had to manage the system. We knew that making just one person responsible for the whole thing would limit the buy-in of others, while a large team would be unwieldy and spread ownership too thin. The answer for us was to create a small "breakthrough" team consisting of the heads of our different functions: marketing, sales, R&D, and manufacturing.

Along with establishing the breakthrough team, this CEO also created incentives that encouraged a radical change in the team members' points of view. They not only looked down the stovepipes of their own separate functions, they also worked together across functions. With their new horizontal perspective, the managers could see what had previously been hidden: a no-man's land between functions where the change process got derailed. The team was able to spot problems in communication, learning, and performance between and within functions and make the necessary adjustments to keep the process moving in a productive and constructive direction.

In most large companies, change is a complex, constantly evolving process that requires constantly evolving solutions. It's natural to want to simplify a complex problem in order to solve it—that is the seduction of reductionist thinking. But when the simplification turns the dynamic problem into a static one, you no longer have an accurate picture of the problem—and therefore your solution can't possibly work. A checklist, after all, is only a simple solution for a simple problem.

The right approach is to accept the complexity of change and to manage accordingly. A dedicated and empowered breakthrough team can manage the company's momentum as it enters the swirling waters of change and ensure that it is moving with the current, not just treading water.

CHOICES, AGAIN

BARRY JONES AND LARRY SHULMAN, 2003

When demand is high, the bar is low. Almost everybody can get over it. But in leaner times, the bar rises, and only the fittest competitor can clear it. We need to choose more carefully where and how to compete.

In boom years, prices are determined by the ability to supply—that is, by the full cost-plus return of new capacity. Industry profitability rises, most competitors make money, and most expansionary moves appear to offer good returns. Barriers come down, business boundaries blur, and industries converge. Choices seem trivial, and business complexity explodes.

In more normal times, however, with no shortage of competitors vying for the business, prices are determined by the full cash costs of the marginal competitor—or even, if exit costs are high, by the marginal cash costs of the marginal competitor. Only those with a real competitive advantage make money. There are some big choices to make.

The first set of choices concerns where to compete. It requires understanding the competitive landscape. How many discrete businesses or business segments do we compete in today? In how many do we have competitive advantage and earn good profits? How long is the tail of unprofitable customers or products or locations, where we are disadvantaged and lose money? Can we exit unprofitable segments, simplify, cut the tail? Will doing so make us both more profitable and a stronger competitor?

The second set of choices concerns how to compete. It requires exploring alternatives to the current way of doing business. As we focus and simplify, taking complexity out of the business, can we radically restructure our cost base? What would be the impact if we eliminated all costs and assets that don't contribute to competitive advantage or customer value? What would our profitability and balance sheet look like? Integrating the where with the how often leads to a radical rethinking of the business, its boundaries, and its operations. The result can be the creation of a whole new way to compete.

Companies that have had the vision and courage to ask these questions and rethink their businesses after the boom years have been through a tough process. They have focused aggressively on areas of advantage. They have eliminated loss-making activities, become leaner and fitter, and made their businesses simpler. They have driven up their profitability and, more important, have rediscovered what they are good at. By doing so, they have found that they can expand share in their areas of strength. They have earned the right to grow and have started back on the virtuous circle of growth, improved efficiencies, lower prices and better value, and further growth.

In normal times, only the fittest competitors can get over the bar. These competitors focus on the things they do best. They spend more time practicing, more time competing, and more time winning. In the process, they continually improve, and they widen the gap between themselves and those that aspire to challenge them. By making choices, they are able to take an increasing share of the winnings in their chosen field.

THE HARDBALL MANIFESTO*

GEORGE STALK JR. AND ROB LACHENAUER, 2004

The winners in business have always played hardball. When companies play hardball, they use every legitimate resource and strategy available to them to gain advantage over their competitors. When they achieve competitive advantage, they attract more customers, gain market share, boost profits, reward their employees, and weaken their competitors' positions. Then they reinvest their gains in their businesses to improve product quality, expand their offerings, and sharpen their processes to further strengthen their competitive advantage.

When they can continue this virtuous cycle of activity for a prolonged period, companies can transform their competitive advantage into a position even more powerful and desirable: they can achieve decisive advantage. With that, they put themselves into a far more powerful and influential position than just that of the market leader. They can use their decisive advantage to bring about fundamental

* This is adapted from the authors' book, *Hardball: Are You Playing to Play or Playing to Win?* (Harvard Business School Press, October 2004).

change in an entire industry, put their competitors into a reactive position, cause their partners and suppliers to make adjustments, and deliver so much value to their customers that their market share grows larger still.

Winning through competitive advantage may sound like nothing more than good, serious, and sensible business practice. But hardball companies are further distinguished by their attitude and behavior. They play with such a commitment to the game, such a fierceness of execution, and such a relentless drive to maximize their strengths that they look very different from other companies that have admirable performance and sound business skills. Hardball players always play to win, in every aspect of the game. They always seek decisive victory. They don't want to win a 2–1 squeaker. They would prefer a 9–2 rout.

Softball players have no competitive advantage or, if they have one, may not know what it is or may be unable to exploit it. Some softballers can drift along for years, finding ways to stay afloat from quarter to quarter—through trade loading, for example, or cost cutting. A few may seek to disguise their poor performance through activities that are questionable, if not illegal, such as creating shell customers. In the parlance of pitching, such companies are throwing junk.

Fundamental Corporate Purpose

We believe that the fundamental purpose of companies in our society is to compete as hard as they can against one another. In the September 13, 1970, issue of the *New York Times Magazine,* Nobel laureate Milton Friedman quoted from his book *Capitalism and Freedom:* "There is one and only one social responsibility of business—to use its resources and engage in activities designed to increase its profits so long as it stays within the rules of the game, which is to say, engages in open and free competition without deception or fraud."

Friedman's comments sparked a debate about corporate purpose that raged in corporate suites across the United States and around the world, in the halls of academe, and in the influential "chat societies" of Washington and other power centers. The debate continues to this day.

Bruce Henderson, founder of The Boston Consulting Group, fundamentally agreed with Friedman but placed even more emphasis on the importance of competition. In 1973, troubled by the antitrust actions taken against IBM and AT&T in the name of competitive "fairness," Henderson wrote: "The dominant producer in every business should increase his market share steadily. Failure to do so is prima facie evidence of failure to compete."*

Henderson went on to describe the virtuous cycle that creates decisive advantage: "Competitors' market shares should be unstable. Low-cost competitors should displace higher-cost competitors. Customers should share the benefits of lower cost with those suppliers who make it possible. Any failure to gain market share even with lower cost is self-evident restraint of trade."

In Henderson's view, a failure by companies to strive for decisive advantage would lead to a failure of their industry to "concentrate" (consolidate and improve), which would lead to an even larger failure—"a failure of the national economy to optimize productivity and reduce inflation." In other words, as self-centered as playing hardball and seeking to win may appear to be, they are, in fact, essential to the health and strength of the larger economy and society.

Our book follows in the tradition of Milton Friedman, Bruce Henderson, and many others who believe that it is the function of companies to compete as hard as they can to gain customers and profits, with the goal of achieving the greatest advantage they can over their competitors.

A Never-Ending Cycle

From our experience working with clients over many years, in many industries, and in many countries, we know that the leaders of the world's most successful companies—the hardball winners—believe it is their obligation to their shareholders, customers, employees, and society to seek and exploit their competitive advantage to the fullest. And, when possible, the hardball leaders will push that advantage to the point where competitors are squeezed and even feel pain.

When competitors find themselves in this position, they have two choices. They can play softball, using nonstrategic means to get society to bend its rules to hobble their hardball opponents. Or they can look for the chinks in the armor of the hardball players to change the rules of the game in their favor. We advocate the second approach. Business, like life, goes on as a never-ending cycle of achieving advantage, facing threats from bold and innovative competitors, and adjusting to or succumbing to those challenges.

* "Failure to Compete," *BCG Perspectives* (1973), reprinted in Part Five of this book, on page 383.

But when an organization achieves advantage, it develops a tendency to continue operating with the same strategy or model that produced the advantage. The leader's main role, then, is to keep alive the quest for advantage. As Roger Enrico, former chairman of PepsiCo, said to us, it's impossible for an organization to "shadowbox" its way to continued advantage building. The leader's task is to make his or her people understand that their company's advantage is always in peril and, if necessary, to create an opponent against which the organization can focus its efforts.

In addition to strong leaders, hardball competitors also have what is generally called "good management." In the development of our book and in the writing of the Harvard Business Review article that preceded it, however, we were criticized for downplaying the importance of the "soft" issues, such as culture and employee relations.* We do not mean to downplay them but rather to place them in the context of strategy.

Good management is a necessary but insufficient condition of business success. Differences in profitability correlate very strongly with differences in competitive advantage. We believe that a management team that can provide a hardball strategy and push the organization to use it to gain competitive advantage is the most likely to deliver benefits—emotional, intellectual, social, financial, and professional—to its people.

By championing hardball, we are not advocating that we discard or ignore all we have learned about how to create good relationships with people both inside and outside the organization. On the contrary, we believe that people who work for and with hardball players are exceptionally well rewarded and among the most fulfilled people you will find in business.

---

*George Stalk Jr. and Rob Lachenauer. "Hardball: Five Killer Strategies for Trouncing the Competition," *Harvard Business Review* (April 2004).

PART FIVE

Social Commentary

AMONG THE MANY *Perspectives* that Bruce Henderson wrote are a set that consider the motivations and effects of various U.S. social and economic policies. All of these were written in the 1970s and address public policy and the harsh economic realities of the time.

Inefficiency drove Bruce crazy, as much in the public sphere as in the corporation. He believed that rules analogous to those making for efficient and successful businesses could be applied to macroeconomic issues—and that by pointing out the opportunities to do so, he could contribute to the betterment of society. A classic was his 1973 piece on U.S. energy policies and their likely impact on supply, which turned out, sadly, to be prophetic. The most direct application of his business theories was to antitrust policy, which he believed to be deeply anticompetitive, and he extended this line of thinking to tax and trade policies. He wrote prolifically and originally on inflation, bringing fresh insight to its causes and consequences.

Over the years, Bruce wrote more than 20 *Perspectives* that can be categorized as social commentary. Their contents are highly personal—

they reflect Bruce's character and beliefs, and not necessarily the views of The Boston Consulting Group. We have chosen one on each of his favorite topics for inclusion here. In addition, there are more recent pieces on health care policy and corporate governance, reflecting BCG's intention to continue to make our voice heard on policy issues when we feel we have something useful to contribute.

FAILURE TO COMPETE

Bruce D. Henderson, 1973

The dominant producer in every business should increase his market share steadily. Failure to do so is prima facie evidence of failure to compete.

Cost and market share are inversely related. The highest market share should produce the lowest cost as a result of the experience curve effect. At least part of that superior cost should be passed on to the customer in lower prices or better quality. That in turn should lead to faster growth of the leading competitor.

Failure to gain market share even with superior costs is failure to compete. This failure is also a failure to achieve even lower costs.

Competitors' market shares should be unstable. Low-cost competitors should displace higher-cost competitors. Customers should share the benefits of lower cost with those suppliers who make it possible. Any failure to gain market share even with lower cost is self-evident restraint of trade.

Displacement of high-cost competitors by lower prices benefits the customer. It leads to benign monopoly. No monopoly can be justly accused of exercising monopoly powers if it does not raise prices more than the extent of inflation.

Failure of an industry to concentrate is failure to compete and a failure of the national economy to optimize productivity and reduce inflation.

Public policy note: See your lawyer before gaining market share if you are a leader. What is best for the customer and the country is not necessarily legal.

INFLATION AND INVESTMENT RETURN

BRUCE D. HENDERSON, 1974

Financial growth as a result of inflation requires the same financial funding as physical growth. That is why profit margins must widen in proportion to inflation or business will concentrate in the low-cost producer.

Inadequate profit eventually results in shrinkage of capacity as retained earnings become an inadequate source of funds. The alternatives are decreased dividends, increased debt, or reduced sustainable growth.

All assets of a company except its land must eventually be replaced at inflated levels. This includes working capital as well as depreciable assets. The rollover of fixed assets is delayed by the life of the asset, but the effect is the same on trend. Either debt or net worth must be increased as an offset to inflation.

The eventual effect of increased inflation on business is therefore predictable if profit margins are kept constant.

The first most likely consequence is an increase in the ratio of debt to shareholder net worth. This occurred on a massive scale in the United States between 1966 and 1974. Following such occurrence, dividends must be cut or margins increased or debt/equity ratios continually increased.

Marginal companies with high debt and no dividends begin to fall behind. They cannot finance the growth in assets forced by inflation. Their relative growth starts to decrease. Over time their relative costs become less favorable. Eventually the marginal companies are squeezed out.

The implications for public policy are obvious but unpopular. "Encourage high prices and discourage dividends." By doing so, the government will increase its cash income from corporate profits. The increase in retained earnings will be deflationary, both short term and long term.

For business, the policy implications are equally obvious. Each and every strategic business unit should compound its own assets at a rate in excess of the inflation rate plus industry physical growth. If the promise of the future is less than this, then the business must be controlled to generate cash, rather than managed for profit. It is a cash trap. Delay in liquidation is a compounding loss.

For the investor, the warning is clear. Historic growth rates and competitive relationships are misleading. A comparative evaluation can be made by subtracting the actual inflation rate from the actual reported earnings as a percentage of net worth.

Higher inflation will slow real growth. It will increase effective tax take compared to shareholders' receipts. It will shake out marginal competitors and concentrate business. Yet with all of its undesirable side effects, increased inflation can have consequences that are beneficial to the economy and the consumer as well. For this to happen, business must eliminate its cash traps and stop investing in them. The pressure to do so will be great. Leading profitable companies must fully utilize their potential debt capacity to further increase their competitive advantage. Leverage, for them, can be used to offset inflation as well as increase profit, even at high interest rates.

Inflation can force many successful companies to do what they should have done for their own benefit and their customers' benefit under normal competition.

CONFLICTING TAX OBJECTIVES

BRUCE D. HENDERSON, 1975

Taxes raise money to finance government spending. That is obvious. Taxes also redistribute income and control the creation of wealth. This may be the more important consequence.

The universal worldwide drive toward leveling of personal consumption by use of taxes has created layer on layer of taxes on income and wealth as well as on the basic flow of commerce itself.

Such tax practices do raise revenue and they do reduce the after-tax income of those who are the most productive. But such policies may substantially curtail productivity and leave the average man much worse off than he needs to be.

It is possible to encourage capital formation, capital investment, and the creation of wealth and to increase productivity by the direction of tax policy. It is possible to redistribute the power to consume and at the same time to limit that power as much as desired. Someone must own all the wealth of every nation. Ownership of productive wealth confers no real benefit except future security until it provides an opportunity to consume. A progressive income tax for individuals can be restrictive enough to put any desired limit on the ability to consume, if that tax is based on consumption instead of income itself.

Capital can be left untaxed and protected as long as it is productively employed. To do this, several changes in tax policy would be very healthy:

- Corporations should not be taxed at all. They are only surrogates for individuals, not the ultimate consumer. Tax the consumer, not the producer.

- If corporations are to be taxed at all, then tax the dividends, not the paper profits of reported earnings and the capital still employed productively in the business.

- If dividends are to be taxed (instead of income), then eliminate the double taxation and make the corporate income tax on dividends a direct tax credit for the recipient of the dividend.

- Eliminate capital gains taxes. Instead, credit all net investment as a direct decrease in ordinary taxable income. Likewise, tax all net disinvestment as a direct increase in ordinary taxable income.

- Eliminate direct estate taxes and death duties. Instead, make all benefits received as legacies or gifts ordinary income in the year actually realized and disinvested.

These rather unorthodox proposals need not reduce tax receipts at all. The progressive personal income tax can be increased as necessary to equate tax revenues.

Those who provide capital must defer consumption to make the capital formation possible. Those who use capital must have a return above the cost of capital to justify its use. Many tax laws are extremely destructive to both capital formation and capital use:

- Any tax that reduces the return on capital to the supplier of capital reduces the supply of capital and increases its cost.

- Any tax that reduces the return on capital reduces the demand for capital and raises the effective cost of production of products and services.

Taxes that reduce both supply and demand for capital while raising the cost of capital are truly self-defeating and punishing beyond measure to the general public. This is not necessary.

High productivity requires high capital investment. Anything that produces a wider differential between the payoff to the supplier of capital and the return to the user of capital inhibits the formation of capital as well as its use. Taxes should be levied when, and only when, individuals disinvest in order to consume. Capital still at work should not be taxed at all. Our taxes could be made both to increase average income and to level actual consumption by individuals.

DUMPING

BRUCE D. HENDERSON, 1978

Dumping should be encouraged. It is a gift from the nation that provides the products. Dumping reduces inflation for the buyer. It permits the same money to buy more. But dumping is never intended to be a gift. It is, in fact, a realistic and often superior business strategy.

No one ever invested in added capacity in order to sell more output below cost. Therefore, dumping occurs only when the buyer gets a lower price and the seller makes more profit on the same transaction.

Dumping may be the sale of temporary excess capacity at marginal cost. Such overcapacity can exist only temporarily except in dying industries. Consequently, supplies will inherently be intermittent. Available quantities will inevitably be limited. Such spot sales can be made only in markets where prices are not permitted to respond to the normal forces of supply and demand for some reason.

Dumping can continue forever and be profitable to the seller if the seller is the lowest-cost producer. It is immaterial and irrelevant that the selling price in some markets may be lower than it is in the country of origin. The lowest-cost producer's prices should be set to meet and better the local competition. Similar segmentation pricing is the basis for competition in the whole universe of business, from fashion goods to airline fares to automotive options.

Dumping can be a deliberate investment to buy market share and reduce future costs. It should be done wherever it will accomplish that purpose sufficiently well. Such investments in the future are the basis for lower prices in the future as well as the present. Every product, every business, and every industry requires ever increasing investment until its growth slows. Rare indeed is the business that generates more cash internally than its reinvestment rate as long as financial growth continues. Investment in higher market share and lower cost may be a prerequisite for future competitive capability. The consumer is always the beneficiary. That competitor who misjudges the return on the investment in penetration pricing subsidizes the consumer with his own losses.

The principal victims of dumping are those competitors who attempt to stabilize price levels instead of responding to marketplace supply and demand. Such artificially stabilized prices avoid the extremes in highs and lows inherent in market-sensitive commodities. However, stabilized prices lead to cyclical shortages and periodic allocations. They require prices high enough to support and protect the inefficient competitors. On average, they make both prices and costs higher then they otherwise would be. Such pricing policies by any industry are a major handicap, perhaps a fatal handicap, to effective competition in products with international markets.

The appropriate response to dumping is to respond in kind. Sell at marginal cost into the markets of competitors who are dumping into your markets. The dumping will stop! If other things are equal, the low-cost competitor will survive and prosper regardless of the country of origin. However, this kind of competition requires national government support in equalizing any barriers to trade. Effective competition of this kind also requires a recognition and acceptance of the inherent price volatility of a free marketplace.

The world must be a free marketplace without artificial barriers if we are to achieve our potential for productivity. The alternatives are not attractive. Increasing government regulation and intervention into the marketplace has always led to nationalization of the industry in the past. Perhaps that is inevitable. But nationalized industries seem to lead to major degradation of productivity based on the record of most past experience.

The existence of dumping as a political issue is a measure of the barriers to world trade and the extent to which government regulation and intervention prevent effective competition.

ADVERSARIES OR PARTNERS?

BRUCE D. HENDERSON, 1983

The labor wars must end. Hostile confrontation between members of the same organization is a barbaric legacy of a past that we should put behind us. It is a fundamental defect in Western productivity. A company divided against itself cannot compete.

The Japanese are teaching the West a humiliating object lesson. One by one the Japanese have entered industries in which the United States has led the world. Now Japan is becoming the new world leader in these industries. It is doing this without significant resources or advantages except the ability of its people to cooperate. The time is overdue for the West to reexamine its fundamental assumptions about business cooperation and competition. The starting point should be cooperation, coordination, and teamwork within the firm.

Philosophy is not a substitute for action. The action must come after rethinking:

- The labor/management hostility

- The logic of labor monopolies, industrywide bargaining, and the social sanctity of labor negotiation by threat, strike, and inter-family war

- The lifetime role and mutual commitment of employers and employees in an increasingly specialized society

- The role of the face-to-face group and its function in our society

The debilitating "English disease" of labor strife is the bitter fruit of the Industrial Revolution. In the beginning the need for production equipment and machinery required factories. But factories broke down the intimate and personal communication of the farm families, the tradesmen, and the artisan guilds. The factory substituted the faceless indifference and jostle of a crowded city. The small groups that formed within the factory banded together to control the hostile, prisonlike environment within which they struggled. The factory itself became the enemy.

The upper Clyde River near Glasgow was once the greatest shipbuilding complex in the world. Eventually, small groups of organized craft unions found that by respecting one another's picket lines each in turn could hold for ransom every ship under construction. Cooperation led to suicidal destruction.

In Japan, cooperation led to the opposite result. The production of the ship became the common cause, rather than the welfare of the small group at the expense of the common purpose. Each worker, to the limit of his ability, did whatever was needed most at a given time. Japan became the world's dominant shipbuilder.

During World War II, the British rose to the heights of courage, heroism, and cooperation. Against impossible odds, they fought, survived, and won against the enemy. But with the return of peace, the cooperation ended and the English disease slowly reduced the United Kingdom from the greatest of the industrial powers to the most stagnant.

Perhaps Japan was favored by skipping the Industrial Revolution and going almost directly from feudal baronies to a modern industrial society. For Japan the process from world isolation to world leader took less than a hundred years.

Constraints on Productivity

Deep in the heart of our self-inflicted constraint on productivity is the myth that we must decrease our individual productivity in order to create additional jobs so more people can share an unchanged total net output. Every society should take care of its own to the best of its abilities, regardless of the capabilities of its individual members. But anything in a culture that suppresses the productivity of any individual or limits achievement of any individual's potential is destructive of the common good.

Where industrywide labor-bargaining monopolies are supported by law, competition between corporations based on productivity is suppressed. The whole industry suffers. Where competition is worldwide, as it is in steel and automobiles, the whole industry withers whenever labor acts as a monopolist. Competitively, the result is that such an industry cannot supply value equivalent to that of foreigners.

Parasitic work practices that kill the host are not uncommon. Railroad work rules required a fireman for an engine with no fire. Railroad work rules limited the mileage of a train crew per day no matter how fast or steadily the train ran. These practices were major contributors to the decline and decay of the railroads. Strikes by such public services hold the entire economy for ransom regardless of the damage done to innocent third parties.

Corporations have prospered and grown to towering heights of achievement, then sunk into obscurity and been forgotten. All of them started with small groups with extensive face-to-face exchange and consensus on goals and values. All prospered as extended families with shared objectives and a common cause. All failed when they became pitted against themselves internally instead of coordinating and cooperating to achieve common purposes.

Whatever the services of organized labor have been in the past, its role as an adversary is self-defeating. Its future role must be that of communicator. Whatever the perceived role of management has been in the past, its future role must be as internal coordinator and external interface. All employees of a corporation, like the crew and passengers of a ship, have a common destination.

The Social Commitment

The payments and benefits of a company to its employees are typically many times greater than those to its shareholders. For that reason, employees are the true beneficiaries of a corporation's prosperity. But the changes in benefits to employees that are practical, or possible, are trivial unless matched by a change in productivity per employee when compared to the company's competition.

The ever greater specialization inherently required for increased productivity means that labor skills are not ordinarily transferable or fungible without very high cost. The labor market becomes increasingly thin and inefficient. The relationship eventually represents mutual dependency.

The long-term services of any organization's employees represent a substantial investment by both the individual employee and the organization. The knowledge, skills, background, organizational fit, and teamwork interactions are often not transferable to another organization. Even if they are transferable in some measure, they have far less value. These capabilities represent a major investment on the part of both the organization and the employee.

That investment is the true basis for the Japanese commitment to lifetime employment. That commitment must represent a social contract. The obligation of the employee to the firm can be no stronger than the obligation of the firm to the employee. For it to be effective, it must be part of the firm's culture, not public law.

The Japanese have set a standard of achievement and internal integrity others cannot match unless they rise above their past cultures and make common cause. Non-Japanese can outperform their competitors by learning from the Japanese just as the Japanese learned from Westerners. The Japanese did not copy Western practices. Instead they learned from us, adapted our practices to their own culture, and then began to outperform us. We can do the same, perhaps even better.

A whole new culture must be built in Western business if it is to realize its potential. True cooperation is based on mutual commitment. True commitment is based on mutual purpose, mutual evaluation, and mutual trust. For that to be possible, the corporate purposes and the implicit responsibilities of each member of the organization must constantly be reaffirmed. For that to happen, management must be more than coordinator; it must be leadership. In the future this probably means that:

- Industrial organizations will move steadily toward smaller and smaller separate factories of 500 or fewer employees with work teams of 10 to 25 members.

- Labor unions will become primarily company unions in those companies that survive.

- Work rules will become a relic of the past. Instead, each member of the team will do whatever is most valuable.

- Permanent employment will come after an extended courtship that leads to long-term mutual commitment and responsibility to the members in an extended family.

- Productivity will become a measure of corporate citizenship and status.

- Corporate stature will be measured by the corporation's ability to provide personal security to its employees, outperform its competitors, and support the norms of its society and culture while repaying its moral obligation to those who make its existence possible.

These things can all be done. They are a matter of will, morality, energy, and culture. Those who can and do will be the survivors. Failure to achieve them in real time is to invite mutually assured destruction.

THE PROMISE OF DISEASE MANAGEMENT*

Joshua Gray and Peter Lawyer, 1995

Disease management is an approach to patient care that coordinates resources across the entire health care delivery system and throughout the life cycle of a disease. Traditional approaches focus mainly on discrete medical episodes, attempting to minimize the expense of individual cost components, including hospitalization, physician services, and pharmaceuticals. Disease management takes a more systemic approach, focusing on the patient with a disease as the relevant unit of management, with an emphasis on quality as well as cost. Early experience suggests that disease management can lead to demonstrably better outcomes, as measured by clinical results, patient satisfaction, and cost.

The Elements of Disease Management

The three primary elements of disease management are:

- *A knowledge base* that quantifies the economic structure of the disease and describes care guidelines (what care should be provided, by whom, and in what setting) for discrete patient segments

- *A delivery system* of health care professionals and organizations, closely coordinating to provide care throughout the course of a disease, breaking down traditional boundaries between medical specialties and institutions

- *A continuous improvement process* that measures clinical behavior, refines treatment standards, and improves the quality of care provided

From a competitive perspective, disease management creates system value and allows the company successfully coordinating the care—the disease manager—to capture a share of the value created.

Many industry players have high expectations for disease management. They believe that focusing on patients grouped by their common

* Excerpted from "The Promise of Disease Management," a booklet published by The Boston Consulting Group in 1995.

medical conditions will control costs, improve clinical outcomes, and create system value. Can disease management live up to these objectives? Can organizations generate profits and improve their competitive position by pursuing disease management? As with any new direction, the potential benefits will sometimes be exaggerated. Early evidence clearly reveals, however, that the approach shows great promise for reduced costs and better health care.

A Comparison with the Traditional Approach

When health care professionals first hear of disease management, typical reactions are, "How is that different from other health care techniques?" or "We already do that." Its unique qualities become clearer when disease management is compared with component management— the primary traditional approach to managing health care costs.

In component management, the individual health care transaction— a doctor's visit or a procedure—is viewed as the relevant unit of cost. The treatment cycle's various transactions and component categories are analyzed to establish statistical norms for unit cost and frequency in a population or a provider's practice. Incentives and penalties encourage compliance with the norms, thereby reducing some of the extreme practices, such as nonessential operations, excessive tests, and too many pharmaceuticals. The unit cost of each component is then driven as low as possible through aggressive contracting, utilization management, case management, and other cost control techniques.

Component management provided one of the first tools to address the relentless growth of health care costs. Its limitations, however, became evident in the late 1980s, as component management successes were relatively meager and medical costs continued to outpace inflation. Component management's process and limitations are summarized in the figure on the next page.

The distinction between disease management and component management is critical from a competitive perspective. Component management can be a powerful approach in the first phase of cost and quality management. For example, using mostly component management techniques, some physician groups in Southern California have driven down hospital utilization dramatically. Successful systems have used a combination of utilization profiling and powerful financial incentives, especially capitation. Clearly, many health systems can become more efficient using these conventional techniques, but they can only progress so far.

The road map for component management is well articulated, and a significant portion of the value it can create has already been captured by progressive organizations. Building competitive advantage in the future will require a more fundamental redesign of care than is possible with a component-based approach.

Several industry and technology trends have helped identify disease management as the way to move beyond component management. Total quality management (TQM), originally developed in manufacturing settings, increasingly is being applied with great benefit to health care. The realization that key business processes can be mapped and measured, best practices identified, and variation reduced has provided major insights in the emergence of disease management. Improved measurement techniques and more flexible information technology systems have helped physicians and health managers make substantial contributions to outcomes research. In addition, the emergence of integrated delivery vehicles, such as physician-hospital organizations, has provided an appropriate structure and incentives to encourage disease management. Finally, increasing cost pressure on payers and public frustration with the health care system have increased organizational willingness to try new approaches.

Disease Management Advantages

In disease management, the unit of analysis is a patient with a disease, not an individual transaction. The most important segments are groups of patients with the same disease. This perspective gives disease management several advantages over component management:

1. Disease management provides a clean-sheet, systemic view of health care management that can fundamentally change practitioners' perspectives. Component management is incremental. It assumes that the overall structure of health care is directionally correct, but the mix of individual components of care may need adjustment.

2. Disease management approaches unit cost and use of products and services according to clinical need and systemwide economic impact, while component management attempts to decrease cost and use without regard to underlying clinical drivers. Component managers, for example, may take aim at the aggregate cost of drugs and specialist consultations for all asthma patients. Contrast that with a disease manager, who may

Traditional cost control efforts focused on components.

initially invest in higher drug and specialist cost for a severely ill segment of asthmatics in order to reduce downstream emergency room and hospital costs.

3. Disease managers work closely with physicians to develop more creative and effective solutions with a higher level of buy-in. Component management typically employs a confrontational approach, policing physician and hospital care.

4. Disease management emphasizes the optimal deployment of resources, ensuring that patients receive the care they need, in the most appropriate setting, from the right physician or practitioner. It does so with continuous self-correction. A disease management approach may implement a specialized diabetes program to monitor brittle patients and educate them so they can self-manage elements of their treatment, such as diet and insulin injections. Component management typically does not address the issue of how an overall health system should be designed and managed, nor is it a learning system.

Disease management, summarized in the figure at the bottom of this page, goes deeper and forces more fundamental rethinking than component management, with potentially more enduring results. Traditional tools, such as case management and utilization review, may still be used, but in the context of an overall system approach designed to address the unique economic, clinical, and resource requirements of specific diseases. The tools are not ends in themselves; they are merely building blocks in an overall disease management strategy.

Strategic Roles

For organizations deciding to pursue disease management, there are several strategic options. A health care organization can generate tremendous value if it can effectively coordinate and deploy a group of providers around a specific disease, or if it can help other health care players to do so. The approach to disease management taken by a pharmaceutical company will necessarily vary from that taken by an

Next generation of managed care: Organize care management by disease.

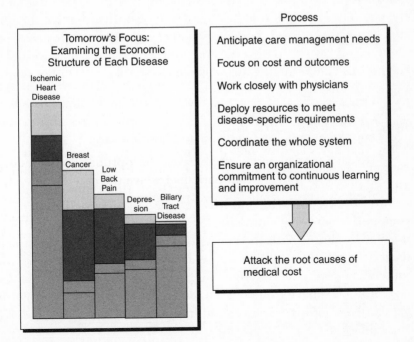

HMO or a hospital, and even competitors within the same sector will find different success formulas over the coming years. No single approach to disease management is inherently superior.

Broadly speaking, we see three roles for organizations focusing on disease management:

- *Integrated disease manager:* Provides care across the spectrum of diseases.

- *Carve-out disease manager:* Assumes responsibility for providing a range of services for a specific disease.

- *Enabling disease manager:* Provides critical services, products, or information to integrated and carve-out disease managers.

The integrated and carve-out managers typically deal directly with payers, providing full service for either the full range or a limited number of diseases. The enabling manager plays a supporting role, as shown in the figure on the next page, perhaps offering disease guidelines or information technology services to the full-service organizations.

Choosing the best role is a critical strategic challenge that must reflect a realistic assessment of each organization's capabilities. We expect successful players to emerge in each of the three groups outlined above, with many partnerships and hybrids coalescing along the way. The choice of role has significant ramifications for the type of partners required and who makes up the competitive set. Depending on the path chosen, some companies may well find themselves competing against customers, suppliers, or other emerging competitors.

Redefining Health Care Success

Many of today's leading health care companies are embracing disease management. They are investing heavily to build the capabilities and infrastructure required to compete in this evolving area. We believe disease management will be a potent approach to building competitive advantage, but not all companies will succeed. Although it is hard to argue with the concepts underpinning disease management, its application presents an enormous challenge. For those that succeed, however, the reward will be a sustainable competitive advantage built on superior outcomes. Disease management will widen the gap between industry leaders and laggards, and accelerate industry consolidation.

Strategic roles of disease management.

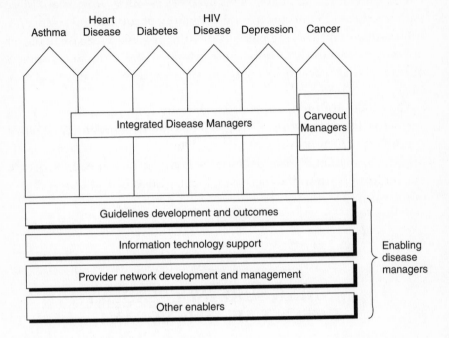

Excelling in disease management often requires a broader array of capabilities than individual organizations can marshal. Consequently, we believe that much of the activity in disease management over the next several years will focus on partnering arrangements. The potential partners with unique expertise or structural position will be courted first, offering early movers a substantial advantage if they choose correctly and implement effectively.

The challenge of assessing prospective partners, negotiating arrangements, and ultimately integrating elements of the health care delivery system is likely to consume tremendous management time and attention. Although partnerships will clearly be part of the solution for many players, we expect many companies to overestimate the value their partners bring to the table and to underestimate the resources required to capture the ultimate opportunity.

Disease management implementation presents a major communications challenge. The customers for disease management services will have a great deal to gain, but they will not necessarily understand the concept, nor will they automatically attribute improvements to disease management. Disease managers must forge links with patients and payers. The disease management approach must be made user-friendly and understandable. This becomes especially important when patient education and behavioral commitment are central to successful treatment. By drawing patients into the process, a disease manager not only motivates them to become informed and rational consumers of care, but also creates a competitive advantage by building a consumer franchise.

The stakes are high. Many organizations attempting disease management will fail because of insufficient analytical insight or a lack of financial, informational, or managerial resources to bring their insights to market. Those that succeed will be positioned to assume market leadership in the increasingly integrated health care industry of the future.

MAKING SURE *INDEPENDENT* DOESN'T MEAN *IGNORANT*

COLIN CARTER AND JAY W. LORSCH, 2002

Whatever the final outcome of the current wave of corporate reform, one thing is clear: corporate boards will be seeing many more independent directors. The New York Stock Exchange, for example, recently approved recommendations mandating that a majority of a company's directors have "no material relationship" with the company, and that these independent directors meet regularly without the CEO.

It's hard to argue with independence as a value. After all, boards exist to oversee management and to make sure the company is run in the interests of its shareholders. But a big question remains: Will independent board members have enough knowledge of the companies they are governing to be effective?

Outsiders who are genuinely independent find themselves at an enormous information disadvantage. Paradoxically, the more independent the board, the more it must rely on management for information about the business. In a worldwide survey of CEOs' attitudes about their boards, we found that less than half the CEOs were confident that independent directors really understood the factors driving performance in their business. Little wonder when you consider that the average U.S. director spends only about 100 hours per year on the job. (European directors spend even less time.)

So how to ensure that *independent* doesn't just mean *ignorant*? Consider the following six recommendations.

Widen the Talent Pool for Directors

To begin with, widen the talent pool of candidates and seek more diverse skills. The most important determinant of a board's effectiveness is the quality of its directors. In addition to the attributes that everybody is talking about—integrity, accountability, and sound commercial judgment—a good director must also have the intellectual capacity to dig deep into the details of an unfamiliar business.

Furthermore, instead of just considering current or former CEOs (the typical approach at many companies), think in terms of filling specific slots or functions. A few directors should be chosen with the explicit goal, to put it bluntly, of keeping everybody out of trouble—someone who really understands financial numbers, obviously, or someone with operating experience in areas of major environmental or financial risk. Others should have in-depth knowledge about specific challenges to the company's main businesses. And at least one board member should possess broad strategy skills.

Design Processes that Build Understanding

Too much time at board meetings is spent listening to formal presentations and "ticking" procedural boxes, and not enough time engaging in the substantive issues affecting the business. Instead, think of board activities as vehicles for directors to learn about the business. For example, board meetings should have at least half of their time allocated to a discussion of major issues affecting the company's future. And business unit heads, not the CEO, should report on financial results. That way, directors can get valuable exposure to the broader management team.

It's also important to encourage directors to spend more time outside the boardroom. Our experience suggests that nonexecutive directors spend the vast majority of the time they devote to their task—roughly 90 percent—either alone reading their board papers or seated around an impressively large table with other directors. They spend hardly any time meeting with line managers, visiting plants or key customers, or talking to industry experts about competitors or overseas trends. So give new directors a license to travel around the business. It's a great way for them to learn what is really going on.

Develop Specialist Expertise

Most directors see themselves as generalists. Because they are liable for everything, they reason, they need to be involved in everything. To the degree that board roles have become specialized, this specialization has usually been limited to issues of conformance—for example, the work of audit committees or environment committees—and not performance.

That is a mistake. Individual directors should be encouraged to develop more specialized knowledge in a couple of areas important to the company. Be prepared to establish temporary subcommittees to explore critical questions in greater depth. For example, if major investment in Eastern Europe is a priority across the portfolio, assign one or two directors to learn about the experiences of other companies investing there. These directors should create a personal network of experienced contacts and talk occasionally to consultants and peers involved in the region. Going deeply into one area does more than build specialist expertise: directors will learn more about the business at large while exploring a narrow slice of it.

Encourage Constructive Dissent

Even when independent directors are knowledgeable about the business, they may feel inhibited about expressing their views lest they go against perceived consensus. An effective board, however, both supports *and* challenges management. Boards can encourage constructive dissent by designing it into their process. For example, on contentious matters, assign one board member to be a "designated critic" in order to foster legitimate dissent and debate without creating the ill feeling that can arise if a director asks too many questions. Or set up a due-diligence committee with the freedom to probe an important issue.

Match the Time to the Task

For all the recent attention paid to corporate governance and board performance, remarkably little has been given to the question of how boards can possibly do their job in the time they spend on it. All these changes will require directors to devote far more time to the job than they have in the past. The typical 100 hours per year is the bare minimum. If a board genuinely intends to monitor company performance and discuss major strategy issues, then directors need to commit time far beyond the current norm.

Don't Make a Fetish of Independence

A good board must have the capacity for independence. But that doesn't mean that every director needs to be independent, in the strict sense of having absolutely no material relationship with the company. It can be a great advantage to have one or two directors who know a lot about the business, even if in some respects they are conflicted. It will be necessary, of course, to make sure their position is clearly understood and to develop protocols to deal with it. But tolerance for a small amount of conflict can pay dividends in terms of expert advice and understanding. As one chairman told us: "The most useful director on our board has a conflict of interest. But if management wants serious advice, that's who they go to."

The challenge facing public companies will be to reinforce independence without sacrificing expertise. The effectiveness of their boards will be determined by how well they strike that balance.

Index

THE BOSTON CONSULTING GROUP

Join The Boston Consulting Group's Online Subscription Service

BCG regularly publishes short reports and papers that it shares with clients and subsequently with the broader public. If you would like to receive notification when these publications become available, you are welcome to join our online subscription service. Sign up at www.bcg.com/subscribe and choose your areas of interest. You will then receive e-mail alerts and links to relevant publications. There is no fee for this service.

Since its founding in 1963, The Boston Consulting Group has focused on helping clients achieve competitive advantage. Our firm believes that best practices or benchmarks are rarely enough to create lasting value and that positive change requires new insight into economics, markets, and organizational dynamics. We consider every assignment a unique set of opportunities and constraints for which no standard solution will be adequate. BCG has 60 offices in 36 countries and serves companies in all industries and markets. For further information, please visit our Web site at www.bcg.com.

BCG
www.bcg.com